AIR BASE DEFENSE
IN THE
REPUBLIC OF VIETNAM
1961 – 1973

Roger P. Fo

OFFICE OF AIR FORCE HISTORY
UNITED STATES AIR FORCE
WASHINGTON, D.C., 1979

Library of Congress Cataloging in Publication Data
Fox, Roger P 1924–
Air base defense in the Republic of Vietnam, 1961–1973.
Bibliography: p.
Includes index.
1. Vietnamese Conflict, 1961–1975—Aerial operations. 2. Air Bases—Vietnam. 3. Airbases, American—Vietnam. 4. United States. Office of Air Force History. II. Title.
DS558.8.F68 959.704'348 79–10317

For sale by the Superintendent of Documents, U.S. Government Printing Office
Washington, D.C. 20402

FOREWORD

This book explores the unique problem of defending air bases during the Vietnam War. It centers on the primary efforts of the United States Air Force and allied air units to defend 10 key air bases within the Republic of Vietnam. Bien Hoa, on 1 November 1964, was the first base to be attacked and until the cease-fire in January 1973, these bases suffered a total of 475 attacks.

Although there were initial deficiencies in staff support for base defense in such key areas as intelligence, motor vehicles, weapons procurement and maintenance, communications, and civil engineering, significant improvements had been made by the end of the Air Force's part in the war.

The author, Lt. Col. Roger P. Fox, USAF (Ret.), wrote this volume while assigned to the Office of Air Force History. He brings judgments to his research based on his personal experience as a base security officer during the conflict. Thus, early on the morning of 4 December 1966, he rallied Air Force and South Vietnamese security forces to repel an enemy attempt to penetrate Tan Son Nhut Air Base, the center of Air Force operations in South Vietnam. For his gallantry in action on this occasion, he was awarded the Silver Star. This personal experience formed a foundation upon which he developed a keen insight into exploring the entire spectrum of air base defense, and upon which he has built a strong case for testing future plans and operations.

Colonel Fox's volume is one of a continuing series of books dealing with the war in Southeast Asia which are being written in the Office of Air Force History.

JOHN W. HUSTON, Maj Gen, USAF
Chief, Office of Air Force History

Cover designed by
Warren P. Wildermuth

Contents

Page

Foreword iii

I. AIR BASE DEFENSE BEFORE VIETNAM
The First World War and After 1
The Second World War 2
The Korean War 5
The New Look 7
The Flexible Response 8

II. EMERGENCE OF THE AIR BASE DEFENSE MISSION
The Combat Advisory Phase 11
The Political Scene 12
U.S. Security 13
U.S. Ground Forces Deploy for Defense 20
U.S. Ground Forces Employed for Offense 23
The JCS Rebuffs the Air Force 26
A Mission at Odds 27

III. THE THREAT
The Role of Intelligence 32
Ground Reconnaissance 36
Electronic Warfare 39
Reconnaissance by Fire 41
Standoff Attacks 41
Sapper Raids 46
Battalion-Size Attacks 50
Sabotage 54

IV. THE TARGET AIR BASES
The Geographic Impact 55
Location and Layout of Air Bases 60
Active Defense Facilities, 1961-1972 64
Passive Defense Facilities, 1961-1972 68
Vegetation Control 73

V. USAF GROUND DEFENSE FORCES
Tactical versus Nontactical Organization 79
Manpower Authorizations 81
Personnel Management 84
Training in RVN and the United States 88
Individual Clothing, Equipment, and Weapons 91
Organizational Weapons 93

Page
Motor Vehicles 96
Sentry Dogs 100
Tactical Security Support Equipment 104
Concept of Operations 107
Safe Side Program 110

VI. OTHER U.S. AND ALLIED GROUND DEFENSE FORCES
U.S. Army 115
U.S. Navy and U.S. Marine Corps 116
Free World Forces 119

VII. AIR OPERATIONS
The USAF Gunship Program 125
Rocket Watch 132
The Helicopter Gunship and Air Base Defense 137

VIII. SHORT SUPPORT
Intelligence 139
Motor Vehicles 145
Weapon Procurement and Maintenance 150
Communications 152
The Self-Help Syndrome 153

IX. GETTING IT TOGETHER: DEFENSE ORGANIZATION IN PRINCIPLE AND PRACTICE
Command and Control of U.S. Forces 155
Relationship of U.S. and RVN Forces 158
Elements in Allied Operations 162
The Tactical Situation—A Vital Element 168
The Experience in Perspective 168

APPENDIXES
1. Chronology of VC/NVA Attacks on the Ten Primary USAF Operating Bases in RVN 172
2. Summary of Attacks 206
3. Summary of Losses 207
4. Viet Cong/North Vietnamese Army Weapons Employed in Operations Against Air Bases 209
5. Herbicides Employed in Air Base Defense Operations 214
6. Security Alert Conditions 218
7. Rules of Engagement and Guard Orders 219
8. Tactical Situation Reports, 12-18 January 1969 220

NOTES 233

GLOSSARY 246

BIBLIOGRAPHIC NOTE 254

INDEX 258

PHOTOGRAPHS

Brig. Gen. James E. Fechet 2
French Premier Joseph Laniel, President Dwight D. Eisenhower, and British Prime Minister Winston Churchill 7
President John F. Kennedy and Gen. Curtis E. LeMay 9
U.S. Marines land at Da Nang 10
F–4B Phantom II jet being launched from the USS *Constitution* 14
Ambassador Maxwell D. Taylor 15
Lt. Gen. John L. Throckmorton, USA 17
Saigon officers' quarters damaged by explosion 19
Gen. Earle G. Wheeler, President Lyndon B. Johnson, and Secretary of Defense Robert S. NcNamara 20
Gen. John P. McConnell, Ambassador Henry Cabot Lodge, and Lt. Gen. William W. Momyer 22
Gen. William C. Westmoreland 25
Perimeter of Nha Trang Air Base 36
An Air Force sentry and his dog patrol Tan Son Nhut Air Base 38
Smoldering hulk of a C–123 after a Viet Cong rocket attack 40
Improvised rocket launchers 42
Display of three basic rocket launch methods 44
Launch trenches for 122-mm rockets 45
Aftermath of 1968 Tet attack on Bien Hoa Air Base 52
Security check 54
Vietnamese fishing village 59
Tan Son Nhut Air Base 60
Flight line at Tan Son Nhut 62
Fuel storage bladders adjacent to Pleiku Air Base perimeter 63
Southern perimeter of Tan Son Nhut Air Base 64
Mine field on the perimeter of Phu Cat Air Base 65
Base control tower and "big light" at Phu Cat 66
Sandbag bunker at Cam Ranh Bay Air Base 67
F–100 Super Sabres in revetments at Tan Son Nhut 69
Damaged revetments at Bien Hoa Air Base 70
Brick revetments about billets at Pleiku Air Base 71
Dikes protecting petroleum supplies at Tuy Hoa Air Base 73
A C–123 sprays defoliation chemicals 74
U.S. Air Police and Vietnamese soldiers guard Tan Son Nhut 86
Mortar pit at Phu Cat Air Base 89
Spike barrier 92
Punji stake booby trap 93
Jury-rigged lighting system 96
Motor vehicles used by Air Force security police 98
Rennie, German Shephard dog, gets his teeth capped 102
Infrared warning device 105
Starlight scope 106
Mortar firing 107
Security police using an M–113 armored personnel carrier 113
Gen. Lewis H. Walt, USMC 116
A portion of the double cyclone fence at Da Nang Air Base 117
Antipersonnel directional mines at Tan Son Nhut Air Base 119

Brig. Gen. William O. Quirey, USA 121
Gunships flown in Vietnam 126
VC/NVA rocket launching position 129
Gunship wiping out enemy weapons position near Long Binh 130
Time exposure of action at Bien Hoa Air Base 131
An Air Force O–2 aircraft in flight over South Vietnam 133
A–37B attack aircraft 134
Security policeman checks a Vietnamese worker 138
Maj. Gen. George J. Keegan, Jr. 140
Maj. Gen. Rockly Triantafellu 140
Vietnamese and U.S. police patrol near Bien Hoa 145
Air Force security police vehicles 146
Col. Frank L. Gailer, Jr. 149
Maj. Gen. Jonas L. Blank 149
Weapons used by security police in Vietnam 150
Security police control center at Pleiku Air Base 152
VC/NVA prisoner 157
Enemy soldier killed at Binh Thuy 157
Joint Defense Operations Center at Tan Son Nhut Air Base 163
Fuel tanks destroyed by rockets at Cam Ranh Bay 164
Flares light up flight line at Tan Son Nhut 167
An Air Force security guard watches takeoff of a USAF F–4C 169
Security forces fire into suspected enemy positions 169
An airman examines the body of a Viet Cong terrorist 170
Tower, sandbagging, "toten poles," and fencing at Bien Hoa 170
Mass grave of VC/NVA soldiers 205
Captured enemy 61-mm mortar and ammunition 208
Air Force C–123s spray defoliation chemicals 215
A Vietnamese soldier tests effectiveness of defoliation by fire 216
Effects of aerial defoliation 216

MAPS AND CHARTS

Southeast Asia x
Vietnamese Communist Organization for South Vietnam, 1970 30
Province Party Committee, 1968 31
Typical Sapper Force for Attack without Infantry Support 48
Typical Sapper Force for Attack without Infantry Support (Composition of Assault Teams) 49
Primary USAF Operating Bases 56
Infiltration Routes, 1968 57
Typical USAF Security Police Squadron in Republic of Vietnam 80
A Typical Air Base Defense Sector 109
Combat Security Police Squadron Organization 111
Combined Organization for Defense, Tan Son Nhut Air Base 114
Typical VNAF Air Base Defense Organization 114
Basic Gunship Principle 128
Typical Net Structure, Area Source Program 141
United States Military Assistance Command, Vietnam, 1967 156
Organization of the Air Force Advisory Group 160

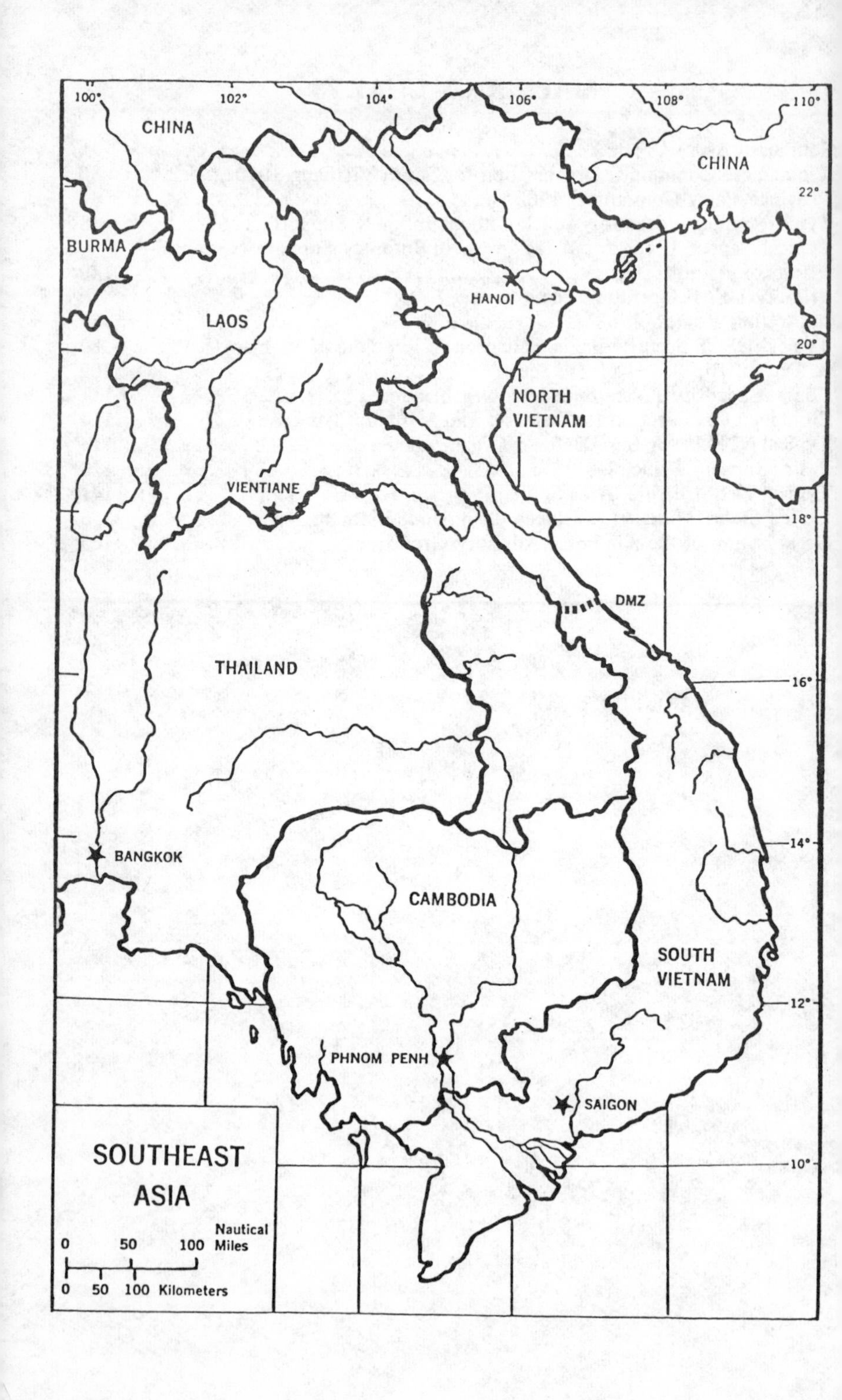
100°
102°
104°
106°
108°
110°
22°
20°
18°
16°
14°
12°
10°
CHINA
CHINA
BURMA
LAOS
HANOI
NORTH
VIETNAM
VIENTIANE
DMZ
THAILAND
BANGKOK
CAMBODIA
SOUTH
VIETNAM
PHNOM PENH
SAIGON
SOUTHEAST
ASIA
0
50
100
Nautical
Miles
0
50
100
Kilometers

I. AIR BASE DEFENSE BEFORE VIETNAM

You can never plan the future from the past.
Edmund Burke, 1791.

Between 0025 and 0035 local time on 1 November 1964, Vietnamese Communist (VC) troops attacked Bien Hoa Air Base, 25 kilometers northeast of Saigon. Positioning six 81-mm mortars about 400 meters north of the base, the enemy gunners fired 60-80 rounds onto parked aircraft and troop billets. The VC then withdrew undetected and unmolested, leaving behind damage all out of proportion to the effort expended. The barrage killed 4 U.S. military personnel and wounded 30. Of 20 B-57 jet bombers hit, 5 were destroyed, 8 severely damaged, and 7 slightly damaged.[1] Increasingly thereafter, U.S. air bases in the Republic of Vietnam (RVN) became routine targets for enemy ground attacks. The Air Force was ill-prepared to meet such an enemy threat.

The First World War and After

The Bien Hoa attack of November 1964 by unconventional ground forces was without an Air Force precedent. Throughout the history of U.S. military aviation, U.S. air bases have been largely immune to hostile ground action. During the First World War, allied and enemy air units operated from bases behind a massive complex of trench lines which rarely shifted more than a few hundred meters. So situated, air bases enjoyed almost absolute security from attack by conventional ground forces.[2]

As for unconventional forces, they were virtually unknown in World War I.* No guerrillas, insurgents, or other irregular combatants disturbed the security of air bases or other rear-area installations. Consequently, air base security measures never progressed beyond the venerable interior guard system.

In the following years, official air base defense policy was based on experience in the recent war. This policy ignored military aviation's expanding role that enhanced the importance of air bases and made them vulnerable targets. The views of Lt. Col. James E. Fechet,* Chief of the Training and Operations Group, U.S. Army Air Service, mirrored the prevailing attitude. In 1921 he said aircraft mechanics and other technicians need not be infantry-trained. Rather, "since their duties were entirely different from those of the Infantry, they should receive only that portion of infantry

*There were two conspicuous exceptions. In the Middle East, Col. T. E. Lawrence (the celebrated "Lawrence of Arabia") assimilated Arab insurgents into British operations. In East Africa, Gen. Paul von Lettow-Vorbeck led African irregulars in behalf of Germany.

training which would permit them to move in a military manner from place to place." In the event of a domestic emergency," he added, "enlisted men of the intelligence usually found in Air Service organizations could be quickly instructed and equipped to perform their part creditably."[3]

Fechet's views, formalized in 1927 by War Department General Order 7, persisted at least until November 1941. Just 1 month before Pearl Harbor, Maj. Gen. Frederick L. Martin, commander of the Hawaiian Air Force, complained bitterly to Maj. Gen. Henry H. Arnold, Chief of the U.S. Army Air Forces.† He objected to the plans of Lt. Gen. Walter C. Short, Commanding General of the Hawaiian Department, to train Air Corps personnel for ground defense missions.[4]

The Second World War

In World War II the Nazis unleashed a new mode of mobile warfare—the blitzkrieg. This "lightning war" relied on sudden smashing attacks by land and air to overwhelm opposing forces. As the German army swept across Europe, it often used paratroops and airborne forces to seize or destroy in advance Allied air bases and other vital rear-area installations. During the spring of 1940, seizure of air bases in this manner speeded the whirlwind Nazi conquest of France, Norway, Denmark, Belgium, and the Netherlands.[5] Likewise, in 1941, the decisive episode in the loss of the island of Crete to the Germans was their capture of the British air base at Maleme.[6]

At this point, German tactics against Allied air bases had become fairly standardized. Bombers attacked the base periphery from medium altitude to drive enemy antiaircraft (AA) gunners to cover. Dive-bombing and strafing kept the gunners and other defenders in their shelters. Paratroops then dropped on the air base, and defenders "coming up for air" found themselves looking into the muzzles of German guns. Finally, transports bearing airborne infantry began landing on runways carefully spared by the bombers.[7]

*Later promoted to major general, he was Chief of the Air Service from 1927 to 1931.

† The U.S. Army Air Forces (USAAF) was created on 20 June 1941.

Brig. Gen. James E. Fechet

By mid-1941 one could theorize with some assurance on the role of air base security in the Second World War. Clearly air power would be crucial in the war's outcome. Nevertheless, air power was firmly bound to bases which were vulnerable, lucrative, and priority targets. The enemy could attack an air base to achieve one (sometimes both) of two quite different objectives. He might destroy aircraft, facilities, and materiel to deny them to the defenders, or seize the base essentially intact and convert it to his own use. Lastly, air bases were really nothing more than large fields. They could not be long defended if the surrounding land area and/or airspace fell to the enemy.

The German seizure of Maleme and the occupation of Crete in May 1941 led Prime Minister Winston Churchill to review British air base defense policy. In a scathing memorandum of 29 June 1941 to the Secretary of State for Air and to the Chief of the Air Staff, the Prime Minister catalogued the shortcomings of the Royal Air Force (RAF) and ordered them corrected. Churchill flatly declared he would no longer tolerate a half-million air force personnel without a combat role. All airmen were to be armed and trained, ready "to fight and die in defense of their airfields; . . . every airfield should be a stronghold of fighting air-ground men, and not the abode of uniformed civilians in the prime of life protected by detachments of soldiers."[8]

Action from this powerful stimulus swept away divided control, tangled responsibilities, and all sorts of improvisations. Full responsibility for local air base defense operations was lodged in the Air Ministry. To execute this mission, the Royal Air Force Regiment was created in February 1942. The regiment reached a peak strength of 85,000 officers and airmen, with 240 field and light AA squadrons deployed to RAF airfields worldwide.[9]

The United States early followed the British lead. On 12 February 1942 Gen. George C. Marshall, the Army Chief of Staff, approved an apportionment of 53,299 blacks to the Army Air Forces with "the stipulation that air base defense units 'for the number of air bases found necessary' be organized and that Negro personnel be used for this purpose as required."[10] Thus, formation of the AAF air base security battalions beginning in June 1942 was influenced by racial as well as military considerations. Designed to defend against local ground attacks, these units were armed with rifles, machineguns, and 37-mm guns.

Peak planning called for 296 air base security battalions, 261 of them black. But a diminishing need defeated this goal, and in 1943 the inactivation began of units already formed.* By this time, the widening Allied control of the air and ground had largely removed the enemy threat to air bases. The last sizable one in the European theater was the German assault on Maleme in Crete previously cited. In the Pacific the U.S. Navy victory at Midway in June 1942 permanently crippled Japan's naval air power and curtailed her ability to seize the offensive. At no time or place did guerrillas or other irregular forces pose any particular danger to U.S. air bases. The only real threat came in China between April 1944 and February 1945 when a quarter-million Japanese troops overran the so-called eastern air bases.[11] A ground offensive

*In a parallel development to prepare for the second front, the RAF Regiment lost 40,000 trained airmen by transfer to the Army. (The Allies invaded Normandy on 6 June 1944.)

of this size was clearly beyond the scope of local defense operations.

Following the Japanese surrender to the Allied Powers in September 1945, the AAF lost all its ground defense forces with the closing out of its air base security battalions.*

Two years after World War II the National Security Act of 1947 established the U.S. Air Force as an independent department equal with the Army and Navy, but under the authority, direction, and control of the Department of Defense.[12] It soon became necessary to spell out the responsibilities of the Air Force as a separate service, among whose missions was defense of its bases. Subsequent controversy over the base defense mission led to a further refinement of responsibilities.

A 1947 Army-Air Force agreement said that "each department will be responsible for the security of its own installations." [13] As then defined, security meant those "measures taken by a command to protect itself" including" measures against air, mechanized and chemical attacks." [14]

The Key West Agreement of 21 April 1948 described basic Service roles and missions.† It identified base defense as one of a number of functions common to all the Services—the responsibility "to develop, garrison, supply, equip and maintain bases," [15] In the joint military vocabulary then emerging, "garrison" embraced "all units assigned to a base or area for defense, development, operation and maintenance of facilities." An "Air Force base" was a facility "for which the Air Force has operating responsibility, together with interior lines of communication and minimum surrounding area required for local security. (Normally not greater than an area of 20 square miles.)" [16] Navy and Marine bases (including air bases) were depicted in much the same terms but their extent was fixed at 40 square miles. Neither standards nor size limits were set down for Army bases.

The Agreement made no mention of an Air Force ground combat mission. In contrast, the Army's key responsibility was "to seize, occupy and defend land areas." Similarly, the Navy and Marine Corps were "to seize and defend advanced naval bases and to conduct such land operations as may be essential to the prosecution of a naval campaign."

Nowhere did the Key West Agreement assign the Air Force the mission of defending its air bases. It also neglected to tell how base defense (common to all Services) would tie in with area defense (chiefly an Army duty). Instead, the Agreement charged the Joint Chiefs of Staff (JCS) with shaping policies and doctrines for joint operations. Reconciling the different Service viewpoints slowed efforts of the Ad Hoc Committee for Joint Policies and Procedures of the Joint Chiefs of Staff.[17] Not until 19 September 1951 was Joint Action Armed Forces (JAAF) published.* [18] Amended from time to time the JAAF was superseded on 23 November 1959

* The Royal Air Force decided at the close of the war to retain the RAF regiment as an essential element of a "balanced Air Force."

† The first Secretary of Defense, James V. Forrestal, held a conference with the Joint Chiefs of Staff at Key West, Fla., in March 1948 to define service responsibilities and missions.

*Earlier guidance was provided by a JCS paper of 4 April 1951, which described itself as "an interim measure pending final approval of the completed Joint Action Armed Forces Publication."

by Joint Chiefs of Staff Publication Number 2 (JCS Pub. 2), Unified Action Armed Forces (UNAAF).

The UNAAF made no significant change in the "principles, doctrines and functions of the Armed Forces . . . acting together" in the matter of base defense. Dealing in broad general terms, JCS Pub. 2, defined base defense as one of several "special operations" not tied to a single Service. The new directive required unified or specified commanders to assign responsibility for local base defense, define its areas, and see that proper relations were set up between area and local defense commanders. The commander of an area that encompassed an air base needed to give it overall protection against the interference or threat of nearby and distant enemy forces. Regardless of Service, the base commander was charged with local defense. He exercised operational control over forces of all Services while they were actively engaged in the local base defense mission. This was in essence the sum total of JCS guidance in the planning and conduct of joint base defense operations.[19]

Largely because of this broad approach, the Air Force found the JAAF and UNAAF "filled with 'semantic compromises' which left 'gray areas' of meanings . . . . which in times of crisis 'could prove costly in delay and indecisiveness in military action.' "[20] For example, the geographical limits of the local base defense mission were undefined. Moreover, guidance was missing on the type and size of the combat forces called for by this function. Hence, from the outset the Air Force's defense role had been vague in terms of joint doctrine.

The Korean War

The outbreak of the Korean War in June 1950 focused urgent operational concern on air base defense. The Air Force immediately began a buildup of ground combat forces for self-defense. As the nucleus of this force, the Air Police establishment expanded from 10,000 personnel in July 1950 to 39,000 in December 1951. Crash procurement of armored cars, machineguns, recoilless rifles, and other infantry-type weapons was initiated.[21]

Yet after 1 year of war, The Air Provost Marshal could still report to the Air Staff that "the Air Force is without policy or tactical doctrine for Air Base Ground Defense."[22] Nearly another year passed before the Air Force Council approved a statement of base defense doctrine.[23] As the conflict drew to a close, this doctrine was formally implemented by Air Force Regulation (AFR) 355-4, 3 March 1953. It defined local ground defense "as all measures taken by the local Air Force installation commander to deny hostile forces access to the area encompassing all buildings, equipment, facilities, landing fields, dispersal areas, and adjacent terrain" from which the installation could be neutralized. This purely emergency mission excluded "sustained ground defense operations."[24]

Performance of this mission fell to provisional base defense task forces organized and equipped like infantry. They consisted for the most part of airmen not directly linked to flight operations. Air Policemen acted as a cadre for these forces, with the base commander or his provost marshal exercising command. At Headquarters USAF, the Deputy Chief of Staff for Operations had primary responsibility for base defense. The technical responsibility for security troops and security systems development was assigned to The Air Provost Marshal.[25]

As this policy evolved within the Air Staff, the Strategic Air Command (SAC) had formulated its own base defense guidance.* In fact, the most lucid statement of prevailing Air Force base defense rationale appeared in the October 1952 edition of SAC Manual 205-2. It rejected the notion that the USAF ground defense mission conflicted with Army functions, because self-defense is an inherent responsibility of all commanders. Moreover, normal Army campaign strategy and tactics for defending land areas inevitably left small areas or points open to attack by small enemy forces. Because the Army was and must remain an offensive force, its doctrine contemplated taking the defensive in a given area only to reach a decision elsewhere. Consequently, the Army's limited and temporary defense role might well run counter to, or coincide only accidentally with, the USAF mission at specific air base locations. The Army in such instances could scarcely be expected to confine its operations to the defense of Air Force elements not vital to its own mission.

Conversely, SAC officials felt that success of the Air Force mission might require point defense of elements which the Army could not afford to protect. Further, as joint defense plans would most likely rely on distant troops, air installations would be vulnerable to surprise attacks pending their arrival. And these defensive forces might not come at all if an overriding Army offensive mission developed at the decisive moment. Hence, the SAC rationale held that ground defense must inescapably remain an organic USAF function.*

With the end of the Korean War in July 1953, Far East Air Forces (FEAF) assessed and documented its experience in a summary report. Among other things FEAF found that "effective security against sabotage and a workable ground defense system was [sic] never fully developed on most Air Force installations in Korea" because plans "were not correlated with the threat. . . . or were beyond the unit's capability to execute effectively."[26] This serious shortcoming, however, did not spell disaster, because in actual practice the main Air Force security mission was to protect resources from theft and pilferage, not to defend bases from ground attack.† Although at times from 32,000 to 35,000 North Korean guerrillas were operating in United Nations territory, they ignored air bases as key targets.[27] The FEAF report cited no air base attacks by guerrillas or other irregular forces and no aircraft lost or damaged by such action.

---

*A detailed review of the SAC defense concept by Air Staff and SAC officials found it in "complete accord" with the Air Staff position. [Ltr (U), Lt Gen Curtis E. LeMay, Commander in Chief, SAC, to Maj Gen William F. McKee, Asst VCS, 13 Aug 51.]

*These views echoed and were possibly inspired by those of Air Marshal Sir Arthur S. Barratt and his committee in their report recommending the permanent retention of the RAF Regiment. [Report of *a Committee on the Future of the RAF Regiment,* Great Britain, Air Ministry, 1 Dec 45.]

† One Air Police officer informed The Air Provost Marshal that during the first six months of the Korean War "the major portion of our time was occupied by interior guard, prevention of thievery, ever present and always successful pilferage, trespassing and securing property at unloading points or in transit." [Ltr, Capt Garland H. Jarvis to Brig. Gen. Joseph V. Dillon, 2 Jan 51.]

Air bases were overrun or threatened when major enemy units ruptured the front, a contingency that was clearly an Army rather than a local base defense responsibility.

The New Look

By 1953 the Air Force had created a foundation in doctrine, manpower, equipment, and training for building a refined, organic, local ground defense capability. However, this program fell victim to the ambivalent experience of the Korean War, reduced resources, a new national strategy, and revised intelligence estimates.

A telling lesson of the war was the inconsistency between the actual combat threat to air bases and that envisioned in AFR 355-4. This contradiction deeply eroded the regulation's credibility.

Also, the extraordinary growth of Air Police manpower drew critical congressional attention during a postwar scrutiny of defense appropriations. And when USAF spokesmen, unversed in security and defense concepts, could not convincingly explain why the Air Force needed so many more policemen than the Army, Navy, and Marine Corps, only a prompt USAF pledge to reduce Air Police strength by 20 percent restrained Congress from imposing a statutory ceiling.[28]

During this same period, a basic switch in national military strategy led to a "new look" at air base defense concepts. Containment or communism, the Eisenhower Administration decided, would be achieved by "brinksmanship" diplomacy, backed by a public avowal that the United States would resort to massive nuclear

Brinksmanship diplomacy of the Eisenhower plan brought a "new look" at air base defense concepts. At the Bermuda Conference in December 1953 are (left to right) French Premier Joseph Laniel, President Dwight D. Eisenhower, and British Prime Minister Winston Churchill.

retaliation if its vital interests were imperiled. This policy did not envision further U.S. involvement in limited wars like the one in Korea. It assumed that a future conflict would be decided by an immediate exchange of nuclear strikes during a fairly short period followed by exploitation by the victor to end the war. The assumption stressing the initial phase required a force-in-being to deliver the nuclear weapons. But, because U.S. policy was retaliatory, not preemptive, the USSR was afforded both the initiative and the element of surprise.

Reflecting this new strategy, intelligence estimates calculated that enemy action would probably include attacks by clandestine teams of highly trained agents against the U.S. nuclear strike installations. Overt ground assaults were deemed unlikely.[29]

Under these circumstances, a 1957 Air Staff study found existing base defense doctrine completely unsound. The study scored reliance on early warning, unattainable training standards, manpower waste, emphasis on an implausible threat, and other failings. AFR 355-4 was therefore condemned as "impractical, unmanageable," and incapable of yielding "defense-in-being consistent with up-to-date estimates and war planning concepts." [30]

The study asserted that quality base defense could best be achieved by the Internal Installation Security Program, originally established in March 1951 by AFR 205-5. This program centered on protecting critical weapon systems, equipment, materiel, and facilities from sabotage. It applied solely to bases with a combat or combat support mission and, with such bases, only to areas that contained vital combat equipment or facilities. Protection of these areas was provided by strict Air Police enforcement of personnel circulation controls, with access based upon a validated "right and need." A 24-hour back-up capability was supplied by small, mobile, sabotage alert teams of Air Policemen. The emergency reserve was comprised of off-duty Air Policemen or other qualified base personnel. Essentially, the entire system was manned by Air Policemen alone, an alluring feature considering the failures to implement the earlier AFR 355-4 concept. To cope with a threat that exceeded this security capability, the study concluded that "the base must be garrisoned by friendly ground forces or evacuation . . . must be accomplished."[31]

Following Air Staff approval of this appraisal, AFR 205-5 replaced AFR 355-4 and was expanded to include protection against small hostile groups. The term "local ground defense" became "reenforced security." This shift in USAF base defense policy revoked the concept of a limited ground combat capability for defense against an overt external threat. In its stead, the Air Force adopted a concept calling for an expanded interior guard system to counter a covert threat from within. The change was probably inevitable at the time, but the political and military factors behind it did not outlive the Eisenhower Administration.

The Flexible Response

The inauguration of President John F. Kennedy in January 1961 signaled another major change in national policy. The new chief executive proclaimed to the world that the United States, mindful of its "ancient heritage," stood ready "to support any friend, oppose any foe to assure the survival and the success of liberty."[32] Militarily, this policy was to be upheld not by nuclear retaliation alone, but by a strategy of controlled, flexible

President John F. Kennedy and Air Force Chief of Staff Gen. Curtis E. LeMay

response that spanned the total spectrum of conflict. "We have rejected," Kennedy told Congress, "any all or nothing posture which would leave no choice but inglorious retreat or unlimited retaliation."[33] Because so-called "wars of national liberation" were one of the most menacing forms of Communist subversion, the President personally directed that the principles and techniques of counterinsurgency* warfare be especially emphasized.[34]

Forewarned by President Dwight D. Eisenhower, the Kennedy Administration from the outset riveted its attention on Communist inroads in Southeast Asia. As a Viet Cong overthrow of the legitimate Government of Vietnam (GVN) appeared ever more imminent, the President authorized a buildup of the U.S. Military Assistance Advisory Group (MAAG). One element of this enlarged effort was the first long-term USAF deployment of forces to the RVN on 15 November 1961, when Detachment 2, 4400th Combat Crew Training (CCT) Squadron, arrived at Bien Hoa AB.* By setting the stage for the VC attack of 1 November 1964 and the ensuing transformation of USAF air base defense operations, this event opened a new and eventful chapter in the history of USAF air force defense operations.[35]

*Those military, paramilitary, political, economic, psychological, and civic actions taken by a government to defeat subversive insurgency.

*This operation was nicknamed Farm Gate. An all-volunteer unit, the 4400th CCT Squadron was formed in April 1961 at Eglin AFB, Fla. Its announced mission was to train foreign air force personnel in counterinsurgency operations. Equipped with T-28, B-26, and SC-47 aircraft, the 4400th attained operational readiness in September 1961.

United States Marines of the 9th Marine Expeditionary Brigade land at Da Nang, Vietnam, March 1965

II. EMERGENCE OF THE AIR BASE DEFENSE MISSION

> I expect that our combat battalions will be used primarily to go after the VC and that we will not be forced to expend our capabilities simply to protect ourselves. . . . Therefore, ... all forces of whatever service who find themselves operating without infantry protection . . . will be organized, trained and exercised to perform the defense and security functions.
>
> —Gen. William C. Westmoreland, 1965.

The Combat Advisory Phase

President Kennedy believed that the South Vietnamese themselves would have to defeat Communist insurgents in the Republic of Vietnam. Thus, in November 1961 he stressed that U.S. military personnel sent to the RVN were there not to fight but to help the indigenous armed forces to help themselves. If such U.S. aid resulted in a strong local effort, U.S. combat units would be unnecessary. Without this effort, U.S. forces could not prevail against insurgents operating in the midst of a population hostile or apathetic to the legal government.

At the same time, the President was profoundly interested in building on counterinsurgency capability within the U.S. armed forces. He repeatedly urged that the JCS utilize the situation in South Vietnam to study and test techniques and equipment for use in a guerrilla war environment. Hence the military services received a dual mandate. They would continue to stress the training and employment of indigenous armed forces for joint operations in support of other friendly countries.[1]

General LeMay, the new Air Force Chief of Staff, accordingly approved a plan accenting counterinsurgency. The Air Staff took steps to devise special equipment, tactics, and skills; to orient and train personnel; and to improve operational intelligence collection. This program did not actively consider the impact of insurgency warfare on air base defense. It overlooked the need to prepare indigenous forces to defend their own air bases, and to develop an organic USAF counterinsurgency ground defense capability. Insofar as air base security was concerned, the Air Staff remained preoccupied with the cold war threat.

The landing of Marines at Da Nang in March 1965 brought the first U.S. ground combat troops to the war. Until their arrival, the United States relied upon the Government of Vietnam to protect American personnel and resources. This policy was clearly a calculated risk, considering the Republic of Vietnam's dwindling capacity to cope effectively with the Communist threat. The initial desire of Kennedy and Johnson administrations to avoid a ground combat role explains why U.S. forces were withheld from this mission. But it does not account for the absence of an Air Force advisory effort to upgrade Vietnamese Air Force (VNAF) base defense forces nor the failure to begin creation of an organic USA ground defense capability at this time.

During 1961-1964 the chief operating locations (OLs) of Air Force advisors were the VNAF air bases at Da Nang, Bien Hoa, and Tan Son Nhut. In general the Army of the Republic of Vietnam (ARVN) was charged with the perimeter and external defense of these bases. The ARVN parceled out this mission to a miscellany of tactical and service units of both regular and regional forces. Internal security, a VNAF responsibility, was provided by small detachments of military police (Quan Canh). All these security forces reflected the shortcomings of the Republic of Vietnam Armed Forces (RVNAF) as a whole. Under weak and unreliable leaders, they were as a rule understrength, ill-trained, undisciplined, and poorly motivated. Lacking any standard concept of operations, local air base defense actions were largely unplanned, uncoordinated, and uncontrolled. The few physical security facilities and safeguards in use were inadequate or in disrepair. Scant support came from military intelligence agencies or the civil organizations responsible for national internal security.

Throughout this early period the Viet Cong/North Vietnamese Army (VC/NVA) chose to ignore these air bases. Thus, RVNAF base defense capabilities were untested, their weaknesses hidden, and the importance of the air base defense mission obscured from U.S. civil and military authorities.

The Political Scene

South Vietnamese political instability had much to do with the diminishing morale and combat effectiveness of the RVNAF. As the only real center of political power in RVN, the armed forces were directly involved in this trend which was accelerated by the military overthrow of the Ngo Dinh Diem regime on 1 November 1964. Against a background of riots, revolts, strikes, and personal feuds,* all of the successive governments failed to mobilize the population and resources for a concerted counterinsurgency effort on a national scale.[2]

A spinoff of this political turmoil was the emergence of an interservice enmity that gravely jeopardized air base defense operations. On 13 September 1964, when ARVN elements tried to overthrow the Khanh government, the VNAF, on orders from Air Commodore Nguyen Cao Ky, hastened the coup's collapse by threatening to bomb buildings seized by the coup forces. Thereafter, political overtones colored ARVN-VNAF relations and isolated the two services to a degree that crippled coordination between the interior and exterior security forces responsible for the air base defense mission.[3]

One study of the South Vietnamese officer corps concluded that it often seemed that "the military was engaged in a factional struggle to control the government rather than in the struggle in the countryside against the Viet Cong." [4] The frequent shakeups in personnel at the top echelon of

*Between 1 November 1963 and 21 June 1965, there were eight successful or abortive *coups d'etat,* all involving various factions of the RVNAF.

the central government invariably triggered changes in the military commands. These in turn set off a chain reaction that reached down to the lowest levels of the armed forces. Although corps areas were affected, the most drastic changes occurred in III Corps because of its proximity to Saigon. When a political upheaval loomed, U.S. observers noted that the entire officer corps tended to adopt a "wait and see" attitude. Unswerving loyalty to the ruling faction, not professional competence, led to timely promotion and choice assignments. This inveterate linkage of the military establishment to partisan politics impeded both the development of a professional officer corps and the progress of military operations.

U.S. Security

Lulled by the absence of VC/NVA attacks on air bases, the Air Force was generally apathetic to the potential gravity of the physical security threat in South Vietnam, while other USAF elements responded vigorously to Administration desires that South Vietnam be a counterinsurgency testing ground. Security officials ignored this requirement and took no action to formulate base defense doctrine and tactics. Instead, they continued to concentrate their efforts on the development and refinement of internal security measures to counter cold war threats.

For example, in February 1962, Headquarters, Pacific Air Forces (PACAF)—totally disregarding USAFs tenant status in the Republic of Vietnam—directed the 2d Advanced Echelon (ADVON)* to insure that all USAF internal security measures were enforced at operating bases in South Vietnam.[5] With equal wariness, 2d ADVON requested a staff assistance visit by Headquarters, Thirteenth Air Force to define the security needs of USAF detachments at VNAF bases.[6] A model of circumspection, the report of this visit suggested that 2d ADVON rely on standard Air Force procedures to detect and neutralize sabotage. It discouraged the use of ground force defense methods that entailed unfamiliar weapons and created support problems. And, while conceding that a large-scale enemy assault might require active USAF defense measures, the report warned that stocking more than a single basic load of small-arms ammunition might invite a VC/NVA attack.[7]

In essence these views accorded substantially with the position of the U.S. Military Assistance Command, Vietnam (USMACV), which repeatedly declared that it relied on the Government of Vietnam to safeguard American personnel, property, and equipment. Except for personal defense, USMACV ordered that only passive security measures be taken.[8] As practical experience accumulated, acceptance of this quiescent approach waned.

By the end of 1963, U.S. personnel on the scene had a keener insight into air base defense realities and became increasingly critical of VNAF and USAF security roles. They insisted that VNAF local security measures were satisfactory only if judged by the criterion of numbers. Caprice appeared to be the constant factor in these operations. Manning of blockhouses and observation towers was

---

*Established 15 November 1961, 2d ADVON exercised operational control of Farm Gate and Thirteenth Air Force Detachments in South Vietnam. (The 2d ADVON commander also was Chief of the Air Section, MAAG.) On 8 October 1962, 2d ADVON was redesignated 2d Air Division; on 1 April 1966, Seventh Air Force. *See* Chapter IX for details on organization, command, and control of U.S. Forces in the Republic of Vietnam.

erratic. Only at Tan Son Nhut did the VNAF allow the USAF to guard its aircraft. Barred from the flight line at Bien Hoa and Da Nang, USAF air police guarded only cantonment and supply areas.* For perhaps the first time, the USAF security doctrine stressing a cold war threat came under fire. Field commanders asserted that this concept "must be revised and more flexible rules and standards devised for the protection of USAF personnel and equipment in limited war areas." Thirteenth Air Force launched reform proposals in January 1964 but neither MACV nor PACAF acted on them.[9]

*The Air Force at this time had only a token security force in South Vietnam —1 officer and 280 men in temporary duty (TDY) status.

Complacency toward air base defense was largely dispelled, when hostilities suddenly escalated in August 1964. Naval units of the Democratic Republic of Vietnam (DRV)* attacked a U.S. Navy patrol in the international waters of the Gulf of Tonkin, and U.S. aircraft retaliated by striking targets in North Vietnam. It was immediately recognized that the ensuing influx of USAF aircraft into South Vietnam vastly enhanced the target value of Tan Son Nhut, Bien Hoa, and Da Nang. The probability of VC/NVA counter reprisals provoked apprehension in the command chain from 2d Air Division to the Joint Chiefs of Staff.

The 2d Air Division commander urged that the Commander, U.S. Military Assistance Command, Vietnam (COMUSMACV), pressure the Joint General Staff (JGS), RVNAF, to allocate more troops to the base security mission. To reduce the risk at Bien Hoa, where aircraft were parked wingtip to wingtip, he proposed moving one B-57 jet bomber squadron to Clark Air Base in the Philippines.[10]

After personally reviewing the Bien Hoa and Tan Son Nhut defense

*The Government of North Vietnam.

F–4B Phantom II jet being launched from the angle deck of the USS *Constitution*

Ambassador Maxwell D. Taylor

plans, COMUSMACV verified the Thirteenth Air Force finding of January 1964 that there was an "immediate requirement for more formal coordination between U.S. services and VNAF and ARVN forces." He attached four U.S. Army officers to 2d Air Division to advise on air base defense and to coordinate RVNAF actions. He also called on the Joint General Staff to create combined U.S./RVN base defense command posts at Tan Son Nhut and Bien Hoa.[11]

Sharing the concern of onscene commanders, the Commander in Chief, Pacific Command (CINCPAC), warned the JCS that the VC could conduct sabotage or surprise attacks up to battalion size. He cautioned that the United States must be "alert to any slackening of ARVN provisions for security of these air bases," and be "prepared to provide troop support for their protection and be ready to evacuate aircraft for any base under attack by VC or mobs." [12]

Meanwhile, General LeMay directed the Commander in Chief, Pacific Air Forces (CINCPACAF), to check personally the adequacy of defense plans for RVN air bases. At the same time—revealing he knew the token character of the USAF general military training program—LeMay ordered that "the means each individual has for self-protection and weapons qualification" be given special attention.[13]

On 1 September 1964 a summary of the status of air base security in the Republic of Vietnam was presented to the Joint Chiefs of Staff. It reported that the RVNAF Commander had allocated one airborne battalion each to the defense of Tan Son Nhut, Bien Hoa, and Da Nang. He had in addition installed new mine fields and initiated defoliation programs. The U.S. Ambassador, Maxwell D. Taylor, COMUSMACV, and CINCPAC all agreed that American ground forces were not needed in the RVN for base defense. But as a precaution, CINCPAC had positioned naval amphibious forces of U.S. Marines 30 miles at sea off Da Nang and Cap St. Jacques (Vung Tau). The Joint Chiefs judged these measures sufficient to meet the potential threat in the Republic of Vietnam at that time.[14]

Yet, as was frequently the case, these reported RVNAF improvements soon proved to be most illusory. At a joint U.S./RVN meeting at Tan Son Nhut on 10 September 1964, the RVNAF spokesman advised that Bien Hoa and Tan Son Nhut were now organized for a combined ground defense "but the Defense Command Post was operational only in case of alert." He also disclosed the "lack of sufficient personnel to man the outer perimeters of the air bases and the inability of the Joint General Staff . . . to provide more." Moreover, the volatile political situation and the questionable loyalty of individual soldiers also came up. Doubts were expressed about the prudence of continuing to employ Regional Forces (RF)* on air bases.[15]

Three days following this meeting, the attempt to overthrow the Khanh Government took place. As mentioned earlier, it injected an element of enduring mistrust into ARVN-VNAF relations. These and other security developments were duly reported up the chain of command. On 21 October—10 days before the Viet Cong attacked Bien Hoa—2d Air Division informed PACAF that ground defenses at Bien Hoa and Tan Son Nhut were still unsatisfactory. It attributed unpreparedness to "RVNAF inability or reluctance to implement certain of the recommendations made to them and the conflict of interests sometimes dividing VNAF and ARVN."[16]

In the opinion of Ambassador Taylor, "the attack on Bien Hoa marked a turning point in Viet Cong tactics." Hitherto, he observed, the small VC assaults on American personnel and property had been incidental to operations directed against RVNAF units accompanied by U.S. advisors. In this case, however, the Viet Cong targeted a major U.S. operating base for a preplanned attack.[17] The endless post-mortems of this severely destructive raid uncovered no truly productive defense actions taken after the Gulf of Tonkin incidents of the previous August. The sole exception was the evacuation of 14 B-57 bombers from Bien Hoa to the Philippines. The affair demonstrated beyond doubt that RVNAF defense measures were inadequate and uncoordinated. Patrolling by untrained external defense forces was ineffectual, and their reaction time was incredibly slow. Warned in advance of the enemy's presence in the area, the province chief failed to alert U.S. forces, and on the night of the attack he fragmented and weakened the external defenses by withdrawing men for convoy duty.[18]

In a soothing response to a Congressional inquiry on the Bien Hoa attack, the Office of the Secretary of Defense (OSD) omitted direct identification of RVNAF shortcomings and simply stated that there could be no "finite assurance that mortar attacks can be prevented." The legislators were told of renewed efforts to persuade the Government of Vietnam to redouble its security measures. Gen. William C. Westmoreland, COMUSMACV, had urged General Khanh to intensify patrolling, position more and better security troops on major bases, assign special police to enforce movement control in populated areas next to air bases, and create a special purpose air base intelligence system. General Westmoreland had in addition suggested improvement in organization, integration, and alert posture of reaction forces (infantry, artillery, and air), and the need to protect aircraft by greater dispersal and more revetments.[19] In retrospect these actions

*RVN local defense forces recruited and employed within one of the administrative regions into which the country was divided.

Lt. Gen. John L. Throckmorton, USA

clearly constituted a sound program for protecting bases from insurgents. Yet the record reveals that they were never fully or adequately put into practice.

The security problems bared in the Bien Hoa attack would shortly be revealed as intrinsic to all U.S./RVN air base defense operations. The experience of Lt. Gen. John L. Throckmorton, U.S. Army, Deputy COMUSMACV, was an early example. On 15 November 1964 he met with Maj. Gen. Tran Van Don, Deputy Commander in Chief, Republic of Vietnam Armed Forces. The latter agreed to reinforce Bien Hoa's external defense forces with one RF infantry company and one airborne company. Throckmorton learned the next day that the RF company had been duly transferred from internal security duties under the VNAF base commander to the local ground defense force under the ARVN province chief. No action had been taken on the airborne unit. Told of this omission, General Don promised to take up the matter at once with the RVNAF Chief of Staff. On 17 November Throckmorton discovered that the airborne company was moving to the field for a week-long operation and would not be at hand for the base defense mission. This information and General Westmoreland's strong recommendation that the company be returned to defend the base were relayed to Don. He promised to discuss the problem with the RVNAF Deputy Chief of Staff for Operations.[20] Together with expanded enemy offensive operations, repeated episodes of this type increasingly undermined USAF confidence in the security of its RVN air bases.

Gen. Hunter Harris, Jr., CINCPACAF, believed that the time had come to bring in U.S. ground forces. He informed General LeMay that USAF commanders in the Republic of Vietnam deemed external defense inadequate and doubted that the ARVN could do the job. "As a result," Harris declared, "I do not believe we will have security from mortar attack in the foreseeable future unless the U.S. decides to use U.S. Marines or Army security forces to secure and control about an 8,000-meter area around Da Nang, Bien Hoa, and Tan Son Nhut." [21]

Ambassador Taylor and General Westmoreland rejected this proposal out of hand. It would, the latter contended, take at least one battalion per airfield and the presence of U.S. troops "might cause GVN to lose interest in the defense of these major RVNAF bases and relax in its performance." [22]

Other weighty obstacles were the language, political, and psychological problems involved. Westmoreland's only concession to USAF apprehensions was a request that CINCPAC deploy 300 more security policemen to South Vietnam to bolster internal security. He did not foresee that these security police would have any responsibility to defend air bases against organized VC ground attacks.[23]

Nevertheless, USAF agitation on this score was not totally ignored. In December 1964 the Joint Chiefs of Staff expressed views akin to those of USAF commanders. They conveyed to CINCPAC their concern over the chronic instability of the Government of Vietnam and the security of installations there. Pinpointing perimeter and area defense of airfields as critical problems, the JCS ordered CINCPAC to reassess the adequacy of RVNAF defense operations.[24]

The day before Christmas 1964, VC/NVA terrorists went into action once again, this time detonating a 300-pound explosive charge in the Brink Bachelor Officers' Quarters (BOQ) in central Saigon, killing 2 and injuring 71 U.S. military personnel. A committee appointed by COMUSMACV to consider the Communist threat in the Saigon-Cholon-Gia Dinh complex identified 60 installations requiring protection. But there was disagreement within the committee as to how this could best be provided. The USMACV Provost Marshal recommended that a tailored U.S. Army military police battalion be deployed to augment existing GVN security forces. Dissenting strongly, the United States Overseas Mission (USOM) representatives insisted that the Government of Vietnam retain undiluted responsibility for the security of U.S. property, personnel, and installations.[25]

Saigon officers' quarters damaged by an explosion on Christmas Eve 1964

This MACV decision was in due course reflected at PACOM. In his response to the Joint Chiefs of Staff, CINCPAC confirmed that outer perimeter and area defenses of air bases were still inadequate, but concluded that "the RVNAF are still considered the best qualified to correct the deficiencies." [26] For the moment these views prevailed because the JCS "demurred from recommending the introduction of U.S. combat troops in RVN for air base defense unless the unified commander requests the action." The Air Staff therefore exhorted CINCPACAF "to press CINCPAC for employment of U.S. forces in RVN . . . or other such actions as you believe essential to enhance airbase defense." [27]

In any event, this guidance had been anticipated. A month earlier, CINCPACAF had proposed to CINCPAC a base defense concept fully consistent with USAF objectives. This was an eclectic production culled from JCS Pub. 2, base defense doctrine of Korean War vintage, USMACV directives, and sundry other sources. It confined USAF responsibility solely to the internal security of Air Force personnel, equipment, and facilities. The most vital and extensive responsibilities were allocated to local ground defense forces, which in the PACAF scheme should consist of the RVNAF augmented by U.S. Army and/or U.S. Marine Corps units. Their immense task would be to constantly observe and patrol a zone extending 8,000 meters from the base perimeter, in order to block the approach of enemy ground forces and prevent the emplacement of standoff weapons such as mortars and rockets.[28]

This PACAF package did not rouse much enthusiasm at the unified headquarters. After a 6-week delay, CINCPAC sent the proposal to COMUSMACV with an indorsement that totally but tactfully quashed it. "This concept," he told General Westmoreland, "is approved in principle, however, those measures that are not in consonance with current assignment of responsibilities are not approved." [29] The only practical significance of this episode was that the PACAF concept articulated, for the first time, the air base defense policy resolutely pursued by the USAF throughout the war. That is, USAF security responsibility ended at the perimeter, and within that perimeter it was restricted to USAF resources.

Despite U.S. advisory efforts, public order and security under the Government continued to deteriorate at an ever increasing rate. Still there was no public change in U.S. security policy. Immediately after the February 1965 attacks on Army facilities at Pleiku and Qui Nhon, General Throckmorton, Deputy COMUSMACV, told reporters:

> We are operating under the policy that defense of these key installations is a Vietnamese responsibility. Of course we are providing a certain amount of internal security of our own, but defense of the outer perimeter is definitely the job of the Vietnamese.[30]

Yet, 2 days later Throckmorton took the opposite view in a private memorandum to Westmoreland. He noted the vital importance of Da Nang AB, doubted that the RVNAF could defeat a determined attack, and recommended landing the 9th Marine Expeditionary (ME) Brigade to secure the installation.[31]

With Ambassador Taylor's reluctant concurrence, Westmoreland approved his deputy's estimate of the situation and on 22 February forwarded it through CINCPAC to the JCS. Coupled with the VC/NVA attacks on American bases and the imminent collapse of the RVNAF, this recommendation by the field commander hastened the decision by the Johnson administration to commit U.S. ground troops to the Vietnam War.

U.S. Ground Forces Deploy for Defense

On 7 March 1965 the Joint Chiefs of Staff directed CINCPAC to land "at once" at Da Nang specified elements of the Marine Expeditionary Brigade

> to occupy and defend critical terrain features in order to secure the airfield and, as directed, communications facilities, U.S. supporting installations, port facilities, landing beaches, and other U.S. installations in the area against attack. The U.S. Marine Force will not repeat not engage in day to day actions against the Viet Cong.[32]

As the first contingent of the 9th ME Brigade came ashore, Gen. Earle G. Wheeler, JCS Chairman, publicly announced the reason for the deployment and its limited mission. For some time, he told Congress, officials from the President on down "have been increasingly concerned about the security of our people and our facilities in Vietnam." As the enemy threat grew progressively more ominous,

> General Westmoreland recommened to us that we move a force of Marines into the Da Nang area to provide local security and to guarantee, in effect, that the place would not be overrun by a concentration of Viet Cong, our people killed and our aircraft destroyed.[33]

Secretary of State Dean Rusk stressed the same theme. On the television program, *Face the Nation,* he pointed out that "the purpose of those Marines is to provide local close-in security. . . . It is not their mission to engage in pacification operations." By taking over the security mission, the Secretary explained, the Marines would free the RVNAF to focus on offensive actions.[34]

News stories of the Da Nang landing surmised correctly that the dispatch of U.S. Army combat units for similar security duties would soon follow. On 3 May the 173d Airborne Brigade arrived in Bien Hoa/Vung Tau to protect the American air and logistic bases in the III Corps Tactical Zone (CTZ). At the same time, Westmoreland was formulating plans for more large-scale deployments to cope with the security threat.

In July 1965 President Lyndon B. Johnson sent Secretary of Defense

Gen. Earle G. Wheeler, Chairman of the Joint Chiefs of Staff, President Lyndon B. Johnson, and Secretary of Defense Robert S. McNamara

Robert S. McNamara to Saigon to appraise the situation directly. Upon his arrival, Westmoreland presented a USMACV "shopping list." Heading the list was an urgent request for 44 more infantry battalions in 1965 and another 24 in 1966. Of these 68 units, 21 were earmarked for base and site defense. Four air bases, Tan Son Nhut, Bien Hoa, Da Nang, and Nha Trang were said to require such support immediately. Five others, Pleiku, Binh Thuy, Qui Nhon, Phan Rang, and Cam Ranh Bay would need it by October 1965. According to USMACV, security of these installations demanded that

> a zone enclosing each base and site contiguous to its boundaries, must be defended continuously to a depth and degree of saturation that will serve to prevent enemy penetration or employment of artillery or mortars. The defense capability must be responsive to the needs of the USAF commander on the base.[35]

The local base defense role of the forces in the so-called 44-battalion proposal was stressed during discussions with the Secretary of Defense. When McNamara asked where and how these units would be employed, the USMACV response was that the majority would be deployed to base areas located at Hue, Phu Bai, Da Nang, Chu Lai, Qui Nhon, Binh Khe/An Khe, the Dong Ba Thin/Cam Ranh Bay complex, and the Bien An Khe, the Dong Ba Thin/Cam Ranh Bay complex, and the Bien Hoa/Tan Son Nhut complex. Once in place,

> the initial mission of these forces is to secure the base and its internal LOC's through a combination of static defense and vigorous patrolling. After security has been established . . . those forces not required for base security will conduct offensive operations in the immediate vicinity to expand the Tactical Area of Responsibility (TAOR) around each base area. . . . As the base becomes more secure through the foregoing actions, the forces *(over*

and above those required for security of the base) will be available to conduct offensive missions from the base area.[36]

McNamara was told that base defense ground forces were programmed on the basis of three battalions for each major base, two for every minor one. Clearly, base security was central in the USMACV justification for additional ground forces.

President Johnson again underscored the primacy of the security mission in late July 1965 when he announced his approval of the 44-battalion proposal. Johnson assured the newsmen that these additional troops did not signal any change in U.S. policy or aims within the Republic of Vietnam.[37]

In August Westmoreland published a 3-phase concept of operations that spelled out actions to stave off immediate GVN defeat, resume the offensive, and destroy enemy troops and bases. In each phase the security of major military bases, airfields, and communications centers was identified as the primary task.[38] During November Westmoreland informed Defense Secretary McNamara that 29 of the 97 U.S. and third-country battalions requested for calendar year 1966 would defend major U.S. bases.[39]

At a January 1966 Mission Council Meeting, Westmoreland announced that "about 50%" of U.S. ground forces were then "tied down in securing base areas." As the buildup continued, he saw this number falling to "about 30%," a figure consistent with the data given to Secretary McNamara 2 months earlier.[40] On 1 October 1966, according to Ambassador Henry Cabot Lodge,* 40 percent of American troops were "guarding bases" while the rest engaged in "offensive operations" against the enemy's main force units.[41] And in the 1967 Combined Campaign Plan for U.S. and RVN military operations the security of bases and surrounding areas was specified a primary mission.[42] Thus, as far into the war as 1967, classified

*Lodge succeeded Taylor as Ambassador to RVN in August 1965.

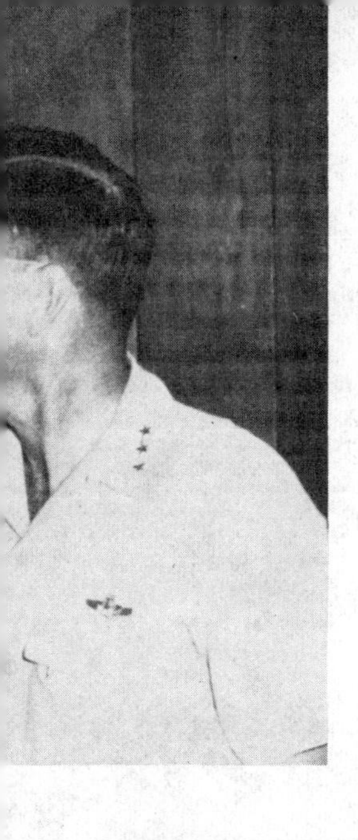

Gen. John P. McConnell, Air Force Chief of Staff, Ambassador Henry Cabot Lodge, and Lt. Gen. William Momyer, Seventh Air Force commander

lans and official public statements ways offered the security rationale, long with other reasons to justify the eployment of more ground combat nits to South Vietnam.

U.S. Ground Forces Employed for Offense

In the spring of 1965 the Air orce's hopes for base defense ran igh. With the Marines at Da Nang nd the Army at Bien Hoa, it seemed nere would soon be more than enough merican ground forces to protect SAF operating bases. This sanguine rospect, however, soon withered as ne Government of Vietnam remained naky and its armed forces weak. VC/ NA attacks stepped up. In response these attacks, President Johnson in arly February 1965 ordered selected r strikes against North Vietnam. The everely limited bombings failed, howver, to change the policy of the Demcratic Republic of Vietnam. Coulled by his advisers in Saigon and ashington that additional measures ere required, the President moved a ep closer to committing U.S. ground forces to combat. He authorized the introduction of additional troops and approved their use in limited offensive operations while continuing the slowly ascending tempo of the Rolling Thunder air strikes against the North.*

On 1 April 1965 the President expanded the primary mission of U.S. ground forces in the RVN. By authorizing their more active use under conditions to be agreed upon by the Secretaries of State and Defense and by the Government of Vietnam.[43] As Ambassador Taylor understood the Presidential decision, the Marines could now conduct mobile insurgency operations, and in addition act as reserve support for the ARVN up to 85 kilometers from Da Nang.[44] If all went well the forming of other enclaves along the coast would be considered. Each enclave would have a brigade-sized garrison for limited offensive operations. On instructions of the President, there was no public announcement of these developments.

The second expansion of the ground force offensive mission coincided with the arrival of the 173d Airborne Brigade at Bien Hoa in May 1965. In his memoirs, President Johnson recalled that

---

*See Department of Defense (The Pentagon Papers), *United States-Vietnam Relations, 1945-1967* (Washington, 1971), Bk 4, Section IV-C-5, pp 55-62 and pp 124-6, and Lyndon B. Johnson, *The Vantage Point* (New York, 1971), pp 139-41.

> the basic mission of the U.S. forces in Vietnam up to mid-May had been to secure the base areas to which they were assigned. This mission had been broadened somewhat to permit active and aggressive patrolling near those bases. In May General Westmoreland asked permission to use his forces in combat support if it became necessary to assist a Vietnamese unit in serious trouble. I granted that permission and announced it in a White House statement on 9 June.[45]

This White House statement was not voluntary but compelled, by a State Department spokesman who inadvertently publicly disclosed the facts.* In contrast to the "broadened mission" acknowledged in his memoirs. President Johnson at the time flatly denied any change. He vigorously asserted that "the primary mission of these troops is to secure and safeguard important military installations like the air base at Da Nang," which included "active patrolling and security action." His statement ended with the assurance that the discretionary authority of the COMUSMACV to employ U.S. troops in support of hard-pressed RVNAF elements "does not change the primary mission of United States troops in South Vietnam." [46]

Nonetheless, most journalists and members of Congress viewed the White House statement (in retrospect, correctly) as an enlargement of the U.S. ground combat role. It is now known that even before the public tumult over this episode subsided, President Johnson had secretly removed the last practical curb on the use of U.S. ground forces. "Late in June," Johnson subsequently revealed,

> General Westmoreland requested and received additional authority. This permitted him to commit U.S. troops to combat "independently of or in conjunction with" Vietnamese forces if asked by the Vietnamese and if Westmoreland himself judged that their use was "necessary to strengthen the relative position of GVN forces."[47]

With this decision the shift of ground force strategy from the defense to the offense was completed.

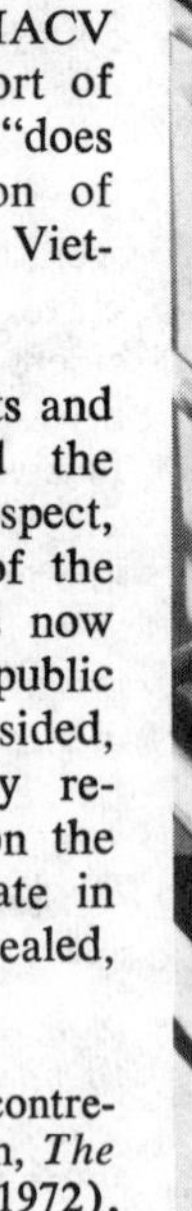

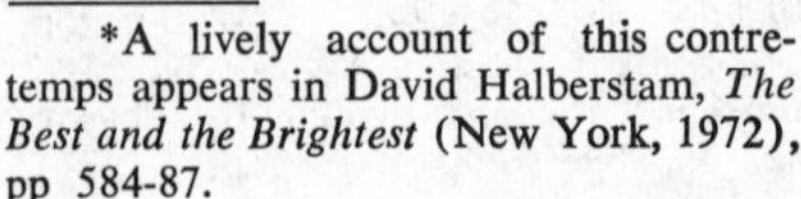

*A lively account of this contretemps appears in David Halberstam, *The Best and the Brightest* (New York, 1972), pp 584-87.

The strategy of security, tied as t was to the defense of air bases sup- porting the Air Force's Rolling Thun- der strikes, expired along with early hopes that this aerial campaign could ucceed by itself. Its demise was sig- naled by the 1 April 1965 decision reeing the Marines to undertake of- ensive operations against enemy orces. The original enclave strategy, ailored to test the counterinsurgency kills of U.S. troops in a controlled ituation, never got off the ground. Disfavored by the Army because it placed ground forces in an almost ntirely defensive role, the enclave concept waned rapidly as it became nore and more apparent that the RVNAF could not alone prevail gainst the VC/NVA. The final step n the evolution of U.S. military pol- cy was taken when President Johnson nvested General Westmoreland with he widest latitude in directing surface ground operations. This set the stage or the search-and-destroy strategy—a ustained ground offensive against the VC/NVA at any location within the RVN.

At this point the enemy again urned his attention to air bases. On July 1965 the VC/NVA penetrated Da Nang in a combined standoff and apper raid, destroying three F-102 ighters and three C-130 transports on he ground. Lt. Gen. Lewis W. Walt, Commanding General (CG), III Marine Amphibious Force (MAF),* responded with his "Ink Blot" process, a concept which aimed at reaching out from the base to conduct offensive operations, expand the TAOR, and achieve pacification without abandoning the local base defense mission. Walt then at once coordinated with ARVN a 7-kilometer extension of the Marine TAOR to the south, the area from which the attack was launched.[48] The clear intent of the Marines to build a solid local defense operation did much to allay USAF concern for the safety of Da Nang. The Army's handling of security at Bien Hoa produced quite the opposite reaction.

Gen. William C. Westmoreland

Exercising his new authority, General Westmoreland in late June 1965 began to deploy the 173d Airborne Brigade in whole or in part to other locations. Between 27-30 June he sent the unit into War Zone D (east of Bien Hoa) to support ARVN. Next, a protracted deployment to the central highlands near Pleiku absented the brigade from its Bien Hoa TAOR from 10 August to 6 September. During this period the air base on 23 August became the target of a standoff attack that damaged six A-1Es, three O-1Es, one F-100, and one U-10 aircraft. This assault starkly revealed how an unrestricted search-and-destroy strategy exposed USAF installations to the enemy. Alarmed at the long-term consequences, the USAF sought a policy change that would assure unequivocal allocation of U.S. ground forces to the local air base defense mission, inasmuch as base security was cited repeatedly in justifying additional ground force deployments to the Government of Vietnam.

---

*The 9th Marine Expeditionary Brigade was renamed the III Marine Amphibious Force in May 1965 because of an alleged imperialistic inference in the original designation.

The JCS Rebuffs the Air Force

Among the first to seek high level clarification of local air base defense was General Harris, CINCPACAF. In a personal message to Gen. John P. McConnell, USAF, Chief of Staff, Harris pointed to the sizable deployment of ground forces and assurances given Secretary McNamara that defense of major and minor bases held first and second priority. Nevertheless, he reported there was still no reasonable level of air base protection. He predicted a steady reduction in base security as ground operations shifted to the offensive. Bien Hoa, he asserted, was a foretaste of things to come. "It would seem logical," Harris observed, "for the VC to plan attacks to coincide with U.S. ground probes that reduce further already inadequate base defense forces." He deemed the "present organization for base defense . . . inadequate, the responsibility unclear, and resources not under centralized control." [49]

Harris further advised that his talks with the CINCPAC and COMUSMACV left him pessimistic about any solution favorable to the USAF. Hence he asked McConnell to act through JCS or secretarial channels to enhance the external defense. In his view, this meant deploying to each base adequate U.S. ground forces under a single commander, whose sole mission was to defend the base. Lastly, Harris proposed that McConnell consider the "development of an Air Force security force along the lines of the RAF Regiment." This, he contended, would rivet high-level attention on USAF security needs, and sort out the priorities for utilizing U.S. ground forces in South Vietnam.[50]

General McConnell replied that he agreed completely and intended "to hold the Army to its mission of pro- viding adequate external base secu- rity." If Inspector General finding supported such action, he said h would address the problem to the JC or the Army.[51]

Though not yet conveyed to Mc Connell, these findings had alread been reached. USAF inspectors on 2 August 1965 questioned Genera Throckmorton, Deputy COMUS MACV, who confirmed General Har ris's gloomy prediction. USMACV, h explained, took the position that th VNAF was responsible for interna security and the ARVN for externa security. Unfortunately, jealousy an distrust between the air and groun commanders obstructed coordination So despite USMACV efforts, he ex pected no improvement in the securit supplied by the RVNAF.[52]

Nonetheless, General Throckmor ton declared, "there is no intent t secure air bases with US troops* suc as the Marines are doing at Da Nang, because "we could use up all the U troops assigned to RVN" in this fash ion. Asked about the priorities for th defense of air bases as given to Secre tary McNamara the preceding month Throckmorton stated that "the ques tion of priorities had not come to hi attention before." "It is true," he con ceded,

> major installations have priority for defense, but only against a strong VC mass attack. There are no plans to tie down US troops to defend US air bases against mortar and sneak attack, it costs too much in troops.[53]

As an illustration, the Deput COMUSMACV cited Bien Hoa AE where the U.S. Army protected th area where a mass attack would mos

---

*Read "U.S. Army troops" here an in Throckmorton's quotations below.

kely originate. Not so at Tan Son
hut AB, however, even though its
ocal defense had been identified to
Ir. McNamara as justification for
aore ground troops. There, General
hrockmorton explained, "the only
.S. personnel participating in any
ecurity/defense effort were Air Po-
ce," because

> Tan Son Nhut should not be protected by US troops against this mass attack threat. GVN troops must be able to defend their own capitol [sic]. Tan Son Nhut is in sufficient proximity to Saigon that it should be protected by GVN troops.[54]

JSMACV policy, Throckmorton
ointed out, was to hold the Govern-
ient of Vietnam to its responsibility
or static defense and to take a calcu-
ated risk on air base security. This
vould free U.S. Army forces for of-
ensive operations and thus success-
ully conclude the war.

Word that the COMUSMACV
itended to treat air base security as a
alculated risk led General McConnell
refer the issue to the Joint Chiefs
f Staff. He proposed on 14 Septem-
er 1965 that the JCS request the
INCPAC to re-examine the air base
efense problem to assure that U.S.
round forces gave first priority to the
efense of bases, protected base pe-
imeters against VC infiltration/pene-
ation, and defended external areas in
nough depth to eliminate mass at-
acks and minimize standoff as-
aults.[55] Though this proposal merely
choed the ground force role set forth
the USMACV shopping list of July
965, it was disapproved by the other
ervice chiefs. Instead they authorized
AcConnell to discuss base defense
vith the CINCPAC and COMUS-
IACV during a forthcoming visit to
he Pacific Command.[56] This was the
ast time the USAF addressed the
VN base defense issue in the joint
rena.[57]

A Mission at Odds

Soon after the McConnell visit, Westmoreland dispelled any lingering illusions that U.S. Army troops would be utilized to fulfill the earlier USMACV proposition that "a zone enclosing each base . . . and contiguous to its boundaries must be defended continuously to a depth and degree of saturation that . . . will prevent any penetration or employment of artillery and mortars." As a subordinate unified commander under JCS Pub. 2, Westmoreland defined and fixed local base defense reponsibilities anew. In a December 1965 letter he directed commanders to give "personal and immediate attention" to the primary task —ongoing, aggressive, offensive operations to wipe out enemy main force units.[58]

Westmoreland next dealt with the corollary task of installation security. Acknowledging the difficulty and complexity of the security problem "in a war with no front lines," he rejected out of hand the use of ground forces for this task. Their commitment to static defense would cripple decisive offensive operations and delay enemy defeat. Therefore, he instructed his commanders,

> we must call upon all of our troops to perform not only on a defensive role around our installations, but also they must take certain additional measures which we all know to be essential in achieving real security. I have in mind the necessity for patrolling, for outposts and for reaction forces. . . . I desire that all

> service units and all forces of whatever service who find themselves operating without infantry protection . . . will be organized, trained and exercised to perform the defensive and security functions which I have just discussed. . . . I reiterate that their participation in self-defense is not an optional matter, but an urgent necessity.[59]

With this letter General Westmoreland wrote the formal epitaph of the security strategy from the standpoint of actual operations. He also voided his previous assurance that USAF security policemen need not defend air bases against organized VC/NVA attacks. Notably and refreshingly absent was any reference to the absurd principle that the United States relied on the GVN to defend and secure its operating bases. There was an implicit but obvious assumption that, even in modern sophisticated warfare, every U.S. military member must be prepared to engage the enemy in combat. In the final analysis, Westmoreland's base defense policy was not new. It merely revived the venerable maxim that each commander bears the ultimate responsibility for the security of his command. A commonplace in joint operations and in the ground forces, this principle had only a limited application in the USAF concept of air base defense. And it soon became evident, the Air Force did not intend to abandon its stand on the matter.

After a 6-week delay Lt. Gen. Joseph H. Moore, 2d Air Division Commander, disseminated Westmoreland's letter accompanied by the USAF interpretation of the actions directed therein. At the outset, Moore told his air base commanders that the letter applied "specifically to US ground forces." Then, expressing agreement with the USMACV intent to stress offensive operations, he underscored the need for Air Division to support this objective with "all feasibl *internal** security for self-defense a tions." Moore ordered commanders t keep in close touch with ground forc that assisted external defense, and t build the "maximum possible capabi ity for self-defense of . . . perim ter [s] over and beyond . . . that re resented by Air Police forces." [60]

To bolster defenses in the absenc of external ground forces, he su gested manning more positions alon the base perimeter or setting up a internal defense line. Concentrating o internal and perimeter security, Moo omitted any implementing instructio for patrols, outposts, and reactic forces—the extra external defens measures directed by Westmoreland. Thus the Air Force too was prepare to take a calculated risk on base sec rity rather than assume extern ground defense duties. Henceforth t the end of the war, this became fixe USAF policy and practice. Except f air operations, the Air Force loc ground defense mission did not exten beyond the legal perimeter of its i stallations.

The upshot was to leave in limb the security of air base approach later called the rocket belt.

Rejected alike by USA and USA and relegated wherever possible to th uncertain competence of RVNAF, l cal external defense constituted a indeterminate element in the overa base defense function which, as a co sequence, was a mission at odds wi the concept of unified action pr scribed by joint doctrine. Under th anomalous but enduring arrangemen our bases were for the most part u protected by any external defens forces, so that the VC/NVA we largely free to mount attacks at tim and locations of their choice.

---

*Author's emphasis.

III. THE THREAT

It is easier and more effective to destroy the enemy's aerial power by destroying his nests and eggs on the ground than to hunt his flying birds in the air.

Giulio Douhet, 1921.

The deployment of Farm Gate to the Republic of Vietnam in November 1961 marked a milestone in USAF history. For the first time, the Air Force conducted sustained aerial operations from bases in a territory pervaded and widely controlled by well organized, aggressive, hostile insurgents. This movement commonly known as the Viet Cong (VC)* sprang from the December 1960 creation of the National Liberation Front (NLF) of South Vietnam. It was a product of Communist doctrine on protracted social-revolutionary warfare. Conceived by Lenin, this form of conflict was refined and shaped to conditions in China and Vietnam by Mao Tse-tung, Ho Chi Minh, and Vo Nguyen Giap. The insurgency in the Republic of Vietnam was directed by the People's Revolutionary Party (PRP),† that is, the South Vietnam Communist Party. Executive control from the Central Office for South Vietnam (COSVN) pervaded all political and military activities.[1] No segment of the VC rebellion worked apart from the North Vietnam Communist Party* or the Democratic Republic of Vietnam.

Although this organization was intricate and hierarchical, it did not function with monolithic coherence. In theory and practice, the Communists agreed that successful insurgency warfare demanded a high degree of flexibility at the tactical level. Mao Tse-tung stressed that "while general plans are made by higher commanders, the nature of actions is determined by inferior commanders . . . . Thus the inferior groups have more or less complete local control."[2] Therefore, the charts below show merely the general command and control structure of the insurgency. They should not be construed to mean that all tactical details of individual operations were controlled from or even known to Hanoi.

Under this arrangement the military arms were the Viet Cong and the North Vietnamese Army. The VC consisted of RVN nationals who joined up or were forced into service. Being a conventional conscript force, the NVA was generally the better trained, equipped, and motivated. The

*Viet Cong (Vietnamese Communists) is the generic term applied herein to all elements of insurgency.

† Dang Nhan-Dan Cach Mang.

*Lao Dong party.

Vietnamese Communist Organization for South Vietnam, 1970

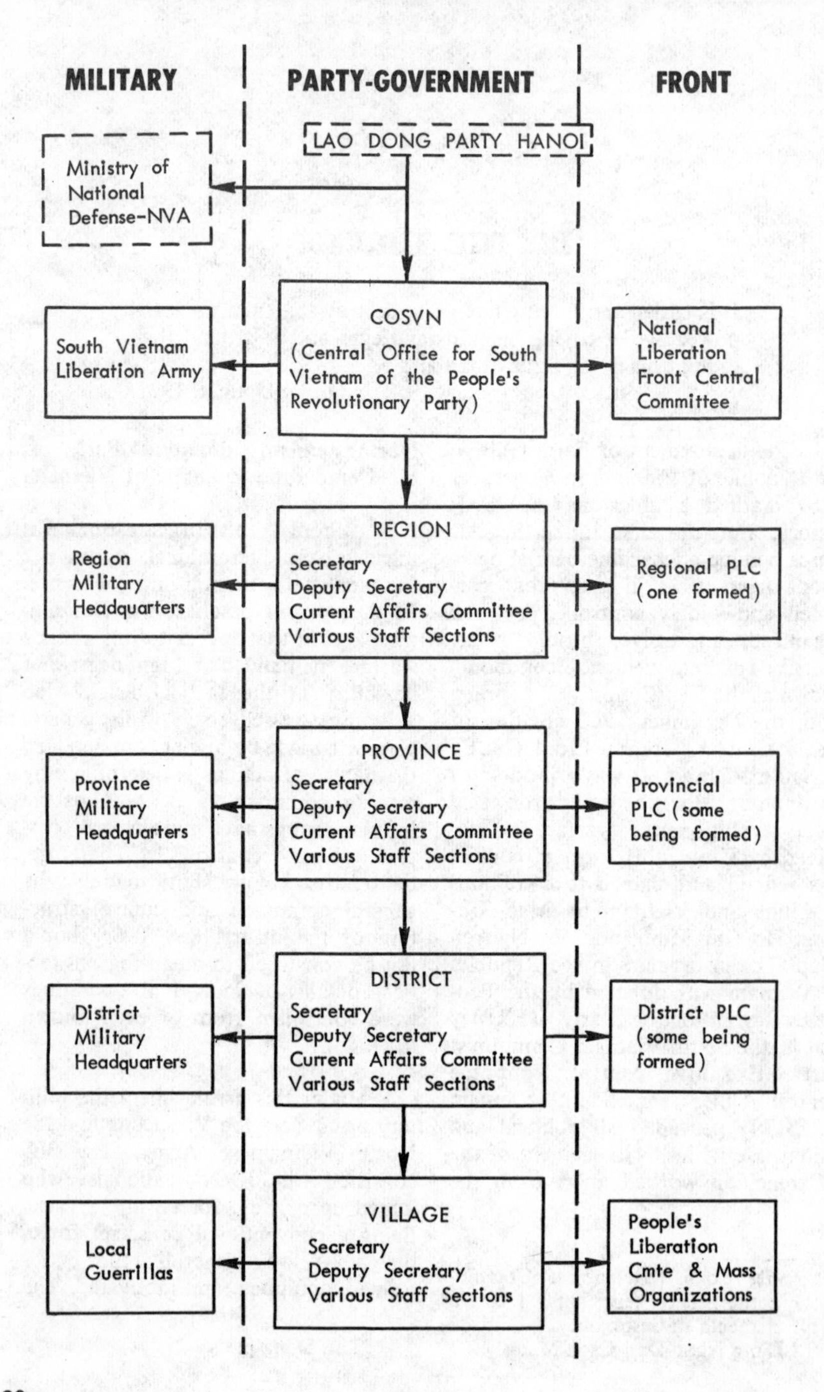

Province Party Committee, 1968

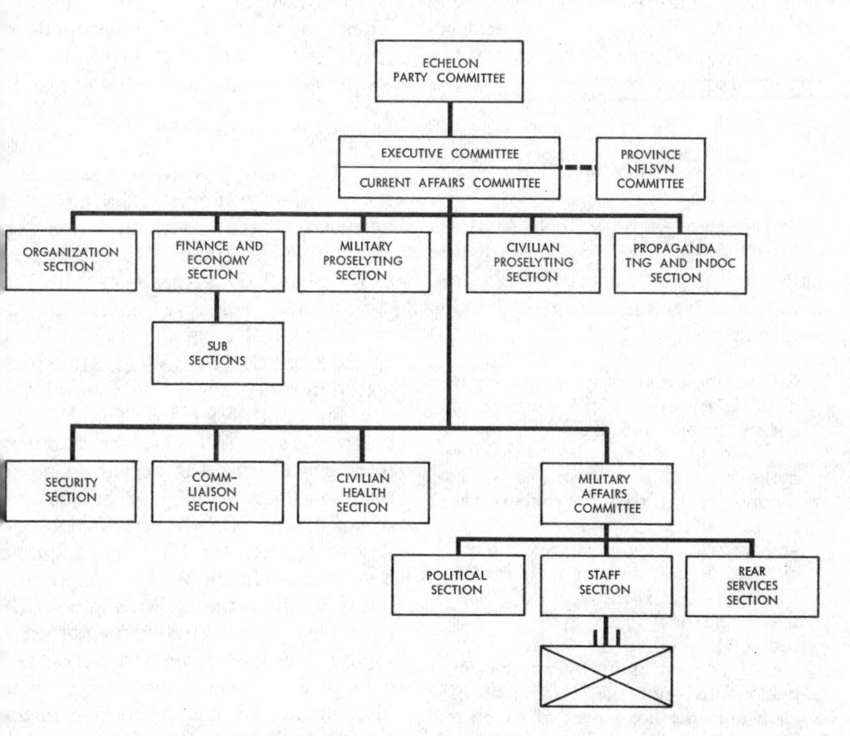

Viet Cong planned and executed most local operations such as attacks on U.S. bases. The NVA began by helping out but after the 1968 Tet Offensive* virtually took over from the VC.[3] The two as a rule strove for a common aim, responded to a single control, and used the same tactics, weapons, and equipment. Hence no distinction is drawn between the two in discussing the Communist threat to American air bases. They are dealt with jointly as VC/NVA.

By striking at USAF air power on the ground, the VC/NVA hewed to a military concept old in theory and application. As early as 1921, Giulio Douhet, an early and most influential prophet of air power, theorized that the only effective way to counter enemy air power was to destroy it at its bases on the ground.[4] Combat experience during World War II and the Korean War confirmed this concept.[5] Even more germane to the later USAF deployment to the RVN was the adaptation of Douhet's formula by the insurgency forces in the 1946-1954 Indochina War. Employing

* An attack by the VC/NVA in the early hours of 30 January on Saigon, many other cities and towns, as well as numerous RVN and U.S. military bases and airfields.

the simplest weapons and techniques, the Viet Minh* routinely mounted successful ground assaults on French air bases.[6] That this was not achieved by air strikes as envisioned by Douhet was of no practical consequence. All that really mattered to the French and the Viet Minh alike was the destruction of aircraft and/or essential air support facilities.

The Role of Intelligence

Basic to every VC/NVA attack on a U.S. air base was the advance collection of intelligence. For example, a captured training document emphasized that

> before mounting any attack, you must learn exactly the number of enemy troops and their armament. . . . [and] all you can about the commander. . . . You should also study the morale of the enemy soldiers, the location of their strong points . . . and heavy weapons emplacements, and the organization of their forces. Find out what is the chain of Command and how many men are in a squad, a section, or a company; identify enemy units by number or name. Find out the equipment of each unit, the fire power of which it is capable, and the political and military training received by the enemy troops.[7]

Also accented was the need to collect data on communications ("Do they have radios or telephones?"), the best approach and withdrawal routes, and how the local people feel toward the enemy troops. Since raids on enemy bases required more careful and precise planning than ambushes, the document said that agents must be planted on the installation beforehand to ferret out key details such as the defense layout, weapons, the guard system, and the availability of reinforcements.[8] Thus espionage as well as ground reconnaissance were employed by the VC/NVA to gather tactical intelligence.

The VC/NVA espionage apparatus was fairly simple. Like all other agencies of the insurgency, the top echelon was in Hanoi. There the Central Research Directorate (a Ministry of Defense Agency) exercised supreme control over the VC Military Intelligence Service (VCMIS), which was nominally under the Central Office for South Vietnam. The VC Security Service (VCSS), the counterintelligence arm, was organized along the same lines. Though technically an organ of the COSVN, the VCSS took its orders from the Ministry of Public Security in Hanoi. Within the Republic of Vietnam the VCMIS and VCSS paralleled VC district, province, and region administrative structures. At each of these levels, both services were also linked with and responsive to the corresponding echelon of the People's Revolutionary Party. This was standard practice in the Communist world to insure Party supremacy.[9]

The VCMIS directly assisted VC/NVA tactical operations by gathering intelligence on military plans, organization, and activities of the United States and its allies. Agents of the VCMIS were usually (but not always) of the low-level variety whose inputs added to those acquired by reconnaissance. The VCSS focused on internal security but also engaged in limited espionage devoted chiefly to the recruitment of RVN officials with access to sensitive information. Other

*The Vietnamese abbreviation for League for the Revolution and Independence of Vietnam. Ho Chi Minh and Vo Nguyen Giap organized and led this Communist insurgency movement. [Bernard B. Fall, *Street Without Joy* (Harrisburg, Pa., 1963, p 24.]

insurgent military agencies likewise passed intelligence to VC/NVA commanders.[10]

From the few known details, it would seem that this espionage apparatus had three distinct but dovetailed systems. One made use of local VC/NVA cadre* to report information upchannel through the district, provincial and regional military hierarchy. Another specialized in recruiting South Vietnamese who held sensitive positions on Allied installations. The third system used informants living in villages and hamlets near target bases.

Under the first system the VCMIS at the provincial level formed control groups for local or "in-place" cadre. The cadre's job was to maintain contact with the local VC Infrastructure (VCI),† enlist informants from the workers on Allied installations, and to send intelligence data to the control group. Allegedly from 1 to 4 in-place cadres were inserted in the vicinity of every Allied air base within the Republic of Vietnam.

An in-place cadre first established himself in the community as a legal resident with lawful employment. He next secured from the VCI a list of Vietnamese workers at the base and selected likely prospects as informants. Usually these were known to the VCI as Viet Cong sympathizers or relatives of VC members. Any number might be chosen in a deliberate effort to develop informants in the maximum number of base activities. A maid employed in officer or airmen billets was in a position to acquire information on troop strength, unit designations, and the construction or location of buildings, bunkers, or defenses. With a better grasp of English she might also get details on casualties, troop movements, and offensive or defensive operations. Grasscutters working in or around the flight line, bomb dump, fuel storage, and base perimeter could report the number of aircraft and their parking areas; the position and size of munition and supply stockpiles; the type and location of weapon emplacements, barriers, and minefields; and the siting of powerplants, communications centers, and command posts.

Informants as a rule were organized into 2- or 3-man teams with one member acting as agent net chief. The latter received information from the others and relayed it to the in-place cadre. New targets for intelligence collection and other instructions flowed to all net members through this same channel. The net chief and the cadre met off base, generally after work and in one another's home. But in the time of danger or to escape counterintelligence detection, it was not unusual to communicate by couriers who were family members.

A glimpse of this espionage pattern was gained in early 1968, when RVNAF counterintelligence officials arrested two South Vietnamese employees of an American construction company on Bien Hoa AB. They con-

---

*"A phenomenon of the Communist world, the cadre acted as combination priest, policeman, and editorial writer. He led the people in the struggle movement . . . translated village committee plans and . . . programs into reality. In general he was a native of the village, worked full time either for an administrative or functional liberation association (or in the Party itself), and was supported by the villagers and NLF or Party funds." [Douglas Pike, *Viet Cong* (Cambridge, Mass., 1966), p 230.]

† The VCI was the shadow government that directed the insurgency and competed with the legal RVN government for control of the people. [Hist, USMACV, 1968, 59-60.]

fessed to having been recruited as VC informants by a third employee of the firm. After each of five attacks on the base, they had passed damage and casualty reports to the Viet Cong. At other times they had furnished numbers and locations of parked aircraft. Extra evidence of Bien Hoa spying came to light in a captured VC document, locating 27 onbase targets by grid coordinates accurate to three decimal places.[11]

In the same fashion the VC/NVA sought to subvert RVNAF members and recruit them as informants. One convert was an airman correspondence clerk in 74th VNAF Wing Headquarters at Binh Thuy AB. In a 4 May 1969 statement he admitted passing to his net chief details on the frequency of patrols, perimeter barrier system, exposed areas, watchtowers, alarm sirens, troop morale, discord between RF and VNAF personnel and post-attack damage and casualty assessments.* [12]

The in-place cadre did not evaluate such reports, but delivered them in person or by courier to the VCMIS control group. From there they went by encrypted radio transmission to the province-level VCMIS unit for evaluation. Reports deemed accurate were radioed to the COSVN Military Intelligence Detachment or to the sub-regional military intelligence section.

Little is known about the espionage effort that placed or recruited VC/NVA sympathizers in sensitive positions affording easy access to air base security and defense details. Two events lend some insight into the matter. The first came to light in May 1969, when the capture and interrogation of a VC/NVA cadre by Gia Dinh District Police laid bare an enemy intelligence net on Tan Son Nhut AB. Key man of the net proved to be an RF second lieutenant working in the intelligence section of the Joint Defense Operations Center (JDOC), the control point for all U.S. and RVN air and ground base defense actions.

The lieutenant had been recruited through his father, himself an informant, Viet Minh veteran, local VC sector chief, and employee of the base's 377th Civil Engineering Squadron. Information he supplied the VC/NVA included strength figures on RVNAF security units at the base and on National Police elements at the Saigon International Airport; the number of tanks operated by RVNAF security troops; the number and location of onbase artillery pieces and antiaircraft emplacements; and a count of parked aircraft by model designation. The lieutenant had also furnished descriptions of the perimeter fence complex, minefields, and bunker positions. Finally, he had identified to the VC/NVA by grid coordinates all Allied units committed to base defense.[13] Enjoying free access to these data in the JDOC, this agent worked skillfully and undetected until exposed by the blunder of another agent.

A second revelation occurred in May 1970 when ARVN infantry seized collections of VC/NVA documents during the Cambodian cam-

*Past incidents confirmed these activities. A USAF counterintelligence report issued just prior to the clerk's statement noted the close VC/NVA attention paid postattack assessments. It cited Binh Thuy as an illustration. A shelling of the base on 9 April 1968 caused only slight damage because all rounds fell along the perimeter. But during two attacks on the 13th, the shells hit vital areas. The report concluded that the better accuracy of enemy fire was probably due to an onbase spotter. [OSI CID, 10 Mar 69, pp 1-2.]

paign. These disclosed a large, competent, and well-financed intelligence effort that showed a signal interest in Tan Son Nhut and Binh Thuy Air Bases. Under COSVN direction an estimated 195 agents collected "tactical information and political and military information of strategic characteristics" within Military Regions (MRs) III and IV.* They were given identity papers, top pay,† generous expense accounts, and extras like autos, motorcycles, and motorboats. Specific targets at Tan Son Nhut were in VNAF Headquarters, 33d VNAF Wing, 2d and 4th Security Companies, and the bomb depot. Despite this focus on the Vietnamese Air Force, sensitive USAF information could also be compromised. An apt example was installation security. Integrated U.S./RVN planning at these bases gave the VNAF information covering all facets of base defense operations.‡[14]

The third air base intelligence collection system used VCI and VC district forces. It was tied closely to standoff attack planning. Inputs came from the local Vietnamese who acquired information through onbase jobs, offbase observation, and association with U.S. and RVN military personnel who frequented the countless small shops clustered around every military installation. Initially collected by the VC hamlet or village chief, these informant reports were dispatched first to the district then to the provincial VCMIS office. At the latter they were evaluated and became a factor in target selection and attack planning. The workings of this low-level system is documented in many U.S./RVN counterintelligence reports.[15]

In 1966, for example, the Police Chief of Dong Ha City * reported that the VC/NVA were advertising an offer of 10,000 piastres (about $85) for each American-made map of RVN areas delivered to them. Apparently the VC/NVA were receiving advance warning of U.S. air and artillery strikes but were plotting them on French or Vietnamese maps that sometimes differed from American maps. The latter were therefore required if VC/NVA units were to receive accurate warning. This report was prompted by the discovery of 13 U.S. maps of Quang Tri Province in a trash dump near Dong Ha AB and by word that the VC/NVA had ordered their informants to hunt for official documents in dumps and other disposal areas.[16]

Another report concerned a VC district chief's wife. In early 1969 she was seen sketching in a notebook at the perimeter of Bien Hoa AB near the VNAF bomb dump. Arriving by taxi, she drew while the driver feigned repairs on his vehicle. After an interval she reentered the cab and was driven back to the village. The VC/NVA had shown keen interest in the

---

*Formerly Corps Tactical Zones III and IV.

† One hundred times the salary of the average VC/NVA soldier.

‡ Since the fall of the Republics of Vietnam on 30 April 1975, the deep VC/NVA penetration of U.S. and RVN ranks has been spotlighted by longtime Communist agents breaking cover. Before being deported by the Provisional Revolutionary Government (PRG), the Saigon bureau chief of United Press International reported a number of such cases. A chief translator and interpreter for the Central Intelligence Agency (CIA) is now a province chief and wears the insignia of a VC/NVA lieutenant colonel. A military police officer worked years inside the RVN intelligence apparatus while waiting for the enemy to win. A chief surveyor who drew up plans for Allied ammunition storage sites and military bases is currently a member of the PRG. [Alan Dawson, "Saigon Regime Riddled with Viet Cong Before Its Fall," *Washington Star,* 9 Sep 75, p A3.]

* Situated about 25 kilometers south of the Demilitarized Zone (DMZ).

Bien Hoa bomb dump since August 1968, when a 122-mm rocket attack caused secondary explosions that detonated 200,000 pounds of munitions.[17]

Another incident in the area of Bien Hoa AB shed light on the VC/NVA method for conveying intelligence collected by this system. In September 1968 ARVN rangers captured a suspected VC/NVA cadre 8 kilometers northeast of the base. His notebook contained a sketch map of the base area, labeling the ARVN compound and the U.S. Army's Hawk missile sites. Also recorded were the location and manning of the 57th ARVN Battalion, RVN civil defense units, and elements of the Popular Forces (PF).* Other data concerned the security measures in villages adjacent to the air base, the internal layout and defenses of the base ammunition storage facilities, and the number and type of assigned aircraft. The suspect conceded he was Chief of the VC Military Intelligence Section in Vinh Cuu District,† but he claimed to be merely a runner who gathered data from VC village chiefs, secretaries, and villagers within an 8- to 14-kilometer radius of Bien Hoa AB. He made his collection rounds on foot usually every 3 days, unless time factors or the information's importance called for a scheduled change. As a whole, therefore, the workings of this apparatus convincingly disclosed an intelligence collection, mirroring an overall VC/NVA spy setup system that was sophisticated and professional.[18]

* The PF were voluntary, locally recruited volunteers, organized into squads and platoons, and used chiefly as security forces in villages and hamlets.

† The central and northeast portion of Bien Hoa Province.

Ground Reconnaissance

In seeking intelligence on Allied air bases, the Viet Cong/North Vietnamese Army did not depend entirely on espionage. Equal or greater reliance was placed on visual observation by military ground reconnaissance patrols. Since such reconnaissance of the objective was crucial to offense planning and operations, men were specially trained for this mission.[19]

Reconnaissance trainees underwent up to 3 months of instruction in the techniques of observation and patrolling.* Of the sundry subjects

* Perhaps in some cases the training lasted longer. Taken prisoner in 1968, a NVA reconnaissance platoon leader said that NVA recon personnel received at least 1½ years of instruction and training [*Maj Billy J. Biberstein, A Monograph of 2Lt Nguyen Van Thong, Plt Ldr, Recon Co. 320th Regt, 1st NVA Div* (13th Mil Hist Det, USARV, undated).]

Perimeter of Nha Trang Air Base, separated from the city by two concertina fences on either side of a drainage ditch

covered, greatest emphasis fell on movement, penetration, and observation methods, noise/light discipline, camouflage, mapreading, and reports preparation. Particular attention was paid to personal motivation. Because the work was specialized and hazardous, trainees were told they must be quick, intelligent, skillful, and courageous. For reconnaissance cadre* the cardinal virtues were loyalty, discipline, bravery, modesty, and the patience to bear hardships and overcome difficulties.

Trainees took part in frequent practical exercises to apply what they learned from lectures and manuals. Realism was the keynote. In practicing penetration of enemy installations, it was not unusual to construct a mockup complete with wire barriers and other obstacles. Split in two groups, the trainees alternated as penetrators and defenders. Each exercise was critiqued and repeated until instructors were satisfied by the performance.

Reconnaissance units manned by these men were standard in VC/NVA military forces. It appears tables of organization prescribed one reconnaissance squad for each Local Force (LF)† company and each LF battalion organic to a regiment. One reconnaissance platoon was authorized for each Main Force (MF)‡ battalion and each independent LF battalion. Each regiment was entitled to a reconnaissance company. However, the size of an actual reconnaissance patrol reflected the mission and the availability of personnel. A squad of not more than 10 sufficed in most cases.

Usually, a squad was broken down into three cells of three men each and a squad leader. It was customary for one member to observe and take notes while the other two provided security. It was also common practice for key operations personnel (such as the battalion operations officer and one or all of the company commanders) to accompany the reconnaissance patrol on a mission.

A VC/NVA reconnaissance of an air base paid close attention to obstacles. This included the structural pattern, height, length, and depth of barbed wire. It also recorded the location and specifics of minefields, bunkers, and emplaced weapons. Other considerations were how firepower was combined with obstacles, and any obstruction that blocked the view from the interior of the base. Due to allied air and firepower superiority, every effort was made to learn the location and reaction time of artillery support, the likelihood of helicopter and tactical air support, and the strength and response time of reserve forces. The terrain in the base's vicinity was studied to pinpoint landing zones for heliborne reaction forces, probable approach routes for Allied reinforcements, and areas most exposed to allied air strikes. At the same time, the VC/NVA patrols determined those areas best suited to their own troop deployments, taking into account the daily routine of the target installation—particularly sleeping and eating times, patrol operations, and guard changes.

---

* A leadership position of squad leader or higher.

† VC Local Force units were those directly under a provincial or district Party committee. They generally operated within a specified VC province or district. [Hist, MACV, 1967, I. 54.]

‡ VC Main Force units were directly subordinated to the COSVN, a VC military region or subregion, and normally operated within the corresponding territory. [*Ibid.*]

If the VC/NVA judged the information from espionage and/or observation to be unreliable or insufficient, they sent reconnaissance elements into the base. Such a penetration was usually carried out by a single cell of three men clad only in loin cloth or shorts and camouflaged with mud. Their standard gear was an automatic weapon, one set of wirecutters, a single knife or bayonet, a sharp metal rod to probe for mines, bamboo sticks to prop up barbed wire, and a quantity of small pins to disarm mine fuzes.

Infiltration called for a high degree of concentration, skill, and coordination. Generally, one cell member stayed outside the perimeter barriers while the other two penetrated. The lead man propped up the wire with bamboo sticks then disarmed the mines. His partner followed him under the wire and removed the props. Crawling meticulously to escape detection, each used hands and feet to probe the ground for wire that might reveal mines, boobytraps, tripflares, or other warning devices. After examining the base, the men withdrew by the same route, with the lead man repropping the wire and second man removing the props and rearming the mines. Wirecutters were a least resort because the intent was to avoid all trace of entry. Having completed withdrawal, all cell members met at a prearranged location to prepare their report to the commander.

VC/NVA reconnaissance of U.S. air bases was verified repeatedly. VC/NVA prisoners taken during the 4 December 1966 sapper raid on Tan Son Nhut told of a 2-month prestrike reconnaissance of the base by a 7-man team. Whether information was gathered from onbase or offbase locations was unknown, but the effort was a successful one. Enemy intelligence was good on the base periphery, good on one munitions area, and poor near the runway and aircraft parking aprons. It successfully identified a point to infiltrate the perimeter and cut three wire fences without detection. It also accurately assessed infiltration cover afforded by excavation work, fixed the positions of aircraft parking areas, and traced out routes for undetected access to three munitions bunkers.

But the prisoners also revealed fatal flaws in their intelligence. First, they were discovered by sentry dog patrol and surprised by a security alert team. This proved that security police patrol patterns had not been charted. Second, their intelligence failed to

An Air Force sentry and his dog patrol Tan Son Nhut Air Base

locate a barbed wire barrier along the runway's south edge and they became entangled in it. Finally, VC/NVA intelligence failed to locate security police guard posts in the flight-line area. As a result, nine sappers died when they tried to enter the parking ramp by passing directly in front of a machinegun position.[20]

In January 1967 an ARVN ranger company turned up fresh proof of enemy reconnaissance during a sweep of Khanh Hoa Province near Nha Trang AB. The rangers came upon a recently abandoned VC/NVA campsite in the Dong Ba Mountains about 6 kilometers southwest of the base. Among the camp's structures was an observation platform that commanded the entire Nha Trang area. From here with minimum effort and risk, it was possible to map the air base in detail and to observe air traffic and troop activities.[21]

Apart from being detected and one cell member captured, a VC/NVA penetration attempt at Bien Hoa in early May 1967 proceeded by the book. According to the prisoner, he was a member of a 10-man reconnaissance squad belonging to C-238 Company.* When the squad arrived at a point 4 hours from the air base, he and the other two cell members separated from the squad and began their final approach to the target. Each man left behind all clothing except small camouflaged briefs and a head cover, both of nylon. They were provided with a submachinegun, one .45-cal pistol, and a Soviet handgrenade and were permitted to study a base map created from photos snapped from nearby Buu Long Mountain. Their orders were to count the cargo aircraft on the west parking ramp, and to find out the contents of a number of 200-liter barrels in the same area. But the operation failed when security police spotted the enemy penetration of the perimeter fence. Evidently this abortive reconnaissance was offset by a number of more successful efforts that presumably resulted in the devastating standoff attack of 12 May 1967.[22]

* This reconnaissance sapper unit was believed responsible for the successful October 1966 and February 1967 attacks on the U.S. Army Long Binh Ammunition Depot.

Electronic Warfare

To supplement intelligence data collected by espionage and reconnaissance the VC/NVA carried on a limited form of electronic warfare. This fell into three general categories: intercept, jamming, and imitative deception.

Intercept (called technical reconnaissance by the VC/NVA) was the most common and important of the three. It was nearly impossible to detect. In this technique the intercept operator simply tuned his receiver to the target station's frequency, and copied the traffic by hand or recorder. The intercept station never transmitted on this frequency, because strange signals might lead the target station to take evasive action. Of course, the success of intercept operations varied with the degree to which the target stations adhered to communications security. Results also hinged on the location of the intercept station. It had to be close to a target station using a short-range radio, chiefly the FM (frequency modulation) kind. An AM (amplitude modulation) radio could be intercepted at a greater distance. Moreover, weak or intermittent AM signals could be partially compensated for by a highly sensitive receiver.

Jamming introduced disturbances the same language as the target station,

Smoldering hulk of a C–123 after a Viet Cong rocket attack on Da Nang Air Base in July 1967

depriving it of radio communication. The simplest techniques worked. "When jamming," a captured VC/NVA document instructed, "play with the dials, whistle, make noise or simulate sounds."[23] To produce a signal that could completely override the frequency, the jamming station was placed as near as possible to the target station.

In using imitative deception, the VC/NVA operator transmitted messages on the same frequency and in the same language as the target station, hoping they would be received as friendly communications. Such deceptive messages were usually orders to move troops, redirect artillery fire or air strikes, or to take other steps favorable to enemy operations.

An event at Da Nang AB showed the successful use of imitative communications. After killing a U.S. guard undetected, the VC/NVA used the guard's unsecured telephone to announce briefly in English that the far end of the base was under attack. When U.S. forces responded to this information without demanding authentication, the VC/NVA attacked, met little resistance, and inflicted an estimated $15 million damage on aircraft and base facilities.* [24]

At Pleiku a similar venture failed. By tapping a field telephone circuit linking the perimeter defenses of a large storage area, the VC/NVA expertly imitated the Spanish accent of a guard sergeant. The imitator asked for a count of the troops in each of the operating bunkers so he could bring them hot food. But at this point, the deception was perceived and the ruse was defeated.† [25]

Intelligence analysts never did precisely determine the number, strength or equipment‡ of VC/NVA

---

* The source does not say, but this incident apparently happened during the raid of 1 July 1965.

† This episode took place in late 1966 or early 1967 at Camp Holloway on the outskirts of Pleiku.

‡ One study concluded that 50 percent of an estimated 795 radios in the hands of the enemy were captured U.S. equipment. [Study 67-061, *VC/NVA Electronic Warfare Capability* (Combined Intelligence Center, Vietnam (CICV), 1 Jul 67, p E-1.]

electronic warfare units. Nor did they settle how well electronic warfare helped enemy operations. Still, captured documents and prisoner interrogation reports clearly confirmed that units or cells were created for this purpose. From the incomplete evidence at hand, however, it could only be surmised that the enemy valued and exploited electronic warfare as a subtle but useful means of collecting intelligence and causing confusion.[26]

Reconnaissance by Fire

Reconnaissance by fire was one more way that the enemy secured pre-attack air base information. VC/NVA forces engaged the base defenders in light tactical contact—sniper or harassing fires or small unit probes—to find out the strength and disposition of base defense forces; the number, type, and location of automatic weapons; the placement of prepared positions and the reaction time of artillery, tactical air, and reserves; or to register their weapons. Small unit probes, unlike reconnaissance penetrations, deliberately sought to attract attention and draw fire in order to provoke a practical demonstration of the base defense capability for study and analysis.[27]

For the most part, the Viet Cong/North Vietnamese Army system to collect and process tactical intelligence information illustrated the maturity and expertise gained during the Indochina War. The apparatus was a blend of the simple and complex. Although quite a few agencies had to do with intelligence, counterintelligence, and internal security, there was no sign of unsure direction or bureaucratic bickering. The setup on the contrary featured direct command lines, well-defined functions, and a closely controlled information flow. Consequently, the VC/NVA commanders who planned and conducted combat operations against U.S. air bases could generally count on competent intelligence support.

Standoff Attacks

Counter-air base operations carried out by the Viet Cong/North Vietnamese Army can for all practical purposes be grouped into four categories—standoff attacks, sapper raids, battalion-size assaults, and sabotage. Of these the most common, simple, economical, and effective was the standoff attack. It used "a weapon . . . launched at a distance sufficient to allow the attacking personnel to evade defensive fire from the target area." [28] In this way the VC/NVA exploited the Air Force's dependence on large fixed installations and the allies' incomplete control of the surrounding countryside. Thus, at least risk to themselves, the Communists could inflict damage on costly combat resources, striking at times and places of their choice. International news coverage of the attacks consistently portrayed the VC/NVA as successful and the allies as inept. Finally, standoff attacks undermined the morale of the men on installations, and often diverted Allied troops from the offensive to the defensive.[29]

At first the enemy had only mortars and recoilless rifles as standoff weapons, but rockets entered the inventory in 1966. The rockets brought the Communists greater and more flexible firepower, since they possessed longer range and could be fired in salvo from improvised launchers. The peak standoff range well-nigh doubled, from the 5,700 meters of 120-mm mortars to the 11,000 meters of 122-mm rockets. Now the VC/NVA arsenal of standoff weapons boasted

Improvised rocket launchers used to fire into Phu Cat Air Base

60-, 82-, and 120-mm mortars; 57-, 75-, and 82-mm recoilless rifles; and 107-, 122-, and 140-mm rockets furnished mainly by the Peoples Republic of China and the Soviet Union.* [30] Specialized units handled these weapons.

Mortar, recoilless rifle, and heavy machinegun companies were part of the standard VC/NVA infantry combat support regiment, and operated at all echelons. Such regiments usually had one 82-mm mortar company, one 12.7-mm heavy machinegun company, and one 57-/75-mm recoilless rifle company.[31] These and rocket artillery units had little in common. The latter more closely resembled field artillery units in training, organization, and tactics. Every rocket regiment contained a headquarters company, a signal and reconnaissance company, and three rocket battalions. Within the standard rocket battalion were a headquarters company and three rocket companies. The latter were equipped as follows:

Rocket Company	*Launchers*	*Rockets*
107-mm	12	24
122-mm	6	18
140-mm	16	16

If need be, all rockets could be fired from improvised launchers. In large-scale standoff attacks, rocket units were sometimes supported by elements of an infantry combat support regiment.[32]

Despite their differences all VC/NVA mortar, recoilless rifle, and rocket units shared one key attribute—superior mobility. All weapons and munitions could be man-packed to just about any launch location. When circumstances permitted the use of waterways, oxcarts, bicycles, or trucks, mobility was further increased, the requirement for porters decreased, and weapon effectiveness markedly improved.

Minute planning and preparation preceded an enemy standoff attack. This customarily included collection of target intelligence, identification of

* Appendix 4 briefly describes each weapon.

firing locations, prepositioning of munitions, selection of approach and withdrawal routes, movement of weapons into position, and preparation of weapons for firing.

Drawing on the intelligence collection methods discussed above, a target base was usually reconnoitered at least three times during the planning phase.[33] Normally, the rocket company commander(s) performed a last reconnaissance before the final decision and the attack preparation. To maintain maximum security, few people saw the approved plans. Launch crews, for example, were told neither the time nor the target until arrival at the firing sites.[34]

Perhaps the most arduous of the preparatory requirements was prepositioning munitions in the target area. Major stockpiles of munitions and other materiel were maintained along the VC/NVA lines of communication. This network of paths and roads, known collectively as the Ho Chi Minh Trail, extended from North Vietnam through Laos to Cambodia. The resupply point for I Corps Tactical Zone was thought to be in the A Shau Valley; for II CTZ, in the B-3 Front area near the Tri-border* in the Central Highlands; and for III CTZ, in War Zone D about 30 kilometers northeast of Saigon.[35]

The enemy transported munitions from these resupply points to staging areas and launch sites by one or more of the modes mentioned above. Travel time between staging areas and launch sites rarely exceeded 1½ hours. Movement usually took place at night, 5 to 30 days in advance of an attack. Munitions so prepositioned might be stored a few meters or as far as 5 kilometers from the launch sites. Storage points could be situated along the banks of rivers, streams, and canals; in tunnels, graveyards, and abandoned villages or hamlets; astride boundary lines between units of the RVNAF and its allies where surveillance was often poor; and next to or within inhabited areas, depending on the attitude of the people. Great care was taken to camouflage these caches.[36]

Prior to each rocket attack, a survey team from the responsible rocket artillery unit staked out and aligned the rocket positions. This survey, the sole site preparation before the night of the attack, commonly took place the preceding afternoon to minimize detection by aerial observation. Since the attack's success turned upon the survey's accuracy, the team computed firing data with precision instruments such as theodolites and transits.* When the job was done, stakes in and on the ground marked the position, azimuth, and elevation of every launcher or rocket.[37]

After dark the rocket launch crews equipped with simple tools like shovels, scoops, and picks moved into the launch site. Using the reference stakes placed by the survey party, they positioned and aligned the launchers or rockets, readied the firing pits, wired the launch system for firing, and loaded the rockets. Individual rockets were spaced about 10 meters apart, with about 20 meters between each group of six rockets. This work required from 20 minutes to 3 hours, depending on the number of crewmembers, the type of launchers, and the distance to the rocket storage point.[38]

---

* The area west of Dak To, South Vietnam, at the convergence of the Cambodia, Laos, and South Vietnam borders.

* Much of the accuracy of the 122-mm and other rockets came from these precise calculations.

Preparations for employment of mortars and recoilless rifles resembled those for rockets, except that aiming stakes were put 20-30 meters in front of the mortar firing positions. These normally formed a semicircle with the recoilless rifles on the flanks. It was customary to site mortars in a circular foxhole about 1.7 meters deep and about 2 meters in diameter. The spoil formed a bern around the position, while foliage and other material served as camouflage. As a rule, the recoilless rifles occupied high points offering concealment.[39]

Where conditions allowed, the VC/NVA often positioned standoff weapons to exploit the standard base layout and thus inflict the most damage. Mortars and rockets, for example, were set up along the long axis of the main runways to take advantage of the small deflection error* and relatively large range dispersion of these weapons. To expedite approach and withdrawal, proximity of trails and other transportation routes was always a factor in the final setting of weapons positions.[40]

* The distance to the right or left of the target between the point aimed at and the shellburst, or the mean point of a salvo burst.

As experience accrued, the Allied forces identified the general principles behind the VC/NVA's tactical deployment of standoff weapons. Rarely were rockets, recoilless rifles, and mortars combined in the same attack unless the enemy intended to penetrate or overrun the air base. However, when standoff weapons were employed for this purpose, rockets normally preceded all other attack activities. Next the mortars, recoilless rifles, and rocket-propelled grenades (RPGs) hammered automatic weapon positions, bunkers, or other specific targets on the base. When used solely for standoff purposes, mortars and recoilless rifles concentrated on area targets such as ammunition dumps, aircraft parking ramps, POL (petroleum, oil, and lubricants) tank farms, and troop billets.[41]

Rocket attacks frequently lasted from 2 to 20 minutes depending on attack force size, rounds on hand, and the speed and accuracy of Allied counterfire, such as artillery, helicopter or fixed-wing gunships, or strike aircraft. It was enemy practice to employ rockets in salvos of 3, 6, 12, 18, and on occasion 2 battalions of 18 rockets each. In the February 1967 attack on Da Nang AB, 130 140-mm rockets were emplaced at a single site. But due to malfunctions only 66

Display of the three basic methods used by the Viet Cong to launch rockets: launch tube, earth embankment, and crossed sticks

Launch trenches for 122-mm rockets fired into Pleiku Air Base in January 1968

were successfully launched with 56 striking the air base, 8 hitting an adjacent village, and 2 falling outside the target area. Any fire adjustment was made after two or three rounds if counterfire permitted. A forward observer transmitted corrected launch data to the rocket company commander by radio or field phone.[42]

In 1968 the VC/VNA rocket units introduced a new standoff tactic. It consisted of attacking an installation from two or more launch sites, either simultaneously or in alternating salvos with the intent of confusing friendly counterfire. This technique, a captive rocket company commander explained, was devised to offset allied aerial observation and quick-reaction air strikes that limited the number of rockets that could be fired. Allied countermeasures were greatly aided by rocket exhaust trails which, clearly visible as far as 300 meters from ignition to burnout points, greatly aided these Allied countermoves, pinpointing the launch site locations. In consequence, the Communists turned to hit-and-run tactics. No more than 5 rounds in 20 minutes were fired from any single tripod launcher. And no more than 2 salvos in 10 minutes were fired from improvised launchers. Rocket crews were trained to pick up all equipment and vacate a launch site in about 5 minutes, traveling along preplanned routes at top speed to the staging area.[43]

Mortar and recoilless rifle units operated individually as independent forces, jointly as a composite force, and as elements in rocket standoff attacks. When employed individually, the VC/NVA took pains to site their weapons in well-concealed positions. Often they were sited near hamlets, villages, churches, or inhabited dwellings. Twice in 1967 the Communists set up mortars in buildings in central Saigon. In February an 82-mm mortar so located fired on Headquarters USMACV then housed on Rue Pasteur. The shells bracketed but failed to hit the building. Again in October the enemy positioned a 60-mm mortar on the upper floor of 141/43 Tan That Dam Street. Firing through an opening created by peeling back the tin roof, this mortar lobbed four rounds at Independence Palace nearly 1,100 meters to the north, where a reception for Vice President Hubert H. Humphrey was underway.[44] During the 1968 Tet Offensive there were several reports of mortars shelling Tan Son Nhut AB from buildings in Saigon.[45] The clear intent of this method was to deter friendly counterfire.

In rocket standoff attacks not involving penetration of the installation, VC/NVA mortar and recoilless rifle units generally furnished follow-on fire to the first rocket barrage. Under cover of this fire, the rocket unit withdrew from the launch site. Due to their greater mobility, recoilless rifle units were as a rule the last to leave the target area.

Sapper Raids

Sapper raids on U.S. air bases stood second only to standoff attacks in frequency and gravity. The first one took place against Da Nang on 1 July 1965. Covered by a mortar barrage, the sappers infiltrated three perimeter fences before detection and reached the aircraft parking ramp. Using demolition charges and handgrenades, they destroyed three C-130s and three F-102s, damaged three F-102s, then withdrew with the loss of only one man.[46]

As described in captured VC/NVA documents, the rationale of the sapper raid was "the use of small numbers of men to inflict extensive damage on enemy installations rather than to inflict casualties." So sapper operations did not employ firepower or large forces but relied on undetected infiltration of defenses to reach and destroy with explosives preselected targets. Lightly armed, sappers shunned extended contact with base defenders and usually sought to complete their mission and withdraw from the base within 30 minutes after detection.[47]

The sapper was a well-trained, highly disciplined, combat engineer. He was not a guerrilla, and though often used in terrorist activities, he was not truly a terrorist. As in other forms of warfare, skill in sapper tactics depended on the training, experience, and determination of the individual sapper and his leaders. The VC/NVA leadership understood this and strove to "make both cadre and soldiers aware that to serve in the special sapper arm is a great honor" and that "although this is a new arm, it already has a victorious background." At the same time, the sapper arm was pictured as "'the hard-core special unit' playing an important role with our armed units on all battlefields."[48]

While these units were officially classified as elite organizations, not all sappers were volunteers. Many times the cadre culled them from honor graduates of the basic military training courses.[49] Officer volunteers accepted for sapper duty were stripped of rank during training. In contrast, enlisted candidates commonly received promotions when training commenced.[50]

A basic phase of sapper training covered reconnaissance techniques and skills such as land navigation, negotiation of natural and manmade obstacles, observation, penetration, and withdrawal. Next came intensive drill in assault tactics based on the 3-man cell, a tactical organization concept highly esteemed and widely applied by the VC/NVA.* According to official doctrine the 3-man cell, due to "its close organization and its close inner command and control structure," was uniquely fitted for day or night, offensive or defensive, and independent or coordinated operations. However, when employed in combination "the capabilities and qualities of each cell in relation to other cells" required the combat effectiveness of the overall organization. Instructors were warned that "the organization of cells is different from the organization of squads, platoons, and companies as employed in infantry." [51]

Because explosive charge was the key to sapper effectiveness and because survival might well depend on competence with this weapon, demolition training was exhaustive. Sappers were taught to recognize, arm, and disarm conventional explosives as well as those of local manufacture. Instructions included the characteristics and uses of detonators; the characteristics, properties, maintenance, and force of all available explosives; and the quantity and position of explosives required to destroy fences, buildings, bunkers, aircraft, fuel tanks, and munitions. Sappers were also instructed on the details of Allied mines, flares, and boobytraps, which they were taught to disarm, and convert to their own uses. In short, the trained sappers were specialists in the employment of explosive charges.[52]

Against air bases, sapper raids were almost always independent operators without participation by infantry or other forces.* To insure the success and secrecy of these raids, the VC/NVA exercised extreme care in the preparatory phase. This entailed reconnaissance of the target installation, formulation of the attack plan, and rehearsal of the unit tasked with the mission.

Reconnaissance was generally conducted by the special VC/NVA reconnaissance units discussed earlier. Planners also made full use of reports from espionage agents working on or near the target base. At some point in the preparatory phase the sapper unit commander usually made a personal reconnaissance. Information in these various ways was a major factor shaping the attack plan. As it evolved, the focus was chiefly on the size, disposition, strength, and weakness of air base defense forces. When completed, it set the priority of targets, the approach, infiltration, and withdrawal routes, and the size, composition, organization, and armament of the sapper raiding party.

The standard VC/NVA policy of tailoring organizations to meet the needs of changing circumstances prevents a uniform definition of a sapper

---

* In name, cohesion, and function these cells appear closely related to those that once were the basic organizational unit of the Communist Party of the Soviet Union. Cells are clearly in keeping with the Bolshevik revolutionary tradition.

* Only sappers in attack without infantry will be discussed herein, since it was the form of tactical deployment most relevant to air base defense. However, there were five other distinct forms—sappers in support of infantry attack; sappers in attack with infantry support; special action sappers trained in urban terrorism, sabotage, and propaganda; marine sappers targeted against ships and bridges; and mechanized sappers trained to seize and instantly employ enemy mechanized equipment. [Study 69-10, *VC/NVA Sapper Tactics* (CICV, 23 Oct 69), pp 8-17; USMACV CE 4-69, 1969, pp. 12-14; OSI CIM, South Vietnam: Sapper Tactics and Threat Against the USAF, 6 Apr 71, p 6.]

unit. Apparently, however, its structure was akin to that of the VC/NVA infantry battalion (itself an undeterminate organization) since it consisted of four or five 40- to 50-man companies. A company contained up to three 15- to 20-man platoons, each split into two squads. Within each squad personnel were organized into cells. A cell of three sappers was considered ideal but in practice that number might vary from two to five.[53] But, from the air base defense standpoint, the formal organization was far less important than the variable structure of the VC/NVA sapper raiding party.

Sapper raiding parties were tailored to the mission, VC/NVA resources, and the capability of the opposing forces. They normally consisted of assault, security, and fire support elements. On occasion a reserve element was included in a representative sapper raiding party structured for attack without infantry support.

In principle all elements of the raiding party were built from 3-man cells. The concept was that two cell members would carry out the assigned mission while the third provided cover and replaced either of the first two if one became a casualty. Armament commonly included various explosive charges as the primary weapon, an AK-47 assault rifle, and rocket-propelled grenades. This 3-man cell and the explosive charges composed the nucleus of the sapper unit, but current conditions determined how the cells would be grouped and what additional armament, if any, would be used. A given situation might demand a modification of the cell itself.

Typical Sapper Force for Attack without Infantry Support

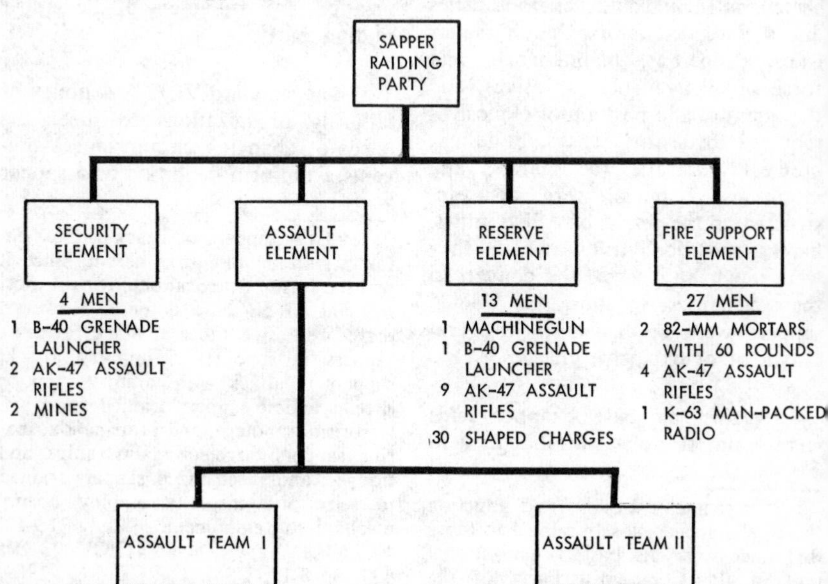

Typical Sapper Force for Attack without Infantry Support

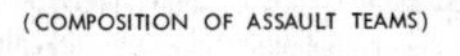

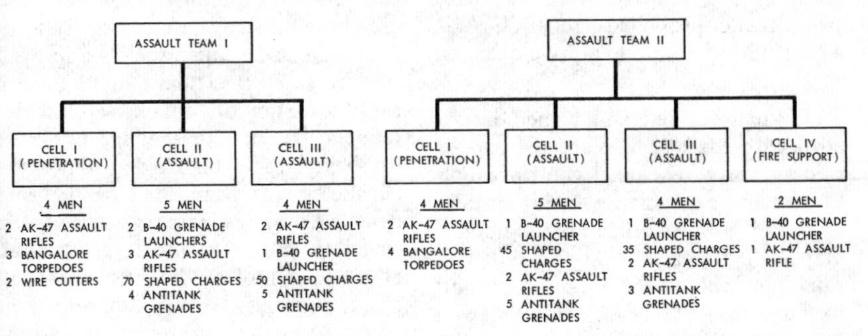

The assault element was the key feature of the sapper raiding party. Normally it was composed of two or more assault teams, or "arrows," each responsible for a single approach route to the target. The size of the mission and the men available determined the number of assault teams in the assault element. Standard practice called for three types of cells in each assault team: assault, penetration, and fire support. The number and kind of targets governed the number, composition, and armament of assault cells. The complexity of perimeter defenses controlled these same factors for penetration cells, as did defense force strength for fire support cells. It was at this point that the 3-man cell lost some of its basic configuration as it was fitted to mission needs. In lieu of explosive charges, a penetration cell might carry wirecutters, bangalore torpedoes, stakes, tape, and probing devices. It might also dispense with the AK-47 assault rifle or drop one man from the cell. A fire support cell might use rocket-propelled grenades (RPG-2s or RPG-7s) in place of explosive charges. But in the assault cells the basic 3-man configuration was usually maintained or augmented.[54]

A fire support element was included in all but the simplest attacks. Its task—as distinguished from that of the assault element's fire support cell—was general support of the entire raiding party. Like other elements, fire support composition and armament was suited to the mission. Strength in most instances was limited to weapon crews (cells), protected at times by a security cell. Standard weapons were the 60- and 82-mm mortars because heavier armament was not suited to fast-paced operations of this kind. Rarely were more than two mortars committed to a single raid.[55]

The smallest element of the raiding party was usually the security element which seldom exceeded one reinforced cell. Its task was to keep Allied reinforcements from entering the battle area. Its normal armament consisted of direct fire weapons such as RPG-2's and RPG-7's and sometimes M-79 grenade launchers and directional mines.

Only under unusual circumstances was a reserve element included in the raiding party. Generally small, it acted as a reinforced infantry squad to furnish close-in support and assistance when and where required. Its weapons were machineguns, rocket-propelled grenades, AK-47 assault rifles, and explosive charges.

When formed and armed in accord with the attack plan, the sapper raiding party rehearsed the operation to acquaint each man with his specific task. Full use was made of sandtables, maps, diagrams, mockups, and terrain like that of the target area and its environs. VC/NVA cadre viewed dry runs as vital to success, since the plans were usually complicated and all sapper elements mutually supporting. Hence failure of any one part of the plan could well endanger the entire enterprise. Once the attack got under way, there was little or no opportunity for further coordination or change. Each sapper was expected to know and do his job precisely and automatically without onscene direction.[56]

The required standard of performance was formidably illustrated by an incident of February 1969. During a raid on Phu Cat AB, a wounded sapper was taken prisoner by security police. When interrogated, he described the rehearsal phase of the operation. He said his company commander had warned that anyone endangering the mission's success would be shot. Accordingly, when the prisoner inadvertently triggered a tripflare while trying to penetrate the perimeter fence, the company commander shot him.[57]

Sapper tactics in the attack without infantry were designed to eliminate the need for fire superiority and to thwart the massive defensive fire usually at the disposal of the allies. Secrecy, stealth, and surprise replaced fire superiority in the attack.* Deep thrusts into the base interior and simultaneous assaults on several targets curbed friendly firepower and greatly confused defense operations. One standard sapper tactic employed the fire support element to disguise a raid as a standoff attack, so that defenders would take shelter and leave the base largely unguarded. Once the perimeter was penetrated or the raid detected, the sappers moved at top speed to and from the targets, in an effort to complete the mission in 30 minutes or less. After attaining their objective, the sappers withdrew through the perimeter, generally at the same point where they had entered. Fire support or reserve elements covered the withdrawal. All elements of the raiding party then moved to a rallying site, normally the same place as the assembly area. Then they quickly regrouped for rapid return to their base camp.[58]

Battalion-Size Attacks

During the 1968 general Tet Offensive, battalion-size forces struck Tan Son Nhut and Bien Hoa in the most sensational and highly publicized of all VC/NVA operations against U.S. air bases. Without precedent or sequel, these two simultaneous attacks were unique in the history of air base defense in the RVN. For this reason there is no basis for reliable generalization on the tactics and techniques used in this form of operation.

Tan Son Nhut and Bien Hoa Air Bases were situated in III Corps Tac-

---

* At one U.S. Army installation, the VC/NVA sappers devoted over 8 painstaking hours in an undetected stealthy movement across the last 100 meters to the perimeter and into the wire of the barrier complex. [USMACV CE 1-69, 1969, p 1.]

tical Zone near Saigon, a city of immense political, economic, and psychological importance. Probably the VC/NVA regarded the seizure of these two bases essential to the seizure of Saigon—apparently the key objective of the entire offensive. So, in contrast to the hit-and-run tactics of earlier standoff attacks and sapper raids, the VC/NVA at this time aimed at overrunning and holding the two installations. At Tan Son Nhut the VC/NVA committed one sapper and four infantry battalions and at Bien Hoa two infantry battalions and one reinforced infantry company.* Evidently, the enemy meant to subdue the U.S./RVN defenders by sheer numbers.[59]

The terrain facilitated infiltrations by large VC/NVA units to the areas surrounding Saigon. Save for a few radial roads, the city is bounded on the north, west, and east by a combination of paddies, jungles, and swamps interlaced by waterways. Routes for clandestine approach to the city were excellent. This plus VC/NVA skill in camouflage, concealment, and tunnel construction for storage of arms and supplies rendered it virtually impossible to secure all avenues of approach.[60]

Traversing this terrain, the units that engaged Tan Son Nhut, Bien Hoa, and other objectives in the Saigon area made formal tactical marches over set routes and through prepared base camps. They were held in assembly areas 9 to 12 hours marching distance from their targets until time for the coordinated assault.[61] One prisoner at Bien Hoa placed the VC/NVA staging area at 29 kilometers, a 9-hour march, due east of the air base. Upon arrival, they immediately cut through the perimeter fences and attacked the base.[62] Except to avoid detection on approach, these forces (unlike the stealthy sappers) moved openly against their targets, preceded or accompanied by supporting fires. The main attacks at both bases were supplemented by secondary ones.

By mounting their general offensive during the 1968 Tet holiday, the VC/NVA hoped to achieve the maximum tactical surprise. In this they were disappointed. Indications from a variety of sources (captured documents, prisoners, and ralliers) all pointed to a winter-spring offensive, spearheaded by attacks on population centers and Allied military installations. This intelligence convinced USMACV and RVNAF that a mid-January attack was certain, and caused them to concentrate forces in the Saigon area. What the Allies did not foresee was the true magnitude of the impending offensive.[63] This was slightly offset by a serious error in judgment by the VC/NVA command.

The VC/NVA security measures to guarantee surprise proved so severe that vital coordination among tactical units was blocked. In consequence, the forces in I and II CTZs launched their portion of the general offensive between 0030 and 0500 on 30 January 1968—24 hours before operations were initiated in the rest of the RVN. Targets for two of the seven premature actions were located at the air bases at Da Nang and Pleiku which were shelled by 122-mm rockets. These ill-timed events further confirmed that the awaited enemy offensive was imminent. Accordingly at 1125 local time 30 January 1968, COMUSMACV canceled the Tet cease-fire, ordered that "all forces will resume intensified operations," and directed that "troops will be placed

* An estimated 60 percent of the troops attacking Bien Hoa were North Vietnamese nationals.

Aftermath of the 31 January 1968 VC/NVA Tet attack on Bien Hoa Air Base. The attempt to destroy the base was thwarted by timely preparations by the base defense force. Damages, and allied losses, were minimal while the attackers suffered heavy casualties; many were captured.

(Below) Viet Cong map of Bien Hoa Air Base.

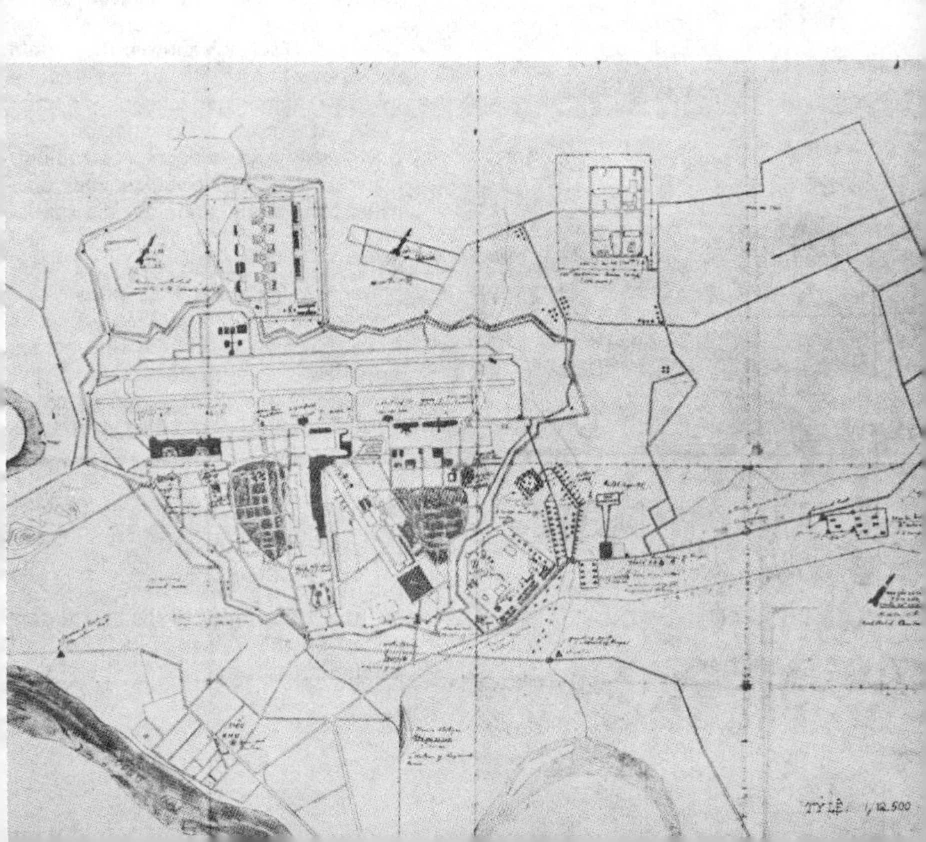

on maximum alert with particular attention to the defense of headquarters complexes, logistical installations, airfields, population centers, and billets." [64]

The enemy unleashed his main attack between 0300 and 0400 local time on 31 January with about 84,000 troops. In addition to Saigon they assaulted 36 of the 44 provincial capitals, 5 of the 6 autonomous cities, 64 of the 242 district capitals, and 50 hamlets.[65] Responding to USMACV alerting orders, the Seventh Air Force Commander directed all bases to adopt Security Condition Red (Option 1), a readiness posture in which all base defense forces were mobilized and deployed to repel an impending attack. Hence at both Bien Hoa and Tan Son Nhut, the VC/NVA forces found themselves opposed at once by U.S. defenders.[66] It was generally agreed that this fact alone accounted for the successful defense of the two bases.

Security check

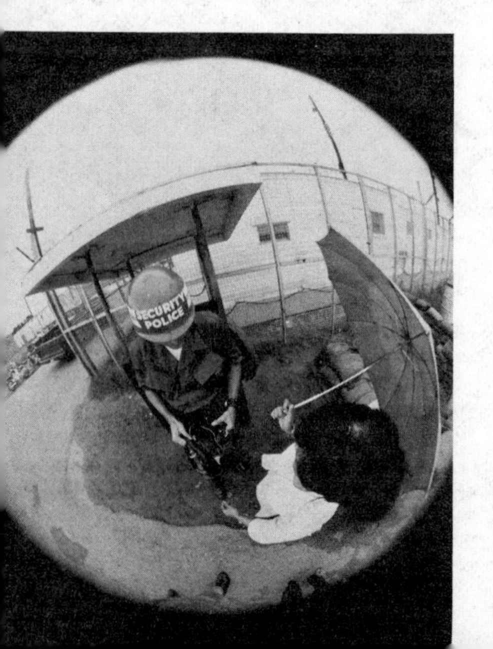

Sabotage

Of the four threats posed by the VC/NVA to the local security of U.S. air bases, sabotage was the least significant. Despite unlimited opportunities for sabotage afforded by the thousands of Vietnamese civilians working on these installations, this classic weapon of insurgency warfare was a curiosity rather than a commonplace. Records reveal but one notable case of sabotage at an American base during the entire war. On 8 February 1967 at Bien Hoa, Soviet-made explosive devices, secretly planted, destroyed about 2,600 napalm bombs valued at $342,000.[67] During 1968, a year of intense enemy activity, not a single instance of actual or attempted sabotage was reported at any Seventh Air Force base.[68] Why the VC/NVA all but ignored this simple and potentially highly rewarding tactic cannot be explained by available evidence.

The VC/NVA showed they could do serious damage to air bases, notably by standoff attacks and sapper raids. Much of their capability derived from a high degree of military expertise that reflected sound doctrine, meticulous planning and preparation, deeply instilled discipline, and an aptitude for fusing available manpower and weapons with proper tactics to produce a mission-effective force. Such ingenuity and skill helped surmount many of the inherent advantages of the defense and to retain a broad initiative to strike at ground-deployed U.S. air power at times and places of their choice. Accordingly, it is perplexing that the VC/NVA never sought to redress more vigorously the air power imbalance by fully exploiting their notable counter-air base capabilities to the extent permitted by the vulnerability of Allied defense measures.

IV. THE TARGET AIR BASES

> The majority of bases do not have a positive approach or active planning program for the protection of their operational assets. . . . There are no criteria established for the construction of air bases in a combat environment. New construction and redesigning is [sic] based on peacetime criteria.
>
> Seventh Air Force Base Defense Study Group, 1967.

Major targets for Viet Cong/North Vietnamese Army attacks embraced the 10 primary bases that supported USAF operations in Southeast Asia. Da Nang, Phu Cat, Tuy Hoa, Nha Trang, Cam Ranh Bay, and Phan Rang are located in the narrow coastal zone bordering the South China Sea. (See page 56.) Pleiku is situated in the Central Highlands less than 70 kilometers from Cambodia. Tan Son Nhut and Bien Hoa are in the environs of Saigon. Binh Thuy, the southernmost base, lies on the outskirts of Can Tho in the middle of the Mekong Delta.

The Geographic Impact

Geography had a vital bearing on all facets of the war. Its impact on local ground defense of these bases came chiefly from the conformation, topography, climate, and vegetation of the Republic of Vietnam.

A geopolitical principle holds that a compact country is much easier to defend than a large sprawling one. Clearly, the Republic of Vietnam fits the latter category. Slightly larger than Florida, the country extends more than 1,300 kilometers from north to south, while its width from east to west varies from 50 to 200 kilometers. Saigon, usually considered an east coast city, lies less than 60 kilometers from the Cambodian frontier to the west.

The Republic of Vietnam is a classic example of exposed territory. So lengthy are its boundaries in relation to its size, that points for infiltration by land and sea are almost unlimited—a circumstance fully exploited by the VC/NVA. The Ho Chi Minh Trail, stretching the whole length of the western boundary with branches extending into most interior areas, was their main route for infiltration of men and materiel throughout the war. Secondary but much more limited infiltration occurred along the 1,300-kilometer sea frontier. Hence, due in part to the physical conformation of RVN, logistic support for VC/NVA operations against USAF bases was available along well-established lines of communication reaching from North Vietnam to within tactical striking distance of the target installations.

Topography also favored the insurgency forces. Nearly 60 percent of RVN consists of relatively high mountains and plateaus rising to 2,500 meters. These mountains, the Annamite Chain, extend southeastward from China forming the border between RVN and Laos and, further south, between RVN and Cambodia. They terminate at a point in the Mekong Delta about 80 kilometers north of Saigon. Numerous spurs extending to the east insure broken and rugged terrain in close proximity to all USAF bases but Binh Thuy. Low-

Primary USAF Operating Bases

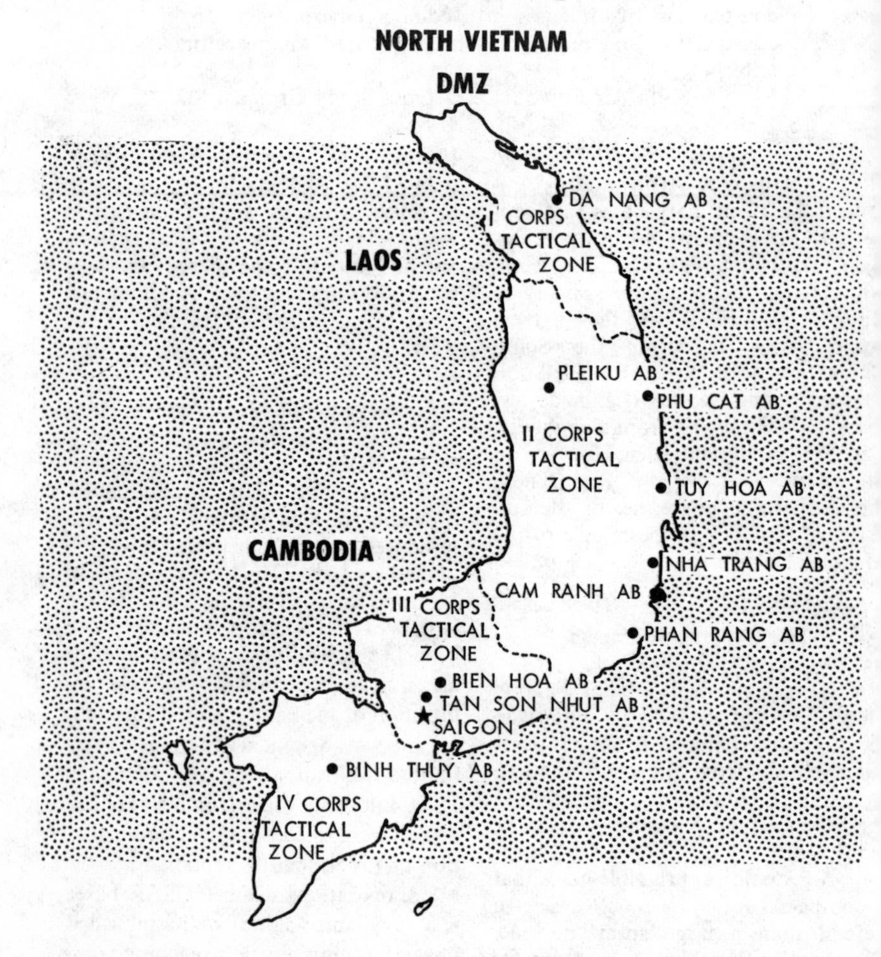

NOTE: CORPS TACTICAL ZONES WERE REDESIGNATED MILITARY REGIONS IN 1970.

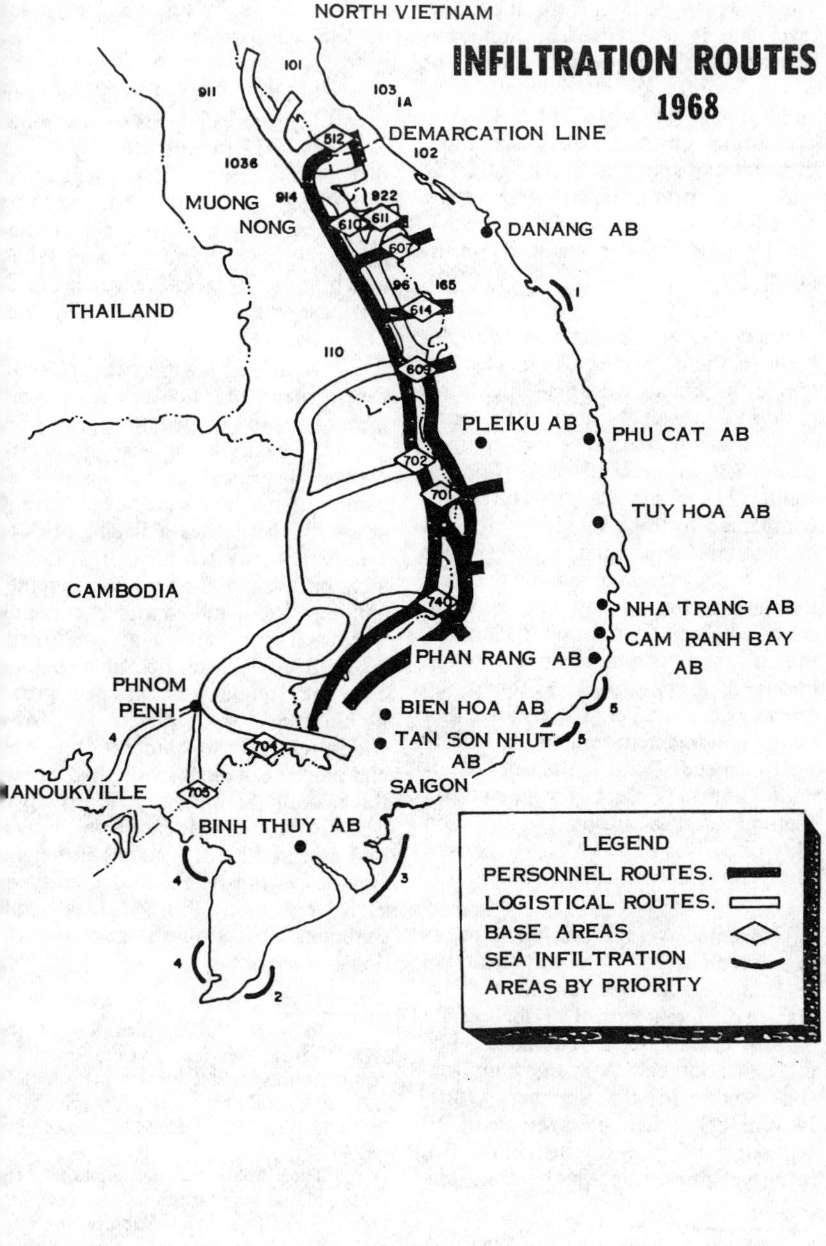

INFILTRATION ROUTES
1968

NORTH VIETNAM
101
911
103
1A
512
DEMARCATION LINE
102
1036
914
922
MUONG
NONG
610
611
DANANG AB
607
96
165
THAILAND
614
1
110
609
PLEIKU AB
PHU CAT AB
702
701
TUY HOA AB
CAMBODIA
740
NHA TRANG AB
CAM RANH BAY
AB
PHAN RANG AB
PHNOM
PENH
BIEN HOA AB
5
4
704
TAN SON NHUT
AB
5
IANOUKVILLE
705
SAIGON
BINH THUY AB
4
3
4
2

LEGEND
PERSONNEL ROUTES.
LOGISTICAL ROUTES.
BASE AREAS
SEA INFILTRATION
AREAS BY PRIORITY

lands with little or no relief comprise the remaining 40 percent of the country and are located chiefly in the Mekong Delta where the land is seldom more than 4 to 5 meters above sea level and is intersected by numerous waterways. Consequently, almost the whole countryside offered cover and concealment to the VC/NVA while presenting obstacles to observation, penetration, and movement by RVN and Allied ground forces. Each of the 10 USAF primary bases was accessible by land and/or water to insurgency forces.

Except in the mountains and plateaus of the Annamite Chain—for example the Pleiku AB area—high temperatures prevail throughout the year, the average annual range varying only from 77°F in the north to 81°F in the south. There high temperatures accompanied by high humidity create a climate that saps human energy and enormously increases maintenance requirements for all equipment. As in other countries with similar climates, the afternoon siesta is an institution observed, except for U.S. forces, by friend and foe alike. It appeared that by tacit agreement mutual hostilities were suspended during the early afternoon hours. Except for about six standoff attacks during the Tet and May offensives of 1968, air bases were rarely threatened during siesta.*

Annual average rainfall is heavy in all regions of RVN and torrential in many. It is heaviest in the Da Nang-Hue area with 128 inches. At Saigon it amounts to 80 inches. For most of Southeast Asia the rainy season occurs in the summer (June-November), when an average of 10 typhoons off the South China Sea bring yet more rain. In the Da Nang area the wettest period lasts fron December through January. Thi heavy rainy season crippled Allied an VC/NVA operations alike an marked the yearly low point in attack on U.S. air bases.*

Abundant rainfall joins the year round high temperatures to give much of RVN a 12-month growing seaso that results in luxuriant vegetation More than 80 percent of the country has a natural cover of rain forests monsoon forests, and savanna lands which provide extensive concealmen for insurgents.

Around and within the U.S. ai bases, plant life flourished in over whelming and unwanted profusion Several varieties of grasses and weed created a critical problem for bas defense. Especially widespread is tranh grass which reaches a height of 1 t 2 meters, easily tall enough to hide a man or even to imperil a helicopte landing. Yen-bach, another commo weed and a serious countrywide pest grows from 1.25 to 1.60 meters. Lau cane of frequent occurrence grow in clumps 2 to 3 meters tall. Als widespread are the bamboos, the mos common of which, mai pha, occur throughout Southeast Asia to form dense, almost impenetrable brake that ascend 12 to 16 meters in height Obviously, the height and density o such vegetation afforded ideal con cealment for ambush and infiltra tion.† [1]

---

* Siesta, it appeared, was the preferred time for launching a coup d'etat.

* John F. Fuller, historian of th Air Weather Service, gives a good ac count of the impact of weather on mili tary operations in his monograph, Wea ther and War (Hist Ofc, MAC, Decembe 1974).

† The botanical designations fo these plans are: tranh grass (*Impert. cylindrica*), yen-bach (*Eupatorium odo ratum*), lau (*Saccharum spontaneum*) and mai pha (*Bambusa arundinacea*).

Vietnamese fishing village engulfed by dense tropical vegetation

Effective vegetation control was nade vastly more urgent and onerous y the year-long growing season and he exceptional growth rate. The lat- er was a truly incredible phenomenon nd one on which information is sur- risingly incomplete.[2] Security Police t Tan Son Nhut recorded that vege- ation grew 1½ to 2½ inches per day luring the rainy season,[3] an observa- ion consistent with the findings of lant life specialists. A botanical study f one giant bamboo (*Dendrocalmus iganteus*) established that growth ould occur as rapidly as 46 centi- neters within 24 hours.[4]

Vegetation was probably least roublesome at Tuy Hoa where the en- ire eastern perimeter fronted directly n the South China Sea and where round cover around the remainder f the circumference was the lighter ariety common to savannas. The nost extreme vegetation problem ex- sted at Binh Thuy, the smallest USAF perating base. Situated in the center f the waterlogged Mekong Delta near Can Tho, it had an elevation of only 75 to 1.5 meters above mean sea level. The base was ringed by excep- tionally dense tropical vegetation 3-4 meters high. This growth engulfed the perimeter fences constructed on the outer face of the levee that enclosed the installation. Likewise concealed were navigable canals, used occasion- ally by the VC/NVA to float muni- tions and weapons to the base perim- eter. In the interior of Binh Thuy the same vegetation flourished.

At other bases vegetation growth fell somewhere between the extremes represented by Tuy Hoa and Binh Thuy. At all bases, however, it was a permanent security threat that varied only in the urgency of its impact.*

So on the whole, the geography of RVN greatly favored the VC/NVA either directly by facilitating their military operations or indirectly by restricting activities of Allied forces. In the case of air base defense, the tacti- cal imbalance was perpetuated and

* The combination of dank vegeta- tion and abundant rainfall created a breeding ground for mosquitoes and other disease-bearing insects.

accentuated by other factors, notably decisions on location and layout of USAF operating bases.

Location and Layout of Air Bases

Among the most critical decisions affecting air base defense was the determination to make maximum use of existing airfields, however inadequate, in order to speed the introduction of USAF combat elements. The six bases in question were Da Nang, Pleiku, Nha Trang, Bien Hoa, Tan Son Nhut, and Binh Thuy. All dated from the French regime and all were located in or near population centers.

Tan Son Nhut with its southern and eastern perimeters abutting metropolitan Saigon and with numerous villages and hamlets situated to the north and west was literally engulfed in a sea of humanity. Da Nang AB joined and shared the name of the second largest city in RVN. At Nha Trang the perimeter fence bordered upon civilian dwellings and often served as a clothesline. Nor were conditions radically improved at Phu Cat, Tuy Hoa, Cam Ranh Bay, and Phan Rang—bases expressly built for the USAF. All four were close to settlements of varying size. In the spring of 1969 a study compared an old and a new base in this regard. It found that clearing a 1-mile security zone around Bien Hoa would displace 13,998 people, 2,478 homes, and 55 shops. A like strip circling Tuy Ho would expel 16,180 persons and Don Tac, a refugee village newly erecte by the Agency for International De velopment (AID).[5]

Relocation of all people inhabit ing air base approaches was probabl the ideal technical solution to the de fense problem. But politically it wa out of the question, even though man of those concerned were squatter without legal title to the land the occupied. There was the unacceptabl risk that those relocated would b alienated from the Government o Vietnam and converted to the VC NVA cause. Such an outcome woul have simply aggravated an alread unsatisfactory situation.

As it was, problems of this natur faced the Air Force at Phu Cat, Tu Hoa, and Phan Rang where construc tion had forced small landowner from their property. Many did no desire to sell in the first place, o feared that family graves might b disturbed or the land gods displeased Some owners were underpaid or no paid at all. After waiting 2 years former residents of Phu Cat petitione the GVN to compensate them fo their property. Such grievances cre ated a receptive audience for VC NVA propaganda and bred a distinc antipathy toward U.S. forces.[6]

Tan Son Nhut Air Base

Vietnamese so displaced posed fresh security problems. Former residents frequently desired to return to the base to worship at pagodas left standing, to care for graves, to harvest tree or garden crops, or to tend to other affairs. Security personnel had to accompany the returnees and to search for boobytraps after their departure. At one USAF base under VNAF control, the faithful regularly came on the base without clearance or escort to visit a pagoda located near unguarded VNAF napalm stocks and ordnance-loaded aircraft.[7] This episode will illustrate the exasperating and hazardous idiosyncrasies encountered in security operations at the six old airfields where VNAF had primary responsibility for base defense and exercised control over base access.

Concentrations of civilian dwellings adjacent to the 10 USAF operating bases afforded the enemy an absolute tactical advantage since they provided cover and concealment to the threshold of the target base. These same conditions seriously restricted defense forces by prohibiting or limiting use of boobytraps, tripflares, sensors, freefire zones, and exclusion areas around base perimeters. Also totally or critically curtailed was the delivery of artillery, aircraft, or helicopter counterfire. Thus, like the Allied conduct of the overall war, base defense operations were profoundly influenced by the necessity to enlist the widespread active support of the population.

The USAF and VNAF buildup soon saturated the six older air bases to a point that invited enemy attack. Near the peak of the war, 76 percent of the total aircraft and 60 percent of all USAF aircraft operated from these more vulnerable airfields, whose target value was further heightened

Aircraft Assigned To Primary RVN Bases
3 January 1969

	RAAF	*VNAF*	*USAF*	*USA*	*USN*	*USMC*	*Total*
*Bien Hoa		75	220	220			515
*Binh Thuy		43	52				95
Cam Ranh Bay			117		22		139
*Da Nang		59	158	59	2	69	347
*Nha Trang		47	110	89			246
Phan Rang	8		141				149
Phu Cat			90				90
*Pleiku			48				48
*Tan Son Nhut		77	105	48			230
Tuy Hoa			97				97
Total	8	301	1,138	416	24	69	1,956

* Older bases.

SOURCE: USAF Management Summary Southeast Asia, 3 Jan 69, p 39.

by large stores of munitions and aviation fuel. At many of them, conditions were further aggravated by the presence of major military headquarters and/or key political facilities. The ARVN II Corps was at Pleiku and the USMACV I Field Force Vietnam (FFV) at Nha Trang. Da Nang hosted the ARVN I Corps and the III Marine Amphibious Force.

But in this respect Tan Son Nhut was unique. It not only supported an aerial combat mission but housed the headquarters of the Vietnamese Air Force, Seventh Air Force, and United States Military Assistance Command, Vietnam.* The base was also Saigon International Airport and in 1965 became the VNAF induction center. For much of the time, it served as the residence for the RVN premier or vice president. Location at the seat of government gave Tan Son Nhut a far-reaching political and psychological importance as a military target. Population saturation was noted as early as August 1965 in an Air Staff report which stated that the base was designed for 3,000 people but had 25,000.[7] An April 1968 estimate placed the permanent population at 25,000 but that the influx of daily workers and military members living off base raised this number to 55,000 during duty hours.[8]

Overcrowding seriously degraded security at the older bases. As congestion mounted, new combat-support facilities for the expanding aerial mission had to be sited solely on the basis of unoccupied real estate without regard to security factors. Dispersal to protect parked aircraft was impossible due to lack of space to enlarge or decentralize the ramps. At Tan Son Nhut, Da Nang, and Pleiku aviation fuel tanks and bladders were sited within 10-30 meters of the base perimeter. On every older base except Da Nang, munitions were stored in equally exposed locations.[9]

The USAF tenant status greatly complicated these troubles. As host, the VNAF insisted on exercising approval authority over all new construction. Thus a command change like that at Tan Son Nhut in early 1966 often necessitated renegotiation of many planning actions previously approved by the former commander. Agreements were also subject to cancellation for routine reasons. As one USAF base civil engineer plaintively observed, "Boy it's discouraging to get a project all set to go and then have the host say 'Sorry about that, you'll have to put it some place else.'" Usually no alternative site was offered or, if one were proposed, it was invariably in the rice paddies and required extensive fill before use.[10] The task of unsnarling

* USARV Headquarters was housed at Tan Son Nhut until it moved to Long Binh in July 1967. At that time, USMACV Headquarters relocated most of its activities from various points in Saigon to the newly built "Pentagon East," situated on Tan Son Nhut near the Saigon International Air Terminal.

View of the crowded flight line at Tan Son Nhut

Vulnerable fuel storage bladders adjacent to the Pleiku Air Base perimeter

these tangles fell to the base engineer, one of the much-abused heroes of USAF deployment to RVN.

Because there were no USAF criteria for constructing air bases in a combat area, peacetime standards governed the design of Tuy Hoa, Cam Ranh Bay, Phan Rang, and Phu Cat.[11] Some of the more glaring drawbacks of this approach showed up in the siting and configuration of these bases.

Perhaps from a location standpoint, Phan Rang was the most vulnerable because it received its water and aviation fuel from offbase sources through pipelines exposed to enemy interdiction.* In contrast, a peninsular site made Cam Ranh Bay the most defensible base in the Republic of Vietnam.

Critics, however, leveled their sharpest barbs at the internal layout of the four new installations. Security police officials, themselves partly to blame for the lack of proper planning guidance, pointed out that although the bases had "ample real estate to permit the locations of critical resources consistent with optimum security/defense criteria . . . this was not done." As a consequence, they asserted, vital resources and facilities were without exception sited at vulnerable locations or were so positioned that excessive manpower were required for their protection.[12]

Munitions were stored in the northwest and aviation fuel in the southeast corner of Phan Rang, both within easy small-arms range from the base perimeter. At Cam Ranh Bay combat essential facilities were so scattered that additional multiple guardposts were created. The security police claimed that a little forethought in planning could have incorporated dispersal into the general scheme while grouping resources in a tighter-knit layout that would have reduced manpower, increased security, and simplified defense operations.[13]

The siting of noncritical facilities also impaired base defense. For example, at Tuy Hoa a raised railroad bed along the south and west perimeters afforded excellent cover and concealment to enemy forces approaching from the rice paddies in these areas. And base defense forces launching a

* Of the older bases, Pleiku and Binh Thuy also relied on vulnerable offbase sources for water. [Final Report, 7th AF Base Def Study Gp, 17 Aug 67.]

counterattack were placed at a disadvantage, since the flat terrain from the track inward provided no cover against an enemy operating from the shelter of the embankment.[14] As these and other incongruities reveal, new bases were located and laid out with scant concern for security.

Active Defense Facilities, 1961-1972

After siting and layout, the most critical physical element in base defense operations was the status of security facilities—fences, barriers, lighting, sensors, minefields, towers, bunkers, and roads. But, from 1961 to 1965 USMACV viewed base defense as a primary responsibility of the overextended and hard-pressed RVNAF. Therefore the USAF did little more than post a few interior guards around parked aircraft and/or base billets, and file periodic reports on the unsatisfactory status of security safeguards.

As early as November 1961, the Farm Gate Commander at Bien Hoa informed CINCPACAF of security problems posed by uncontrolled vegetation and the need to lay "adequate concertina wire and mines throughout the perimeter."[15] During 1962 a USMACV survey rated Da Nang's perimeter fence as inadequate.[16] In anticipation of VC/NVA reprisals for U.S. air raids on the DRV, USMACV and 2d Air Division in late 1964 jointly inspected the physical defenses at Tan Son Nhut.

This inspection revealed that the base perimeter fence—none too sturdy when new—was in an advance state of deterioration. There were improvised gates and numerous holes which permitted uncontrolled access by civilians and military dependents. Three-quarters of its length was overgrown by foliage so dense that a company-size unit could have infiltrated undetected. Minefields laid in 1957 along some sections were not chartered or maintained, and livestock grazed in allegedly mined areas. No perimeter lighting system existed, and from 40 to 50 percent of the 18-kilometer perimeter was neither under surveillance nor covered by fire, due to the distance between observation posts and bunkers.[17] As Tan Son Nhut was the most prestigious air base in RVN, its defenses were likely the best to be found.

USAF assumption of responsibility for base defense facilities dated from December 1965 when COMUSMACV directed 2d Air Division and all other Service components to initiate measures for the local defense of their RVN bases.[18]

Southern perimeter of Tan Son Nhut Air Base. In May 1968 the VC/NVA attacked the base through this area, abetted by the overgrowth on the fences and the close proximity of private dwellings

Progress was halting and meager. After 18 months, a detailed survey by a Seventh Air Force Base Defense Study Group in the summer of 1967 reported widespread defects in physical security safeguards.[19] Of the 10 primary air bases, Da Nang alone boasted both permanent perimeter fencing and lighting systems installed by the USMC in early 1966. This double cyclone-type fence was the only one of its kind at RVN air bases.* At Tan Son Nhut a new but less durable perimeter barrier complex had been installed at the direction of COMUSMACV, after the 4 December 1966 sapper raid. It consisted of from one to three lines of triple-tier concertina wire, minefields, and permanent lighting.[20] Both Da Nang and Tan Son Nhut possessed good observation towers and fighting bunkers. Elsewhere the picture was bleak. Perimeter sighting was unsatisfactory at six bases; fencing was inadequate at 2; minefields were not utilized at 4; and bunkers were inadequate or unsafe at 5.

* The French considered the best obstacle a vertical fence, 2 meters high. imbedded 40 centimeters into the ground to prevent tunneling, made of barbed wire with a maximum mesh of 20 cm, and equipped with a conventional double-apron fence at its base. [V. J. Croizat, trans, *A Translation from the French: Lessons of the War in Indochina* (RM-5271-PR, The RAND Corp, May 1967), 11 138-39.]

By February 1969 Phu Cat and Tuy Hoa were still "aggressively pursuing" fencing programs. Phu Cat had constructed a single line of triple-tier concertina wire along 16 kilometers of its main line of resistance (MLR),* but its perimeter fence remained in the programming stage. Tuy Hoa's perimeter was 68 percent fenced, but the beach area was still unenclosed. Plans for a perimeter fence at Cam Ranh Bay were abandoned due to scope, configuration, and soil conditions, and an approved fencing project was confined to the MLR alone.[21] Perimeter

* A line at the forward edge of a battle position, designated for the purpose of coordinating the fire of all units and supporting weapons. It defines the forward limits of a series of mutually supporting defensive areas.

Mine field on the perimeter of Phu Cat Air Base

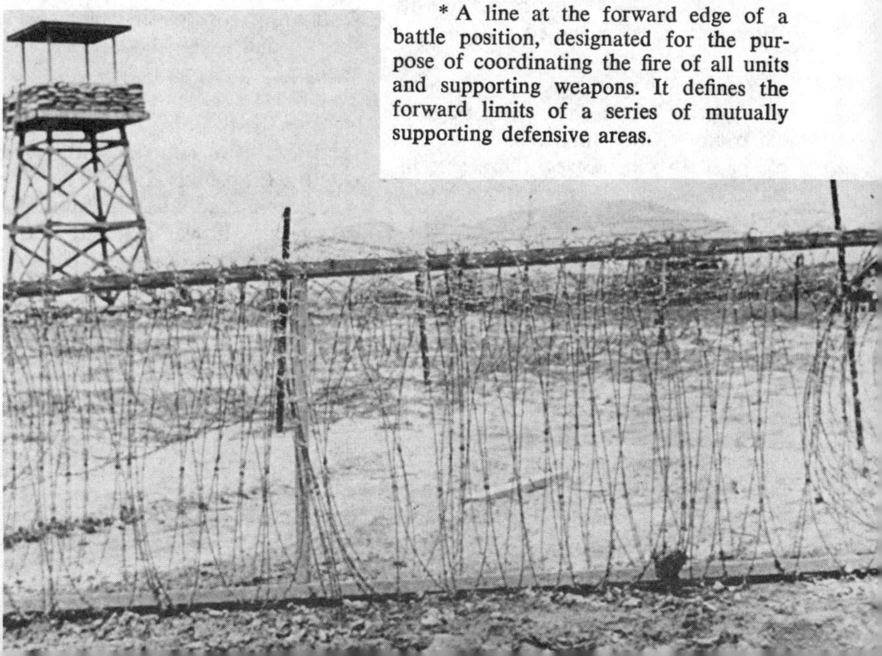

Base control tower and "big light" used in defense of Phu Cat Air Base

lighting continued to lag at five bases. Thirty-two percent of Tuy Hoa's perimeter was unlighted. As with fencing, the lights programmed for Cam Ranh Bay were limited to the MLR. Procurement delayed Phan Rang's permanent lighting system, and the one planned for Bien Hoa in July 1969 was never installed.

A basic obstacle to adequate security lighting was a chronic shortage of electricity from sources both on and off base. In most cases, therefore, installation of a permanent perimeter lighting system included an organic power source. Field expedients were widely used as substitutes. These makeshifts ranged from mobile Fresnel units to jury-rigged flares that had been condemned for aerial use.

However, the most common interim answer was the NF-2 Light-All unit. One generator fed up to 10 floodlights spaced along 100 meters of perimeter. Each NF-2 unit cost $1,090, and a requirement of 100 for a single base was not unreasonable. But the initial outlay was only the beginning. Not designed for continuous 8- to 12-hour daily operation, these units required daily maintenance service, a task which at a large base employed two airmen full time. The NF-2s were also vulnerable to small-arms fire, and the loss of a single unit darkened that segment of the perimeter it serviced.[22]

Hand-held slapflares* and 81-mm mortar illumination rounds supplemented lighting at all bases and constituted the primary source at some. Air-dropped flares routinely enhanced these ground efforts. In April 1969, Seventh Air Force reported to PACAF a monthly cost of $81,000 for slapflares and $100,000 for mortar shells.† [23]

At best, none of these interim solutions, even coupled with sophisticated night observation devices, provided more than a bare minimum level of lighting. It was asserted that "the cost of aircraft destroyed by sappers at one base [Tuy Hoa] in July 1968 would have been sufficient to ade-

---

* A slapflare looked like a paper towel cylinder with a cap on the bottom. The steps for igniting were to remove the cap, hold the flare in the left hand, and slap the bottom with the right hand.

† Cost data on the air-dropped flares was not available.

Sandbag bunker at Cam Ranh Bay Air Base

quately fence and light all our bases in RVN.* [24]

Construction of fighting bunkers was equally troublesome. Experience and experimentation led to the use of a wide assortment of materials and designs. Initially bunkers of sandbags were nearly universal. But deterioration due to weather and hard usage normally necessitated replacement of the bags every 90 days and created a monumental work load. Waterproofing was not feasible and all timbers were vulnerable to rot and termites. Accordingly, the trend was to replace sandbags with more durable materials.

By 1968 each base had for the most part produced a bunker best adapted to local conditions. The French had found the ideal to be a facility of permanent construction and low silhouette. At Cam Ranh Bay, however, the shifting sands rendered this type undesirable. And at Binh Thuy, because of the high water table of the delta, bunkers had to be built above ground. Accordingly, building materials adapted to varying conditions and terrain, but most bunkers were designed to withstand a direct hit by a B-40 rocket. Most but not all bunkers at the bases had some type of overhead protection. All enjoyed a standoff weaponry screen, usually cyclone or other heavy fencing. Placed 3-4 meters forward of the bunker, the screen predetonated rocket propelled grenades.[25]

In the spring of 1969, bunker construction was least advanced at Phu Cat and Cam Ranh Bay. At the former limited fire necessitated shifting bunkers from perimeter sites to the MLR, where in conjunction with the planned fencing and lighting, they would contribute to a sound defense complex. At Cam Ranh Bay bunker construction was deferred pending action on programmed MLR fencing and lighting.

After 4 years of massive USAF involvement, physical safeguards in 1969 were still judged inadequate by the Director of Security Police, Seventh Air Force. This was attributed to profound USAF disinterest as reflected by the lack of an active planning program and the absence of any criteria for air base construction in a combat area. General apathy and indifference were only intermittently dispelled by a near-disaster such as the 1968 Tet Offensive, or by a destructive sapper raid like that on Tuy Hoa

---

* This sapper raid on Tuy Hoa on 29 July 1968 resulted in 2 C-30s destroyed, and 5 C-130s, 1 C-47 and 1 F-100 damaged. Four USAF personnel were wounded. (7AF/IGS WEINTSUM, No. 68-13, 27 Jul-2 Aug 68, p 23)

in July 1968. Contributing to the problem was the continuous turnover of commanders at all echelons. New commanders not exposed to enemy attack usually stressed more spectacular but less vital construction. Highly visible recreation facilities received top priority while defense works at obscure or remote locations were ignored. For example, at the time of the Tuy Hoa sapper raid the perimeter was only partially fenced and totally unlighted. Yet, a year before, the base had been equipped with air-conditioned recreation facilities that included a base exchange, open messes for officers and noncommissioned officers, a library, and a recreation center. The latter offered a poolroom, reading room, and complete snackbar. Under these conditions which prevailed at all bases, security police undertook the construction of security safeguards as a self-help project with a corresponding degrading of their primary security mission capability.[26]

By 1970 construction projects in support of base defense had been overtaken by events. Shortly after assuming office in January 1969, President Richard M. Nixon decided to Vietnamize the war and to begin the phased withdrawal of U.S. forces from RVN. His decision was swiftly reflected in such actions as the Nha Trang Project which, begun in 1969, aimed at early USAF relinquishment of that air base to VNAF.[27] Consistent with this policy, the Secretary of Defense refused Military Construction Program (MCP) funds for the perimeter fence at Phu Cat. Because concertina wire was an expendable item, he recommended that construction be accomplished with Operation and Maintenance (O&M) funds.[28] This policy was soon extended by USMACV to other security fence projects. Seventh Air Force instructed base commanders to draw fencing material through base supply and install it by self-help.[29] At the same time security lighting requests were also deleted from the MCP with the recommendation that they be resubmitted in the O&M Program, "selecting the most critical area for accomplishment within the $25,000.00 limitation." [30] Clearly, for all practical purposes, USAF construction of physical safeguards at RVN air bases was at an end.

Passive Defense Facilities, 1961-1972

Passive defense facilities directly complemented the physical security safeguards of active defense operations. Their purpose was to reduce the probability of and to minimize the damage from enemy action without taking the initiative. In RVN such facilities consisted chiefly of shelters, revetments, and hardened structures installed to protect USAF personnel and resources not engaged in a base defense mission.

From 1961 through 1965 the only USAF passive defense construction to speak of was the erection of aircraft revetments. The stimulus for this program came initially from the necessity to reduce explosive safety hazards arising from wingtip-to-wingtip parking a bomb-laden aircraft. On 16 May 1965 at Bien Hoa, an accidental explosion aboard a B-57 triggered a series of blasts that killed 28 and injured 77 people. The aircraft toll reached 10 B-57s, 2 A-2Hs, 1 A-1E, and 1 F-8U destroyed, plus 30 A-1Hs and 1 H-43 damaged. Also demolished were 12 pieces of aerospace ground equipment (AGE), 10 vehicles, and the JP-4 fuel dump. This one incident was more destructive than any single VC/NVA attack on any air base during the entire war.[31] It resulted in a USAF directed emergency program for revetment construction.

F–100 Super Sabres parked in aircraft revetments at Tan Son Nhut Air Base

For revetment construction the Air Force chose a prefabricated facility, developed by the Air Force Logistics Command (AFLC) and produced by the American Rolling Mill Company (ARMCO). It consisted of earth-filled corrugated steel bins 12 feet high and 5.5 feet wide. Built up on three sides of an aircraft hardstand, the bins afforded considerable protection against such dangers as near-miss blasts, secondary explosions, fragmentation effects, surface ordnance, and secondary damage and proliferation. Three 28-man Prime Beef* teams were deployed to RVN to do the work, the first one arriving in August 1965. Aided by troop and local-hire labor, they erected 12,040 linear feet of revetments at these bases by the end of the year.[32]

Tan Son Nhut	4,700
Bien Hoa	3,800
Da Nang	3,540

During 1966 through 1969, USAF interest in passive defense facilities continued to center chiefly on aircraft revetments which totalled 506 at all bases by 30 June 1967.[33] However, the Seventh Air Force Base Defense Study Group reported on 17 August the improper siting of many revetments. Explosives-laden aircraft stood face to face, their forward-firing weapons pointed toward maintenance facilities or other planes. The study group asserted that this arrangement severely curtailed protection against blast or fragment damage, and could not prevent an explosive chain reaction from aircraft to aircraft. Of the

---

* Prime Beef (Base Engineer Emergency Forces) are worldwide base civil engineer forces. They are organized to provide trained military elements, used in direct combat support or emergency recovery from natural disaster.

Damaged revetments at Bien Hoa Air Base following an attack in June 1969

10 primary bases, Bien Hoa alone had positioned its revetments so that the bay opening of one faced the rear wall of another.[34] The corrective action action recommended by the study group was rejected by Gen. William W. Momyer, Seventh Air Force Commander, because "we are too far committed to change now. Cost in time and manpower is prohibitive." [35]

Static aircraft protection embarked on a new phase in 1968 as the Air Force launched a crash shelter construction program. The switch from revetments to shelters stemmed from the VC/NVA spring offensive when standoff attacks had destroyed 25 (valued at $94 million) and damaged 251 USAF aircraft. These strikes bared the weaknesses of revetments, mainly the absence of overhead cover. The adopted shelter design called for a double corrugated steel arch with a poured-in-place concrete cover 18 inches thick. An added freestanding backwall extended protection equal to the cover's and included an opening to let out jet exhaust. A small number of the shelters were also fitted with a front closure device. Production of materials began in CONUS in mid-1968, and the first concrete cover was poured in RVN in October 1968. Civilian contractors such as Raymond-Morrison-Knudson and Brown-Root-James (RMK-BRJ) erected a few of these shelters. But USAF civil engineer Red Horse* squadrons augmented by troop labor built the majority.[36] In contrast to revetments, siting of shelters received careful consideration. Wherever possible they were placed nose to tail with the front ends oriented away from the most likely direction of a ground attack.[37]

The capping of the last shelter at Tuy Hoa on 13 January 1970 completed the program. Seventh Air Force

* Red Horse (Rapid Engineer Deployment, Heavy Operational Repair Squadrons, Engineering) are controlled by Headquarters USAF. They give the Air Force a highly mobile, self-sufficient, rapidly deployable civil engineer capability required in a potential theater of operations.

then owned about 1,000 revetments and 373 shelters for a total 1,373 protective structures. This number compared favorably with the 1,164 USAF aircraft permanently assigned at that time to RVN air bases.[38]

The protection afforded aircraft by hardened shelters confirmed the soundness of the program. Responding to a PACAF query, Seventh Air Force on 3 June 1969 cited two cases in which aircraft parked in shelters escaped destruction by direct rocket hits. On another occasion shelters saved several aircraft from damage or destruction when a nearby munitions storage area exploded. In spring 1970 a USN EC-121 crashed and burned at Da Nang, but adjacent hardened shelters saved three USAF F-4Ds from destruction and two others from major damage. The estimated dollar savings attributed to shelters in these incidents more than paid for the $15.7 million program in RVN.[39]

Men, like aircraft, were for much of the war without safe shelter. Inspection by the 1967 Seventh Air Force Base Defense Study Group found personnel bunkers unroofed and in disrepair. They were often too dispersed to give real protection. Revetment construction to safeguard the lower floors of barracks was slow, and no one had come up with a way to exit quickly from the unprotected upper floors. Quarters of key personnel were equally unsafe, and working areas were unsheltered.[40] Popular response to these exposed conditions were echoed in these earnest lines:

I arrived at Da Nang and my heart felt a pang
As I viewed my new home for the year
For the sheetmetal top, I was told would not stop
The rockets intended for here.

. . . .

When the sirens go off, or the rocket tubes cough
"Get under your bed!" reads Directive
But try (and I strive), I can't stop the drive
To seek shelter a bit more protective.[41]

The steps to a final solution of the barrack-revetment problem were drawn-out and wasteful. Initially revetments consisted of earth-filled sandbags, stacked to a height and thickness necessary for protection and stability. These bags as a rule deteriorated within 90 days and were replaced with new earth-filled ones. As local conditions stabilized and further replacement was required, plywood shells packed with earth took the place of the sandbags. These wood revetments also

Brick revetments constructed about billets at Pleiku Air Base to protect against shell fragments. Such revetments were useless against direct hits

rotted, and the substitute became brick or concrete materials that lasted for the useful life of the facility protected. By 1968 precast concrete slabs were adopted as the least expensive revetments for both personnel and equipment. A forklift operator and a welder were the only skilled labor required to erect them.[42]

Concrete slab revetments promised impressive savings. At Da Nang, for example, more than 40,000 linear feet of sandbag revetments shielded barracks and operational facilities. An estimate showed that replacement of sandbag revetments by concrete slabs around the barracks alone would save $521,340 in 1 year.[43]

The delay in protecting essential facilities and services matched that in sheltering personnel. Again, in the absence of combat construction criteria, most bases made no plans for such protection. For example, in 1967 all bases were constructing centralized electric powerplants, but only Cam Ranh Bay had a protection plan for this facility. Even at that base, less than 25 percent of all mobile and alternate generators—those used chiefly for ground controlled approach (GCA) and other navigational aids—were protected. Disregarding the principle of dispersion, alternate generators were frequently located next to primary power sources.[44]

USAF munitions storage areas—priority enemy targets—were adequate at all bases except Pleiku and Binh Thuy. However, those of the VNAF were substandard at each base, save Bien Hoa. Large unprotected quantities of munitions cluttered every VNAF parking ramp, a serious hazard to USAF personnel and resources. Barring the bases of Tan Son Nhut, Phan Rang, and Cam Ranh Bay, munitions at aerial ports awaiting shipment had little or no protection. Storage was either on or immediately adjacent to aircraft parking areas.[45]

Security of petroleum storage tanks—also priority enemy targets—needed upgrading. Other than at Tan Son Nhut, the protection of these storage tanks was after the fact. It relied on earthen dikes to contain escaping fuel and head off a holocaust. When rockets struck Da Nang on 27 April 1971 and Cam Ranh Bay on 25 May, the dikes let firemen limit the blaze to tanks taking direct hits.[46] On Tan Son Nhut the tanks belonged to commercial petroleum companies who encased them in costly masonry shells. The wisdom of this move was doubtful, due to the high silhouette of the tanks and the deep penetration of rocket propelled grenades. Fuel storage in rubber bladders became widespread in South Vietnam. Often set adjacent to aircraft hydrant fueling systems, the bladders posed a grave fire hazard.

No shielding from blast or fragmentation existed for most aircraft maintenance and civil engineering control centers, supply control systems using UNIVAC 1050 computers, and base command posts and communications centers.

Fire and crash vehicles crucial to damage control were normally parked in rows at one central open area on each base. Few bases had any plans to disperse this critical recovery equipment. None provided a hardened parking area.

Water sources, purification equipment, and storage points were unprotected at all bases. Pleiku, Phan Rang, and Binh Thuy depended on water from vulnerable offbase sources. Several bases put in fire hydrant systems, but only Bien Hoa had dispersed emergency water storage. Two water

Dikes constructed to protect petroleum supplies at Tuy Hoa Air Base

storage points at Cam Ranh Bay were situated in the fighter aircraft area, a choice target for enemy attack.[47]

The stimulus given passive defense by the 1968 Tet Offensive carried over into 1969. But this momentum focused almost exclusively on protection of aircraft with only limited attention to personnel and facilities. As the year wore on, the program began a gradual phaseout, owing to the decision to begin withdrawal of American forces and the cutback in funds for RVN operations.

With the completion of the last hardened aircraft shelter on 13 January 1970, significant USAF passive defense construction in RVN came to an end. Thereafter, general policy was to perform minimum maintenance on the minimum number of existing facilities needed to protect the diminishing USAF forces.

Vegetation Control

No element of the Vietnamese environment was more detrimental to base defense than the invincible ground cover described earlier. This rampant vegetation hid the enemy, shut off friendly observation and fields of fire, neutralized fencing and other defense barriers, slowed security forces, and nullified detection by sentry dog teams. The need to control this jungle was evident and urgent—how to do it was the sticking point.

Clearing approaches to the base was the first order of business. This meant defoliating a zone around the outside circumference of the installation, an area outside the Air Force's accepted defense responsibility. Hence it became the task of the Allied ground commander whose TAOR was confined to the base. Actually internal and external security overlapped in this zone, creating a joint and at times unequal interest in common defensive measures. This diffusion of military responsibility and the necessity for political clearance vastly diminished the prospects of winning approval for any defoliation program.

Another critical area calling for the most complete defoliation was the air base perimeter. Here physical factors crippled or canceled out progress. From the outset the six old bases took security steps, and the four new bases followed. These safeguards embodied fencing, tactical wire, minefields, and tripflares set in divers numbers and mixes along the perimeter. The skill of the VC/NVA sapper in clearing manmade obstacles and in disarming explosives devices dictated that this complex be kept free of concealing vegetation. Ignoring the French experience, the USAF discovered anew the problems associated with defoliation of the perimeter barrier system.[48]

Rarely if ever charted, the minefields of the perimeter barrier prohibited use of manual labor to cut and remove the vegetation. The mines, fencing, and wiring prevented mowing or scraping by mechanized equipment. Burning was unsatisfactory on several counts. Vegetation was highly fire resistant, particularly during the rainy season when growth was most rapid. It ignited slowly, even if sprayed with a flammable such as contaminated jet fuel. Because fire hardly ever consumed the vegetation, the residue went on obscuring the barrier system and offering cover to penetrators. Burning also detonated or destroyed mines and flares within the complex.

Next in importance was defoliation of the base interior. Here too, the ideal was to clear the ground cover that concealed penetrators and reduced surveillance by defense forces. For example, the defense vegetation negated sentry dog detection—the base's most reliable alarm. And the exertion in plowing through this thicket sapped dog and handler. Because the interior was without the perimeter's hazards or obstructions, it seemed that the clearing methods mentioned earlier could be given full play. In practice this was not the case. Safety factors forbade burning in or near fuel and munitions storage areas. The immense labor entailed in clearing a sizable area in a reasonable time curtailed manual cutting. Cutting by hand nonetheless left the root system intact, and so was well-suited to Cam Ranh Bay's very unstable soil. Elsewhere, however, an undisturbed root system meant rapid regrowth of vegetation. Even though scraping served well in the base interior, the conventional USAF civil engineer squadron usually lacked the needed mechanized equipment. In light of these facts, the answer to vegetation control in the interior as on the perimeter appeared to be herbicides.

By the time the Air Force turned to herbicides for base vegetation control, they were in full-scale military use in support of other ground operations. The dispensing of defoliants centered on foliage along thoroughfares to deny the enemy ambush cover. Spraying also focused over VC/NVA camps and assembly areas, as well as over crops intended for feeding the foe. The acreage treated with agents from the 1,000-gallon tanks of USAF UC-123 (Ranch Hand) aircraft rose from 17,119 in 1962 to 608,106 in 1966.[49]

None of these herbicides was believed to endanger humans or animals. All had been widely used in the United States for more than 20 years on foods and other crops, rangeland, and forests. None persisted in the soil and periodic respraying was required to kill regrowth. All were liquids. Those dispensed in RVN were designated Orange, White, and Blue. Appendix 5 gives general data on their composition, application, effect, and safety precautions.

The use of these herbicides was a GVN program supported by the United States. The U.S. Ambassador and COMUSMACV acted jointly on GVN requests for herbicide operations on the basis of policy formed by State and Defense Departments and approved by the President.[50] Senior U.S. Army advisors at ARVN corps and division level were delegated authority to approve requests in which dispersal of the herbicides was limited to hand or ground-based power-spray methods.

A herbicidal defoliation request from a USAF air base was prepared and documented by the base civil engineer, using a set checklist. (See page 77.) It was then processed through U.S. military channels to the senior U.S. Army headquarters in the corps tactical zone. If approved there, it was sent on to the ARVN commanding general of the same CTZ for military approval and political clearance. It was at this point that delay most frequently occurred, due to opposition from the district and/or province chief. These officials were influenced by such things as superstition, concern for local crop damage, and possible propaganda value to the VC/NVA. Final action on requests for ground-delivered herbicides was taken at this level. If aerial delivery was desired, the request could only be approved at USMACV/JCS level.

A C–123 sprays defoliation chemicals over South Vietnamese jungles

Technical factors also entered into the dispensing of herbicides. Dry weather was essential, because rain quickly washed chemicals from the target vegetation to nearby crops and other desirable growth. Ideally, spraying was done between dawn and 1000, at ambient temperatures under 30° C (86° F), and in calm or very low wind conditions to minimize drift. Storage and mixing points had to be kept to a minimum, isolated from cultivated areas. Empty herbicide drums required close control to avoid accidental contamination.[51]

Approval and execution of herbicidal defoliation projects were time-consuming and uncertain. In February 1968 Phan Rang requested defoliation of a 200-meter strip both inside and outside the perimeter, around the entire circumference of the base. The approving authority reduced the scope of the project to one-half the perimeter. In addition, problems in obtaining herbicide and other obstacles delayed completion of the project for 1 year.[52]

Excessive vegetation at Tan Son Nhut and Bien Hoa hindered the base defenders throughout the 1968 Tet attacks.[53] At Bien Hoa the approval process for aerial defoliation was termed "hopelessly complicated," one

Checklist for Defoliation Requests

1. Overlays or annotated photographs depicting the exact area.

2. Target list:
    a. Area—province and district.
    b. UTM coordinates.
    c. Length and width.
    d. Number of hectares.
    e. Type of vegetation.

3. Justification:
    a. Objectives and military worth.
    b. Summary of incidents.

4. Psychological warfare annex (prepared by sector):
    a. Leaflets.
    b. Loudspeaker texts.

5. Civil affairs annex (prepared by sector):
    a. No crops within 1 kilometer.
    b. Contingency plan to provide food or money to families whose crops are accidentally damaged by the defoliation operation.

6. Certification by province chief:
    a. Province chief approval.
    b. Indemnification will be made by the Republic of Vietnam for accidental damage to crops.

SOURCE: Lib of Cong Rprt, 8 Aug 69, to the House Subcommittee on Science and Astronautics, 91st Cong, 1st sess, *A Technological Assessment of the Vietnam Defoliant Matter: A Case History*, p 19.

that might take two or more months. Plant growth meanwhile continued unabated. Even when authorized, a project was apt to be fettered with restrictions. Thus aerial delivery of Orange was denied at Bien Hoa, and only parts of its perimeter were approved for chemical defoliation. Accordingly, because Blue and White were not suited to local conditions, Orange had to be dispensed from a tank truck by a power spray that did not reach beyond the second fences. Local terrain made it impossible to go outside the third and fourth fence and spray inward.[54]

As noted earlier, Binh Thuy faced the most extreme defoliation problem. Here the one herbicide approved for use was Blue, which killed only those portions of plants with which it came in contact. With the root systems left intact, regrowth was rapid. In 1 month, 2,420 gallons of Blue valued at $22,000 were sprayed over limited areas of the interior and a narrow zone around the perimeter of the 550-acre installation without making any significant inroads against the teeming vegetation.[55]

Herbicides for air base defense seldom if ever improved the horizontal view at installations by the desired 40 to 60 percent.[56] Defoliation needs of the 10 primary bases were specific, permanent, and known in advance. Still no ongoing long-term program to satisfy them was ever set up. Instead the job was done piecemeal, with each base handling defoliation requests. Despite administrative and technical controls, chemical agents remained the single sure way to control vegetation in places where other means could not—notably in the critical perimeter complexes. As the war drew to a close, however, curbs on the use of herbicides grew more and more rigid. The last herbicide mission by fixed-wing aircraft was flown on 7 January 1971. On 1 May, a presidential directive ended *all* U.S. herbicide operations.[57] In the ensuing months, mines killed eight and injured seven Army personnel who were trying to clear vegetation by hand from wire entanglements and fields of fire.[58] With the Ambassador's full backing, COMUSMACV urged Washington to alter at once the ban on chemical herbicides because immediate defoliation was "essential to security of bases." [59]

On 18 August the President permitted the resumption of chemical defoliation until 1 December 1971. He authorized the use of Blue and White but not Orange. Approved herbicide operations were restricted to the perimeters of firebases and installations, with delivery limited to solely helicopter or ground-based spraying equipment, under the same regulations applied in the United States.[60] As the expiration date for this authority neared, COMUSMACV asked for an extension. On 26 November 1971 the President authorized continued use of herbicides and set no termination date. At the same time, he stipulated that U.S. defoliation assistance to the Government of Vietnam be confined to "base and installation perimeter operations and limited operations for important lines of communications." This policy prevailed until the last U.S. forces departed RVN in 1973.[61]

No defoliant method tried for air base defense purposes in South Vietnam proved to be at once efficient, economical, and politically acceptable. The practical value of herbicides was much impaired by technical, administrative, and political constraints. For chiefly technical reasons, the same could be said for techniques such as burning and scraping. For the United States—as it had for France—vegetation remained a major unresolved problem.

V. USAF GROUND DEFENSE FORCES

> The enormous mass of non-combatant personnel who look after the very few heroic pilots, who alone in ordinary circumstances do all the fighting, is an inherent difficulty in the organization of the air force. Here is the chance for this great mass to add a fighting quality to the necessary services they perform. Every airfield should be a stronghold of fighting air-groundmen, and not the abode of uniformed civilians in the prime of life protected by detachments of soldiers.
>
> Sir Winston Churchill, 1941.

By late 1965 it became certain that U.S. ground combat forces would take part in offensive operations, and that the Air Force would be expected to protect its own installations. The USAF reaction to this unwelcome task was alien to the U.S. armed forces.[1] It was to ship the basic means of air base defense to South Vietnam—man by man and item by item. Then in the combat zone the Air Force assembled, organized, and trained these troops. More than 8 months passed before this process began to turn out forces that showed elementary skill in executing their unit mission.[2] Security police squadrons were formed in this manner at the 10 major bases in RVN. These units became the focal point of USAF ground defense during the entire war.

Tactical versus Nontactical Organization

The governing USAF directives* were silent on how to organize and employ security police in a hot war. Hence USAF ground defense forces in RVN were structured to cope with CONUS contingencies in a cold war. A security police squadron in RVN

* Air Force Manual (AFM) 207-1, Doctrine, and Requirements for Security of Air Force Weapons Systems, 10 June 1964 (superseded by AFM 207-1, 10 Jun 68, and in turn by AFM 207-1, 10 Apr 70); AFM 205-3, Air Police Security Operations, 15 February 1963 (replaced by AFM 207-2, Handbook for Security Forces, 15 Jul 66, which was supplanted by AFM 207-2, 15 June 69).

differed little from its stateside counterpart. The police did, however, add intelligence and maintenance/construction functions and delete the correctional one. (See chart.) The standard squadron consisted of four security and four law enforcement flights. These employed most of the personnel and performed the primary mission. The duty day consisted of three 8-hour shifts, rotated from flight to flight every 3 days. A 3-day break came after each cycle of 9 duty days. Within any flight there was little further subdivision. In keeping with good management, the personnel were rotated frequently among the various posts and duties. This promoted cross-training, expedited skill upgrading and equalized assignment to onerous or unpopular posts. The upshot was a flight shaped largely by administrative needs, not tactical considerations.

Limited modification of this structure began with the 1965 buildup and was due less to experience than to insufficient manpower. The flight structure in both security and law enforcement functions was reduced from four to three. Each was assigned permanently to one of the three 8-hour shifts. At the same time, it became standard practice to allocate 50 percent of the present-for-duty strength to the 2000-0400 shift, which coincided with the high-threat period. Job rotation in the flights ceased as stability was stressed. This policy sought to make every security policeman a specialist on a specific post or duty during a single shift, so he would more readily detect any irregularities. It also sought to stabilize a personnel situation rendered chaotic by the 12-month tour of duty. Off-duty time was handled on an individual basis within each flight. A member might get 1 out of 15 days off, if the threat was low and manning was adequate. But every base often canceled off-duty time for 6 to 12 weeks at a stretch. When guard mount and

Typical USAF Security Police Squadron in Republic of Vietnam

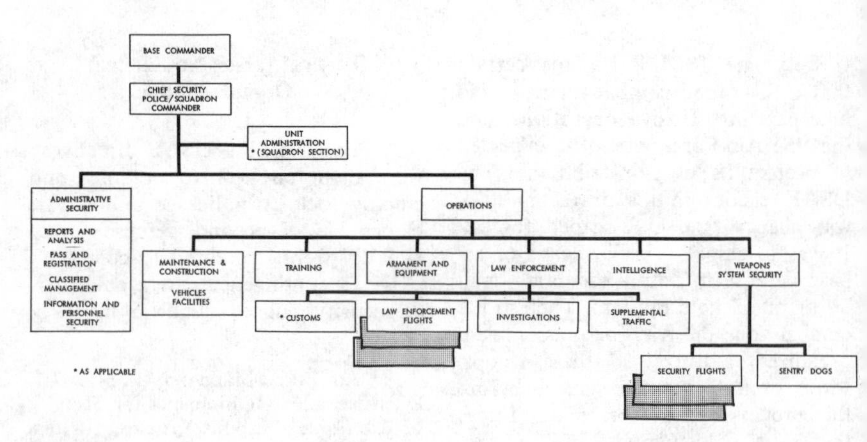

posting were added to time on post, the duty day averaged 10 or more hours.

These changes left the basic structure of security police squadrons in RVN untouched. As one Army officer observed:

> Security police are deployed as individuals much as peacetime interior guards along based perimeters, without unit integrity. Yet they have been required repeatedly to fight, as small tactical units, locally superior hostile tactical forces.[3]

Security police flights contained no element analogous to the fire teams of USA or USMC rifle companies. The closest thing to a tactical element in a security police squadron was the 13-man quick-reaction team, an *ad hoc* formation employed as a standby reserve. Except for the 3 combat security police squadrons organized in the United States under the Safe Side II program (discussed later), USAF made no effort to reorganize units already in SVN along tactical lines. The explanation appears to have been a desire to avoid compounding the disruption caused by the annual 100 percent turnover in personnel. For the future, however, tactical organization for security police units in insurgency surroundings was made part of official USAF doctrine.*

The most creative change in security police organization came not in the operating units but at staff level. In Seventh Air Force Headquarters, the chief staff responsibility for air base defense belonged to the Director of Security Police. Standard USAF organization at the time placed him under the supervision and direction of the Inspector General.† Until 1968 the Security Police Directorate performed as a conventional staff agency. In that year, however, the scale and intensity of attacks on air bases during the Tet Offensive thrust it into an operational role.

To discharge its new role, the Directorate of Security Police added a Base Defense Operations Center composed of both Intelligence and Operations sections. To improve advance detection of enemy action, the Intelligence Section tapped all Allied sources at hand. From them it compiled and published a weekly evaluation of the enemy threat, along with the friendly order of battle at each of the 10 USAF operating bases.* The Operations Section checked command-wide base defense activities around the clock, from a desk in the combat operations center (COC) of Seventh Air Force's tactical air control center (TACC). When so ordered by the Security Police Director (acting with his commander's approval), the section directed and coordinated the security police mobile contingency forces. This setup (mainly the idea of Maj. Gen. Robert L. Petit, Seventh Air Force Chief of Staff) mirrored the deep concern for protection of USAF aircraft on the ground. The Director of Security Police came to play in ground defense operations a role much like that of the Director of Operations in aerial offensive ones.[4]

Manpower Authorizations

When the JCS refused to dedicate U.S. ground combat forces to the local defense of air bases in RVN, the USAF in late 1965 began a crash buildup of security police forces for this mission. This action continued

---

* AFM 206-1, 30 June 1969, Local Ground Defense of US Air Force Bases.

† During 1965 and early 1966, the Security Police Directorate was a staff agency directly under the command element.

* The 7AF/IGS Weekly Intelligence Summary.

until mid-1967 when authorized strength leveled off at slightly less than 5,000. (See table.) Under the circumstances, this program had to be based on existing cold war manning standards.

Until Vietnamization progressively reduced USAF air base defense responsibilities, there was consensus among security police officials that manpower authorizations were inadequate. As early as 1962 the Director of Security and Law Enforcement, 2d Air Division protested—with good reason—that the 84 security policemen then authorized were "simply not enough . . . to provide internal security for all our mission equipment." [5] His successor in 1969 asserted that an authorized strength of 4,712 was "inadequate for effective accomplishment of the air base defense mission." [6] Blame for this deficiency was ascribed to "the absence of basic USAF Security Police doctrine for a hostile environment" from which realistic manning standards could be developed.

It was correctly pointed out that existing manpower spaces were arrived at by applying systems security policies and standards designed for cold war conditions and tied to operational resources. For example, one security policeman was authorized per one B-52 aircraft for close-in protection. Security police officials in RVN judged these standards irrelevant there and wanted new ones based on a concept of tactical operations adapted to a hot-war threat. The new criteria were to address manpower needs of local air base ground defense to include such key factors as terrain, size, and shape of the defended area, rules of engagement, political constraints, and enemy aims, strength, and tactics.[7] Some

Security Police RVN Manpower Authorizations

	PCS	*TDY*		*PCS*	*TDY*
Jan 65	250		Jan 69	4,712	515 [2]
Jul 65	700		Jul 69	4,712	485 [2]
Jan 66	2,100		Jan 70	4,960 [3]	
Jul 66	4,000		Jul 70	4.460	
Jan 67	4,490	200 [1]	Jan 71	3,840	
Jul 67	4,712		Jul 71	3,035 [4]	
Jan 68	4,712		Jan 72	2,385	100 [5]
Jul 68	4,712	540 [2]	Jul 72	1,292	

[1] Safe Side test unit: 1041st USAF Security Police Squadron (Test).

[2] Safe Side units: 821st 822d, and 823 d Combat Security Police Squadrons.

[3] This increase represents the PCS transfer from TAC to PACAF of the 821st Combat Security Police Squadron with an authorized strength of 250. Unit was inactivated on 15 February 1971.

[4] Seventh Air Force at this point had relinquished perimeter defense responsibility to VNAF.

[5] Emergency CONUS to RVN deployment to strengthen Seventh Air Force security capability.

SOURCE: Compiled by author.

security officials faulted this approach for assuming that all bases faced an equal threat, even though experience had proved the contrary. They believed too little was known to determine why the threat varied from base to base and what the decisive factors might be.[8]

The deterrent aspect of air base defense operations was another element that should enter into any estimate of manpower requirements. A study by Lockheed Missiles and Space Company stressed that the defense mission would be achieved if the latent threat was discouraged before it became real. But more specifics on VC/NVA operations were needed to measure the role of manpower as a deterrent.[9]

The insurgency manpower standards set forth by PACAF in May 1968 were predicated on a stated "need for a marked increase in security police over and above those authorized in a nonhostile environment."* Though these standards, like their cold-war counterparts, were tied extensively to the resources to be protected, they were equally linked to the concept of operations defined in the same publication. Gone was the mechanical checklist compliance directed by the cold war standards. The striking thing about the new insurgency standards was the leeway in applying them. They gave security police commanders wide latitude in using people to best serve local defense needs.

In terms of increased manpower, however, the insurgency standards were less liberal than the cold war standards commonly blamed for the inadequate security police manning at RVN air bases.[10] A 1967 PACAF survey utilizing cold war standards validated a Seventh Air Force requirement of 7,033 people for base defense.[11] A similar survey in 1968 using insurgency standards confirmed a need for only 6,057 or almost 1,000 fewer spaces.[12]

Standards aside, a realistic view could consider the authorized security police strength adequate, on the whole, for the USAF base defense mission. It seems implicit that this was the appraisal of decision-makers at the highest level.

The position of the Joint Chiefs of Staff was clearly revealed by their action on a USMACV request for 7 U.S. Army physical security companies and 5 U.S. Army air base defense units included in CINCPAC force requests for the fiscal years 1966-1967. The Joint Chiefs applied manpower spaces for the 7 security companies against another USMACV requirement for add-on rifle companies. They disapproved the 5 air base defense units because the proposed use was not "a profitable one" and

> the combined assets of this force would be better employed in an offensive attitude as a part of a larger force and not tied down permanently to a base area. MACV requirements for internal security must be met by improved passive defense measures, by assignment of appropriate security tasks, and through the provision of minimum MP/AP physical elements as augmentations to tenant unit guards.[13]

These comments were consistent with the security concept of the other Services, namely, that every military unit is responsible for its own security and defense, and every serviceman is first a combatant and second a specialist. Air policemen (as they were then known) were merely to supplement the primary defense effort of all other

---

* PACAFM 207-25, Security Police Guidance for Guerrilla/Insurgency/Limited War Environments, 20 May 1968.

base units. This approach was of course at serious odds with the USAF concept that assigned to security police units the primary security/defense mission of the base, augmented temporarily by noncombatant technicians. The opposite views of the Joint Chiefs and the Air Force on this score explain in part the problem in securing spaces for security police units in RVN.

If security police strength was insufficient, it was not due to cold war manpower standards. The real constraint was the Department of Defense (DOD) headspace ceiling established in successive SEA Deployment Programs. An apt example of how this ceiling affected defense force manning occurred at the time of the Tet Offensive in the spring of 1968. The Seventh Air Force Commander stated an urgent requirement for an additional 448 security police spaces "to be distributed to the bases to increase firepower and defense capability." [14] Noting that USMACV operated under a manpower ceiling, General Westmoreland withheld his approval for immediate deployment "unless Seventh AF can identify an appropriate number of trade-off spaces to absorb this number within their presently established ceiling." [15] He agreed to weigh this new Seventh Air Force requirement with all others and give CINCPAC by 31 March a complete statement of additional USMACV manpower requirements for calendar year (CY) 1968.

The upshot was that on 6 April 1968 the Secretary of Defense approved SEA Deployment Program 6, raising the USMACV manpower ceiling from 525,000 to 549,500.[16] The Seventh Air Force share of this increase was 2,832 spaces, none of them allocated for defense forces. The latter remained frozen at the 1967 level of 4,712 spaces, so that any increase would have to come from a tradeoff within the Seventh Air Force ceiling. Owing to the low priority of the defense mission, this did not occur until January 1970, when large CONUS redeployments arising from U.S. withdrawal permitted the conversion of the 821st Combat Security Police Squadron from a temporary to a permanently assigned status in RVN.

Personnel Management

Clinging to the Korean War precedent, the Johnson Administration early in the war decided to limit the duty tour in RVN to 1 year. By so doing, it created a permanent obstacle to the attainment of an effective base defense capability. Directly related was the "hump" problem which arose from the crash buildup of security police in late 1965, and from the subsequent mass infusions of personnel as new manpower authorizations were approved *en bloc*. The lurching operation of the rotation replacement cycle was epitomized by the experience of the 35th Security Police Squadron at Phan Rang. In the spring of 1966 unit authorized strength was increased from 183 to 580 in anticipation of a tactical fighter wing's arrival. Personnel buildup was rapid. In March 100 security policemen arrived, and between 15 April and 2 May 251 more reported for duty.[17] More than half of the total squadron strength arrived in a space of 8 weeks and 1 year later departed with the same speed. This inefficient practice was still in operation 3 years later.[18]

At yearly intervals, security police and most other units at each base were seriously crippled by the mass exodus and influx of personnel. The hump came with clockwork precision —at Tan Son Nhut, for example, during November-December; Pleiku, April-May; and Phu Cat, March-

April. Shuffling people between the bases had no impact on the problem and reduced further their already limited productive time. The obvious solution on extensive one-time curtailment/extension of tours, was never attempted or considered.

As designed by the professional personnel managers, the rotation/replacement program also led to a marked variation in the numbers of assigned and present-for-duty personnel. Normally, CONUS officers and airmen selected for RVN duty requested port call dates as late as possible in the assignment month. Those rotating to the United States, anxious to return home, asked for travel dates early in the month. When an airman rotated, the RVN unit carried him on its strength until completion of the customary 30-day leave and expiration of his CONUS reporting date. Therefore, for reporting purposes, the assigned strength of RVN units might be 100 percent, while in reality the personnel physically present might be only 70 percent, and those available for regular duty just 60 percent. This last 10 percent loss in production strength was a fairly constant factor due to in/out administrative processing, unit indoctrination and training, and rest and recreation and RVN in-country leave for veterans of 6 or more months.[19] Clearly, then, the personnel managers in CONUS who regulated and monitored the rotation replacement program did so on the basis of incomplete and inaccurate data.

Severe problems were also encountered in the management of security police officer manning also centrally controlled by the United States Air Force Military Personnel Center (USAFMPC). Midway through the war, a Seventh Air Force Director of Security Police spelled out the difficulties in his end of tour report. Existing procedures, he remarked, prevented rather than promoted proper manning, and amounted to little more than the assignment of numbers to vacancies. Frequently officers arrived with no advance notification. When such notice was received it was rarely sufficient to verify the officer's fitness for the job given him by USAFMPC. Thus a number of officers, even though unqualified by experience, training, or performance, were frequently placed in critically responsible positions. When an officer failed in his job, he could not be replaced out of cycle.[20]

The experience of one hapless officer illustrates the haphazard quality of this remotely controlled personnel system. Without experience or training, he was installed as security police operations officer at Bien Hoa, just in time to participate in repelling the mass enemy attack of Tet 1968. Though he successfully surmounted this challenge, the officer scorned his treatment at the hands of the personnel managers:

> I came to Vietnam as a security police officer with no idea of what a security police officer was supposed to do. I was taken from another career field, given no training and shipped to one of the most important bases in Southeast Asia where I was responsible for the protection of over 5000 lives and millions of dollars in vital equipment. Even though the base and I have survived so far, I still believe the assignment was a mistake. . . . I do not think Vietnam is the place for anyone in a position of authority to start from scratch in a new career field.[21]

There were comparable cases where security police officers who reached senior grade during long service in CONUS ceremonial units or in highly specialized joint service assignments, suddenly they found themselves commanding security police squadrons in RVN, much to their dismay and that of their subordinates.

Nor were personnel procedures geared to the quick replacement of casualties in advance of the annual rotation cycle. An emergency action to replace an officer wounded on 31 January 1968 demonstrated the inertness of the system. The replacement got word of his impending transfer on 6 March and arrived in-country on 27 April. Three months (one-quarter of a complete tour) were consumed on a matter that in a combat zone should have been handled as routine support.[22] Fortunately, security police casualties were few.

A positive step toward solving these and other officer manning problems took place in spring 1968. As part of a USAF wide program for all career fields, a well-qualified security police officer was assigned to USAF-MPC to participate directly in the management of security police officer resources. Other aspects of the rotation/replacement program remained fundamentally inchanged.

Through 1966 most security policemen sent to RVN were fully qualified and so carried Air Force Specialty Code (AFSC) 81150.* But the ceaseless demand for 100 percent annual replacements soon exhausted the pool of skilled airman and more and more apprentices (81130) and helpers (81010) were shipped to RVN air bases.[23] This trend triggered a vastly expanded on-the-job training (OJT) program.

* The next-to-last digit of the AFSC designated the skill level—for example, "5" (fully qualified), "3" (apprentice), and "1" (helper).

Designed as a thrifty substitute for formal training, OJT was a do-it-yourself procedure to upgrade airmen in their specialties. The trainee learned the work by actually doing it under the supervision of his trainer. But he acquired the theory, principles, and basics of the job through self-taught career development courses (CDCs).[24] Success depended on a sizeable amount of off-duty study, and the maintenance of extensive and complex records. Tailored to an orderly peace-time environment, the OJT program created serious problems under the turbulent conditions prevailing in the combat zone. As early as August 1965, the combat support group commander at Bien Hoa admonished a visiting Air Staff party to "tell everyone that Vietnam is not the school house."[25] The message never got through.

U.S. air police and Vietnamese soldiers guard the perimeter of Tan Son Nhut Air Base

The Air Staff soundly assumed that combat operations could be carried out by skilled men, then unwisely chose to build these skills by emphasizing the OJT program in RVN. To assist Seventh Air Force, major commands were told to counsel airmen on OJT before RVN assignments, review and update training records, and forward OJT materials to reassigned trainees. Consolidated base personnel offices (CBPOs) were authorized additional clerical personnel, and actions on career development courses were speeded up. The Director of Personnel Training and Education, USAF, believed "the basic criteria for upgrading which apply in non-conflict areas must also be applied in the conflict area to assure that personnel receive the practical and knowledge training required for skilled performance within their Specialty." By January 1967, of the total 46,000 airmen in RVN, 14,000 (30 percent) were enrolled in the OJT Program.[26]

Security police commanders in South Vietnam did not share Air Staff enthusiasm for on-the-job training. They branded it "not conducive to effective manpower management and utilization in a combat area." One commander with 40 percent of his security policemen undergoing OJT acidly observed that "with the extensive requirement for OJT in the combat theater it is quite evident that security-wise we are not adequately prepared for war."[27] He asked for a training specialist (751XX) at squadron level to assist in the program. PACAF manpower and security staff agencies approved a security policeman space instead. They said a specialist could solely keep OJT records but a security policeman could in addition give training. The core of the commander's request was utterly ignored—assignment of a technical specialist to care for the excessive administrative workload linked to on-the-job-training.[28]

At Da Nang the program was condemned for diverting both trainers and trainees from the primary mission, and for infringing upon airman off-duty time during an uninterrupted 2 months of 12-hour work shifts.[29] At Phan Rang it was necessary to send airmen on TDY to other bases to borrow OJT regulations, standards, and forms.[30] Nor were living conditions, especially at the six old bases, conducive to off-duty study. At Tan Son Nhut, for example, each airman was allocated just 40 square feet of barracks space.[31]

The Director of Security Police, Seventh Air Force, summed up the feeling of the command. He saw the OJT Program as "wasteful, time-consuming, and frustrating," and "wholly irrelevant to the primary air base defense mission," hindering rather than furthering it. Nonetheless,

> because OJT is a significant factor in selection for promotion it cannot be neglected. And so, Security Policemen, who normally work 10 hour shifts and who frequently do not receive a day-off for as long as 2 months, are forced to devote what free time is available to memorizing material on such subjects as industrial security, safeguarding classified documents, and game conservation. Quite apart from the adverse impact on the mission, there are indications that the obvious irrationality of these requirements contributes to the low retention rate among first term Security Policemen. Clearly this is a matter which requires correction at USAF level.[32]

These comments remained valid for the remainder of the war.* [33]

Training in RVN and the United States

As the headquarters most physically concerned about enemy attack, 2d Air Division was the first to come to grips with the problem of air base defense training. To counteract the 8-year hiatus in such training, the 2d Air Division launched a program, in late 1965, that stressed weapons training such as night firing, fields of fire, fire discipline, and grenades. It also featured small unit tactics like fire and movement, fire and maneuver and cover. And it required that each security policeman fire 600 rounds with the M-16 rifle during his first 2 months in-country, then 100 rounds each month.

The program was a motley one due to shortages in qualified instructors, range facilities, and training publications, together with the overriding demands of the primary mission. A 1967 study sponsored by the DOD Advanced Research Projects Agency (ARPA) reported that

> the USAF Security Police essentially have no training in the types of infantry tactics useful in base defense before they arrive in Southeast Asia, and there is no standard program set up to provide this type of combat training . . . when they arrive. . . . Programs vary in scope and quality from base to base; at some bases no training of this type exists.[34]

* The limitations of on-the-job training were late to be recognized in Washington. In January 1976 the Secretary of Defense reported to Congress that "we could train more of our skills in units through so-called 'on-the-job' training than we currently do. However, experience has indicated that a combat unit cannot both train new men in basic skills and maintain combat readiness. . . . We therefore provide essential skill training in a centralized training establishment." [Report of Secretary of Defense Donald H. Rumsfeld to the Congress on the FY 1977 Budget and Its Implications for the FY 1978 Authorization Request and the FY 1977-1981 Defense Programs, 27 Jan 76, pp 271-72.]

Mortar pit at Phu Cat Air Base

With the continuing inadequacy in the formal security police training conducted in CONUS by the Air Training Command (ATC), the unit training program in RVN was expanded and formalized, becoming a major task of all security police squadrons. In its final form the program consisted of a 4-day initial phase for new arrivals and a recurring bimonthly refresher phase. The initial phase dealt with the enemy threat and the concept, tactics, and techniques of air base defense as spelled out in PACAFM 207-25. Most time was devoted to small unit tactics and weapons proficiency. Men assigned to crew-served weapons, such as the 81-mm mortar and 90-mm recoilless rifle, were trained accordingly. The refresher phase was a less intensive coverage of the same subjects.[35]

Adding enormously to the training workload was the requirement that each security police squadron conduct the same training for other airmen designated to augment base defense forces during periods of high threat or low manning.* Augmentees averaged 100 airmen per base. These were part of that "enormous mass" of Air Force personnel who, from basic training on, were taught to perform a noncombatant role and given only token instruction in basic military skills. They knew even less than security policemen about ground combat methods.[36]

---

* Augmentation was the panacea for manpower shortages in all functional areas. On one occasion at Tạn Son Nhut *all* combat support group units were ordered to furnish airmen for the civil engineer, transportation, and security police squadrons. Only informal coordination between these latter units prevented a meaningless exchange of personnel.

The lag in crew-served weapons training spurred the Director of Security Police, Seventh Air Force, to set up a mortar school at Phu Cat on 1 April 1969. The instructors came from the 37th Security Police (SP) Squadron. However, the Army's 41st Artillery Group lent a technical hand to get things rolling. On 9 September 1969, by direction of Seventh Air Force, the 821st Combat Security Police (CSP) Squadron started a heavy weapons and small unit tactics school at Phan Rang. And in February 1970, the mortar school moved from Phu Cat to Phan Rang and merged with the weapons and tactics school, still controlled by the 821st CSP Squadron. When the 821st was inactivated on 15 February 1971, the school stayed in business until 1 February 1972 as a detachment of the 35th SP Squadron.[37]

The 10-day weapons and small unit tactics course riveted on weapon skills and tied them in with the right ways to deploy security alert teams (SATs) and quick reaction teams (QRTs). As set by his parent unit, every student specialized in either the .50-cal M-2 machinegun or the 7.62-mm M-60 machinegun. All students learned to use the XM-174 grenade launcher, M-72A1 light antitank weapon (LAW), M-26A1/Mk-II fragmentation grenade, and the M-18A1 antipersonnel directional mine (Claymore). Also taught were the means used by the ground observer to direct fixed-wing and helicopter gunship fire.[38]

Also lasting 10 days, the mortar and fire direction center (FDC) courses were conducted together in the classroom phase and jointly in the practical application phase. They were designed to certify gunners for the 81-mm mortar and computers for the fire direction centers. Live-fire night missions were directed by FDC students and fired by mortar students.[39]

The weapons and tactics school over its final year trained USAF security policemen in South Vietnam and those from Thailand, as well as personnel of the U.S. Army, U.S. Navy, and Vietnamese Air Force. From April 1969 through January 1972, the number of graduates reached 1,500.[40]

From 3,000 to 4,000 security policemen were sent to South Vietnam in 1965 and the first part of 1966. Their CONUS training amounted to little more than a few hours on the operation and maintenance of the 5.56-mm M16A1 rifle. This took place en route at the staging area, as a rule at Hamilton AFB, Calif., or Clark AB, Philippines. If at Clark, the troops were also exposed to a taped 15-minute orientation on Southeast Asia.[41] Such skimpy training was the fruit of 8 years neglect.

In 1956 ATC's Air Base Defense School at Parks AFB, Calif., had closed down. This ended school training within the Air Force in ground combat skills and techniques basic to air base defense operations. Revival of such training did not come until 2 August 1965. The Director of Security and Law Enforcement, USAF, proposed to Air Staff training officials that a course be formed to prepare Air Policemen for duty in Southeast Asia.[42] Ten months in the making, the Air Police Combat Preparedness Course (AZR77150) was born at the 3275th Technical School (ATC) Lackland AFB, Tex. The course's 5 days of instruction borrowed heavily from internal security courses offered in basic Air Police training. For example, the student spent 10 of his total 40 hours on the O'Neal method of unarmed defense (highly favored at the time). In 1968 the course was extended from 5 to 9 days and in July 1970 was further stretched and split into two courses. One (0ZR8124) was designed for the grades of Technical

Sergeant (E-6) through Lieutenant Colonel (0-5), and the other (AZR-81150) for Staff Sergeant (E-5) and below.[43]

Several stumbling blocks kept the 3275th Technical School from ever shaping the course to SVN needs. Land set aside for tactical exercises was too small and fenced with restrictions. Lean budgets and low priorities ruled out the buying of critical items in needed numbers—chiefly weapons, ammunition, and tactical vehicles. And safety checks cut back weapons training.

Under these circumstances, it was not surprising that repeated revisions of the Combat Preparedness Course failed to stifle critics in South Vietnam. They faulted the course for not forging the basic weapon and ground tactics skills, judging it "inadequate in substance and depth." [44] A silent rebuke lay in the continued operation of the Seventh Air Force weapons and tactics school. In short, the Combat Preparedness Course reaffirmed a forgotten lesson of the Korean War, that is, "Training programs in the zone of the interior must be geared to the immediate needs of field organizations under combat conditions." [45]

Individual Clothing, Equipment, and Weapons

While on duty the typical security policeman wore a green or camouflaged two-piece, tropical weight, cotton poplin, fatigue uniform. By early 1967 this had largely replaced the heavier and less comfortable standard utility uniform, made of USAF green herringbone twill. Thanks to the laudable intervention of the Seventh Air Force Flight Surgeon, it was permissible to roll the sleeves above the elbow. Sleeves usually came down at night, however, due to the swarms of mosquitoes and other insects. Every security policeman was issued five sets of the tropical uniform (an item of organizational equipment). This let him make the frequent clothing changes demanded by the climate, working conditions, and prevalence of infectious diseases.

Headgear was the U.S. steel helmet, commonly worn with a camouflage-patterned fabric cover. A heavy rubberband—cut from an innertube—often encircled the helmet and served as an unsanctioned carrier for such sundries as cigarettes, lighters, pencils, security instructions, and eating utensils. In daytime, sunglasses (also organizational equipment) were customarily worn. At night, sentries on the more remote posts regularly used headnets to ward off bugs.

The security policeman's footwear was the excellent mid-calf jungle boot with a porous nylon top and a black rubber sole with deep tread. A steel plate in the sole protected against punji stakes, caltrops, and similar hazards.* For free escape of water, the interior edge of the instep had two screen-covered drainage ports. An innersole of plastic mesh could be inserted to foster ventilation and dry feet.

A web belt of olive drab, supported by web suspenders of the same color, was worn over the uniform as an equipment carrier. Pouches fastened to the belt held 270 5.56-mm cartridges, the basic load for the M-16A1 rifle. Also hung on the belt or

---

* The punji stake could penetrate the soles of most footwear, and the caltrop could puncture vehicle tires as well. Made of fire-hardened and sharpened bamboo, the punji stake was smeared with excrement. The caltrop was a device with four metal points. These were so arranged that when any three were on the ground, the fourth projected upward.

attached to the suspenders were a portable radio transceiver, flashlight, poncho, survival knife or bayonet, canteen, and first-aid kit. Certain posts or duties might call for more gear, such as a starlight scope* for an observation post, or a muzzle, leash, and choke chain for use by a sentry dog handler. Since he was not spelled for meals, every security policeman took along a package of C-rations.

Available around the clock, flak vests helped screen the wearer from shell fragments. The vests were worn mostly at night, when the enemy threat was the highest. During daylight they were less used because of the high temperatures and low enemy activity.

When the troop buildup began in 1965, the M-16A1 rifle replaced the M-1 and M-2 carbines as the basic security police shoulder weapon.* Lightness, durability, high performance, and ease in markmanship training rendered the M-16A1 right for air base defense operations. The early models did tend to jam but this was laid to "poor cleaning and maintenance procedures." [46] Colt therefore went to work on a better version that could withstand long usage with least upkeep. While this action delayed mass production, it resolved the maintenance problem.

* An image intensifier using reflected light from the stars or moon to identify targets.

* Developed by Armalite (as the AR-15) and later made by Colt, the M-16A1 is gas-operated, automatic or semiautomatic, with a box-type magazine holding twenty 5.56-mm rounds. The rifle's muzzle velocity of 3,270 feet-per-second gives the bullet tremendous striking power and a top effective range of 460 meters. The weapon fully loaded weighs just 7.6 pounds.

Spike barrier around a strategic hamlet

Among the base defense forces, sentry dog handlers found the M-16A1 rifle wanting. Their criticism was first documented in the after action report covering the Tan Son Nhut attack of 4 December 1966. It was suggested that the sling be attached to the top rather than the underside of the rifle. This would let the handler sling the weapon from his left shoulder and carry it in a firing position on his right side. By so doing he could more easily manage the dog and still stay at the ready. Then, too, the overall length of the rifle was in itself a problem. Colt surmounted these objections by coming up with a modified M-16A1 having an 11.5-inch barrel, telescoping stock, sturdier flash hider,* and reworked handguard. Called the CAR-15 and afterwards the GAU-5A/A submachinegun, it became the authorized weapon for sentry dog handlers. The Seventh Air Force Director of Security Police reported that both the M-16A1 and the GAU-5A/A were dependable in combat and "well liked by all field troops."

The regulation security police handgun in South Vietnam turned out to be the .38-caliber revolver, due simply to its being already in stock and issued to CONUS security police. The gun's open-face design exposed the working parts to foreign matter and its shock power was weak. Save for the infrequent use of the .38, these faults would have barred it from combat service.[47]

The typical security policeman in South Vietnam toted about 50 pounds of needed gear to his post.

Organizational Weapons

The security police adopted the 7.62-mm M-60, the substitute for the .30-caliber air- and water-cooled machineguns of World War I vintage.

* A device attached to the muzzle of a gun to conceal the muzzle flash.

Punji stake booby trap

The new machinegun weighed 23 pounds (counting shoulder stock and bipod), compared to 32 and 42 pounds for the older ones. Forty-three inches long, the M-60 had a peak useful range of 1,100 meters and a top efficient fire rate of 200 rounds-per-minute. It was fed by a disintegrating* metallic gun belt, and the quick-change barrel featured an integral gas system. Fashioned of new metals, the barrel enjoyed a much longer useful life and the simple design eased cleaning and maintenance. Fairly light and almost free of recoil, the M-60 could be fired from the shoulder or hip (and of course from the bipod or tripod). This trusty and potent general purpose weapon became standard for security alert and quick reaction teams. It further guarded key fixed positions on the perimeter and in the interior of the air base.[48]

The first grenade launcher operated by air base defense forces was the percussion-type, single-shot M-79. Light, compact, and easy to handle, the M-79 fired a 40-mm round as far as 400 meters—plugging the gap between longest handgrenade and shortest mortar range. The launcher looked like a short (29-inch) shotgun and was hinged to break open for loading and unloading. Rifling in the 14-inch aluminum barrel added a spin that steadied the round's flight. The rounds came in such types as high-explosive, buckshot, and illumination and signal flares. They and the M-79 itself were secured in fixed numbers from Army sources in RVN.[49]

For its regular grenade launcher, the Air Force settled on the 40-mm M-203. Fitted to the M-16A1, this semiautomatic launcher could fire three M-79 grenades in succession. The intent of linking the M-203 and M-16A1 was to win rifle point fire and M-79 launcher area fire* from a single weapon. As with other multipurpose ordnance, the M-16A1/M-203 could indeed perform both point and area tasks. Even so, the results were inferior to those of weapons designed to do one or the other of the two jobs. In late 1969 a third kind of 40-mm grenade launcher (the XM-174) entered the scene. This one gave semiautomatic or automatic fire, its 40-mm grenade cartridges being fed by a 12-round magazine. But apart from the magazine feed and automatic fire, the XM-174 differed little from the M-203 or M-79.[50]

Grenade launchers were thought best for security alert and quick reaction teams, and for men in static posts like bunkers and towers. In point of fact, however, these weapons got most use in harassment and interdiction fire (H&I). Such fire took place where free-fire zones were authorized outside the base perimeter for example, at Phu Cat and Tuy Hoa. H&I firing at random was meant to keep enemy troops near the base off balance.† Grenade launchers seldom served as antipersonnel weapons. It seemed that when enemy and friendly forces tangled, the distance between the two was less than the lowest safe launch range of 31 meters. Hence handgrenades came into play.

The least adequate weapon was the Stevens Pump (Savage), Model 77, 12-gauge shotgun. It was issued to sentries in South Vietnam who pa-

---

* As the linked ammunition ran through the breech mechanism, the links and cartridge cases separated.

* The M-79 launcher's performance was judged to be far superior to the M-203's.

† Harassment fire was designed to disturb the rest of the enemy troops, to curtail movement and, by threat of losses, to lower morale. Interdiction fire was placed on an area or point to prevent the enemy from using the area or point.

trolled in the vicinity of aircraft and other high-value resources. Jamming grew persistent, due chiefly to the weapon's being designed for civilian and not military duty. Most of these shotguns had the tubular rather than the box-type magazine that would have simplified loading. Moreover, ammunition troubles were major. In the high humidity, brass shell casings corroded and paper ones expanded and rapidly rotted. During the enemy's 4 December 1966 assault on Tan Son Nhut, Air Police in the aircraft revetments fired Savages. Three of them jammed, "preventing VC who had penetrated the area from being taken under fire." Because the Savage was unreliable, of short range, and awkward in loading, it was almost totally replaced by the M-16A1 rifle.

The 1968 Tet Offensive drove home the need for heavier security police weaponry. Thus the air base defense arsenal acquired the M-67 90-mm recoilless rifle, the M-29 81-mm mortar, the M-72 66-mm high-explosive antitank (HEAT) rocket, and the M-2 .50-caliber heavy-barrel machinegun. This ordnance helped the security police to deal with VC/NVA forces fighting from prepared/overrun positions or from armored vehicles. The chance to do so did not come however, and the new weapons joined the rocket launchers in H&I fire. The M-2 machineguns and M-29 mortar also took part in combat operations, the mortar being widely used for illumination. On the other hand, there is no documented combat employment of the recoilless rifle or the HEAT rocket after Tet 1968.[51]

Another class of weapons consisted of those informally secured or locally made by the security police at certain bases. At Tan Son Nhut two gun units were thus obtained, each made up of four M-55 .50-caliber machineguns and a M-45C armored mount. With these units bolted to their beds, two 2½-ton trucks parked every night in revetted positions at either end of the main runway. At Bien Hoa, Phan Rang, and Phu Cat, security police came by several GAU-2B/A 7.62-mm miniguns (the kind of fast-firing machineguns found in AC-47 and AC-119 gunships). Mounted on jeeps or XM-706 armored cars, the miniguns supplied H&I fire and served as mobile weapons for reaction force.[52]

At Bien Hoa—where there was a special talent for this sort of thing—security police came up with an explosive-incendiary-illumination device and nicknamed it Fire Drum. A modified mixture of phougas,* Fire Drum consisted of a metal napalm-filled container, like that used for shipping 175-mm propellant charges. The drum was buried in the ground at an angle, with the protruding open-end covered by a weatherproof plastic membrane and pointing toward the base perimeter. Upon command, an electric circuit touched off the explosive charge under a plunger at the bottom of the container—instantly expelling the napalm that was at once ignited by a white-phosphorous grenade. Range and lateral dispersal hinged on the size and angle of the container and the amount of napalm. The two sizes of Fire Drum at Bien Hoa thrust burning napalm as far as 61 to 122 meters with sideward coverage of 61 to 30 meters. If steel fragments were wanted in the burning napalm, a claymore antipersonnel mine replaced the explosive charge.[53]

Bien Hoa security police further conceived the Totem Pole, a creation for high-intensity lighting of the base perimeter. Aircraft flares rejected for aerial use by munitions inspectors were assembled. Concave reflectors

* A mix of napalm and white phosphorous.

(totem poles) were shaped from the steel shipping containers for rockets or propellant charges. The flares were mounted in the reflectors and set inside the perimeter fence, ignition wires stretching to stakes 30-50 feet to the rear. Sentry dog handlers patrolling such areas commonly carried detonating devices for claymore mines. They could accordingly fire these flares at will, while staying concealed in the darkness. The intense flarelight let defense forces observe, but temporarily blinded anyone approaching the perimeter from outside the base.

Jury-rigged lighting system

It would be a mistake to construe these jury-rigged devices as a reflection on duly authorized weapons. The consistently high quality of the Army weapons furnished air base defense forces formed one of the few bright stars in the support area. As discussed earlier, there were procurement, maintenance, and training troubles. But the weapons themselves posed no real performance problems, for they proved evenly dependable and efficient. According to the AFSC official in charge of air base defense matters, "there never has been a formal request for improved weaponry . . . from SEA or PACAF." [54]

Motor Vehicles

Together with manpower and weapons, the third element vital to air base defense operations was automotive transport. From motor vehicles came that mobility so central to defense force mission success. "Motorization," explained B. H. Liddell Hart, the distinguished British military theorist,

> tends to multiply the strength of defense—by providing the defending force with the power to switch its fire to any threatened spot. Moreover, once the real point of attack becomes clear, it offers the means of thinning out other sectors in rapid time, so that on the vital sector an adequate resistance may be formed, even though the total resources may seem inadequate.[55]

In view of the above, the gnawing problems in the procurement and maintenance of motor vehicles troubled Air Force security police officials throughout the war.*

Before 1965 the sole vehicles available to the tiny security police

---

* These logistic problems are explored in Chapter VIII.

force in SVN were aged and rundown commercial models. These were drawn from the base motor pool—a real auto junkyard. For security alert teams the chief vehicle was the International "Scout," generally kept on hard-surfaced roads because of its 2-wheel drive. Being also 2-door, exiting from the rear seat was no easy job. Further used by security police were Dodge pick-ups, equally road-bound and unreliable. After a while, the doors were taken off the Internationals and Dodges to let passengers dismount quickly under fire. A jumble of other trucks and buses served for posting, guard checks, and quick reaction teams.[56] Not a single vehicle was sturdy enough to survive operational demands.

Emergency handling by Air Force Headquarters of a direct request for 2d Air Division brought 63 M-151 jeeps to South Vietnam in September 1965. These were the first increment of military vehicles authorized for security police forces. From this point on, the jeep was the overburdened vehicular workhorse of air base defense. Designed to haul 500 pounds, it usually conveyed 900-1,000 pounds of cargo in its chief role as a SAT vehicle.* This and around-the-clock operation speeded mechanical troubles and upped maintenance demands to a point unprovided for by the USAF logistic system. It is a tribute to the rugged construction that the M-151 jeep held up as well as it did.

The 63 jeeps signaled no total switchover to military vehicles. All through the war, commercial vehicles of various makes remained a sizable part of the security police fleet. The number of International Scouts and Dodge pickups did dwindle as more jeeps arrived. However, the commercial 1½-ton stake-body flatbed truck was still the mainstay for posting, resupply and quick reaction teams.

The last step in the growth of security police vehicles was the coming of some tactical ones. Drawing on experience from the 1968 Tet Offensive, Seventh Air Force concluded that the M-151 jeeps and flatbed trucks used by response teams were "inadequate and unrealistic" for stepped-up operations during base attacks. "Enemy assaults," it was noted, "have demonstrated the need of armored vehicles for the movement of personnel and the prompt aggressive engagement of the enemy as far away from priority resources as possible." [57] Seventh therefore stated a requirement for a multipurpose vehicle that could serve as a protected platform for mobile weapons, a patrol vehicle able to maneuver on hard-surfaced roads and over cross-country terrain, act as a passenger carrier for 13 armed airmen, and function as an on-the-scene command post.[58]

Since no present vehicle met these demands, the long-term solution called for special design and development. Acquisition of the M-113 armored personnel carrier appeared to be the short-term answer. But production of the vehicles slipped 12 to 18 months behind schedule, forcing Seventh Air Force to request an interim substitute. Called the XM-706, this armored car failed to meet needs for armor protection, passenger capacity, and low silhouette.[59]

By October 1969 about 60 XM-706s and 30 M-113s were in the

---

* A typical SAT vehicle carried this weight (pounds shown in parentheses): 3 security policemen (480) with individual equipment (150); 1 M-60 machinegun (23) with mount (12) and 1,000 rounds of ammunition (105); 1 case of slap-flares (67); 1 M-79 grenade launcher (6) with 18 rounds of ammunition (9); 1 mobile radio transceiver (25); armorplate or sandbags as protection against mines (50-75); and one 5-gallon container of coffee (40).

hands of security police units in SVN. Each air base at first received both types of vehicles on the premise that their distinct features would complement each other. Experience revealed, however, that in some cases neither the M-113 nor the XM-706 lent itself to the environment of a given base. So redistribution was necessary.

While on the move and ready to fire, the XM-706 protected its passengers from small-arms fire and shell fragments. Serving mainly as a security alert team and ammunition supply vehicle, it was highly mobile and could traverse nearly all terrain in and around SVN bases. The inside could hold a 3-man SAT and the team's equipment, weapons, and ammunition. Akin to all other armored vehicles, the XM-706 could not survive a rocket propelled grenade or a landmine. Awkward design included doors that prevented rapid exit of fully equipped airmen, the fuel tank placed in front and thus vulnerable to

hostile fire, and high-maintenance assemblies and parts such as the transmission and the throttle cable.

Like the XM-706, the M-113 afforded occupants but limited armor protection and could not withstand a landmine or rocket propelled grenade. This carrier had a large cargo compartment and proved excellent for cross-country travel, fitting it best for moving fully equipped 6-man quick reaction teams to hostile areas. On the minus side, the heat and noise in the M-113's crew compartment discomforted the riders and hindered communication. Moreover, getting replacement parts was a chronic headache.

The M-113 and the XM-706 were the only tactical vehicles used by the Air Force in South Vietnam. The design and development of a special purpose SP vehicle for air base defense were never carried through.

Motor vehicles used by Air Force security police in Vietnam included (counterclockwise starting with upper photo on page 98) M–151 jeeps, Commando V–100s, M–37 trucks, and M–113 personnel carriers

Sentry Dogs

When the Air Force first became concerned over the protection of personnel and resources in RVN, it viewed detection of enemy intrusions as a key element in any air base defense system. Sentry dogs, however, were the sole detection means instantly at hand.*

The sentry dog program was one outgrowth of the Korean War that survived when the Air Force abandoned its plan for an organic local ground defense. Internal security measures of the mid-1950s featured sentry dogs, and the Air Force became the single Service to procure and train them. Consequently, there was in CONUS by 1965 a pool of trained sentry dogs and handlers available for service in South Vietnam. At first the Director of Security and Law Enforcement, USAF, opposed deployment because he doubted if the animals could take the tropical climate.[60] However, his opposition ended on 3 July 1965 with the creation of Project Top Dog 45.† Headquarters USAF ordered SAC, TAC, Aerospace Defense Command (ADC), and Headquarters Command (HQ COMD) to prepare 40 handlers and 40 sentry dogs for 120 days temporary duty at Tan Son Nhut, Bien Hoa, and Da Nang. These teams assembled at Lackland AFB on 10 July 1965, left for SVN on 13 July, and on 17 July the first ones arrived.

---

* Between March and August 1961, the Sentry Dog Training Center at Lackland AFB, Tex., deployed 2 instructors and 10 sentry dogs to assist VNAF. This program fizzled due to deficient supervision, discipline, training, care, and veterinary support. The dogs became pets of the handlers rather than guardians of air bases.

† Timing of this action suggests it was taken in response to the 1 July 1965 sapper raid on Da Nang.

The dogs had no trouble in adjusting to the weather and working conditions. Top-notch work of the teams led to their permanent assignment with USAF air base defense forces.[61]

When Project Top Dog 145 expired after 120 days, only the handlers returned to CONUS. The dogs were taken over by qualified handlers already in RVN on 1-year duty tours.* Under Project Limelight more sentry dogs were shipped to South Vietnam, every increment being assembled, examined, and tested at the Lackland Sentry Dog Training Center before deployment.† The number of dogs at SVN bases peaked at 476 in January 1967, distributed as follows:

Bien Hoa	46
Binh Thuy	25
Cam Ranh Bay	62
Da Nang	48
Nha Trang	23
Phan Rang	66
Phu Cat	66
Pleiku	28
Tan Son Nhut	66
Tuy Hoa	46

From this high, the number of dogs gradually tapered off. The decline stemmed from the swelling congestion at the six VNAF air bases that compressed the areas where the animals could be productively employed. Another cause was the phased withdrawal of U.S. forces starting in 1969. During this drawdown, sentry dogs surplus to RVN were given a careful medical examination. Those judged sound were rotated to CONUS for further military service.* [62]

* The yearly changeover of handlers generated yet another permanent training requirement (7-10 days) for all security police squadrons in SVN.

† Upon completion of the buildup, replacement dogs for losses through combat or natural causes were furnished by the PACAF Sentry Dog Training Center, situated at Showa, Japan, and later at Kadena AB, Okinawa. This setup shaved costs and speeded response.

* Veterinarian records at the Sentry Dog School, Lackland AFB, show that 190 sentry dogs were returned from RVN to CONUS between April 1971 and April 1972.

Rennie, German Shepherd dog of the 3d Security Police Squadron gets his teeth capped by a U.S. Air Force vet

The care and maintenance of sentry dogs in South Vietnam differed little from that required in the southeastern United States. With but few exceptions, the chief concern centered on kennels, working conditions, and climate.

Through the hectic buildup phase, nearly all the sentry dogs were quartered in shipping crates until security police undertook self-help projects to make kennels. In time at most bases, these kennels were replaced by ones of professional civil engineer construction. At the four new bases (Tuy Hoa, Cam Ranh Bay, Phan Rang, and Phu Cat), kennels that closely conformed to CONUS standards were part of the base facilities constructed by civilian contractors. Comparatively speaking, sentry dog kennels by the close of 1967 equaled or excelled the quality of security policemen's barracks.

Heat posed a problem from the outset. There were many cases of heat prostration wherein the dog's body temperature could not be controlled and death occurred. Security police handlers wisely trimmed base defense training to the required minimum and conducted it as a rule in the cooler night hours when the dog was on post. The furnishing of kennels having enough shade and air circulation further slashed heat-induced illness.

Over 1966 and 1967, inferior food was the culprit in numerous gastrointestinal upsets. The food became tainted and weevil-infested because it remained too long in the logistic chain. The death of eight sentry dogs due to spoiled food sparked actions that went far in wiping out the problem. Procurement switched from yearly to monthly. A brand-name food (Gaines) was bought in lieu of the cereal-based ration usually specified. Refrigerated storage retarded spoilage and weevil buildup. The addition of horsemeat or beef made the dogs' diet tastier and diminished bloat.

Working conditions held a host of hazards. In designating sentry dog posts, scant or no attention was or could be given to dog and handler comfort. Stubble, rocks, deep sand, marshes, and dense coarse grass bred foot injuries. Snakebite was common, but fortunately it was the dog and not the handler who in most cases was bitten. Swift injection of antivenom and sensible treatment usually saved the animal's life. In hauling dogs to post, too few vehicles often meant crowding that led to bruises and scratches when the dogs attacked each other. Letting dogs jump down from high vehicles broke bones, mangled paws, and tore claws (especially dewclaws).* Complete daily grooming was vital to detect and treat such injuries as well as to ward off skin disorders.[63]

Nightly at every air base, sentry dogs were deployed as a detection and warning screen in the zone separating combat resources from the perimeter. Experience forged the common practice of working the dogs in two overlapping shifts. This put twice the number of dogs on post during the hours when the VC/NVA were wont to attack. Besides being detectors, the dogs were a psychological deterrent as evidenced by the training of enemy sapper and reconnaissance personnel. One sapper captured during a penetration of Phu Cat in February 1969 told how his company commander

> discussed at length the dangers presented by dogs. . . . [The commander stressed] that they were very intelligent and were to be respected. If any man heard or saw a dog he was to lie down immediately, hold his breath, and remain motionless until the dog left.[64]

---

* Dewclaws on a dog's feet do not reach the ground.

To conceal their scent from sentry dogs, sappers smeared their bodies with a garlic-like herb (toi) before going into action.

From the coming of the first sentry dog teams in July 1965 until 4 December 1966, no known penetrations took place in areas patrolled by dogs. But on the 4th of December, sappers aided by good weather and the terrain slipped through a sentry dog post at Tan Son Nhut. The infiltrators were spotted when they tried to penetrate a second (backup) post. The alarm voiced by the handler at the second post alerted the air base, triggering a defense force counterattack that staved off major damage and wiped out the enemy raiding party. During the fighting, sentry dog forces in South Vietnam sustained their first casualties: one handler and three sentry dogs killed, two handlers and one sentry dog wounded.* In the ensuing years of the war, the sentry dogs saw no combat of this size. Nevertheless, they quietly showed their value as sturdy, versatile, detection devices.† Their worth sparkled at Binh Thuy, Phu Cat, Pleiku, and Phan Rang where again and again they gave warning of enemy probes and penetrations. The last sentry dog to be killed in the war fell during the 29 January 1969 attack on Phan Rang.[65]

* Nemo, the wounded dog, lost the sight of one eye despite the best efforts of USAF veterinary and medical specialists. By July 1967 Nemo was back at the Sentry Dog Training Center at Lackland. He saw no more security duty but served as a sentry dog recruiter. His myriad of personal television appearances throughout the nation kept the sentry dog "enlistment" rate high enough to satisfy the needs of all Services. Nemo died on 15 March 1973 from a mix of natural causes and war wounds.

† They were likewise invulnerable to theft by friendly but predatory Vietnamese.

Nearly all air base defense personnel agreed that the sentry dog rendered outstanding service in RVN. Most of them would allow that "of all the equipment and methods used to . . . detect an attacking enemy force, the sentry dog has provided the most sure, all inclusive means."[66]

Tactical Security Support Equipment

Tactical security support equipment embraced the various sensor, observation, and sighting devices widely used in air base defense. These electronic, optical, or mechanical aids were hurried into use as standoff attacks heated up. On 4 December 1964—1 month after the initial attack on Bien Hoa—the Marine Corps put in the first countermortar radar at Da Nang to direct counterfire.[67] Also in December, COMUSMACV asked the JCS to approve deployment of eight countermortar radars (AN/MPQ-4A) and three ground surveillance radars (AN/TPS-33) to South Vietnam. These radars arrived after some delay and were parceled out to Bien Hoa, Da Nang, Nha Trang, Pleiku, Vung Tau, Tan Son Nhut, and other bases.[68]

In the course of the war, no countermortar radar attained the ideal scan of 360°. The AN/MPQ-4A covered only about a 40° sector. Thus, the few sets on hand were usually aimed along those axes of fire most likely to become the enemy's approach path. This technique did not always win out, as attested by the 13 April 1966 strike on Tan Son Nhut. The radar was trained slightly off the axis from which the assault was launched, and could not get on target before the 13-minute barrage ended. Sighted accurately, however, the AN/MPQ-4A detected mortar rounds in trajectory and with a few operator inputs computed the location of the foe's mortar position. Such data let mortar and/or artillery counterfire engage targets rapidly and with telling results. Since the AN/MPQ-4A performed poorly against rockets, the enemy could concentrate an attack in a single salvo. In the first such attack during February 1967, 64 rockets slammed into Da Nang AB and the adjacent village in less than 60 seconds.[69]

Detection of infiltrators by the AN/TPS-33 ground surveillance radar was severely impeded. This stemmed from the bulk of the air bases being situated in populated areas, and from the constant movement of friendly personnel in the immediate vicinity.

On 25 November 1965, 2d Air Division submitted Southeast Asia Operational Requirement (SEAOR) 22. The SEAOR set forth an urgent need for intrusion equipment to protect air base perimeters from infiltration by personnel and vehicles. Rome Air Development Center (RADC), AFSC, responded by founding the SEA Intrusion Detection Equipment Program. Its chief task was to evaluate a wide assortment of commercial detection equipment, to see if any could speedily satisfy SEAOR 22.[70]

Infrared warning device used to detect infiltrating Viet Cong

This "buy and try" approach bypassed a great number of customary procedures. The streamlining was justified on the premise that the conduct of operational tests in actual combat would trim leadtime by around 24 months, yield more precise test data, and afford at once a measure of perimeter protection. In practice these assumptions were not wholly borne out. The method was too informal and gave rise to problems.

Among the items tried and turned down was the Oxford Rifle Sight, developed by Sears Roebuck Company to enhance rifle sighting at night. About 40 of these sights with brief instructions were sent to South Vietnam in 1967 for evaluation. After unorganized and unsupervised testing, users reported that they did not like the item. Also subjected to the haphazard testing was the Surveillance and Detection System (SADS 1.5). This was a seismic sensor buried in such a way as to send a sensing line along the area to be safeguarded. SADS 1.5 was ultimately rejected for it was too costly to maintain and could not adapt to climates worldwide. Security police units likewise evaluated IR (infrared) binoculars, a line-of-sight receiver made up of a completely self-contained unit (headset, microphone, binoculars, batteries, and electronics). Test results revealed no need for this equipment.[71]

Evaluation of the Perimeter Detection and Surveillance Subsystem (PDSS) proved the most ambitious by far. This system contained two lines of buried sensors (the Balanced Pressure System and the Magnetic Concealed Intrusion Detector. Two types of antipersonnel radar (AN/PPS-5 and

Starlight scope, mounted on an M–16 rifle, is used to detect night movements at Tuy Hoa Air Base

-12) were included plus a radio data set (AN/GSQ-113) that transmitted buried-sensor alarms and received and displayed alarms on the receiver panel. The Army had never evaluated the PDDS as a system, but had tested and was using most of its major components. In view of this, the Seventh Air Force Commander ordered evaluation of the PDDS in the Idaho Sector of Phu Cat AB prior to installation at other bases.

Construction and trenching burgeoned into a major civil engineering effort as the PDDS was completed at Phu Cat. The system's performance was promising but turned poor during high winds and rain. There were further drawbacks. Too many men were demanded to maintain the PDDS and protect it from the friendly Vietnamese who dug up sensors for curiosity, scrap, or reasons unknown. Studies recommended against placement of the system at Tan Son Nhut, Bien Hoa, and Nha Trang, owing to the terrain, traffic, and other unfavorable factors. Nor did the system save a great deal of manpower, for it supplemented but did not supplant surveillance by sentries. In early 1970, the Seventh Air Force Commander weighed the limited benefits of the PDDS, the foreseen need for more engineering and retesting, and the imminent withdrawal of U.S. forces. He then directed removal of the PDDS from Phu Cat, and dropped plans for installing it elsewhere.[72]

Not all tactical security support equipment evaluated under this program was rejected. A notable example was the Air Force's buying three types of night vision devices that were widely used by air base defense forces. The ANTVS-2 starlight scope served for battlefield surveillance, target acquisition, and delivery of aimed rifle and machinegun fire within 400 meters. The night vision sight (ANPVS-4) did the same for crew-served weapons up to 1,000 meters. The night observation device (ANPVS-5) could scan the terrain and pick out tactical objects as far away as 1,500 meters.[73]

All three were portable, battery-powered, electro-optical instruments that illuminated targets by amplifying available ambient light (moonlight, starlight, or sky glow). Viewing quality suffered when ambient light diminished, and flares, illuminating shells, or searchlights were brought into play. If exposed to intense light, however, these instruments cut off automatically to prevent burnout of the image intensifier tube and to protect the operator's eye. Night vision devices excelled at the new, more isolated, and less well-lighted bases like Phu Cat and Phan Rang. Tan Son Nhut and Da Nang possessed perimeter lighting systems, and were surrounded by lighted urban areas. Hence high-power commercial binoculars gave good results, with night vision devices serving as auxiliary or back up surveillance.[74]

Concept of Operations

Except for the addition of heavier weapons and equipment, security police squadrons had been organized, manned, trained, and equipped at all 10 USAF bases in South Vietnam before a concept of air base defense operations in combat was published. Reliving the Korean War experience, the Air Force commenced in 1961 to send more and more aircraft to these combat-exposed bases. At the same time, there was no policy or tactical doctrine for their ground defense. In Korea this deficiency had been corrected in somewhat less than 3 years (June 1950-March 1953). But more than 6 years (November 1961-May 1968) elapsed in Vietnam before combat tactics and techniques were adopted. In the interim, security operations hewed to the guidelines in AFR 207-1 which dealt purely with physical protection during a cold-war threat.[75] Security police strength passed the 4,000 mark in November 1967 with still no action by the Air Staff. PACAF therefore requested Seventh Air Force to write an air base defense manual based on lessons learned, and zeroing in on security in combat. The manual would set out standards for figuring manpower needs and guidance on the mission and use of security policemen.

Drafting of the manual was nearly completed when the 1968 Tet Offensive erupted, calling for a major rewrite to capture the fresh experiences of that event. Meanwhile, the urgency of the VC/NVA threat goaded the Air Staff to action. It gave PACAF the green light to replace the USAF cold-war security program in South Vietnam with one shaped to air base ground defense needs in combat.[76] PACAF proceeded to build on the spadework of the Seventh Air Force staff to produce Pacific Air Forces Manual (PACAFM) 207-25, Security Police Guidance for Guerrilla/Insurgency/Limited War Environments, 20 May 1968.

An Air Force security policeman covers his ears against the noise of a mortar blast

For the most part, the first and later editions of PACAFM 207-25 reflected the insight gleaned from actual security operations in RVN. Gone was the rigid, checklist approach of the USAF cold-war security program. The new manual went out of its way to be general, to allow elbowroom for down-to-earth action on the scores of variables peculiar to different bases. Yet the combat-tested guidance was sufficiently clean-cut to set exact standards for planning and conducting security operations.

PACAFM 207-25 defined a threefold security mission for the Air Force in South Vietnam: to prevent *close-in* enemy reconnaissance, infiltration, raids, ambushes, and attacks by guerrilla or sapper forces; to contain enemy forces *penetrating* the air base perimeter; and to destroy such forces by counterattack. It was underlined that success of this mission hinged on the linking of internal and external base security operations by means of coordinated command and control. The two were not to be confused however: the Air Force was charged solely with *internal* security; RVN, U.S., or Allied ground forces were responsible for *external* security.*

The internal security concept called for 3-zone deployment of USAF security forces in sectors. (See page 109.) These zones were termed preventive perimeter, secondary defense, and close-in defense. The preventive perimeter traced the base boundary line as closely as possible. Being the first line of defense, it had to detect, report, and engage the enemy as far as feasible from the resources protected. The secondary defense zone separated the preventive perimeter from the locations of aircraft, munitions, fuel, and other operational resources. This line of defense used numerous sentry dogs and security alert teams to detect and block the enemy until reaction forces arrived. The close-in defense positioned sentries on the boundaries of areas harboring operational resources, to guard against sappers and saboteurs stealing in. The original concept reflected the destructive attacks by enemy maneuver units in the 1968 Tet Offensive, and accordingly massed security forces along the perimeter and in secondary defense positions. Later on, attacks by major ground units were judged unlikely and sappers were regarded as the greater threat. When the original concept was criticized as an "egg shell" defense, the emphasis shifted to close-in security or what was sometimes described as "zones of increasing resistance." [77]

Other facets of this concept of operations created a base intelligence section in each security police squadron, changed the counterthreat technique to keep the foe off balance, and daily worked half the present-for-duty security police during the high-threat period (normally from 2000 to 0400).

To help tie internal and external defense together, PACAM 207-25 stipulated that at each base the Aerospace Security Plan (OPlan 207-XX) would be the USAF input to the area or joint defense plan. Patterned after AFM 207-1, the bizarre format of Operational Plan 207-XX differed sharply from that of the plans prepared by other defense forces. To correct this, PACAF adopted the standard 5-paragraph operations plan format prescribed by JCS Pub. 2, the one employed and understood by RVN, U.S., and Allied ground forces.

---

* In a few special cases, Seventh Air Force authorized security police to take part in offbase patrols and ambushes organized and conducted by U.S. or Allied ground forces. [Minutes, 7AF Security Police Commanders Conference, 30 Sep-2 Oct 68, Tab D.]

A Typical Air Base Defense Sector

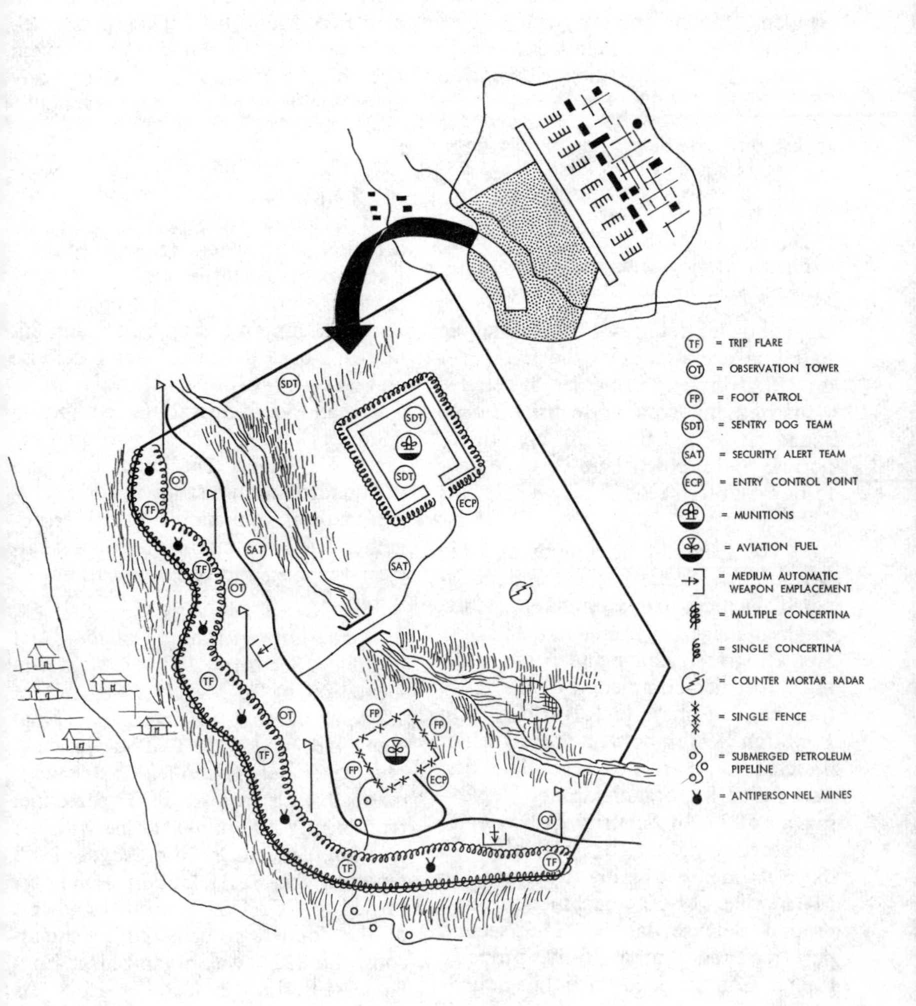

Safe Side Program

The last major step in shaping USAF ground forces in SVN was the introduction of a combat security police squadron as a permanent independent, mobile, countrywide, quick reaction unit. The Seventh Air Force Commander took the initial action on 18 February 1968 by requesting

> that one Safe-Side squadron be deployed immediately to Phan Rang on a TDY basis. The squadon [is] to come under the direct control of my Directorate of Security Police for further deployment and utilization as the situation dictates.[78]

Impelling his request were the telling battalion-size attacks by the VC/NVA on USAF bases during 1968 Tet. He visualized the combat security police squadron as a backup in high-threat periods and a potent and variable day-to-day counterthreat.

The Chief of Staff approved the Seventh Air Force request and designated Tactical Air Command as the single manager to implement the Safe Side Program, which had been marking time since completion of the RVN 6-month test phase in July 1967.[79] On 1 March 1968 the Air Force Chief directed a 2-part program. The first part called for organizing and deploying a "500-man Security Police unit" on temporary duty to SVN, after 30 days of intense training accenting the M-16 rifle, M-60 machinegun, and ground defense tactics. The second part required that a "fully, properly trained Combat Security Police Squadron" replace the hastily trained unit before the latter exceeded the 179-day statutory limit on TDY.* [80] Clearly this was a crash program.

Within 2 weeks following the Chief of Staff's directive, Headquarters 82d Combat Security Police Wing (CSPWg), the USAF Combat Security Police Training school,* and the 821st Combat Security Police Squadron were activated. Manned by TDY personnel, these units were organized at Schofield Barracks, Hawaii, where the Army made facilities and housing available.

The 821st and other combat security police squadrons were organized with an authorized strength of 21 officers and 538 airmen. (See page 111.) Each contained three tactical flights of 6 officers and 538 airmen, responsible for high firepower, mobility, surveillance of base perimeters, and defense and security of internal base areas. Command and operations comprised 3 officers and 4 airmen, headquarters flight, 51 airmen. The latter took care of squadron administrative, food service, medical, and supply functions, together with the maintenance of vehicles, weapons, and communications.

The hurried training of the 821st Combat Security Police Squadron kicked off by 15 March 1968, and on 15 April the unit was in place at Phan Rang AB. The 822d CSPSq was next organized at Schofield Barracks, manned with trained TDY personnel from nearly 100 units. In line with the rotation plan, the 822d in August 1968 replaced the 821st CSPSq which returned to CONUS. The third and last of the combat security police squadrons, the 823d, was organized at England AFB, La., in October 1968. Its personnel, most of whom were permanently assigned, were trained at Ft.

---

*At this time, there was no room under the USMACV manpower ceiling to permit assignment of the combat security police squadrons to SVN on PCS. Hence they were deployed on TDY and rotated home before the 179-day limit was up.

*This school operated under the 82d CSPWg. Together, they organized and trained the combat security police squadrons.

Campbell, Ky., where the CSP Training School had been relocated since August 1968. The 823d took over from the 822d CSPSq at Phan Rang in March 1969 and was in turn relieved by the 821st in August 1969. At this point, the rotation cycle ceased. Because of the progressive withdrawal of U.S. forces and ensuing budget cuts, the Safe Side Program was discontinued in December 1969 and all its CONUS units inactivated. The 821st CSPSq stayed in South Vietnam at a reduced strength of 250 until February 1971 when it too was inactivated.[81]

How well did the combat security police squadrons fit into air base defense operations in South Vietnam? What did they contribute? First off, Safe Side was a crash program of fast-paced actions. Regular staff procedures were by-passed. Refinement of requirements went by the board as did formal implementing directives. Operational concepts firmed up as the program evolved. And from the very beginning, the location of Safe Side at Schofield Barracks made it difficult to communicate with CONUS-located higher headquarters.

Combat Security Police Squadron Organization

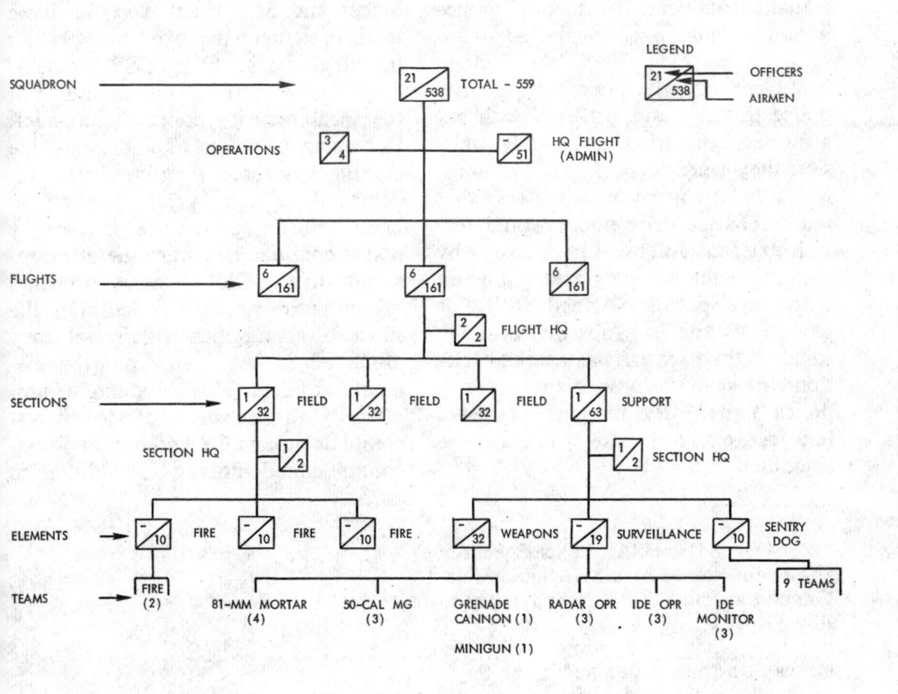

The problems of haste cropped up in the program's training. Because they were at hand, former members of the Safe Side test unit* were pressed into service en masse as instructors. Yet few of these men knew how to teach. All of them were oriented toward U.S. Army Ranger operations and not to the small unit tactics and theory of static defense. Ranger training taught a man "to survive, move and fight at extended distances behind enemy lines." Slight wonder, then, that a sizable chunk of Safe Side instruction dealt with land navigation, long-range ambush and reconnaissance patrols, stream crossing, rappelling,† and like subjects. The teaching of air base defense operations as actually conducted by security police in South Vietnam was neglected.

Consequently, combat security police trainees came to SVN with but a dim and distorted grasp of the mission they were to perform. The most widespread misconception was that the combat security police would furnish external defense for air bases by manning ambush sites and going on long-range patrols. Armed with this ignorance and a superior attitude, some of the new arrivals sparked friction with men of conventional security police units.[82] By the end of 1968, however, many of these problems were smoothed out.

Seventh Air Force Oplan 533-69 covered the use of combat security police squadrons in South Vietnam. In general the in-country unit acted as a mobile, ground defense contingency force, deployed as the Seventh Air Force Director of Security Police saw fit. This took place as a rule in the course of a heightened threat, a significant change in the enemy/friendly order of battle, or a weakening of in-place defense forces (due to a personnel shortage or exhaustion from prolonged duty during an advanced security alert condition).

The combat security police squadron was supposed to operate as one unit, but in practice the section (1 officer and 32 airmen) was the basic tactical element deployed in SVN. At the deployment base, CSP elements came under the operational control of the local security police commander. But being elements of a theater-wide contingency force, they were often redeployed without prior warning to bases with a greater need. Security police commanders were therefore reluctant to put CSP elements in charge of an entire sector. To cushion the shock of a no-notice withdrawal, they preferred to use men from the elements as fillers. This shredding of unit integrity was the source of the bitterest complaints from CSP officers and noncommissioned officers. In addition to

*The 1041st USAF Police Squadron (Test) functioned as a Safe Side evaluation unit at Phu Cat AB from January to July 1967.

† Descending (as from a cliff) by means of a rope passed under one thigh, across the body, and over the opposite shoulder.

Security police using an M–113 armored personnel carrier while developing defense tactics

their tactical mission, combat security police personnel manned Seventh Air Force Base Defense Operations Center, and for a time operated the Weapons and Small Unit Tactics School at Phan Rang.

According to a widely accepted evaluation by a former Seventh Air Force Director of Security Police, the combat security police squadrons

> made a significant contribution to the air base defense mission. Of all the Security Police forces in-country, the CSP squadrons alone possessed a tactical organization and the desired proficiency in the employment and maintenance of crew served weapons. In every instance they were capable of timely response to deployment requirements, in some instances with no more than one hour prior notification. On the whole the integration of CSP elements with Security Police units presented a minimum number of problems. Where problems did arise it was usually due to one of two things: incompatibility of organizational structures and attitude. The tactical organization of CSP elements into fire teams and sections does not readily adapt to the non-tactical organization of Security Police units. The merits in this case are with the tactical organization. . . . When attitudes created difficulties they usually but not always stemmed from the belief of certain CSP personnel that they were members of an elite group superior to the Security Police.[83]

At no time during the Vietnam War did the Air Force try or consider the conversion of "its enormous mass of non-combatant personnel" into "fighting air-groundmen," as urged on the RAF by Churchill in World War II. A limited number* of specially trained personnel augmented security police squadrons in time of low manning or high threat. The tooth to tail (combat to support troop) ratio was low, for the bulk of the officers and airmen who served in South Vietnam were exempt from combat duties. Air base defense effectives—security policemen and augmentees—totaled an estimated 12 percent of all USAF ground personnel. The remainder knew little of ground defense skills and techniques. Any general arming of these officers and airmen was a hazardous expedient, one officially and properly defined as a "desperation type operation." † Clearly, the combat service support demanded by the air base defense mission came from a single tooth in the USAF administrative tail—the security police.

---

* At peak Seventh Air Force strength, an average of 100 men at each of the 10 air bases were designated as security police augmentees.

† Mobilization and arming of all base personnel was the defense posture called for in Security Alert Condition Red (Option II). (See App. 6.)

Combined Organization for Defense, Tan Son Nhut Air Base

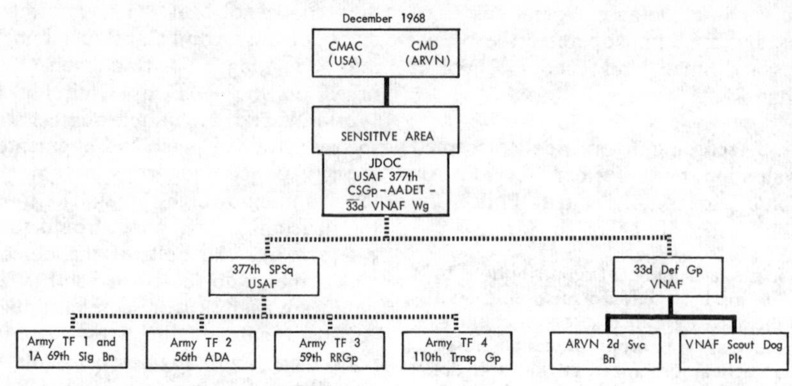

Typical VNAF Air Base Defense Organization

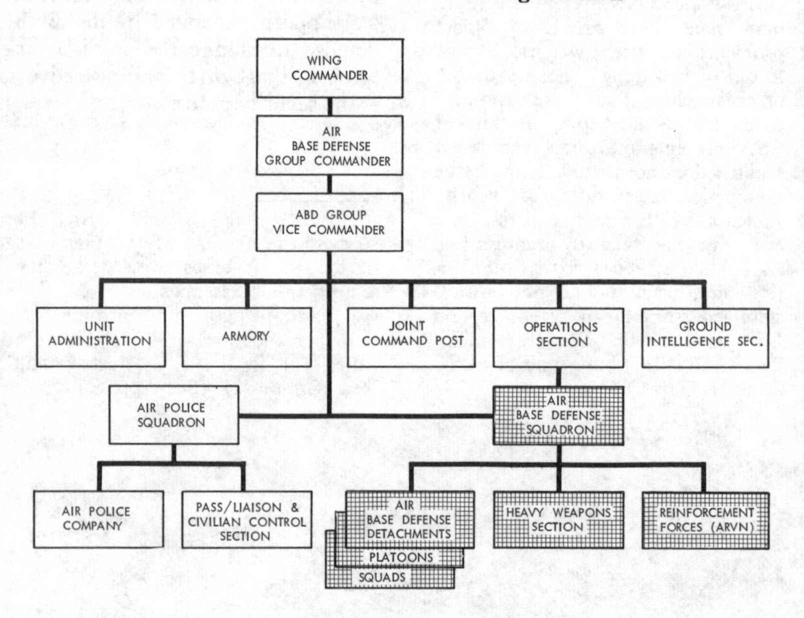

SHADED AREAS DEPICT OPERATIONAL CHAIN OF COMMAND FOR AIR BASE DEFENSE FORCES

VI. OTHER U.S. AND ALLIED GROUND DEFENSE FORCES

Phan Rang Air Base is located within the ROK TAOR. Twenty-six ambushes are emplaced each night by ROK forces along critical approaches to the base. Additionally, Australian Forces conduct night patrols within 1,000 meters of the perimeter fence. Hamlets, bridges, railroads, fixed installations, and check points are secured by RF/PF forces.

Inspector General Report, IFFV, 1969.

Other U.S. and Allied forces were involved to varying degrees in the local defense of all major USAF operating bases. In the case of the Army, Navy, and Marine Corps, the principles of unified operations prescribed by the Joint Chiefs of Staff required such support.

U.S. Army

In South Vietnam the widespread U.S. Army helped defend all 10 air bases. Aid consisted of advisers working with local ARVN/RF/PF units, countermortar radar detachments, fire support, and reaction forces.* At Phan Rang, for example, the main Army tenant units in 1969 included the 589th Engineer Battalion, the 5th Battalion/27th Artillery, and a Logistical Support Activity of the 1st Logistical Command. The base defense plan called for these organizations to furnish countermortar radar and artillery fire support, and to protect their share of the perimeter.[1]

* The vital support of air bases by Army aviation units is dealt with in the next chapter.

The largest linking of Army and Air Force ground defense forces took place at Tan Son Nhut AB. There throughout much of the war, the Army operated from 1 to 3 countermortar radars and fielded Task Force 35. The latter reaction force embodied 3 to 5 platoons of 30 men each, drawn from Special Troops USARV and/or 69th Signal Battalion, 110th Transportation Group, 56th Air Defense Artillery (ADA), and 59th Radio Research Group (RRGp). For about 12 months during 1968-69, a tank platoon of 3d Brigade, 82d Airborne Division, served at the air base as a quick reaction force. These Army/Air Force defense forces plus RVNAF elements composed part of the area defense system for the Capital Military District (CMD). (See page 114.) Headquarters Seventh Air Force was outside the command chain, because the 377th Combat Support Group (CSGp) commander came under the operational control of the Commanding General, Capital Military Advisory (Assistance) Command (CMAC).*[2]

* CMAC coordinated the overall defense of the Saigon area, consisting of Saigon, Bien Hoa, and Tan Son Nhut.

U.S. Navy and U.S. Marine Corps

When in a position to do so, the U.S. Navy lent a hand to air base defense. A case in point occurred on 31 January 1968 at the outset of the Tet Offensive. Lying off Nha Trang, the dstroyer USS *Mansfield* delivered suppressive fire from her 5-inch guns when the air base came under standoff attack. Later under like conditions, the battleship USS *New Jersey* loosed her 16-inch guns at enemy troops threatening Phan Rang.[3]

Beyond question, the U.S. Marine Corps at Da Nang conducted the most distinctive air base defense system and (in the eyes of the Air Force) the most satisfactory. It dated from 8 March 1965 when 9th Marine Expeditionary Brigade (MEB) came ashore "to occupy and defend critical terrain features in order to secure the airfield . . . and other installations in the area against attack." [4] This tactical area of responsibility embraced little more than 8 square miles, confined almost completely to Da Nang Air Base. But as rapport between the Marines and ARVN flourished, the TAOR grew apace until it encompassed 800 square miles containing over a half-million people. Fueling this growth was the 1 July 1965 standoff/sapper attack against Da Nang from a point outside the Marine TAOR.[5] By year's end, the base was enveloped by an expansive protective zone that the Marines observed and patrolled around the clock.

Initially, defense operations at Da Nang were just as disorganized and uncertain as those at other joint U.S./RVN air bases. This state of affairs was soon righted after General Walt, III MAF Commanding General,* took charge of Da Nang's overall defense. His first step was to exercise "a sort of presumptive authority over the tenants," U.S. Air Force and Vietnamese Air Force alike.[6] Thus began the shaping of the most rational and integrated air base defense system within South Vietnam. Very shortly, practical control of all defense operations (external, perimeter, and internal) was concentrated in a single commander. Under the guidance of III MAF, the USAF 366th Tactical Fighter Wing (TFWg) and the VNAF 41st Tactical Air Wing were absorbed into Marine operations. Each wing was tasked to secure 10 percent of the base perimeter and to furnish internal security for its own facilities, personnel, and equipment.

Gen. Lewis H. Walt, USMC

---

* Established ashore at Da Nang on 6 May 1965, III Marine Amphibious Force consisted of 3d Marine Division/1st Marine Air Wing elements. [Hist, CINCPAC, 1965, II, 312.]

A portion of the double cyclone fence installed around the perimeter of Da Nang Air Base

Firming up Da Nang's defense force consumed around 15 months. Defense at first rotated among the infantry battalions of III MAF. To free them from this static onbase role, a provisional battalion was formed in July 1965 of men from various logistic and service units. This procedure so weakened support services that it was ended after 1 month, forcing the infantry to resume the defense job until June 1966. At that time, the 1st Military Police Battalion arrived from CONUS and assumed the base defense mission permanently, having been expressly organized, trained, and equipped for the task.[7]

The strength of the 1st MP Battalion ranged from about 650 to 1,200, a peak held throughout most of 1967. The unit pursued an aggreissive threefold defense concept. Observation, day-and-night patrols, ambushes, and listening posts sought to detect the enemy outside the defensive perimeter. Combined Action Companies (CACs) conducted saturation patrols and kept in close touch with local Vietnamese. Lastly, three companies on the perimeter employed wire barriers, sentry dogs, foot patrols, illumination, and intrusion detection sensors. At high or low strength, the battalion carried out many day/night small unit operations: [8]

	January 1967 (1,200 personnel)	March 1969 (650 personnel)
Ambushes	75	650
Fire-team patrols	234	369
Squad patrols	1,298	16
Platoon patrols	0	48
Listening posts	138	0
Total:	1,745	1,083

The 1st MP Battalion had operational control over two Combat Action Companies—Da Nang and Da Nang East. Their original mission was to bolster base defense by conducting combined Marine/PF saturation patrols. However, these innovative units soon became an alternate means for asserting III MAF control over the countryside. Their personnel were unmatched in setting up civic action programs, since they worked with Popular Forces, lived in village compounds, and met villagers every day.[9] The CACs were likewise an excellent source of intelligence.

Supplementing 1st MP Battalion operations, unique to Da Nang, was the infiltration barrier, built in 1968 to protect the air base and city from rocket and ground attack. The idea was to seize control of the entire rocket belt by enclosing it with outer and inner barrier complexes. Since the South China Sea lay to the east, the outer barrier was a 48-kilometer semicircle around Da Nang on the landward side. This semicircle was sited 11-14 kilometers out from the air base, a radius equal to the extreme range of the enemy's 122-mm rocket. To surmount the outer barrier, the foe had to pass through the two double-apron, triple-tier, concertina wire fences that were sandwiched between three 100-meter cleared strips.

ARVN manned the southern portion of the outer barrier, where towers and bunkers were emplaced for best observation. Towers were absent along the western and northern parts manned by III MAF infantry. In their stead, a continuous chain of Balance Pressure Sensors (BPSs) in 100-meter segments was installed.* This system operated two parallel fluid-filled cables, buried 4-5 feet apart at a depth of 18-36 inches. When people or vehicles moved over the ground above the cables, the change of pressure forced fluid into a recorder that induced an electrical pulse picked up at a monitoring station. Artillery fire was then brought to bear on the site of the movement, if no friendly forces were in the vicinity.

The inner barrier was erected around the outskirts of the Da Nang metropolitan area. It consisted of a minefield 50 meters wide, bounded by parallel barbed wire fences and guarded by bunkers and watchtowers on the side nearest the city. Passage through this complex was permitted at six gateways where all travelers had to prove identity and submit to search. Designed to prevent a repeat of the mass infiltration at Saigon and Hue prior to the 1969 Tet Offensive, these checkpoints enabled the arrest of many VC/NVA personnel trying to enter Da Nang.[10]

The area enclosed by these two barrier complexes was parceled into TAORs and assigned to Marine Corps (and ARVN) infantry battalions. Seeing that a battalion TAOR measured nearly 72 square miles, the ratio of Marines to territory was usually one per 478 square yards. Like the 1st MP Battalion, these Marine units centrally controlled and coordinated military, civic, and political actions.[11] This system did not keep the enemy from striking, but did reduce the number of standoff attacks on Da Nang AB. There were 19 of them in 1968 (the system's first year), 16 in 1969, and 7 in 1970. Equally significant was the reversal of this trend after the withdrawal of all Marine Corps forces from South Vietnam in 1971.

While the Army viewed air base security as an unwelcome distraction,* III MAF saw it as the requisite first step toward rooting out the Communist insurgents. Marine Corps counterinsurgency strategy called for the gradual spread of control over the RVN hinterland, by carefully conducted clear-and-hold operations launched from secure coastal enclaves. Entailed were several interdependent actions — base defense, offensives against large enemy units, expansion of TAORs, and pacification of the countryside.[12] One outgrowth of this approach was a fusion of purpose and effort that distinguished III MAF air base defense operations at Da Nang from those elsewhere. Da Nang was

---

* These sensors were procured but never used for the so-called McNamara's Wall along the southern boundary of the Demilitarized Zone.

* For an expression of the Army's position by General Throckmorton, Deputy COMUSMACV, see page 27.

the first major base to have counter-mortar radar (1964), secure perimeter fencing (1965), permanent perimeter lighting (1965), intrusion detection sensors (1965), and truly unified control over internal, local, and area security operations (1965).

Antipersonnel directional mines installed inside the perimeter fences at Tan Son Nhut Air Base. Sandbags protected defenders from back blast

Free World Forces

Free World Forces (FWF), notably those of Korea and Australia, also helped protect major USAF operating bases in II Corps Tactical Zone. Republic of Korea (ROK) units furnished external defense and fire support for these bases:

1st Infantry Regiment, ROK Capital Division	Phu Cat
ROK 28th Regimental Combat Team	Tuy Hoa
30th Regiment, ROK 9th (Whitehorse) Division	Cam Ranh Bay, Phan Rang

Also assisting in base defense at Phan Rang was Ground Defense Force, 2d Squadron, Royal Australian Air Force (RAAF). This element of about 20

men carried on external perimeter patrols and at night maintained a quick reaction team.

The Air Force shared six joint-use air bases* with VNAF and ARVN defense forces of varying numbers and roles. In principle the RVNAF directives on base defense and security resembled those of the JCS for U.S. armed forces. Thus as a general rule, the senior VNAF tactical commander (wing commander) was formally charged with the internal security and local ground defense of his installation.

To take care of internal security, each base was authorized a Quan Canh (QC) unit for law enforcement and an air base defense unit for physical protection. These organic VNAF elements were for the most part undermanned, ill-organized, meagerly trained, and poorly equipped. Until Vietnamization got under way in 1969, they were virtually ignored by the Air Force Advisory Group (AFAG).†

Local defense, including the base perimeter, was the job of ARVN and/or RF units with occasional help from Popular Forces. These ground elements came under operational control of the VNAF wing commander. In manning,‡ proficiency, and equipment, they were in no better shape than the VNAF units handling internal security. As ground forces, however, they fell within the scope of the U.S. Army advisory effort.

* Bien Hoa, Binh Thuy, Da Nang, Nha Trang, Pleiku, and Tan Son Nhut.

† The roles of USAF and U.S. Army advisors are discussed in Chapter IX.

‡ A common practice throughout RVNAF was for commanders at all levels to keep on unit rolls and collect the pay of a number of "ghost soldiers" who existed only on paper. [DDIIR 1 502 0287 75, 18 Sep 75.]

On the surface, the advantages of a unified command structure seemed to offset in part many of the glaring weaknesses in RVNAF organization for local air base defense. But beneath this facade, unified command was crippled by factors inherent in the politics of the Vietnamese armed forces and in insurgency warfare. Foremost was the political enmity that flared from time to time between VNAF and ARVN, a rancor rooted in the events of 13-14 September 1964* and the personal political rivalries between ranking officers of the two Services.[13] Moreover, complete distrust seethed between the military class and the civilian politicians.[14]

These attitudes and animosities reflected in command arrangements. A case in point was the command structure of the RF and PF who were slated for the key RVN role in local defense. On the pretext that the commander might plot a coup, the command setup was deliberately snarled in redtape, thereby denying proper leadership to 300,000 men.[15] Also for fear of a coup, there was a pronounced reluctance to give any one VNAF commander control of very many men. This was especially so at the politically sensitive air bases, such as Tan Son Nhut and Bien Hoa in the environs of the capital.†

* VNAF helped put down an attempted coup by ARVN elements. (See page 12.)

† The distrust pervading RVNAF now and then appeared in requests that U.S. forces report any troop or aircraft movements not related to known operations and of possible political significance. [Msg, COMUSMACV to CINCPAC, 011245Z Sep 64, subj: Meeting with Gen Khanh; msg COMUSMACV to 7th AF, 190852Z Jan 66, subj: VNAF Counter Coup Flight; msg COMUSMACV to VMAC, 091120Z Mar 66, subj: Reporting of Unusual Activity.]

Brig. Gen. William O. Quirey, USA

Brig. Gen. William O. Quirey, USA, Ret. (a former Deputy Director of the USMACV Combat Operations Center) said that throughout his experience with RVNAF he detected a number of ideas that "ran counter to all doctrine held dear by the American military professional." One off-shoot was the failure to consolidate "command under one commander who could be held responsible for results." General Quirey attributed this to a "fear of placing too much power in the hands of one military commander," a fear "evidenced in the defense of Tan Son Nhut." A further reason "seemed to be the reluctance of some South Vietnamese military personnel to seek and exercise increased responsibilities," probably because of

> the jeopardy in which a career might be placed if a successful attack occurred on the installation for which the commander was responsible. . . . Always there seemed to be the possibility of some future military coup in the back of the minds of personnel with whom one dealt on any problem of command in the Saigon area.[16]

These circumstances demanded that USMACV go all out in persuading the Joint General Staff to drop its "divide and rule" policy, and to place sufficient ground forces for the air base defense mission under VNAF commanders' control. A start was made in 1966 when the JGS agreed to such control over ground troops responsible for external security in "sensitive areas" surrounding the air bases.[17] This did not guarantee, however, that ample ground forces would be positioned in sensitive areas.

The VNAF wing commander faced another hurdle to the timely use of RVNAF air base defense forces in combat. This was the need to secure approval in advance from the province and/or district chief before engaging enemy targets in the sensitive areas.* Seeing that these officials were ARVN officers (usually a lieutenant colonel at province and a captain at district level), ARVN-VNAF tensions strained these dealings. Other than the 33d VNAF Wing commander at Tan Son Nhut, every sensitive area commander had to endure this always time-consuming, often negative, and usually unresponsive procedure.

---

* U.S. forces also had to get this approval.

The persistent USAF doubt that RVNAF could protect the joint-use air bases was rooted in the 1 November 1964 mortar attack on Bien Hoa. Despite strong signs of an enemy threat to the base, RVNAF units took no precautions and neglected to alert the Air Force.[18] Feeding this initial distrust was the string of RVNAF failures to detect or react to VC/NVA attacks* against air bases. The 4 December 1966 sapper raid on Tan Son Nhut led the 377th Combat Support Group Commander to conclude that the

> RVNAF responsible for external defense have not yet attained a reliable capability to detect hostile forces moving against the air base nor can the RVNAF responsible for perimeter defense be relied upon. Hence effective defense of Tan Son Nhut necessarily rests with US Forces.[19]

The above appraisal was reaffirmed 13 months later during the 1968 Tet attacks. At Tan Son Nhut a number of men from ARVN 2d Service Battalion deserted their perimeter bunker posts.[20] Just hours before the assault on Bien Hoa, guard checks of the perimeter repeatedly found RF troops sleeping on post. Behavior of the Vietnamese at Bien Hoa disgusted the 3d Combat Support Group Commander. He recommended that VNAF security forces be disregarded in future security plans, because "experience has proven they cannot be depended upon." [21] Departing Bien Hoa at the end of his tour, Lt. Col. Bernard H. Fowle, 3d Security Police Squadron Commander, declared that joint defense operations was "only a title," since VNAF 23d Defense Group was

> not manned, equipped or trained to participate to any appreciable degree in the defense of the base. Much time and effort was devoted during my tour here in devising training programs for the 23d Defense Group. The Commander of that organization for reasons known only to him made little or no use of our effort. . . . I will not comment on VNAF relations because I could not do so unemotionally. It has been a trying year at best.[22]

The same conditions prevailed at Pleiku. Maj. Perry J. Rawls, Chief of Security Police, reported in May 1969 that the VNAF base commander had "neither resources nor personnel to do more than establish policy. He is able to man only one position on a 24 hour basis." [23]

The Nixon administration's vigorous push of Vietnamization* spurred the first concerted high-level action on the security situation. This was the September 1969 directive cosigned by the Seventh Air Force Commander and the Vietnamese Air Force Commander.† The plan called for VNAF to publish the minimum training requirements for its air police and air base defense units. The aim was an early turnover of all air base defense to VNAF and a speedup in the withdrawal of U.S. forces. Not sharing the sense of urgency, VNAF had to be prodded several times by AFAG

---

* Nha Trang (27 June 1965), Bien Hoa (24 August 1965), Pleiku (16 February and 22 April 1966), and Tan Son Nhut (13 April 1966).

* Vietnamization was defined as "the process by which the U.S. assists the Government of Vietnam to assume increasing responsibility for all aspects of the war and all functions inherent in self-government." [Ltr, USMACV to activities concerned, subj: Vietnamization, 23 Dec 69.]

† Bearing the imposing title, Joint VNAF/7AF/AFAG Plan for Initial and Continuing Proficiency Training of VNAF Air Police/Air Base Defense Forces.

before issuing the requisite directive* on 22 December 1969.

Seventh Air Force's idea was to train a cadre of VNAF supervisors and instructors who in turn would train the mass of VNAF air police and air base defense personnel. Since the Air Force Advisory Teams (AFATs) could not take on this initial training, Seventh Air Force ordered the security police squadron at each joint-use base to furnish one officer and one noncommissioned officer (NCO). These two would develop standards for the VNAF training program at the base, train the VNAF cadre, and otherwise assist the local AFAT. The Air Force Advisory Group was saddled with monitoring and inspecting the entire program.

A milestone in this program was reached on 5 February 1970, when the Seventh Air Force Directorate of Security Police published the Air Base Defense Supervisor's Guide. In rich and comprehensive detail, this manual told how to plan, organize, conduct, and evaluate base defense and security operations. It became the basic training aid of USAF security police instructors and the standard reference for supervisors in VNAF defense groups. It offset, in part, the lack of a VNAF directive giving an air base defense concept of operations and establishing uniform tactics, procedures, and physical security requirements.

At the same time, the Air Force Advisory Group convinced VNAF to draw up a mid-range manpower program for the defense functions. (See table.) Also, a standard organization structure was devised for air base defense groups (see page 114), as was a table of authorization for standardized equipment, supplies, and facilities. It bode ill that VNAF officers had precious little to do with framing these measures, so essential to self-sufficient security/defense operations. Their penchant for the passive role mirrored the strong political orientation of the RVNAF officer corps. The Chief of the Security Police

* Memo 4781/TTM/KQ/PTYC/PCU/K, Technical Training for Servicemen for Defense Groups at all Units.

VNAF Air Police and Air Base Defense Program (1972)

	Officers				*Enlisted*				*Total*
	AP	ABD	SPT	Total	AP	ABD	SPT	Total	Off & Men
VNAF Headquarters	4	2	2	8	1	63	7	71	79
Air Logistics Command	2	2	0	4	0	66	1	67	71
Air Operations Command	0	0	0	0	0	5	0	5	5
Air Training Center	1	2	0	3	0	53	0	53	56
AC&W Group	0	1	0	1	0	30	0	30	31
Bien Hoa Air Base	8	18	2	28	104	445	32	581	609
Binh Thuy Air Base	3	9	1	13	24	229	24	347	360
Da Nang Air Base	8	18	2	28	68	475	28	571	599
Nha Trang Air Base	8	15	2	25	68	442	28	538	563
Pleiku Air Base	5	14	2	21	30	304	29	363	384
Soc Trang Air Base	7	19	2	28	39	446	28	513	541
Tan Son Nhut Air Base	8	14	2	24	102	518	34	654	678
TOTALS	54	114	15	183	436	3,146	211	3,793	3,976

Division in the AFAG reported to the Director of Operations that

> the major problem in advising the Headquarters VNAF Air Police/Air Base Defense Division is that of motivating my counterparts to show initiative and to perform effectively and professionally their staff function. Their hesitancy and apparent inability to make staff level decisions necessitates continual expenditure of time and effort to instill in them the requisite knowledge, confidence, and staff responsiveness.[24]

Energizing VNAF was one of the vital efforts doomed to die when U.S. forces departed South Vietnam.

By the middle of 1971, VNAF had formal control over perimeter defense at the remaining joint-use bases (Tan Son Nhut, Pleiku, Da Nang, and Bien Hoa), save for small segments of the latter two. At once the Air Force's security police operations shrunk to those base areas containing USAF personnel, resources, and facilities.* This transition did not sit well with the American base commanders, whose abiding want of confidence in VNAF made them hesitant to quit all interest in the air base perimeter. Hence they continued to repair fences, control vegetation, and keep up lighting systems. Such concern and fast-dwindling security police forces led, in November 1971, to the emergency temporary deployment of 100 security policemen from CONUS to SVN.[25]

Air Staff visitors in 1971 met old familiar problems, many detected in 1965 during the first such survey of air base defense in RVN. At bases taken over by the Vietnamese, the visitors found an obvious decline of perimeter physical barriers and vegetation control. Because VNAF air base defense groups were undermanned, owned too few vehicles, and had paltry maintenance, they continued to rely on USAF security police for reaction teams. Shortages existed in training, ammunition, radios, and field-phone batteries.

In addition, the defense structure was still plagued with command-and-control troubles. Tan Son Nhut was under the direct scrutiny of VNAF Headquarters and the Joint General Staff. Even so, the ARVN lieutenant colonel in command of the airborne unit guarding most of the perimeter was scarcely on speaking terms with the major commanding the air base defense group. Yet as the wing commander's agent, this major was supposedly in charge of the total local defense operation. The 2d Service Battalion manning the rest of the perimeter was also commanded by an ARVN lieutenant colonel who often bypassed the VNAF commander.[26]

The VNAF air base defense establishment was largely remodeled in the image of its USAF counterpart. Added to inbred shortcomings, therefore, were those of its mentor in doctrine, organization, and staff support. Unlike the Air Force, however, the Vietnamese Air Force failed to redeem these flaws by ingenuity, commitment, and talent for improvisation at the unit level.

* Much the way it was during the combat advisory phase (1961-64).

VII. AIR OPERATIONS

We have the utmost confidence in our ability to destroy a target a few feet from our own troops at night.

Gen. William W. Momyer, 1971.

The Air Force, Army, Marine Corps, and Vietnamese Air Force conducted air operations in support of air base defense. Each furnished that type and degree of support dictated by time, circumstances, and aircraft on hand. Overall, the support consisted mainly of illumination, visual reconnaissance (VR), and fire support.

The USAF Gunship Program

Since most VC/NVA attacks took place under cover of darkness, the air bases needed night air support. The Air Force, however, had not planned for this possibility. The night operations skills forged in the Korean War had been discarded as irrelevant to the role and mission of tactical air power in the mid- and late 1950s. In consequence, the Air Force went into Vietnam ill-equipped to counter a foe whose stock-in-trade was night combat. Starting from scratch, tactics and techniques had to be pieced together from the hard lessons of experience. Many of these lessons stemmed from night air support of hamlets, outposts, and air bases.[1]

The process began with the pioneer use of C-47 and C-123 cargo aircraft to drop flares over hamlets and outposts under night attack. Fire support was linked with this illumination mission when the AC-47 (nicknamed Spooky), a modified C-47, entered the scene. With three 7.62-mm Gatling guns (miniguns)* mounted on its left side, the AC-47 attacked in a pylon turn around the target. (See Figure 3.) The pilot could fire the miniguns singly or in combination as tactical needs dictated. Each gun held 16,500 7.62-mm ball and tracer rounds, and could rake the enemy with 3,000 or 6,000 rounds-per-minutes. As did all later gunships, Spooky carried a stock of Mk-24 flares, each giving off 3 minutes of 2-million-candlepower light.

Modified C-130s and C-119s yielded the follow-on gunships—chiefly the AC-130 Spectre, AC-119G Shadow, and AC-119K Stinger.† Among other refinements, these aircraft featured better performance, greater and more accurate firepower, and an array of sensors for finding the enemy in the dark. Spectre and Stinger assumed an interdiction role, while Shadow aided and then replaced

---

* The initial SUU-11/A gun pods were afterwards replaced by GAU-2B/A ones—both types made by the General Electric Company.

† Spectre, Shadow, and Stinger were the call signs of these aircraft.

Prominent among the gunships flown in Vietnam was the AC–47. The time exposure (above), taken from the ground, shows the AC–47's deadly fire as streams of tracers pour into the target from the circling aircraft. The plane's armament is shown below. Other gunships were (top to bottom page 127): AC–123s, AC–119s, and AC–130s.

Spooky. Of all the gunships, however, the AC-47 shouldered the heaviest load in supporting the defense of hamlets, outposts, air bases, and (during Rocket Watch) areas. Hence in this chapter Spooky occupies center stage.[2]

The 4th Air Commando Squadron (ACSq) became the first operational AC-47 unit in South Vietnam, settling in at Tan Son Nhut AB on 4 November 1965. All through 1966 the 4th ACSq stepped up support of air bases. Lessons learned in the Korean War were rediscovered; for example, a gunship orbiting on station over an air base would often deter VC/NVA attacks. But on other occasions, discouraging the foe required bullets. Thus at Binh Thuy on 20 February and at Pleiku on 22 April 1966, a Spooky braved incoming mortar rounds to hammer the mortar positions and help break up the assault. Again on 8 July the miniguns of two AC-47s silenced another standoff mortar barrage of Binh Thuy. Spooky's success in helping deter and quell attacks on bases inspired the

BASIC GUNSHIP PRINCIPLE

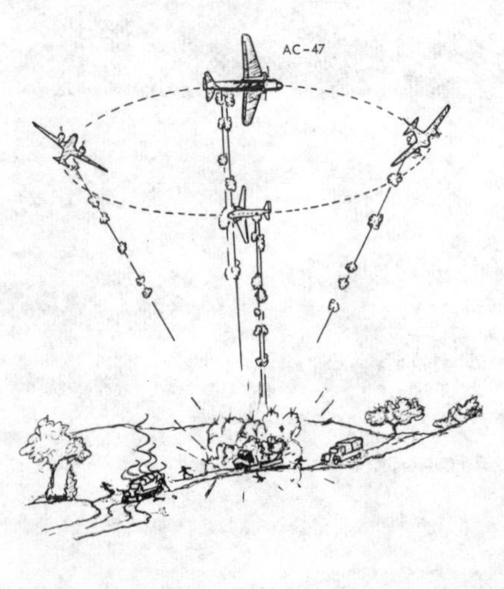

Commander, 14th Air Commando Wing (ACWg), to proudly assert "that the 4th Commando Squadron is the greatest thing since sex, so far as protecting a base is concerned."[3]

The VC/NVA did not delay in switching tactics to cope with the gunship menace. More and more attacks kicked off when the AC-47 was on the far side of its orbit or away from the base on another mission. It was not unusual for the enemy to stop attacking when Spooky approached, showing a healthy respect for minigun fire. Such action also accented the need for more gunships, so that night air cover for every major air base could be expanded during the high-threat period (2000-0400).

Enlarging the USAF gunship fleet grew especially urgent in early 1967. During the 27 February standoff attack on Da Nang, the VC/NVA first used rocket artillery. This new weapon boosted Communist standoff firepower from three to four times, and posed a far grimmer threat to the air bases.

Seeking to detect this threat well in advance, Seventh Air Force quickened visual air reconnaissance of the rocket belt and beyond. Observers looked for indicators that a rocket attack was in the wind. One clear clue was many people moving into the area of the air base and conveying long cylinders. Further telltale signs lay within a 12,000-meter radius of the air base—this distance being the extreme range of the enemy's 122-mm rocket. They included: survey teams staking out and aligning rocket positions; stakes in and on the ground, marking the position, azimuth, and elevation of each launcher and rocket; removal of treetops and other obstructions from line of sight to the air base; and any digging or new excavations

VC/NVA rocket launching position ten miles northwest of Da Nang Air Base

evenly spaced and crossing the line of sight. A sure sign of imminent attack was men working around shallow trenches during the late evening hours. These men were readying the firing pits, wiring the launch system for firing, and loading the rockets.[4]

As an interim move, Seventh Air Force diverted four psychological warfare-equipped C-47s to nightly flare missions.[5] It likewise gave base defense duty to elements of the USAF 20th Helicopter Squadron (Green Hornet) at Nha Trang and Binh Thuy. Every night at these bases, one UH-1F helicopter was kept on 2-minute ground alert or on airborne alert. Attesting to the void in ground defense intelligence, Green Hornet crews were told that "normally the first notification of attack will be when the first round impacts on the base." [6]

In a parallel action, 16 C-47s were secured from VNAF and slated for conversion to gunships by the close of 1967. At the same time (and with strong support from USMACV, PACAF, and Headquarters USAF), Seventh Air Force requested in March 1967 that the AC-47 fleet be built from 22 to 32 planes, if no tradeoff of priority items was required.[7]

While the JCS was pondering this proposal, the Seventh Air Force Commander ordered a commandwide assessment of air operations supporting air base defense. As in most every facet of base defense, air support at Da Nang was better than that found at the other major bases. Three forward air controller (FAC) aircraft, manned by seasoned crews and observers, made daily recon patrols of the surrounding rocket belt. The 13-18 daytime and 4 nighttime sorties* were flown by all U.S. forces operating from the base. Of the day sorties, the Army usually flew five; the Air Force, two to eight; and the Marine Corps, six. At night one USAF AC-47 flew air cover, and the Marines placed two UH-1B gunships and two FAC aircraft on 15-minute ground alert. All sorties were fragged † or requested through the Marine frag section at Da Nang.

---

* A sortie is one aircraft making one takeoff and landing to conduct the mission for which it was scheduled.

† "To frag" means to issue a fragmentary operations order covering the details of a single mission. The frag order was the daily supplement to the standard operations order governing the conduct of the air war in Southeast Asia (SEA).

Gunship wiping out enemy weapons position near Long Binh

Every night at Pleiku, the Air Force as a rule stationed one AC-47 gunship and one C-47 flareship on airborne alert and one Spooky on ground alert. The base commander* did not have operational control over these aircraft. Such control reposed in II CTZ Direct Air Support Center (DASC) at Pleiku or DASC Alpha at Da Nang. Base requests for flare or fire support went to II CTZ DASC for approval and execution, a procedure that rarely raised problems.

Because by 1967 Phu Cat had never been attacked, it received the least support of any USAF base. One AC-47 based on Nha Trang flew nightly air cover, but was often diverted to other missions. When this happened, an alternate Spooky was scrambled † from Nha Trang. Lapses in coverage up to 50 minutes commonly occurred—a serious shortcoming in light of the short duration of VC/NVA rocket or sapper raids.

Air protection of Tuy Hoa was on a par with that of Phu Cat. A Spooky out of Nha Trang supplied coverage each night "but only after the fact—when the rockets were fired."

Phan Rang's air coverage stemmed from one AC-47 Spooky shared nightly with Nha Trang and Cam Ranh Bay. Response time ranged from 5 to 30 minutes. Extra support flowed from organic aircraft of the 101st Airborne Division, whose base camp in 1967 was at Phan Rang. These planes performed dawn-to-dusk patrols of the rocket belt.

Besides part-time aid from the above gunship, Nha Trang derived support from two VNAF A-1E aircraft. Moreover, one UH-1F Green Hornet helicopter stood ground alert. (No revetments protected the facilities for alert aircraft and crews.)

Its peninsular location made Cam Ranh Bay the most secure of the USAF bases. In addition to the Spooky divided with Phan Rang and Nha Trang, this base benefited from the daily FAC recon flights of its land and sea approaches. Also, Army UH-1B helicopter gunships patrolled the rocket belt from dawn to dusk.

---

* Commander, 633d Combat Support Group.

† Scramble—To take off as quickly as possible (usually followed by course and altitude instructions).

At Bien Hoa one USAF AC-47 and two VNAF A-1E's flew nightly cover. Through high-threat periods an Army UH-1B gunship on 5-minute ground alert was added. Even so, timely reaction by aircraft (and by the abundant Army artillery) was regularly thwarted by long delays in getting Vietnamese approval to strike targets.

Every night, one VNAF C-47 flareship orbited Tan Son Nhut and the Spooky covering Bien Hoa was chosen to help out on call. Army kept two UH-1B gunships on 5-minute alert and two more on 30-minute backup alert. (Enemy mortar fire on 13 April 1966 had damaged unprotected alert helicopters. This spurred construction of a revetted and remote parking area for these aircraft and crews.)

At Binh Thuy—jolted by five standoff attacks between December 1966 and May 1967—one USAF AC-47 joined the VNAF's two A-1Es and one flare helicopter on nightly airborne alert. On ground alert was one UH-1F Green Hornet gunship. (Revetted parking space was available only for the VNAF A-1Es.)

The above commandwide status of air support for base defense was detailed in the report of the Seventh Air Force assessment. It revealed the slender mission capability then on hand and confirmed the need for the 10 new AC-47s that had been requested. However, OSD action was delayed 5 months due to controversy over choosing a follow-on-gunship. It took the enemy's ceaseless rocketing of air bases and the appearance of rocket artillery in all four CTZs to convince the Secretary of Defense. On 14 August 1967 he authorized the 10 additional AC-47s.

Now the gunship fleet totaled 32, evenly split between the 4th and 14th

Time exposure of action at Bien Hoa Air Base as the Viet Cong attempt to penetrate the base. Blurred streaks (center right) are flares dropped from an AC–47, Ellipse of light with diagonal lines running to the center of the action is minigun fire from an Army Huey Cobra helicopter gunship

Air Commando Squadrons of the 14th Air Commando Wing. (See table.) For the most part, 4th ACSq supported the bases in I and II CTZs and 14th ACSq covered those in III and IV CTZs.

Rocket Watch

The Tet Offensive in January 1968 touched off a 6-month string of standoff attacks unmatched in number and fury. During the first 2 weeks, the rain of rocket and mortar fire took a stiff toll of U.S. planes—14 destroyed and 114 damaged. Bien Hoa and Tan Son Nhut bore the brunt of the attacks.

Hence General Momyer, Seventh Air Force Commander, directed on 24 February that a night rocket watch be set up over the 25-kilometer rocket belts encircling these two air bases. First flown by USAF O-1 forward air controllers and AC-47 Spookies, the watch later included A-37 attack aircraft. The operation's key feature was relaxation of the rules of engagement for the FACs and Spookies. Heretofore, all targets selected for air strike had to be approved by the province chief directly or through the ARVN chain of command. Either route held up the strike and worked in favor of the enemy. Now under the relaxed rules, O-1s and AC-47s on their dusk-to-dawn mission were allowed to attack VN/NVA positions that were seen firing against friendly forces or bases. Simply stated—return fire with fire.*

So as to engage only hostile targets, FAC and gunship commanders were ordered to keep on board the latest listing of friendly troop locations. General Momyer took the position that curbing the rocket attacks

* Basically these same rules were applied throughout SVN on 1 March 1968.

AC-47 Deployment*

Flight	Air Base Location	Aircraft	Aircrews	Operational Frags
	4th Air Commando Squadron—16 aircraft UE (1 NOA)			
A	Da Nang (FOL)	5	7	4
B	Pleiku (FOL)	4	6	3
C	Phu Cat (FOL)	4	6	3
D	Nha Trang (MOB)	3	5	2
	14th Air Commando Squadron—16 aircraft UE (1 NOA)			
A	Nha Trang (MOB)	3	5	2
B	Phan Rang (FOL)	4	6	3
C	Bien Hoa (FOL)	4	6	3
D	Binh Thuy (FOL)	5	7	4

* Abbreviation key: UE—unit equipment
FOL—forward operating location
MOB—main operating base
NOA—nonoperational aircraft

SOURCE: Lt Col Jack S. Ballard, *Development and Employment of Fixed-Wing Gunships, 1962-1971* (Ofc/AF Hist, Jan 1974), p. 74.

An Air Force O–2 aircraft in flight over South Vietnam

warranted the slight additional risk and was a proper use of the commander's authority to defend his forces against enemy action. On 26 April he further amended the rules of engagement for the Bien Hoa and Tan Son Nhut rocket belts. With certain restrictions, A-37s with a qualified FAC in the right seat of the lead aircraft were permitted to strike rocket sites already firing on friendly troops or bases.[8]

On 2 May General Westmoreland expressed concern over FAC* and gunship crews attacking ground targets without the approval of the ground commander. The COMUSMACV thought this might "result in unacceptable casualties to friendly ground forces," in view of the "fluid tactical situation in the Saigon area" and the extreme difficulty in keeping the aircrews "abreast of exact locations of friendly units and personnel." He therefore requested General Momyer to withdraw the authority given the above crews in February, and reinstate it "only in areas where agreement is reached with the appropriate ground commander and this headquarters." [9]

The Seventh Air Force Commander construed COMUSMACV's request to cover the A-37s alone. On 20 May he notified III DASC, II FFV, and USAF units concerned that the 26 April authority granted A-37 crews was withdrawn. He made clear that FAC and gunship commanders would

* In May the O-1 forward air controllers were joined (and soon replaced by O-2 FACs.)

A–37B attack aircraft

continue to return fire with fire. On the same day, Momyer informed Westmoreland of the A-37 decision.[10]

The Commanding General, II FFV, asked Seventh Air Force on the 26th to rescind the right of FACs and Spookies to attack enemy positions without first clearing through the ground commander. He cited the heavy concentrations of friendly troops in the Tan Son Nhut and Bien Hoa rocket belts, and pointed out that short rounds were on the rise in May.* [11] A discussion of this issue ensued between the Director of Seventh Air Force TACC and his counterpart at USMACV COC. The talks disclosed that General Westmoreland would support the II FFV request and would indorse any agreement reached by Seventh Air Force and II FFV so long as he was kept informed.[12]

On the 28th, however, COMUSMACV called on Seventh Air Force to cancel at once the authority given FACs and AC-47s to engage ground targets.[13] General Momyer did so on the 30th [14] but told General Westmoreland the next day that he definitely disagreed and asked for reconsideration of the decision. Momyer insisted that a Spooky on station "authorized to immediately fire" helped discourage rocket attacks. "I strongly believe," he asserted, that

> if permission for Spooky to fire must be withheld until the ground force commander can approve, the effect of Spooky fire has been negated since either additional rockets have been launched and/or the VC have withdrawn their equipment. This exposes two of the largest bases in Vietnam with eighteen thousand people and 500 million dollars of equipment to additional rocket fire. I feel this is a far greater risk than the possibility of injury to friendly patrols. I realize that friendly patrols could be within 1500 meters of the launch site; however, the Spooky aircraft have been instructed to carefully concentrate their fire on the rocket site and if in doubt to withhold their fire pending ground clearance. Over the past few months Spooky has expended several times on rocket sites immediately after their launch in the Bien Hoa area without endangering the ground troops in the area. Prior to takeoff the Spooky crew is briefed on the location of ground forces. After airborne a refined location is received by radio since final troop disposition for the night has not been determined at the time of the pre-flight briefing. It is believed that these procedures coupled with the accuracy of the Spooky aircraft should protect any ground forces outside of a 200-meter radius of the launch site. . . . My staff will attempt to work out an arrangement with CG II FFV for continued utilization of Spooky in the Tan Son Nhut/Bien Hoa area.[15]

---

* The term "short rounds" referred to rounds of ammunition or bombs that fell short of the target. It was also applied to the inadvertent or accidental delivery of ordnance, sometimes resulting in death or injury to friendly forces or noncombatants. There were three short-round incidents during 1 January-18 July 1968, none involving FAC, AC-47, or A-37 aircraft. [Maj. A. W. Thompson, *The Defense of Saigon* (HQ PACAF, Project CHECO, 14 Dec 68), p 62.]

In his statement the Seventh Air Force Commander came to grips with the key point at issue—protection of air bases versus the safety of ground forces. He nevertheless overlooked the need to avoid playing into the enemy's hands. Captured VC/NVA documents at this time revealed tactics to be used in packed urban areas like those around Bien Hoa and Tan Son Nhut. The foe was to penetrate such zones in order to provoke attacks by U.S. and Allied military forces. These would leave widespread destruction in their wake as well as numerous casualties and refugees. The VC/NVA would then step in and stir up discontent among the refugees by harping on the theme that the United States and the Government of Vietnam were responsible for their plight. The end goal was to incite popular uprisings against the GVN.

Clearly, then, General Westmoreland deemed it vital to steer clear of any actions that could advance the VC/NVA design.[16] In fact, the alarm of the Johnson administration over events in South Vietnam exerted pressure for closest control over rocket watch missions. Owing to "the high level of interest" in Washington, Westmoreland had to furnish "a detailed assessment of damage inflicted [by friendly forces] in the Saigon area during the . . . attacks commencing 4-5 May" and weekly reports of new damage.[17]

COMUSMACV moved against a backdrop woven from protection of air bases, safety of ground troops, enemy aims, and American domestic politics. On 17 June 1968 he clamped the tightest controls on all U.S. weapon firing in the Saigon/Cho Lon/Gia Dinh area, whether by tactical air, helicopter, or artillery. Clearance authority was vested solely in the two U.S. ground force commanders directly involved—the Commanding General, II FFV, and the Commanding General, CMAC.[18] The policy of returning fire with fire was dead.

The rocket watch thereafter operated as part of a broad formal system for the overall defense of the Capital Military District. Directed and controlled by CMAC, the setup also employed U.S./RVN ground troops which by December 1968 numbered 60,000. To sharpen detection and response, wide use was made of watchtowers, ground surveillance and countermortar radars, sensors, and artillery.[19]

Four corridors were formed to correspond with the cardinal points of the compass, boxing in Saigon and Tan Son Nhut AB. Each night from 1900 to 0700, rocket watch aircraft worked these corridors. Army helicopters covered the east, south, and west. The Air Force monitored the north, teaming as a rule one O-2 and one AC-47 gunship.* A second O-2 FAC was added later to patrol the east corridor taken over from the Army.[20]

The CMAC Commanding General made the Army helicopter gunship duty officer responsible for all decisions on rocket watch areas and actions. If, for example, an O-2 forward air controller glimpsed the flash of a rocket launch, he instantly advised the Saigon Artillery Center, the tactical operations center at CMAC, and the duty officer. Next the FAC pinpointed the launch site at 6-digit coordinates (to within 100 meters) and passed them with a strike clearance request to the duty officer. While awaiting the green light, the controller monitored the site and kept a sharp

* The north corridor measured 7 by 14 kilometers, the longer sides of the rectangle running east to west. The FAC and Spooky stayed above 3,000 feet to allow artillery fire through the area.

eye out for any firing already begun by artillery, light fire teams,* and VNAF A-1s. If clearance was granted, he directed the air strike.

To whet the skill of rocket watch teams in spotting and marking launch sites, Army artillery units conducted no-notice "flash tests" every night. A white-phosphorous airburst fired on preestablished coordinates simulated the rocket launch. Watchers in aircraft and on towers tried to fix the flash, convert it to a ground position, and call in the coordinates. By August 1968 the O-2 FACs and Spooky could react within 45 seconds after the flash and place the "launch site" closer than 300 meters to its actual location.[21]

Although opinions on the value of the rocket watch differed, certainly rocket attacks ceased to be a real threat. The 14th of June saw the last attack on Tan Son Nhut in 1968. Throughout the same period, Bien Hoa was rocketed just five times. Still, this decline might have come as much from extensive ground sweeps as from air operations. The sweeps kept the enemy off-balance, and caused him to flee leaving mortars and unfired rockets behind.

Their brief experience (24 February-30 May 1968) in returning fire with fire convinced USAF personnel that it was an excellent concept. They deplored the return of tight control over air operations to the ground force commander: "In effect, each base now has an airborne FAC, rather than an immediate offensive capability." [22] On the other hand, the CMAC air liaison officer considered the rocket watch "well worth the time and effort expended," because the constant air surveillance over potential launch sites and approach routes deterred enemy action. One forward air controller with long experience in the program thought that neither the rocket watch nor VC/NVA rocket operations were very effective.[23]

The III Direct Air Support Center held the view that rocket watch efficiency hinged largely on terrain, natural cover, and population density. Conditions at Bien Hoa and Tan Son Nhut were cited as a case in point. To find level terrain and cover for concealment around Bien Hoa, the enemy had to locate his rocket launch sites north of the Song Dong Nai River. This area was at extreme rocket range from the base and not heavily populated. Rocket watch aircraft therefore poured in suppressive fire without fear of harming civilians, forcing the foe to launch hurriedly and in small volleys. At Tan Son Nhut the environment favored the VC/NVA. Flat terrain offered clear fields of fire, and the dense population frequently ruled out air strikes. Moreover, scores of canals, streams, and treelines made many "rocket positions . . . absolutely undetectable from the air." [24]

In time, the fury of the VC/NVA offensive died down, the number of air base attacks tapered off, and the heat went out of the controversy over rules of engagement. The policy of returning fire with fire was never resurrected. Clearance authority for aircraft to strike ground targets remained with the ground commander. Nonetheless, the rocket watch lasted from 1968 to 1970, linking USAF air power with Army aviation, artillery, and infantry. Along with a like Marine operation at Da Nang, it was at once the most telling countermeasure against standoff attacks and best suited to the Air Force's desire for a minimal part in local ground defense of air bases.

---

* Light fire teams were ground elements that attacked rocket/mortar sites.

The Helicopter Gunship and Air Base Defense

Combat experience through 1968 verified the value of USAF fixed-wing gunships against standoff attacks, but disclosed their limitations against ground assaults. Air Force troops shared Army apprehension about the accuracy of supporting fire from gunships circling at 3,000-4,000 feet. Early evidence of doubt arose in the course of the 4 December 1966 sapper raid on Tan Son Nhut, where the roles of the Air Force and Army were reversed. The COMUSMACV COC described it as a successful USAF ground action with Army close air support. The first of three Spookies arrived on the scene 15 minutes after the attack broke out. Between 0135 and 0650 they dropped 490 flares but did no firing. Army aviation based at Tan Son Nhut likewise rendered instant support with two UH-1B assault helicopter teams of two ships each. These teams attacked enemy targets off base, and two of the gunships also supplied on-call support to USAF security police battling VC/NVA forces within the base perimeter.[25]

A similar episode ensued during the massive VC/NVA attacks on Bien Hoa and Tan Son Nhut during Tet 1968. Timely tactical air strikes on the enemy units probably aided the defenders.[26] At both bases, however, close-in support came from Army helicopter gunships. This support proved crucial in beating back the Communists, thus reducing security police casualties.[27]

In the defense of Phan Rang against the 26 January 1969 sapper raid, Spooky served merely as a flagship. This was due in part to the absence of procedures and practice in coordinating air-ground operations. To protect the base from future ground or sapper attacks, the USAF wing commander asked that Army helicopter gunships fly daily cover from 1900 to 0700. These gunships bolstered Phan Rang's defense for several months.[28]

On 7 April 1969 PACAF sent a required operational capability (ROC) to Air Force Headquarters, proposing the procurement of a helicopter gunship akin to the type used by the Army. The ROC noted that the AC-47 gunship had been deployed to SEA to aid ground defense of bases, forts, and encampments. The Spooky had been "quite successful, particularly in support of special forces camps," but

> of limited effectiveness in a situation where direct support of defending security police forces on-base is required. Since the action takes place in a relatively small area, on or immediately inside base perimeters, comparatively speaking, a relatively fast and high-flying gunship cannot deliver the needed close-in direct fire support on strictly defined and quick-shifting targets.* [29]

On the other hand, a helicopter gunship could provide direct fire support to defense forces within and without the perimeter. It could also drop flares, swiftly transport reaction teams and munitions, and do visual reconnaissance. PACAF figured that every primary base in SEA ought to have two helicopter gunships on 24-hour alert.[30]

The above proposal died on the vine because the Nixon administration was pushing Vietnamization of the war. The AC-47 remained the workhorse for fire and flare support—functions that the VNAF took over bit by bit along with ground defense.

---

* The author's research revealed no instances where USAF fixed-wing aircraft attacked enemy targets within air base perimeters.

Injecting USAF air power into air base ground defense operations was a vital step not tried before. To organic defense it added fire support, illumination, surveillance, and deterrence. Of special note was the ability of aircraft to roam freely over terrain, seeking out the enemy's approach routes and rocket/mortar sites. In addition this employment of air power conformed to the views of the Air Force and the Joint Chiefs of Staff on mission responsibility for local ground defense of air bases.

The Vietnam War experience proved that integrated air-ground defense operations were not only possible but essential for countering overt VC/NVA attacks on air bases. Equipment and communications limitations prevented these unified operations from reaching the refinement of maneuver battalions and tactical air. Still they clearly displayed an equal potential.

Security policeman checks a Vietnamese worker at Tan Son Nhut Air Base

VIII. SHORT SUPPORT

> A review of . . . lessons learned in the Korean War discloses the problems of achieving maximum effectiveness when counteraction is of an extemporized rather than pre-planned nature.
>
> FEAF Report on the Korean War.

The responsibility to plan, organize, coordinate, and conduct USAF base defense reposed in the security police.[1] Proper discharge of this mission hinged on the type of support received from such functional agencies as intelligence, logistics, and civil engineering. As with security police, however, these functions suffered from the prolonged gap in USAF air base defense doctrine. Because the Air Force's basic doctrine saw no need for local ground defense, none of these agencies was prepared to support such a mission when it emerged in 1965. The doctrinal void lasted until 1968, denying the requisite guidance for swift, efficient response to the demands of the Vietnam War.

Intelligence

Local ground defense officials had to have tactical ground intelligence to know what security alert conditions to set, when to deploy contingency forces, and how to counter the enemy before he attacked. Seemingly, Air Force Intelligence should have given this help, but it was absorbed in producing intelligence for air combat operations.

There were two impressive exceptions. The rash of standoff attacks on Tan Son Nhut during 1968 Tet spurred the Deputy Chief of Staff (DCS) for Intelligence, Seventh Air Force, to order an all-out search for VC/NVA launch sites. Photo-recon planes in February combed an 11-mile radius around the base, shooting 140,876 feet of film that was scanned by 100 photo interpreters (PIs). Pinpointed were 176 rocket/mortar launch sites along with numerous bunkers, trenches, and storage areas. Air strikes zeroed in on positions not confirmed as friendly, and coordinated group sweeps seized three huge rocket emplacements and a base camp. A similar crash operation during the enemy's May offensive proved just as spectacular.[2]

Seeking to apply air photo recon to base defense intelligence on a regular basis, the Seventh Air Force DCS/Intelligence asked PACAF for more photo interpreters. He observed that

> it is difficult to argue against having enough PIs to do a similar job every week for all of the bases in SVN. We have lost 45 million dollars worth of aircraft to rocket fire within the past few weeks. I believe 50 PIs could have cut those losses in half had they been available.[3]

Maj. Gen. George J. Keegan, Jr.

Maj. Gen. Rockly Triantafellu

Turndown of this request caused ground defense intelligence support from this quarter to remain meager and sporadic. So of necessity several other means were resorted to.

AF/OSI involvement in the collection of information relating to base defense began when the District Office was located in Saigon, before the move to Tan Son Nhut. The District Office 50 was one of other means enlisted to enhance base defense capabilities when Generals Keegan * and Traintafellu † exchanged letters in 1968. AF/OSI was already deeply involved in its collection programs by 1968.

In the meantime, insurgency had turned the whole country into a combat zone, with friend and foe alike drawn from the same indigenous population. In consequence, the classic distinction between counterintelligence and some aspects of intelligence had disappeared.[4]

To do the intelligence job, OSI District 50 relied a great deal on the Area Source Program (ASP). Formed in 1964 because of the upturn in hostilities ‡ and poor RVNAF air base security, ASP bore the name of OSI Listening Post Program until December 1966. The program began as a bilateral effort. OSI supplied on-the-job-training, advice, materiel, and funds for source information. VNAF

---

* Maj. Gen. George J. Keegan, Jr., Assistant Chief of Staff, Intelligence, 7AF.

† Maj. Gen. Rockly Triantafellu, Assistant Chief of Staff, Intelligence, PACAF.

‡ The Gulf of Tonkin crisis and the first air strike against North Vietnam in August 1964, followed in November by the enemy's attack on Bien Hoa.

Office of Investigations * recruited and administered the sources. These were Vietnamese who reported information on real or potential threats to the installation.

The Office of Special Investigations soon discovered that bilateral operations at some bases were not going well. The core cause lay in OSI's being purely an adviser without power to guide and direct. Air Force funds and materiel tagged for the ASP did not always carry the clout to insure that base defense intelligence needs would prevail over other, often political, VNAF interests. At the same time, OSI realized that it required observers of its own to cross-check supplement, and test data gathered by the ASP. Furthermore, should bilateral cooperation falter or end, collection of information could go on. An ASP under OSI's sole direction and control was eventually set up at each of the 10 USAF operating bases. Whenever possible, this action was taken with the knowledge and consent of the VNAF Security Division. The OSI Area Source Program swiftly became the most fruitful source of base defense intelligence information.[5]

The chief aim of the new program was to give tactical warning of ground attack. To this end, it centered on information related to the plans and order of battle of all VC/NVA forces within striking distance of USAF operating bases. The collection process itself accented passive observation in lieu of more complex methods.[6]

Simplicity marked the structure of a typical OSI Area Source Program at any of the 10 USAF operating bases. (See chart.) An OSI agent at one of the OSI field detachments (2-10 men each) headed a particular ASP. Among his duties were planning for the recruitment of sources, training sources in intelligence techniques, deciding on intelligence needs and targets, funding, and producing raw reports.

The ASP Operation Controller worked directly under the OSI Special Agent. He was either a Vietnamese working for OSI or a member of an RVN counterpart agency. In any case, he directed one or more net chiefs.

Every net chief as a rule covered a specific geographic area, known to be a logical standoff attack site or an access route to a USAF base for

Typical Net Structure, Area Source Program

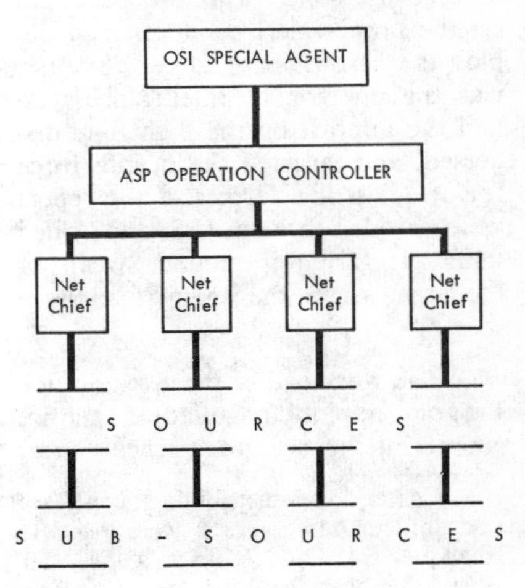

* Redesignated the VNAF Security Division on 24 May 1967. Though nominally under the VNAF commander, this division was an "arm" of and coordinated its intelligence and counterintelligence actions with the Military Security Service (MSS). In the United States the functions of the MSS would have been parceled out to Army Intelligence Command, Naval Intelligence Service, Air Force Office of Special Investigations, Federal Bureau of Investigation, and the police. ["10 Security Agencies in South Vietnam," *OSI CID,* 10 Mar 68, pp 83-86.]

sapper teams. He developed and controlled several Sources.

The Source (a Vietnamese spotter) was usually a farmer, woodcutter, or other menial worker who reported information based on the specific requirements levied on him. He covered part of a hamlet, a land or water access route, or a suspected hostile sympathizer. He also cultivated sub-sources who gave him bits of information.[7]

In essence, the OSI Area Source Program operated as depicted in this fictional episode. About 10 kilometers from one of the USAF air bases, an indigenous observer came upon a group of armed strangers carrying 122-mm rocket launchers. He struck up a conversation with these men and learned of their intention to attack the air base. After departing, the observer reported to his net chief who relayed the information through the ASP operation controller to the OSI special agent at the base. This agent prepared the raw information report, judged the contents important and the observer reliable, then rushed copies to action officials. One was the chief of security police who proceeded to set the proper alert condition and deploy the base defense forces. Another was the director of intelligence who had the aircraft on the flight line dispersed, and targeted the hostile force for an air strike. Copies of the report were speeded to local U.S. and Allied units, triggering a ground sweep of the area where the enemy had been seen.* [8]

The workload of the Area Source Program rapidly engulfed the entire counterintelligence/intelligence effort of District Office 50. From August 1968 through November 1969, ASP generated 78.3 percent of all Department of Defense Intelligence Information Reports and 84.1 percent of the total item in these reports.*

The quality of ASP intelligence outpaced all expectations for an improvised operation. The self-help evinced by OSI workers in the ASP matched that of USAF personnel anywhere in SVN. Moreover, they overcame the bleak handicap that the value of their work was seldom self-evident. In most cases it could be seen solely in the independent action of U.S. and Allied tactical forces. From November 1967 through October 1971, actions brought about by ASP intelligence accounted for an estimated 4,000 VC/NVA killed and 300 assorted enemy weapons captured or destroyed.[9]

The tie-in of tactical forces and ASP intelligence could be seen in the events of October 1970, a typical month. At Da Nang, ground/air forces of ARVN, the Republic of Korea Army (ROKA), and the U.S. Marines achieved noteworthy results on four occasions by using ASP intelligence. Also, the two standoff attacks against the base had been predicted by the ASP. At Pleiku infrared surveillance missions were flown and artillery strikes made "on all OSI/ASP sitings of enemy units" not near villages, towns, and cities. Air Force fighters out of Phan Rang pummeled enemy targets identified by the ASP. Phu Cat intelligence was sparse due to heavy floods, and "many ASP sources were not met by their handlers." At Tuy Hoa maps of enemy positions and facilities, sketched by ASP sources, proved quite accurate and helpful to the success of ROKA

---

* After local distribution, copies of raw information reports were sent to Headquarters OSI District Office 50, where they were consolidated and reproduced as formal Department of Defense Intelligence Information Reports.

* The annual peaks were 1,100 DDIIR's spawned by ASP during 1968 and 14,819 DDIIR items created by ASP over 1970.

search and destroy operations. ARVN reaction forces at Binh Thuy ignored the 127 raw information reports given them—a failure "becoming quite common." Not so at Bien Hoa where 14 source reports furnished tactical forces during 3-13 October sparked U.S. air and artillery strikes. These killed 6 of the enemy, touched off 25 sizable secondary explosions, and wiped out a complex of 46 bunkers and other facilities.[10]

In addition to the OSI Area Source Program, PACAF turned to another self-help intelligence means. In May 1968 it directed that a Security Police intelligence function be created to pull together past and present informal actions. As early as 1965, security police commanders in South Vietnam had traded information with U.S. and Allied units regarding the local threat. Army advisors with RVNAF units having a base defense mission proved a fertile source. So did intelligence elements of Army units in the TAOR that encompassed the air base. By 1968 every base security police squadron had evolved into a focal point for the receipt of base defense intelligence.*

No extra manpower spaces were approved for the new creation that began rounding into shape during spring 1968. The security police intelligence section at base level consisted of one officer and one NCO. Local intelligence responsibility reached out from the base to 30 kilometers. Within this area the mission was to cement ties with Allied intelligence sources, keep an up-to-date order of battle on enemy and friendly forces, maintain a current threat estimate, act as observers on daily air reconnaissance flights, and prepare daily and weekly intelligence summaries.

At Seventh Air Force level, the security police intelligence branch fell under the Base Defense Operations Center (a newly formed division of the Directorate of Security Police). The branch comprised from five to seven security policemen who kept a current threat estimate on a country-wide scale. The estimate rested on data drawn from the bases' daily and weekly intelligence summaries and from Allied intelligence agencies in the Saigon area.* The product of this operation was disseminated in the "7AF/IGS Weekly Intelligence Summary." †

Want of intelligence training was a hurdle that two Safe Side I units helped clear. Arriving in April 1968, the 821st CSP Squadron contained a few men with limited intelligence training. They were the first to man the SP intelligence branch at Seventh Air Force Headquarters and to aid the bases in getting their programs under way. The coming of the 822d CSP Squadron in August yielded some men who had completed the Intelligence Analyst Course (243-96B20A) at the

---

* As in other aspects of base defense, Da Nang AB was a special case. The Marines recognized base defense as a combat mission and charged III MAF with collection of needed intelligence. Thus USAF ground intelligence actions were secondary and supplemented those of III MAF.

* Chiefly the Combined Military Interrogation Center, Combined Document Exploitation Center, Combined Materiel Exploitation Center, MACV Assistant Chief of Staff for Intelligence, and OSI District 50.

† The weekly summary gave a day-to-day record of the base defense mission. It presented data on the threat, order of battle, operations, and items of special interest such as new tactics and weapons. The summary was published as a pamphlet (May 1968-November 1971) and in message format (November 1971-February 1973).

Army Intelligence School, Ft. Holabird, Md. Also, the routine rotation/replacement program was altered to give every security police squadron one officer and one NCO with formal intelligence training. Less than a year after its inception, the security police intelligence program was operating on a fairly professional footing at all 10 bases. There and at Seventh Air Force Headquarters, it was a center for securing base defense intelligence processed by other agencies.[11]

A further method suited to the gathering of base defense intelligence was the Volunteer Informant Program set forth in USMACV Directive 381-2. Vietnamese civilians gained cash or gifts by volunteering information about the VC/NVA. Such informants were the casual or walk-in kind—not permanent agents. Keynote of the operation was simplicity based on best protection of the informant, on-the-spot payment for valid information, and least burden in paperwork and administration.[12] Army advisers and tactical units scored signal success with the system. During 1968-69, the Seventh Air Force Director of Security Police tried to launch the program at bases of the command. It never got off the ground, however, owing to the trouble in obtaining funds.

Another likely source of base intelligence lay in the Civic Action Program (CAP), undertaken by USAF units at the air bases. Conducted in coordination with the USMACV Civil Operations and Revolutionary (Rural) Development Support (CORDS),* the program aimed to win popular loyalty for the Government of Vietnam and to advance the process of pacification. To promote this goal, USAF units sponsored a seemingly endless stream of civic projects.* The program's success was presumed to have a base defense benefit. It would build around the base a friendly cooperative society that few of the enemy could slip through unseen.

These hopes went glimmering. Instances when the Vietnamese warned a base of possible attack were far outweighed by cases to the contrary. Often the presence of enemy raiders in the vicinity went unreported and undetected until the firing began. Bien Hoa and Tan Son Nhut fielded extensive civic action projects in the surrounding countryside. Yet during 1968 Tet, none of the Vietnamese stepped forward to report that large VC/NVA assault units were approaching the two bases. In truth the Air Force never really wrung the intelligence value from the Civil Action Program, a task done by untrained men in their spare time. Too often the projects were merely exercises in altruism, with no thought of securing something in return.

In 1970 the Seventh Air Force Director of Intelligence evaluated the total self-help system for acquiring base defense intelligence. He informed his counterpart on the Air Staff that the effort was "effective and . . . geared especially to operations in Southeast Asia." Consequently, "no major changes are required at either headquarters or base level in the intelligence function as related to base defense."[13] This estimate did not reflect the majority view of the units saddled with the self-help system, who found the appraisal of the Seventh

---

* A joint U.S. civil/military staff that directed U.S. assistance to the Government of Vietnam in support of its revolutionary (rural) development program.

* Including road construction, drilling water wells, medical treatment, high school scholarships, construction of classrooms, sports meets, English language instruction, clearing and/or drainage of land for cultivation, tours of the air base, and assistance to Boy Scouts and orphanages.

Vietnamese military police and U.S. air police patrol near Bien Hoa

Air Force Director of Security Police more to the point. Completing his tour in June 1970, he asserted that the security police were

> plunged into the intelligence business in Vietnam not out of any desire to build empires, but because [the] mission made it absolutely necessary. Evaluation of the entire program reveals that it would be in the best interest of the USAF if the Air Base Defense Ground Combat Intelligence needs could be met by an accommodation with intelligence experts. This will undoubtedly provide a superior product and would free a sizeable number of security police to perform their primary mission.[14]

Motor Vehicles

Among the many logistic problems faced in discharging the base defense mission, none proved more critical or constant than the procurement and maintenance of motor vehicles suited to conditions in South Vietnam.

Seeds of the trouble were sown in the 1950s when the Air Force focused on a clandestine cold war threat and internal security. After 1957—with rare exceptions—security police vehicles were confined to standard production-line commercial models. Military (M-type) vehicles designed for combat operation disappeared from the inventory. The USAF transportation squadrons saw their maintenance function transformed by the wholesale conversion from military mechanics to civilian ones hired locally. Repair parts for the commercial vehicles were removed from the USAF supply network and bought from local vendors.

Rigid minute criteria in USAF Technical Order 36A-170 governed vehicle replacement. Every vehicle bore one of four codes:

A . . . Has reached maximum usage.
B . . . Requires replacement in 1 year.
C . . . Should be replaced in 2 years.
D . . . In good condition, with normal replacement due in 6 years.

Extensive maintenance data was kept on each vehicle. Age, mileage, and repair costs set code changes. For example, a vehicle driven 9,000 miles within the first 90 days was eligible to move from D to C. By accruing 18,000 miles in the first 6 months, the same vehicle could go from C to B.

When a vehicle picked up Code C, Warner Robins Air Materiel Area (WRAMA) budgeted for a replacement. Progression to B told WRAMA to contract for the replacement. When A was assigned, the new vehicle was shipped.*

Designed for peacetime operations, this system worked adequately at the well-manicured air bases in technically advanced areas like the United States, Western Europe, and Japan. But it proved deficient in technically backward, insurgency-riddled South Vietnam.

* Repairs were permitted on Code B but not Code A vehicles.

In August 1965 the Air Staff's first overall survey of base defense in South Vietnam disclosed

> a critical shortage of vehicles in SEA and those on hand vary from 1959-1964 commercial models, some of which were received in very bad condition. The vehicle situation is best exemplified in that vehicles are being rented from local civilian leasing contractors. For example . . . at Tan Son Nhut [1952-1957 model MAP jeep] are rented at $185.00 per month. The commercial type USAF vehicles on hand are not tough enough to withstand the road conditions and because the condition in which received required considerable and in many instances, immediate maintenance. Because of the local terrain/road conditions jeeps are a necessity for security patrols and Security Alert Teams (SAT). Doors, the majority of which will not open, have been removed from the commercial vehicles to facilitate their security use until M-series vehicles are available.[15]

Solution of this problem called for three steps. Military vehicles had to be authorized and shipped to SVN so commercial ones could be phased out. Good mechanics and ample spare parts were required to keep the vehicles running. Current maintenance data and vehicle coding were needed to insure a flow of replacement vehicles from CONUS.

The first M-type vehicles authorized were 63 M-151 jeeps, received in September 1965 and used by security

alert teams. Buses, pickup trucks, and other commercial vehicles continued to be the mainstay for quick reaction teams, posting and checking of guards, and resupply.*

There was hardly any delay in obtaining authorizations for the new military vehicles, but their procurement was drawn-out and uncertain. Security police squadrons in January 1966 had only 94 of the total 233 vehicles authorized.[16] By September 1967 an Air Staff visitor could conclude that "the supply of M-series vehicles and their spare parts" was reaching "a critical stage," and USAF logistic agencies ought to do something about it.[17]

Slow progress could be discerned by the end of 1967, but a complete changeover from commercial to military vehicles never took place. The highpoint came in the fall of 1969 when about 6 XM-706 and 30 M-113 armored vehicles were assigned to the security police squadrons. On the other hand, the maintenance of vehicles and replacement of wornout ones did not go as well.

Vehicle maintenance suffered from a shortage of qualified mechanics and a dearth of spare parts. A typical transportation squadron of a wing in SVN was undermanned for the maintenance workload of the base. Though 104 motor vehicle mechanics were needed, merely 81 were authorized. Of these, 28 were coded for local hire—in a country where the labor market could supply solely untrained or low-skilled people for the job. Filling the 53 military spaces proved just as hard. There was no pool of trained military mechanics to tap, because civilian mechanics were widely used throughout the Air Force. The upshot was that most of the squadron's military and civilian mechanics were apprentices, supervised by journeymen.

Thus crippled, the transportation squadron could not keep up with the maintenance demands. This left the supported units two hard choices. They could stand idly by and watch their vehicles be deadlined for want of repairs, or they could draw on the mechanical talent of their men. Since mobility lay at the heart of base defense, the security police of necessity chose the self-help route. By December 1965 every security police unit in SVN had formed an automotive maintenance section. The number of "mechanics" detailed ranged from two to five, depending on the size and condition of the motor vehicle fleet. The transportation squadron as a rule set aside one of two bays where the security police mechanics could work and shared its slim supply of parts.

* Chapter V discusses security police operations during the military vehicle shortage.

Air Force security police vehicles (left to right): V–100, 2½-ton truck, and ¼-ton truck and trailer

The scarcity of spare parts stymied efforts to keep vehicles on the road. The Air Force had rid the inventory of commercial vehicle parts, specifying local purchase. Parts for the newly acquired military vehicles were slow to show up in USAF stocklists. Since local vendors could not furnish ample spare parts, partial relief came from the Philco-Ford agency in Saigon and the ROX automotive store at Clark AB, Philippines. However, as late as fall 1969, Seventh Air Force sent a team to the San Francisco area to find spare parts.

Transportation squadrons and the self-help units got the lion's share of their parts from the Army.* The formal method was to go to salvage yards and strip parts from battle-damaged Army vehicles set aside for this purpose. The informal way was to hoodwink the Army units for their spare parts. At times when all else failed, machinists in the base aircraft maintenance shops made parts.[18]

During 1967-68 an in-depth study of air base defense in South Vietnam found that

> vehicle spare parts were reported to be in generally short supply at the bases. Current USAF regulations requiring the preservation of a vehicle's identity and log book preclude the cannibalization of vehicles for spare parts. This results in a total complement of vehicles in a questionable state of readiness and a large number of unavailable vehicles.[19]

In the throes of tracking down spare parts and repairing vehicles, the transportation squadrons and self-help units failed to keep records and coding of vehicles up to date. This threw the formal logistic system out of kilter and choked off the normal flow of replacement vehicles to SVN.

Several security police squadrons (notably those at Tan Son Nhut, Bien Hoa, and Da Nang) tried a novel way to get replacement vehicles. As part of their law enforcement duties, they focused on bagging "mavericks" (stolen or misused government vehicles). Daily the gate guards spotchecked vehicles entering and leaving the base, and unannounced "roundups" followed from time to time. If drivers could not produce authorization papers, their vehicles were impounded. Any not reclaimed by proper paperwork within 3 days wound up at the base motor pool. Those beyond economical repair were cannibalized for parts. Those in better shape were given registration numbers, picked up on property records, and returned to government service. Each of the roundups at Tan Son Nhut netted from 15 to 25 mavericks. As one might expect, security police squadrons gained quite a few government vehicles this way, but not enough.

By November 1969 the mechanical condition of the entire security police fleet (chiefly the M-151 jeeps) was once more in crisis. Inasmuch as the majority of these vehicles still carried Code D, Air Force Logistics Command had not procured replacements. A special PACAF technical inspection of all military vehicles selected 105 M-151 jeeps for immediate replacement. Programing was done in December, and by April 1970 the first 38 replacement jeeps had been received and distributed.[20]

In explaining why the USAF motor vehicle logistics system failed to work in South Vietnam, logistic personnel pointed to the self-help meth-

---

* This was not entirely one-sided. An Army agency report showed that three military police units obtained up to 65 percent of their XM-706 armored car parts from USAF sources.

ods adopted for procuring spare parts and performing vehicle maintenance. They insisted that the bypassing of set procedures prevented the tabulation and feedback of detailed data on which the system relied. This diagnosis was certainly correct as far as it went, but it skirted the reason why the system was ignored in the first place.

Geared to peacetime operations, the system simply could not cope with the hectic crash buildup of U.S. forces that began in late 1965. It lost control at the outset and never recovered. In South Vietnam the Air Force was formally directed by COMUSMACV to furnish its own security against an active threat. So it was a bit fanciful to expect combat support group commanders and security police units to accept crippled base defense, while the logistic system adjusted to combat conditions.

Once the system had been bypassed, logistics by self-help became imbedded because at no time did the system show vitality. Also abetting self-help was the austere manning of the transportation squadrons. Though faced with greater mission demands, a transportation squadron of a wing in South Vietnam had fewer officers and men authorized than its counterpart in CONUS or Europe. One wing commander pegged it a situation "without precedent."[21]

Despite yeoman efforts, transportation squadrons could handle neither the vehicle maintenance workload nor the related recordkeeping that energized the logistic system. In practicing self-help the security police knew little about maintenance records and cared less. What mattered was how many SP vehicles were put in running order before sundown each day. Why else were these men diverted from urgent base defense duties.

Col. Frank L. Gailer, Jr.

Maj. Gen. Jonas L. Blank

There can be no quarrel with comments made late in the war by Col. Frank L. Gailer, Jr. 35th Tactical Fighter Wing Commander. "We cannot," he declared,

> support a system in the field when we do not have internal support capability developed in the ZI. There must either be a change in concept for overall vehicle support so that the requirements are predeveloped within the Air Force structure or separate deployable capability developed and fostered in contingencies such as SEA.[22]

Agreement with this appraisal was expressed in 1973 by Maj. Gen. Jonas L. Blank, DCS/Systems and Logistics, USAF. He said the lesson to be learned from the SVN experience was "that the system we develop in peacetime in the CONUS must be workable in a wartime environment overseas."[23]

Weapons used by security police in Vietnam included (clockwise starting above): .50 caliber machine guns, M–67 90-mm recoilless rifles, M–60 machine guns, .38 caliber pistols, and M–148 grenade launchers

Weapon Procurement and Maintenance

The problems of acquiring and repairing weapons proved similar to but not so severe as those of motor vehicles. In the late 1950s the Air Force had purged heavy base defense weapons from the security police inventory. That move and the limited close-in security mission reduced the earliest security police armament in SVN to scarcely more than the .30-caliber carbine and the .38-caliber revolver.

As authorities had perceived the true security police mission, heavier weapons entered the armory. Among them were the M-60 7.62-mm machinegun and the M-16 5.56-mm rifle that replaced the .30-caliber carbine. Jolted by the 1968 Tet Offensive, the Air Force authorized many new weapons before the year was out. These included the Browning M-2 .50-caliber

achinegun, M-67 90-mm recoilless ifle, M-29 81-mm mortar, M-79 40-m grenade launcher, XM-148 40-m grenade launcher, M-72 66-mm igh-explosive antitank rocket, frag-entation handgrenades, and illumina-ion flares.

To obtain the new weapons, the ir Force had to send a Military nterservice Procurement Request MIPR) to the Army. Since the eeds of the two military services ompeted, delay ensued in getting the itial issue (mainly the M-29 81-mm ortars) to the security police squad-ons. By mid-1969, however, USAF equirements were for the most part et.

Spare parts and maintenance pre-ented a stickier problem. Because the arts did not appear in stocklists, they ere next to impossible to secure rough USAF supply channels. Nor ere skilled airmen available to serv-e the ground force weapons. Con-equently, security police units not nly hoodwinked Army units for pare parts but imposed on them for eapon maintenance as well.

Time failed to redress the issue, han Rang in 1972 being a case in oint. Serious shortages in parts and eplacement items persisted. Worn out by heavy use, weapons and night observation devices exacted endless repairs. Parts for M-60 machineguns took 6 months to arrive. Replacement M-60s requested in July 1971 had not been received 9 months later. Foraging reigned as a supply technique. Maj. Milton R. Kirste, then Chief of Security Police at Phan Rang, recalled that

> the supply system never seemed capable of keeping up with the pace of deterioration. . . . Had supply support been there, I'm confident we would have made use of it. . . . A 601B [supply request form] won't stop Charlie at the fence, no matter how vigorously and violently the sentry waves it.[24]

Communications

Reliable flexible communications were central to air base defense. Such communications permitted command and control of defense forces, attuned their actions to those of friendly ground and air forces, and directed fire and illumination support. The Air Force had not foreseen combat communications needs, assuming that what worked for internal security at home would do as well for base defense in combat overseas. So in South Vietnam as in the United States, security police communications consisted of a 2-channel FM net. While this sufficed in peacetime, it proved woefully deficient in wartime. A summary of the standoff attack against Tan Son Nhut on 13 April 1966 said that

> the security force could not have operated effectively against a coordinated infiltration action because its radio frequency was completely saturated with damage reports, artillery impact reports, VIP transmissions and transmissions by other agencies sharing the security frequency.[25]

This experience led to the pruning of all nonvital users from the security police net. Still it struggled to keep up with the normal traffic of nearly 300 stations and bogged down in emergencies. Combat operations after-action reports commented again and again on the net's saturation during attacks.* Furthermore, security police radio communication would cease if the enemy chose to jam the two channels.

Portable, mobile, and base station transceivers † comprised this nontactical net. The Motorola Company leased these off-the-shelf commercial radios to the Air Force and arranged for spare parts and repairs. As cracked cases and broken antennas attested, the sets could not take military treatment. They were poorly weatherized, had too short a range, and could not operate on the tactical radio frequencies of USAF aircraft and friendly ground forces. Often requiring two hands to operate, the portable transceivers were not well-suited to sentry dog handlers.[26]

Packing and shipping were erratic. Sometimes the base station, portable radios, mobile radios, and batteries were all in separate containers. This "in pieces" communications network frequently dribbled in at the wrong destinations—thwarting timely assembly, installation, and operation.[27]

---

* Such as the sapper raid and standoff attack on Tan Son Nhut (4 December 1966), the multibattalion assaults on Bien Hoa and Tan Son Nhut (31 January 1968), and the sapper raid and standoff attack on Phan Rang (26 January 1969).

† A transceiver is a radio transmitter-receiver that uses many of the same components for both transmission and reception.

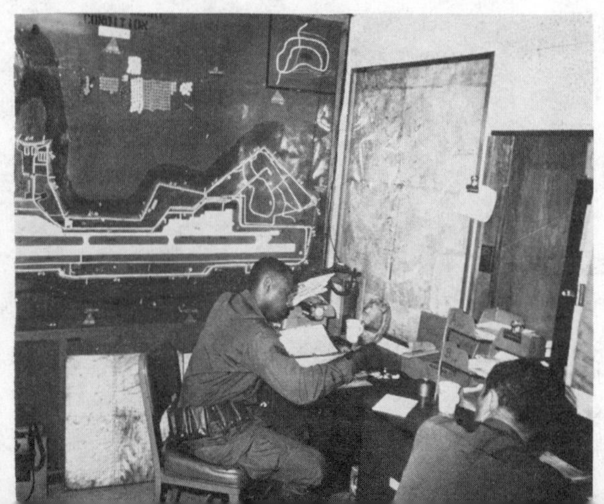

Security police control center at Pleiku Air Base

Tackling the problem, Seventh Air Force in 1967 forwarded SEAOR 127 and updated it after the 1968 Tet Offensive. The SEAOR set out the need for a radio system having several easily switched frequencies and protection from jamming. It would also be compatible with the tactical radios of other U.S. and allied ground forces.[28]

Air Force Systems Command estimated in October 1968 that production prototypes of radios satisfying SEAOR 127 could not be programed for development before fiscal year 1970. Seventh Air Force therefore agreed to the interim solution tendered by AFSC. Four-channel FM radios would be leased from the Motorola Company and shipped commencing in July 1969.[29]

By January 1970 the 4-channel system was in operation at all security police units in South Vietnam. The new net boosted traffic capacity but gave no jamming protection. To reach defense forces other than security police it was necessary to rely on the Army AN/PRC-25 radio—a scarce supply item indeed.*

There was also delay in getting a landline system † as backup for the primary radio nets. Seventh Air Force submitted the communications-electronics implementation plan (CEIP) for the landlines in May 1966. But as of June 1969 only Binh Thuy had the backup system in operation.[30]

* The 377th SP Squadron at Tan Son Nhut requisitioned three AN/PRC-25 radios in July 1968. Oklahoma City Air Materiel Area gave August 1970 as the earliest possible delivery date.

† Telephone or telegraph communication by wire strung over, on, or under the ground.

The Self-Help Syndrome

It is clear from this and other chapters that in too many cases the support given air base defense by other functional areas was utterly inadequate. It is also clear that the single cure-all for the peacetime support system's poor track record was "self-help," a term suggesting a praiseworthy Spartan can-do attitude in the teeth of adversity. This obscured the support failings that required recourse to such an amateurish, inefficient, and wasteful way of doing things.

Self-help did not merely flourish during the swift massive buildup of 1965-67. From first to last, self-help in air base defense was a permanent means of plugging the support holes in critical areas such as ground defense intelligence, logistics, and training.

Even though the USAF intelligence system employed an estimated 60,000 people, it could not furnish the routine support needed by air base defense.[31] The OSI and security police sought to bridge the intelligence gap, and in so doing slighted their primary mission.

The wide sweep of self-help in the logistic support area was documented in detail near the end of the war by Major Kirste, the last chief of security police at Phan Rang. His end of tour report—approved and sent by Seventh Air Force to Headquarters USAF—gives a graphic account of security policemen diverted from base defense to self-help jobs. Two men manned an authorized unit supply section, seeking to keep some semblance of control over a property account wherein the value of the weapons alone surpassed $1 million. Five men did nothing but refuel and repair 66 NF-2 lightall units that generated electricity for a jury-rigged perimeter illumination system. Security policemen had installed this lighting in 1969, operating and maintaining it at an annual cost of around $300,000. One man had the full-time duty of inspecting and replacing the tripflares along the 14.7 miles of base perimeter. Five men constantly repaired motor vehicles. From 7 to 15 men kept up the perimeter and tower access roads, maintained the towers and bunkers, controlled vegetation, and mended fences.[32]

In the same fashion, base defense training for all security policemen and augmentation personnel entailed an extensive permanent self-help program at each base. Advanced training was offered at a weapons and tactics school run by Seventh Air Force. This self-help sought to make up for the consistent failure of stateside security police training to impart the needed proficiency in required skills. The core cause of this shortcoming appeared to be a lack of time and money. For example, weapons training for men slated for SEA stopped at the familiarization level, because of the cost of the extra ammunition required for full-qualification firing.[33] Such firing therefore took place in South Vietnam with bullets rendered even more costly by the shipping charges.

In every one of the above instances, the local security police commander approved self-help to fill a vital support need. Another brand of self-help, however, was undertaken on direction of higher headquarters. This was the evaluation of base defense equipment procured by AFSC under the "buy and try" program.* Experience gained in the Korean War had shown that combat testing should be conducted only if test results could be secured in no other way. Spare parts and supplies should accompany the test item, to lighten the logistic load of the theater commander.[34]

The experience went unheeded in the Vietnam War, a fact pointed up by the evaluation of the Perimeter Detection and Surveillance Subsystem. Testing of the PDSS at Phu Cat in late 1969 differed sharply from the usual combat evaluation of new equipment. Normally the test item was used in combat, and the sole special efforts were to record data on the results. But in the case of the PDSS, combat results hinged on the enemy's penetration of that part of the perimeter where the system was installed. Since the Communists did not cooperate, simulated enemy penetrations had to be staged by friendly troops.

The upshot was that thousands of man-hours were spent on a noncombat evaluation rather than on combat duties. Installing the system called for a major effort by the Ground Electronics Engineering Installation Agency (GEEIA) and Red Horse engineers. The 37th SP Squadron devoted nearly 12,500 man-hours to testing that could have been done in CONUS. The 1883d Communications Squadron placed 4-10 men purely on PDSS maintenance. Civil engineering troops regularly repaired the sensor fields and roads leading to them.[35]

The crowning irony of this episode came after the test's conclusion. In light of the impending withdrawal of U.S. forces, the Seventh Air Force Commander decided the PDSS was no longer needed at any air base in South Vietnam.

Viewed in retrospect, the self-help syndrome cannot be dismissed as simply a short detour from a basically sound way of doing things—after all, self-help went on for 8 years. On the contrary, self-help must be seen as stronger proof that the planning, organization, and response of USAF support services were poorly suited to the combat needs of air base defense in the Vietnam War.

* This program is discussed in Chapter V.

IX. GETTING IT TOGETHER: DEFENSE ORGANIZATION IN PRINCIPLE AND PRACTICE

Only those defenses are good, certain and durable, which depend on yourself alone and your own ability.

Niccolo Machiavelli, 1513.

The local ground defense of USAF operating bases in South Vietnam involved U.S. and Allied armed forces working together. Unity of purpose and action was officially praised as the guiding principle for such operations. In practice, however, principle played a minor role. The degree and depth of security cooperation hinged on how well conflicting policies and procedures could be reconciled and personalities dealt with. These variables stood in the way of clear-cut base defense operations.

Command and Control of U.S. Forces

United State Military Assistance Command, Vietnam (USMACV) was formed on 8 February 1962 as a subordinate unified command of Pacific Command (PACOM). (See page 156.) Its mission was to control U.S. military activities and operations in the Republic of Vietnam. The Commander, USMACV, reported through the Commander in Chief, Pacific Command, to the Joint Chiefs of Staff. In line with joint doctrine, COMUSMACV had operational control over all assigned and attached forces. He exercised this control through the commanders of U.S. Army Vietnam, U.S. Naval Forces Vietnam, Seventh Air Force, and III Marine Amphibious Force.

Except for operational control, Seventh Air Force came under the Commander in Chief, Pacific Air Forces. Thus on logistic, administrative, technical, and other matters of solely USAF interest, the Seventh Air Force Commander took orders from and dealt directly with CINCPACAF. The status of U.S. Army Vietnam, U.S. Naval Forces Vietnam, and III Marine Amphibious Force paralleled that of Seventh Air Force.[1]

This organization guaranteed unified operational control at Headquarters USMACV, but at the lower command levels military services maintained strict unit integrity. Hence to assure interservice coordination in the field, COMUSMACV set up a hierarchy of officials. Their task was to coordinate certain designated functions (including installation and area security), performed by two or more U.S. military services or free world forces in a specific geographic area. This network of coordinators was organized by territory and aligned with the structure of U.S. and RVN ground forces.[2]

There were two area coordinators: The Commanding General, III

United States Military Assistance Command, Vietnam, 1967

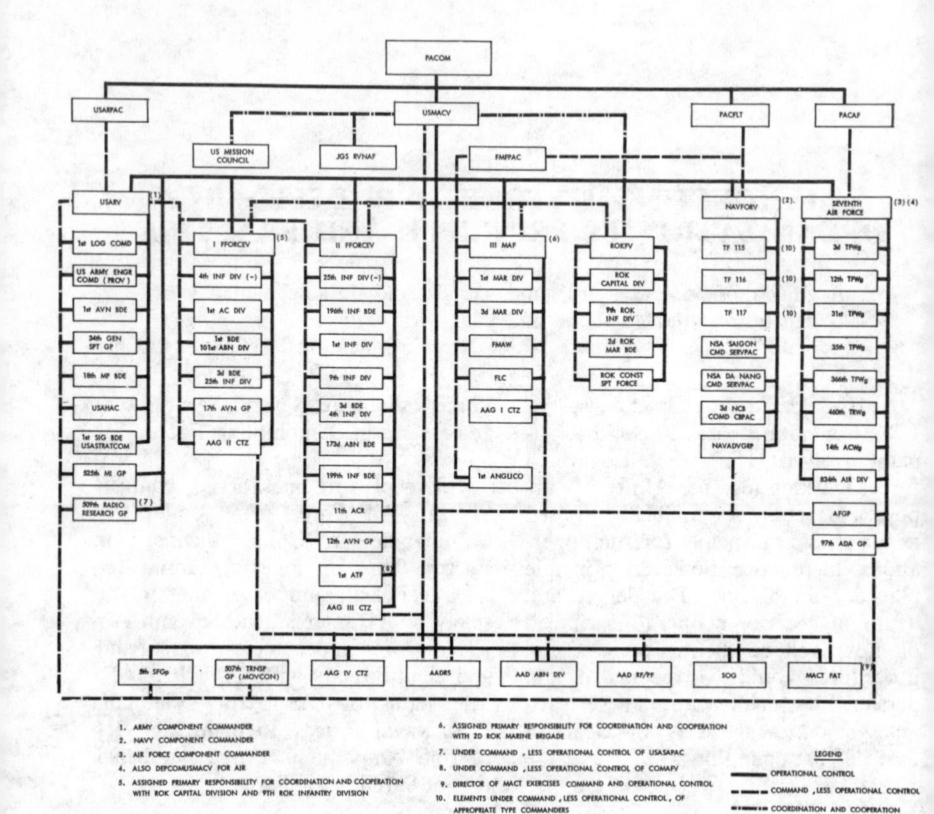

MAF, looked after I CTZ. The Commanding General, USARV, took care of the Capital Military District together with II, III, and IV CTZs. As need be, these two officials designated coordinators at the corps tactical zones, division tactical zones, and installations. The coordinator as a rule was the senior U.S. officer permanently assigned. So at most of the 10 major USAF operating bases, the senior USAF officer had the job as an additional duty.* With these few exceptions, all coordinators were ground force personnel.

Coordinators held no command or operational control over units in their jurisdiction. They could require

* In lieu of the senior USAF officer, the coordinator at Da Nang was the Marine commander; at Tan Son Nhut, the 377th CS Group Commander.

commanders to consult but could not compel agreement. If talking got nowhere, area coordinators referred the matter to USMACV.

In this manner, coordinators at USAF bases were for defense purposes absorbed into the Army structure. The communication channel flowed from base to division or corps then on to USARV and USMACV. Seventh Air Force stayed outside this flow. Of course USMACV resolved no major dispute involving USAF units until Seventh had its say. But such disputes were rare. The upshot was that Seventh Air Force took no hand in the normal coordination of area and base security matters between USAF and Army/Marine units. Bereft of this experience, it could give little meaningful command or staff assistance to its bases.

A partial break in this impasse came at the height of the 1968 Tet Offensive. Upon request, USMACV attached an Army lieutenant colonel to

VC/NVA prisoner taken during the 1968 Tet attack on Bien Hoa Air Base (above).

Enemy soldier killed at Binh Thuy

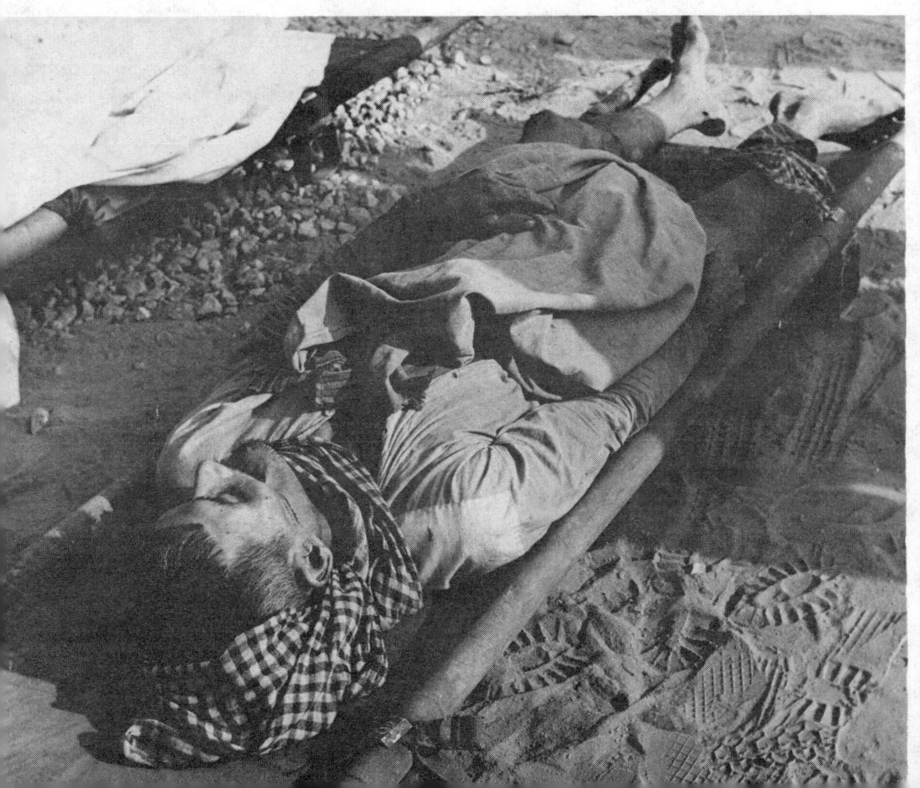

the Directorate of Security Police, Seventh Air Force. This officer advised on defense tactics and techniques, and informally kept in touch with U.S. and RVN ground forces charged with area and local defense of USAF bases. This useful arrangement ceased in spring 1969 as the enemy threat waned and U.S. forces began heading home. Air Base defense duties shifted from American to South Vietnamese ground forces, leaving Seventh Air Force once more outside the flow of events so vital to its security.

Neither the unified command structure nor the coordinator network could span the gap between Air Force and Army thinking on local ground defense of fixed installations. The Air Force believed that the security responsibility of the base commander ended at the base perimeter, and that Army troops should defend the local area. The Army's viewpoint (shared by USMACV and the JCS) insisted that ground forces should engage in offensive operations, not be tied down in static defense of ground installations. The conflict in outlook made it hard for the Air Force and Army to get together on air base defense.* In a nutshell, the unified base defense operations envisioned by the JCS were never quite realized.

Relationship of U.S. and RVN Forces

The operational relationship between U.S. and RVN forces presented a far more tangled problem. Military relations were based on legal terms that crimped clearly defined and well-integrated actions. In South Vietnam the U.S. forces operated from a status of forces agreement on a government-to-government level giving basic guidance for combined military operations. Their military presence rested on the so-called Pentalateral Agreement,* concerned solely with the delivery and use of equipment furnished by the United States as a part of its military assistance program. Faced with these circumstances, COMUSMACV was forced to invent a new formula for the conduct of combined operations.

During the spring of 1965, the U.S. ground forces burgeoned in size and mission. Pressure built for an understanding that would let U.S. commanders share tactical responsibility with the Republic of Vietnam Armed Forces. Secretary of Defense McNamara urged Ambassador Taylor and General Westmoreland to press the Government of Vietnam for a combined command structure along the lines of the ones that worked so well in World War II. This proposal was turned down by the GVN. Still vivid memories of French colonial rule made foreign direction of their armed forces anathema to the Vietnamese. Besides, a combined command would entice the VC/NVA to brand the GVN an "imperialist puppet." As for the United States, extensive experience in an advisory role left it reluctant to put its forces under RVNAF command or control.[3]

To unsnarl the tangle, COMUSMACV proposed and the Vietnamese accepted the formula that the "basic concept underlying command relations between U.S./Allied forces and RVNAF will be one of combat support through coordination and coop-

---

* This clash of concepts is explored in Chapter II.

* The Agreement for Mutual Defense Assistance in Indochina, executed at Saigon on 23 December 1950 by representatives of Vietnam, Laos, Cambodia, France, and the United States.

eration in the mutual self-interest of both commands." [4]

In a directive spelling out the concept, Westmoreland stressed that USMACV and RVNAF were equal and separate entities. At the national level, COMUSMACV and the Chief of the RVNAF General Staff each kept operational control of his forces, and RVNAF retained all territorial responsibilities. This unit integrity of each nation's forces also prevailed at the lower command levels.* It was stipulated that "as a matter of U.S. policy, U.S. forces will not be placed under the command or operational control of Allied Commanders." Only in a combat emergency—and with ground commanders mutually agreeing—could U.S., FWF, or RVNAF commanders give temporary tactical direction to troops of other nations. To war's end, this concept remained a thorn in the side of combined operations.

To promote a coordinated effort without a combined command, USMACV ordered advisory teams at all levels to conduct combat liaison between U.S./free world forces and RVNAF. This duty was in addition to the teams' primary mission of advice, assistance, and support to RVNAF.[5] Thus the advisory network became the intended link in U.S.-RVN military operations. With respect to air base defense, the network's value was tempered by distinctions in Army and Air Force advisory organization. The Air Force Advisory Group reported to Seventh Air Force. (See page 160.) On the other hand, the Army advisory setup bypassed USARV and integrated directly into the joint staff at USMACV Headquarters.[6] At both levels—the USMACV joint staff consulting with the RVNAF Joint General Staff and the AFAG conferring with VNAF Headquarters—the Air Force played a slim part in air base defense liaison.

During 1965-66 the Air Force did have a spokesman for air base defense on the USMACV joint staff. He was a security police lieutenant colonel assigned to the Surface Plans and Operations Division, Assistant Chief of Staff (ACS) Operations (J-3). This billet was nevertheless deleted in January 1967, on the suggestion of the departing officer as agreed to by Seventh Air Force. In the light of later experience, the deletion was recognized as a blunder. It left no one on the joint staff to coordinate USAF base defense plans and operations with those of other U.S. military services or with the Vietnamese. Because of the clash in defense concepts, "serious problems in communication" persisted between the Seventh Air Force Director of Security Police and the Army-dominated Surface Plans and Operations Division. An AF member assigned to the latter could have smoothed communication and working relations with the Army.[7]

In the field, U.S. ground force advisers enlarged their role in air base defense. This trend quickened in early 1967 when the Chairman of the Joint Chiefs of Staff suggested that USMACV assign more U.S. Army advisers to ARVN local security forces of company size and above.[8] These advisers came to be a key factor in USAF-VNAF operations as they aided ARVN, RF, or PF units in perimeter, local, or area defense of air bases. Their worth stood out at bases where

---

* "Only in the area of intelligence was there a combined or integrated effort between US and RVN forces. To take maximum advantage of the resources and information of both, the Combined Intelligence Center, Vietnam was formed." [Maj Gen George S. Eckhardt, *Vietnam Studies: Command and Control 1950-1969* (DA, 1974), p 59.]

the VNAF commander held operational control over RVNAF ground forces. In such cases the Army adviser counseled the VNAF commander on the use of his ground forces and coordinated actions with USAF security forces. At times USAF and VNAF defense forces on the same base communicated with one another through U.S. Army advisory channels. The situation teemed with opportunities for misunderstanding and contention. Hence the indispensable element was the unfailing bond of good will and cooperation that united the efforts of the Army advisers and USAF security police.

The Air Force advisory program to assist VNAF had nearly 500 advisors assigned to AFAG Headquarters and the 10 base-level teams. Not until April 1966 did the program take the slightest notice of air base security or defense matters. Then AFAG added a 1-man security police branch to its directorate of operations. The branch rarely coordinated USAF and VNAF base defense operations, but

Organization of the Air Force Advisory Group

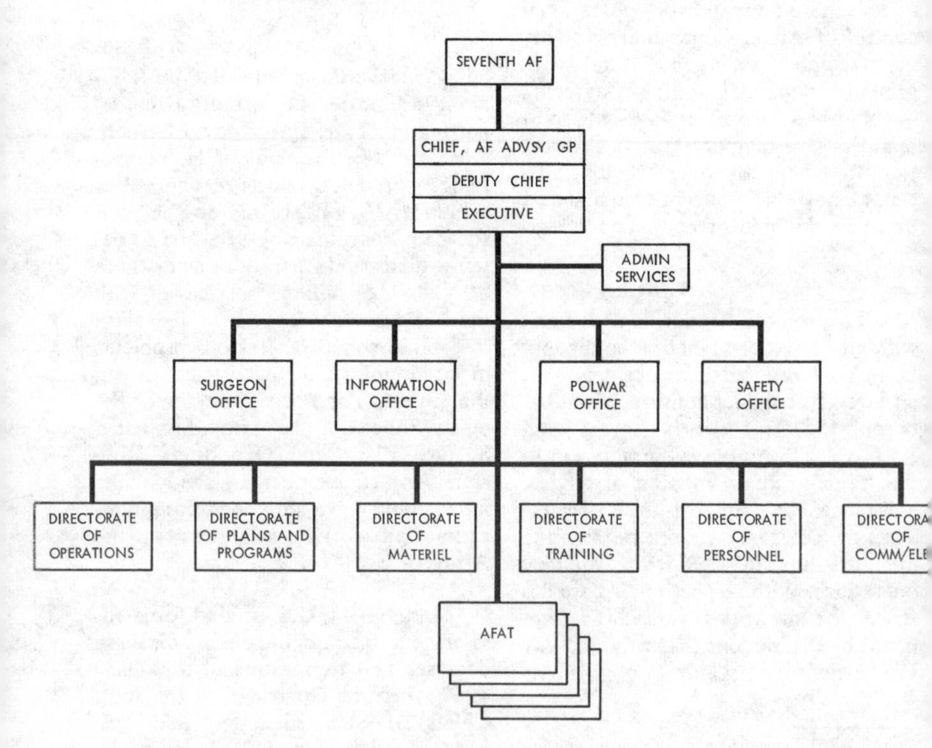

MISSION: (1) To advise and assist the VNAF to achieve a state of combat readiness through application of logistics, engineering, maintenance, communications, planning, air operations, aerospace medicine, and personnel operating procedures; (2) Act in an advisory capacity to COMUSMACV and Comdr, 7th AF, on all matters pertaining to effective use of air power including that of VNAF; (3) To provide for all USAF personnel assigned or attached; (4) Support operations of other agencies as directed or required.

spent a great deal of time reorganizing and modernizing VNAF police and defense forces.* Never did AFAG ready a Seventh AF/VNAF plan to unify defense operations.† As for the Air Force advisory teams, not one carried defense advisers. Small wonder, then, that the program's contribution to Seventh AF/VNAF air base defense operations was sparse at the headquarters level and nil at the base level. Any positive steps by USAF and VNAF officials at the bases lacked the underpinning of prior AFAG-VNAF staffing. Given the extreme sensitivity of the VNAF officer to the real or imagined views of his seniors, the want of explicit top-level approval rendered a local understanding for integrated defense operations shaky indeed.[9]

Nor did the Director of Security Police, Seventh Air Force, figure in the coordination of USAF-VNAF air base defense operations. Unlike the Seventh Air Force TACC, the base defense operations center he set up after 1968 Tet was not occupied by both USAF and VNAF personnel. So aside from the limited, indirect contact afforded by the AFAG channels, the Director stayed aloof from his Vietnamese counterparts.‡ His security police staff officers and those at higher headquarters shared the isolation. When they made inspections and staff visits to the bases, they avoided meeting RVNAF security officers. Consequently, these officers rarely sensed the problems and frustrations peculiar to dealing with the Vietnamese. This led to staff guidance that was at times wide of the mark and now and then hurtful to the cause. Such isolation went a long way in explaining why Seventh Air Force and the Vietnamese Air Force could not firm up a plan for pulling their base defense operations together.

Under these circumstances, changing "coordination and cooperation" from a lofty phrase to a working relationship seemed impossible. As in other combat support, the outcome in base defense hinged chiefly on the attitudes and abilities of the personalities involved. The host VNAF commander and the tenant USAF commander set the tone of relations and degree of understanding. The host was a permanent fixture with extensive experience in dealing with Americans. The tenant was a 12-month bird of passage, used to unfettered command of a CONUS base, eager to win his spurs in the combat zone, and impatient with the niceties of "political warfare" as waged in RVN. As a rule, the relations between the VNAF base defense group commander and the USAF security police commander reflected those of their superiors.[10]

Keeping up appearances by strict observance of host-tenant proprieties was a must. Time and time again, COMUSMACV stressed Vietnamese touchiness on their contribution to the war and their resentment at being bypassed or seemingly ignored. He pointed out that under other conditions Vietnamese displeasure might not matter. In the RVN political climate, however, "we must be alert to

---

* The initial authorization for a captain was afterwards raised to a major and a master sergeant added.

† Later in the war, AFAG developed a Seventh AF/VNAF plan for Vietnamization of the base defense mission.

‡ Near the end of his tour in 1967, one Seventh Air Force Director of Security Police observed that his sole contact with RVN officials had been an introduction to the Saigon Chief of Police at a cocktail party. The officers who followed him in the job were equally isolated. Lt. Col. William T. Luckett, Jr. (1972-73) was the exception. Wearing a "second hat" as Chief of Security Police at Tan Son Nhut, he had daily contact with his Vietnamese counterparts at base level.

all potential divergent influences," lest they be seized on by VC/NVA propagandists to disrupt U.S./RVN relations.[11]

Friendly relations were also required for successful day-to-day operations. There being no combined command, the tenant USAF commander could take few security/defense actions without first getting the green light from the host VNAF commander. These might include building a weapon position, defoliating the perimeter, or putting in security lighting. To proceed without VNAF sanction invited swift and annoying (but seemingly unrelated) reprisals. New access requirements would keep Vietnamese employees of the Air Force from entering the base. Land set aside for USAF facilities would suddenly become unavailable. A rash of incidents might break out wherein VNAF sentries would fire on U.S. military personnel and vehicles. A favorite ploy was to accuse American troops of disrespect toward VNAF officers. The Quan Canh would then apprehend the "offenders" even though the Pentalateral Agreement exempted them from the RVN legal process.

The more seasoned USAF commanders sized up the situation for what it was and acquired an instinct for getting along with their VNAF counterparts. Less astute commanders acted as though they were on their own turf, thus assuring a term of turbulent and barren host-tenant relations. Ambassador Lodge offered wise counsel on this score: "The smart thing to do is to plant an idea in their heads in such a way that it will later emerge as if it were their own creation." [12]

Elements in Allied Operations

The earliest efficient and accepted means for coordinating U.S. and Allied air base defense was the joint defense operations center.* At some air bases it was called the installation coordinating center (ICC). The center housed control/liaison elements of the main U.S./RVN/FWF units having an internal, local, or area base defense mission. In each case the JDOC or ICC reflected the size and complexity of the base's defense operations. At Tan Son Nhut, for example, COMUSMACV ordered a large blockhouse built just for the JDOC. It was constantly manned by a normal complement of 8 to 12 U.S. and RVN military personnel. The center at Pleiku shared space with the corps tactical operations center (CTOC). At Phan Rang (a single-use base) the ICC was at first put with the rear element of 5th Battalion, 27th Artillery Regiment, U.S. Army. To improve and speed up coordination, the center was later moved to central security control (CSC) of USAF security police.

Ideally, every center operated around the clock and had ample radio and landline communications for reliable contact with ground, air, and fire support elements. The participating units were expected to funnel into the center current intelligence and operating data relating to defense of the air base. This would usually include enemy sitings, discovery of weapon caches, evaluations of captured documents and prisoner interrogation reports, status of friendly forces, and maps.

Never in any sense did ICCs or JDOCs become instruments of combined command. In line with the "equal and separate" principle, each center remained a convenient point where U.S./RVN/FWF officials regu-

* The designation should have been "combined defense operations center" because two or more allies were involved.

Joint Defense Operations Center at Tan Son Nhut Air Base with insignia of participating U.S. and RVN organizations

larly met to resolve integrated base defense and kindred problems. Nearly all the units involved continued to have their own command posts—USAF security police, for example, operated central security control. Nevertheless, a well-run center could take on extra duties in an emergency. During an attack on Phan Rang, the ICC coordinated the fire of AC-47 Spookies, Army helicopter gunships, Navy ships offshore, Republic of Korea Army (ROKA) artillery, and USAF security police mortars.[13]

A further aid to air base defense was the joint defense plan, drawn up and agreed to by U.S. and allied commanders. Drafting the plan was never easy, even at joint-use bases where the Air Force and VNAF were the sole parties. The highest hurdles consisted of poor communication between Seventh Air Force and VNAF, national pride, conflicting views, and politics. Thus any plan stating a broad concept of operations, defining tasks in general terms, and spelling out some sort of coordination was seen as an unqualified success. In view of the intricate steps entailed, the plan bore more than a chance resemblance to an international agreement—which in a sense it was.

Strides were made by late 1967. Bien Hoa, Da Nang, and Tan Son Nhut had joint defense plans. Joint "operational instructions" governed perimeter defense and base access at Pleiku, Nha Trang, and Binh Thuy. In the judgment of Brig. Gen. Donavon F. Smith, Chief of AFAG, these plans and instructions buttressed base security and defense throughout the 1968 Tet Offensive.[14]

The forging of joint defense plans moved slowly at bases shared by the Air Force, other U.S. services, and free world forces. The Republic of Korea Army caused the most trouble, for it alone of the FWF was not under COMUSMACV's operational control. At Cam Ranh Bay, for example, base defense fell to the Air Force, Army, Navy, and ROKA. No joint defense plans for the base emerged until 1969, when a surge of enemy attacks supplied the stimulus.[15] Subsequently, the enemy mounted 11 successful attacks against Cam Ranh Bay—4 standoff, 4 sapper, and 3 standoff and sapper. These peaked on 25 August 1971 in one of the most spectacular standoff and sapper operations of the war. The Communists exploded the Tri-Service Ammunition Storage Area, blowing up 6,000 tons of munitions worth more than $10 million. According to the postattack analysis, the joint plan helped base defense hardly at all.[16] The USAF commander said the episode showed that "dependence on other services or agencies for area defense is highly questionable and not recommended if any other alternative is available."[17]

Nor did joint USAF/ROKA base defense operations at Phan Rang go well. The USAF commander during 1968-69 scored the foot-dragging of the local ROKA battalion (the only Allied tactical ground force in the area). He lamented his lack of authority outside the perimeter, asserting that "my experience with the ROKA . . . has been one of frustration and dissatisfaction."[18]

Elsewhere better relations reigned. At Phu Cat, for example, the joint defense plan was smoothly carried out. There, the chief of security police in 1967 praised the readiness of the allies to cooperate in countering

Two of the five 420,000 gallon fuel tanks destroyed by 107-mm rockets at Cam Ranh Bay on 30 August 1970

threats to the base. District officials, MACV advisers, and ROKA commanders in the Phu Cat area gave "exceptional support for external base defense."[19]

In summary, the value of the joint base defense plan waxed or waned in response to the personalities concerned, security force strength, and the local threat. Regardless of the profuse outpouring of esteem and goodwill that went with its signing, the prudent USAF commander never viewed the plan as a stable and reliable base defense tool. For this reason, USAF internal security operations at the bases gradually grew until they nearly took over all internal defense. The single exception was at Da Nang where the Marines had owned the base defense mission since 1965.

A system of security alert conditions (SACONs) was central to joint air base defense. It was a fast uniform means for insuring that bases, areas, or the entire command prepared to repel an actual or anticipated attack. Devised in 1966 by USMACV Assistant Chief of Staff Operations, the system consisted of five security/defense postures (NORMAL, WHITE, GREY, YELLOW, AND RED). Each matched the size and imminence of air enemy threat. (See Appendix 6)

Soon all U.S. and Allied forces save Seventh Air Force used the SACONs. For reasons still not plain, Seventh insisted that the planning and conduct of all USAF base defense operations be keyed to six expanded security postures (ESPs). The ESPs were a keystone in USAF cold war internal security procedures, but they injected vast confusion into the coordination of joint/Allied insurgency defense operations. Not until late 1967 did general discontent at the operational level induce Seventh Air Force to adopt the USMACV system.[20] Now all forces had a common frame of reference for defining defense postures.

Ideally, any change in the SACON of a base triggered a standard, predetermined, and coordinated shift in the strength and disposition of defense forces. (See table.) Most

Bien Hoa Air Base

USAF Base Defense Force
Composition Under Each SACON

	NORMAL	*WHITE*	*GREY*	*YELLOW*	*RED I*	*RED II*
0600-1400	NA	63	81	95		
1400-2100	NA	100	118	125		
2100-0600	NA	178*	178*	287		
0700-1900					132	
1900-0700					401	
0001-2400						2,733†

* The policy at Bien Hoa was to assume a SACON GREY posture daily during the high-threat hours.

† SACON RED II applied solely to Seventh Air Force bases. It was a "forlorn hope" posture that contemplated overrunning of the base by enemy forces, and called for mobilization of all personnel not directly engaged in support of the flying mission. Except for training, SACON RED II was never invoked during the war. The practical value of this posture was extremely questionable, due to the low weapons proficiency and the poor weapons discipline among the rank and file of USAF personnel.

SOURCE: 3d CSGp OPlan 207-69, 29 Mar 69.

obstacles to the system's smooth operation stemmed from the split command structure. The USAF and the VNAF commander at a joint-use base shared the authority to set the SACON. Hope for agreement on the SACON hinged on cooperation and coordination as well as the togetherness nurtured by the JDOC. Sometimes this hope was dashed as USAF and VNAF defense forces on the same base displayed different readiness postures. Blame for the impasse must be placed on both commanders.

On the Vietnamese side, a sure link seemed to join urgent threat estimates with upcoming holidays and liberal leaves. The USAF commander on a base tagged this as a transparent move to entice him into a more advanced SACON. Then his men would have to take up the slack left by those VNAF troops away on holiday leave. At every base in the Saigon area, the USAF commander also had to eye Vietnamese threat estimates closely for hints of an impending coup embracing the base. The Vietnamese commander well knew that USMACV policy was to stay strictly out of politics. So in hope of U.S. assistance, he would paint the activities of the dissident VNAF faction as those of the VC/NVA.

On the USAF side, actions by higher headquarters threw SACONs out of kilter. For example, PACAFM 207-25 called for an automatic SACON YELLOW at Seventh Air Force bases whenever two of them were attacked in a single hour.* But far more disruptive was Seventh Air Force's excessive zeal in directing a given base to assume an advanced SACON (usually YELLOW)—a status that could not be downgraded by local commanders. This action was never coordinated with RVNAF, USMACV, USARV, or III MAF (in the case of Da Nang). Hence the SACON applied only to USAF defense forces and was ignored by all others at no risk to their safety. At Da Nang the 366th TF Wing often looked silly when the III MAF threat estimate failed to support the YELLOW alert imposed by Seventh Air Force. The wing stayed in YELLOW for several days wasting resources, while the rest of the base kept to a WHITE or GREY posture.[21]

Despite these drawbacks, the SACON concept was sound and aided joint air base defense.

Unlike the uniform SACONs, no standard rules of engagement dealt expressly with air or ground forces defending fixed installations—an omission crippling the coordination and conduct of such operations.* The USMACV rules of engagement did not distinguish between the maneuver of ground forces on search-and-destroy missions and the static defense of air bases.[22] However, they closely curbed the latter, because the bases were located in and around cities, towns, and villages. Though never questioning the right of self-defense, the rules usually required that each fire mission receive prior political and military approval from RVN authorities having control over the target area. Many times these officials omitted, delayed, or refused fire-clearance requests—arousing anger and frustration among

---

* Like the ESPs, this requirement was a carryover from the cold war security concept and not the result of counterinsurgency experience in SVN. The greatest number of attacks at one time came during 1968 Tet—3 of the 10 USAF bases were struck in the early hours of 31 January.

* Chapter VII tells of air power's troubles with the rules of engagement.

Flares dropped behind the perimeter of Tan Son Nhut Air Base light up the flight line area, helping prevent enemy infiltration of the base

U.S. forces. Rigid enforcement of the rules of engagement and the glaring publicity given the prosecution of violators made most commanders hesitant about exercising their right of self-defense.

The neglect of reaction forces to fire on the enemy during the 13 April 1966 attack on Tan Son Nhut threw the rigid rules of engagement into bold relief. General Westmoreland, COMUSMACV, accordingly ordered his operations officer to make an in-depth study of Tan Son Nhut's defense. One of the major deficiencies thus brought to light was the delay in receiving clearances to fire on targets outside the base perimeter. Throughout the 13 April affair, response by the clearance authority (Headquarters Capital Military District in central Saigon) was both late and confused. Security police crewing a heavy machinegun saw the muzzle flashes of mortars shelling the base but were forbidden to fire, because CMD approval had not arrived.

The work of Brig. Gen. William O. Quirey, USA, Deputy Director/USMACV Combat Operations Center, went a long way toward righting this situation. He drafted and won Joint General Staff acceptance of rules of engagement authorizing Tan Son Nhut defense forces to strike enemy targets instantly under certain specified conditions.* The Air Force next set out on its own to apply the same rules to every base in South Vietnam—first by a Seventh Air Force supplement to AFM 207-1 and later by PACAFM

* These rules and the accompanying guard orders are in Appendix 7.

207-25. These attempts came to nothing because USMACV and JGS meant the rules for Tan Son Nhut alone. In consequence, the clearance of fire requests continued to be "the single most important limiting factor in base defense operations." [23] On 25 August 1971 the reaction forces at Cam Ranh Bay failed to fire on the foe during a standoff/sapper attack. It was a repeat of what had happened at Tan Son Nhut 5 years before.[24]

For the rest of the war, the use of firepower for base defense was chiefly controlled by the case-to-case action or inaction of RVN military and political authorities. Finishing his tour as Seventh Air Force Director of Security Police in 1972, Col. Jack L. Hughes fingered the lesson learned. He recommended "that the senior in-country headquarters in any future conflict develop rules of engagement to provide specific guidance for defense of a static installation." [25]

The Tactical Situation—A Vital Element

Perhaps the most vital element in shaping air base defense operations was the tactical situation—as the 1968 Tet Offensive clearly confirmed. The latter spurred Seventh Air Force to issue a weekly threat appraisal, based on known or calculated enemy/friendly actions and capabilities. This change injected into air base defense a professional element that had been missing.*

* See Appendix 8 for abbreviated situation reports showing the data and estimates made available to defense forces at typical bases. The week covered (12-18 January 1969) was a representative one, during a period when air base defense operations reached or neared their peak at all 10 USAF operating locations in South Vietnam.

From the operations standpoint, the appearance or anticipation of an urgent threat worked wonders. Friction dwindled, coordination quickened, and morale surged.

And on the support side, nothing surpassed the magic of a damaging attack to stimulate procurement of needed equipment and weapons, speed repair of rundown vehicles, hurry construction of put-off facilities, or energize long-stalled communications projects.

In getting air base defense together, there was no substitute for combat. Prolonged periods of inaction were the bane of this mission. Fortunately, the enemy did not fully exploit that fact.

The Experience in Perspective

Air base defense in the Republic of Vietnam mirrored the total war setting. Rear areas vanished as the enemy turned to insurgency warfare. All of South Vietnam became a battlefield, with installations such as air bases sometimes caught up in the fighting. In past wars, most bases were well behind the lines and free of ground attack. Thus security needs focused on preventing theft and minor acts of sabotage. The situation in South Vietnam differed in every way. Since the enemy hid among the people, he was all around an installation rather than held at a distance by the battlezone's location. He could infiltrate with ease to within rocket range or less.

The VC/NVA threat comprised sabotage, sapper infiltration, ground attack, and shelling by standoff weapons. Sabotage was little used. Ground attacks by battalion-size Communist forces took place at just two bases. Sapper raids posed a more serious threat. But in terms of inci-

An Air Force security guard watches a USAF F–4C fighter-bomber take off from an air base in South Vietnam (above). Security forces at Phan Rang (below) pour machinegun fire into suspected enemy positions

dence and damage, standoff rocket and mortar fire presented the greatest hazard.

Exposed to this threat were nearly 100 installations deemed critical to the American war effort—10 of them USAF operating bases. Their security rested on a single decisive fact: It required about the same resources to carry the fight to the enemy as it did to sit back and protect U.S. installations. COMUSMACV weighed the problem. Neglecting the offensive would repeat the error that cost the French the war. Slighting defense would undermine the U.S. position in South Vietnam. Seeking to strike the proper balance, COMUSMACV directed air bases and other fixed installations to perform their own internal security and other possible defense measures. Under this policy, Army tactical units seldom switched from a search-and-destroy to a security role. When they did, it was usually short-term support or relief for an installation under heavy attack.

For its part, the Air Force slowly carved out adequate internal security from scarce ground resources. It steadfastly rejected any responsibility for external defense on the ground, allocating only air support.* Aside from the Marines at Da Nang, U.S. ground troops rarely took part in external security. Consequently, RVN and free world forces were entrusted with the protection of air bases from standoff attack. Though earlier reliance on the allies had not gone well, the thinking ran that vigorous Army search-and-destroy actions would trim the threat to fixed installations. Apart from the notable 1968 Tet Offensive, this concept of ground operations staved off conventional ground attacks. On the other hand, wiping out elements of the VC/NVA main force failed to deter the foe from mounting small unit attacks against Allied bases whenever he wanted to. Nor could the Allied units charged with external security muster enough patrols to stop these assaults.

An airman (above) examines the body of a Viet Cong terrorist killed during an attempted infiltration of Tan Son Nhut on 4 December 1966

(Below) Tower, sandbagging, "totem poles," and fencing built by the 3d Security Police Squadron at Bien Hoa Air Base

---

* Air support excelled when working with ground forces patrolling the outer limits of the rocket belt.

Hobbling external security was the lack of reliable intelligence on enemy activities within striking distance of bases. This rose chiefly from the Air Force's failure to generate tactical ground intelligence. More crucial, however, was the middling success of the revolutionary development program. Among other things it sought to gird each base with loyal Vietnamese settlers who would give the alarm when VC/NVA forces appeared. While these occupants sopped up the benefits from countless civic action programs, they for the most part kept their own counsel and ignored air base security.

Long-term command and staff shortcomings further hampered air base defense. Foremost was the gap in USAF local defense doctrine that until 1968 denied or delayed the emergence of a proper counterinsurgency. Moreover, sound management was spurned in the administration of counterinsurgency training to security police. Conducting this training in CONUS would have been cheaper and more efficient. It could have spared security police units in SVN the undue drain on their scarce manpower and let them center on the combat mission. A similar dearth of common sense marred the policy banning permanent defense structures at the primary air bases—this at a time when strategic plans projected 3 more years of U.S. involvement. The insistence on temporary construction bred constant repair and replacement, and exacted a stiff price in dollars and manpower. Hardened aircraft shelters became the only notable exception to this rule. They proved at once their worth in protecting against rocket and mortar fire.

Also twisting the shape of air base defense was the USMACV's "counterinsurgency mystique." This theory held that getting on with the war demanded exaggerated deference to a Government of Vietnam openly riddled with dissension and corruption. Such kowtowing flourished in the vital area of external security. The mandatory coordination maze never tired of stifling swift approval of fire-clearance requests, defoliation projects, free-fire zones, and equally essential actions.

All air base defense problems radiated from the core truth of the Vietnam War—to be able to fight in the air, the Air Force had to fight on the ground. Douhet's dictum* on the threat to ground-deployed air power was proven once again, but in a much less-sophisticated way than the author visualized more than a half-century ago. In putting his concept to work, the Vietcong/North Vietnamese Army matched means to ends with consummate skill. They demonstrated "the astonishing effectiveness of the simplest techniques in the age of technological marvels."

---

* "It is easier and more effective to destroy the enemy's aerial power by destroying his nests and eggs on the ground than to hunt his flying birds in the air."

APPENDIX 1

Chronology of VC/NVA Attacks On the Ten Primary USAF Operating Bases in RVN 1961-1973 *

Attacks								US Losses				RVN Losses				VC/NVA Losses	
								Aircraft		Casualties		Aircraft		Casualties		Casualties	
NO	YR	MO	DA	HR	BASE	TYPE	RDS	DES	DAM	KIA	WIA	DES	DAM	KIA	WIA	KIA	POW
1	2	3	4	5	6	7	8	9	10	11	12	13	14	15	16	17	18

Key

Column 1: Sequence of attacks.
Column 2 through 5: Local RVN date and time.
Column 6: Bases: Bien Hoa (BH); Binh Thuy (BT); Cam Ranh Bay (CBR): Da Nang (DN); Nha Trang (NT); Phan Rang (PR); Phu Cat (PC); Pleiku (PK); Tuy Hoa (TH); Tan Son Nhut (TSN).
Column 7: Type of attacks: Standoff (STO); Sapper (SAP); Standoff and Sapper (S&S); Multi-Battalion (MBN); Sabotage (SAB); Automatic Weapons (AWP).
Column 8: Standoff rounds impacting on bases.
Columns 9 and 13: Destroyed (DES).
Columns 10 and 14: Damaged (DAM).
Columns 11, 15, and 17: Killed in Action (KIA).
Columns 12 and 16: Wounded in Action (WIA).
Column 18: Prisoner of War (POW).
All Columns: Not Reported (NR).

* Prepared by author.

	Attacks							US Losses				RVN Losses				VC/NVA Losses	
								Aircraft		Casualties		Aircraft		Casualties		Casualties	
NO	YR	MO	DA	HR	BASE	TYPE	RDS	DES	DAM	KIA	WIA	DES	DAM	KIA	WIA	KIA	POW
1	2	3	4	5	6	7	8	9	10	11	12	13	14	15	16	17	18
001	64	11	01	0026	BH	STO	70	005	015	004	030	002	003	000	000	000	000
001	1964 Sub-Total						70	005	015	004	030	002	003	000	000	000	000
002	65	07	01	0130	DN	S&S	06	006	003	001	003	000	000	000	000	000	001
003	65	08	02	NR	NT	STO	07	000	000	000	000	000	000	000	000	000	000
004	65	08	23	2359	BH	STO	97	000	011	000	024	000	000	000	005	000	000
003	1965 Sub-Total						110	006	014	001	027	000	000	000	005	000	001
005	66	01	25	NR	DN	STO	20	000	000	001	006	000	000	005	025	000	000
006	66	02	20	NR	BT	STO	05	000	001	000	000	000	000	002	006	000	000
007	66	04	13	0027	TSN	STO	243	000	062	007	111	002	000	002	000	000	000
008	66	04	22	0210	PK	STO	79	002	011	000	005	000	000	000	000	000	000
009	66	07	08	0010	BT	STO	40	001	002	001	005	000	002	000	000	000	000
010	66	10	18	2250	BH	SAP		000	000	000	000	000	000	000	000	000	000
011	66	12	04	0110	TSN	S&S	33	000	020	003	015	000	000	003	004	028	004
012	66	12	24	0040	BT	STO	29	000	002	000	007	000	000	000	002	000	000
008	1966 Sub-Total						449	004	098	012	173	002	036	012	051	028	004

Attacks								US Losses				RVN Losses				VC/NVA Losses	
								Aircraft		Casualties		Aircraft		Casualties		Casualties	
NO	YR	MO	DA	HR	BASE	TYPE	RDS	DES	DAM	KIA	WIA	DES	DAM	KIA	WIA	KIA	POW
1	2	3	4	5	6	7	8	9	10	11	12	13	14	15	16	17	18
013	67	01	07	0140	PK	STO	32	000	000	000	000	000	000	000	000	000	000
014	67	01	12	0140	BT	STO	67	000	005	000	009	000	000	000	000	000	000
015	67	02	07	0050	BH	SAB*		000	000	000	000	000	000	000	000	000	000
016	67	02	08	0240	BT	STO	56	000	011	000	000	000	000	000	000	000	000
017	67	02	15	0120	NT	SAP		003	005	000	000	000	000	000	000	000	000
018	67	02	27	0310	DN	STO**	56	000	013	011	124	000	000	035	050	000	000
019	67	03	15	0200	DN	STO	10	000	007	000	000	NR	NR	NR	NR	NR	NR
020	67	03	27	0006	BT	STO	35	000	002	000	000	NR	NR	NR	NR	NR	NR
021	67	05	07	2250	BT	STO	69	000	004	000	000	000	000	000	000	NR	NR
022	67	05	12	0101	BH	STO	189	002	032	006	031	002	NR	NR	NR	NR	NR
023	67	07	15	0020	DN	STO	83	010	049	008	175	000	001	NR	NR	NR	NR
024	67	09	02	0050	DN	STO	09	000	006	000	008	NR	NR	NR	NR	NR	NR
025	67	09	07	0047	TH	AWP		000	000	001	003	000	000	000	000	003	000

*Resulted in the destruction of 2600 napalm bombs valued at $342,000.
**The first time rockets were employed in RVN by VC/NVA.

Attacks								US Losses				RVN Losses				VC/NVA Losses	
								Aircraft		Casualties		Aircraft		Casualties		Casualties	
NO	YR	MO	DA	HR	BASE	TYPE	RDS	DES	DAM	KIA	WIA	DES	DAM	KIA	WIA	KIA	POW
1	2	3	4	5	6	7	8	9	10	11	12	13	14	15	16	17	18
026	67	09	09	0005	DN	STO	03	000	002	002	010	NR	NR	NR	NR	NR	NR
027	67	10	10	0106	NT	STO	16	000	000	000	001	000	000	NR	NR	NR	NR
028	67	11	05	2240	BH	STO	15	000	000	000	002	000	000	NR	NR	NR	NR
029	67	11	26	0010	NT	STO	30	001	003	000	021	000	000	NR	NR	NR	NR
017	1967 Sub-Total						515	016	139	028	384	002	001	035	050	003	000
030	68	01	03	0400	DN	STO	49	001	020	000	002	000	000	NR	NR	NR	NR
031	68	01	20	0040	PK	STO	08	000	000	000	022	000	000	NR	NR	NR	NR
032	68	01	30	0214	PK	STO	13	000	002	000	001	000	000	NR	NR	NR	NR
033	68	01	30	0328	DN	STO	40	005	025	001	000	NR	NR	NR	NR	NR	NR
034	68	01	31	0300	BH	MBN	45	002	017	004	026	000	000	NR	NR	139*	025*
035	68	01	31	0320	TSN	MBN	NR	000	013	023	086	000	000	032	089	157*	009*
036	68	01	31	2318	NT	STO	02	000	000	000	000	000	000	000	000	000	000
037	68	02	03	1930	BT	STO	09	000	000	000	000	000	000	000	000	000	000
038	68	02	04	0300	BT	STO	73	000	016	001	005	NR	NR	NR	NR	NR	NR

*This data is limited to enemy losses incurred inside the air base perimeters.

Attacks								US Losses				RVN Losses				VC/NVA Losses	
								Aircraft		Casualties		Aircraft		Casualties		Casualties	
NO	YR	MO	DA	HR	BASE	TYPE	RDS	DES	DAM	KIA	WIA	DES	DAM	KIA	WIA	KIA	POW
1	2	3	4	5	6	7	8	9	10	11	12	13	14	15	16	17	18
039	68	02	05	0100	BT	STO	45	000	008	000	000	000	004	NR	NR	NR	NR
040	68	02	06	2344	PC	STO	10	000	000	000	000	000	000	000	000	000	000
041	68	02	07	0412	BT	STO	09	000	000	000	000	000	001	NR	NR	NR	NR
042	68	02	11	0003	BH	STO	16	006	026	001	038	NR	NR	NR	NR	NR	NR
043	68	02	12	0301	BT	STO	09	001	006	000	000	000	000	000	001	NR	NR
044	68	02	13	0233	BT	SAP		000	000	000	002	000	000	000	000	001	000
045	68	02	13	0346	BT	STO	44	000	001	000	003	000	018	001	012	000	000
046	68	02	13	2315	BT	STO	26	000	000	000	000	000	000	000	000	000	000
047	68	02	16	0126	BT	STO	25	000	003	000	000	000	006	000	002	NR	NR
048	68	02	16	0157	NT	STO	21	000	000	000	000	000	002	000	000	000	000
049	68	02	18	0100	TSN	STO	60	(Losses are included with those cited for Attack No. 73)									
050	68	02	18	0101	BT	STO	12	000	000	001	000	000	000	000	001	000	000
051	68	02	18	0103	BH	STO	07	001	003	000	000	NR	NR	NR	NR	NR	NR
052	68	02	18	1220	TSN	STO	02	(Losses are included with those cited for Attack No. 73)									
053	68	02	18	1520	TSN	STO	02	(Losses are included with those cited for Attack No. 73)									
054	68	02	18	1755	TSN	STO	01	(Losses are included with those cited for Attack No. 73)									

Attacks								US Losses				RVN Losses				VC/NVA Losses	
								Aircraft		Casualties		Aircraft		Casualties		Casualties	
NO	YR	MO	DA	HR	BASE	TYPE	RDS	DES	DAM	KIA	WIA	DES	DAM	KIA	WIA	KIA	POW
1	2	3	4	5	6	7	8	9	10	11	12	13	14	15	16	17	18
055	68	02	19	0157	TSN	STO	02	(Losses are included with those cited for Attack No. 73)									
056	68	02	19	0352	TSN	STO	02	(Losses are included with those cited for Attack No. 73)									
057	68	02	19	0515	TSN	STO	03	(Losses are included with those cited for Attack No. 73)									
058	68	02	19	0602	TSN	STO	05	(Losses are included with those cited for Attack No. 73)									
059	68	02	20	1203	TSN	STO	01	(Losses are included with those cited for Attack No. 73)									
060	68	02	20	1855	TSN	STO	02	(Losses are included with those cited for Attack No. 73)									
061	68	02	21	1202	TSN	STO	01	(Losses are included with those cited for Attack No. 73)									
062	68	02	21	1634	TSN	STO	03	(Losses are included with those cited for Attack No. 73)									
063	68	02	22	0120	PK	STO	18	000	000	000	001	000	000	NR	NR	NR	NR
064	68	02	23	0105	BT	STO	56	000	000	000	003	000	003	NR	NR	NR	NR
065	68	02	24	0400	TSN	STO	20	(Losses are included with those cited for Attack No. 73)									
066	68	02	24	2255	DN	STO	10	000	004	000	001	NR	NR	NR	NR	NR	NR
067	68	02	26	0001	BT	STO	33	000	000	000	000	001	004	NR	NR	NR	NR
068	68	02	27	0128	TSN	STO	03	(Losses are included with those cited for Attack No. 73)									
069	68	02	27	0525	TSN	STO	04	(Losses are included with those cited for Attack No. 73)									
070	68	02	28	0101	BH	STO	32	000	005	014	024	NR	NR	NR	NR	NR	NR

Attacks								US Losses				RVN Losses				VC/NVA Losses	
								Aircraft		Casualties		Aircraft		Casualties		Casualties	
NO	YR	MO	DA	HR	BASE	TYPE	RDS	DES	DAM	KIA	WIA	DES	DAM	KIA	WIA	KIA	POW
1	2	3	4	5	6	7	8	9	10	11	12	13	14	15	16	17	18
071	68	02	28	0110	TSN	STO	02	(Losses are included with those cited for Attack No. 73)									
072	68	03	01	0145	PK	STO	11	000	000	000	000	000	000	NR	NR	NR	NR
073	68	03	01	0503	TSN	STO	16	004	074	009	151	003	001	000	011	NR	NR
074	68	03	04	2148	CRB	STO	27	000	000	000	000	000	000	000	000	000	000
075	68	03	05	0053	BT	STO	110	000	000	000	001	002	007	NR	NR	NR	NR
076	68	03	06	0210	TH	STO	04	000	000	000	000	000	000	000	000	000	000
077	68	03	06	0250	PK	STO	01	000	000	000	001	000	000	000	000	000	000
078	68	03	07	0105	PR	STO	10	000	000	000	000	000	000	000	000	NR	NR
079	68	03	10	0052	PK	STO	07	000	003	000	000	000	000	000	000	002	000
080	68	03	12	2250	BH	STO	07	000	000	000	001	NR	NR	NR	NR	NR	NR
081	68	03	14	0116	BT	STO	29	(Losses are included with those cited for Attack No. 87)									
082	68	03	14	0318	BT	STO	25	(Losses are included with those cited for Attack No. 87)									
083	68	03	17	0254	BT	STO	65	(Losses are included with those cited for Attack No. 87)									
084	68	03	21	0117	TSN	STO	10	000	007	000	002	000	000	000	000	NR	NR
085	68	03	22	0035	BT	STO	36	(Losses are included with those cited for Attacks No. 87)									

Attacks								US Losses				RVN Losses				VC/NVA Losses	
								Aircraft		Casualties		Aircraft		Casualties		Casualties	
NO	YR	MO	DA	HR	BASE	TYPE	RDS	DES	DAM	KIA	WIA	DES	DAM	KIA	WIA	KIA	POW
1	2	3	4	5	6	7	8	9	10	11	12	13	14	15	16	17	18
086	68	03	22	0138	BH	STO	09	000	005	000	012	000	000	000	000	NR	NR
087	68	03	25	0032	BT	STO	85	001	004	001	001	002	025	000	007	NR	NR
088	68	04	01	NR	TH	SAP		000	000	000	000	000	000	000	000	000	000
089	68	04	02	0301	PK	STO	21	000	000	000	000	000	000	000	000	NR	NR
090	68	04	05	2217	BH	STO	12	000	000	001	014	000	000	000	000	NR	NR
091	68	04	09	2107	BT	STO	30	000	000	000	000	000	000	000	000	NR	NR
092	68	04	13	2250	BT	STO	35	000	000	000	000	000	000	000	000	NR	NR
093	68	05	03	0124	TH	STO	24	000	000	000	000	000	000	000	000	NR	NR
094	68	05	05	0100	PK	STO	11	002	000	009	011	000	000	000	000	000	000
095	68	05	05	0152	DN	STO	01	000	000	000	000	000	000	000	000	NR	NR
096	68	05	05	0259	BH	STO	74	000	013	000	011	000	000	000	000	NR	NR
097	68	05	05	0600	BH	STO	07	000	000	000	000	000	000	000	000	000	000
098	68	05	06	0616	TSN	STO	10	000	000	000	000	000	000	000	000	000	000
099	68	05	07	0343	TSN	STO	11	000	001	000	000	000	000	002	000	000	000
100	68	05	07	1930	BH	STO	01	000	000	000	000	NR	NR	NR	NR	000	000
101	68	05	08	0300	TSN	STO	14	000	000	000	000	000	000	000	000	000	000
102	68	05	08	1806	PK	STO	06	000	002	000	000	NR	NR	NR	NR	NR	NR

Attacks								US Losses				RVN Losses				VC/NVA Losses	
								Aircraft		Casualties		Aircraft		Casualties		Casualties	
NO	YR	MO	DA	HR	BASE	TYPE	RDS	DES	DAM	KIA	WIA	DES	DAM	KIA	WIA	KIA	POW
1	2	3	4	5	6	7	8	9	10	11	12	13	14	15	16	17	18
103	68	05	09	0030	DN	STO	04	000	001	000	000	000	000	000	000	000	000
104	68	05	09	0150	DN	STO	03	000	000	000	000	000	000	000	000	000	000
105	68	05	10	0325	TSN	STO	07	000	000	000	000	000	000	000	000	000	000
106	68	05	11	2355	DN	STO	08	000	006	000	002	NR	NR	NR	NR	000	000
107	68	05	12	1800	DN	STO	03	000	002	000	000	NR	NR	NR	NR	000	000
108	68	05	21	0300	BT	STO	40	000	000	000	002	001	000	000	005	NR	NR
109	68	05	22	1815	NT	STO	05	000	004	000	000	000	000	000	000	000	000
110	68	05	23	2147	BT	STO	03	000	000	000	002	000	000	000	000	000	000
111	68	05	24	2030	BT	STO	40	000	000	000	001	000	000	003	013	000	000
112	68	05	29	0140	DN	STO	08	000	005	000	000	000	003	NR	NR	NR	NR
113	68	06	12	0337	TSN	STO	13	002	008	001	002	000	004	005	005	000	000
114	68	06	14	0340	TSN	STO	04	000	002	001	002	000	000	000	002	000	000
115	68	06	15	0237	BH	STO	09	000	006	000	000	000	000	000	001	000	000
116	68	06	21	0118	NT	STO	11	000	001	000	002	000	003	000	000	000	000
117	68	06	23	0005	PR	STO	18	000	005	000	003	000	000	000	000	000	000
118	68	06	24	0157	BT	STO	10	000	000	000	000	000	000	000	000	000	000

Attacks								US Losses				RVN Losses				VC/NVA Losses	
								Aircraft		Casualties		Aircraft		Casualties		Casualties	
NO	YR	MO	DA	HR	BASE	TYPE	RDS	DES	DAM	KIA	WIA	DES	DAM	KIA	WIA	KIA	POW
1	2	3	4	5	6	7	8	9	10	11	12	13	14	15	16	17	18
119	68	06	26	2206	BT	STO	35	000	000	000	000	000	000	000	000	000	000
120	68	07	23	0204	DN	STO	16	000	005	000	000	000	002	000	000	002	000
121	68	07	23	0602	DN	STO	01	000	000	000	000	000	000	000	000	000	000
122	68	07	27	0245	DN	STO	06	001	004	000	005	000	000	000	000	000	000
123	68	07	29	0137	TH	SAP		002	007	000	004	000	000	000	000	009	000
124	68	08	21	0003	PR	STO	27	000	002	000	002	000	000	000	000	000	000
125	68	08	22	0015	BT	STO	35	000	000	000	000	000	000	000	000	000	000
126	68	08	22	0455	BT	STO	22	000	000	000	000	000	000	000	000	000	000
127	68	08	22	0100	BH	STO	11	000	000	000	009	000	000	000	000	000	000
128	68	08	23	0158	PK	STO	17	000	004	000	002	000	000	000	000	000	000
129	68	08	23	0303	DN	STO	13	000	002	001	007	000	001	000	000	000	000
130	68	08	24	2339	BT	STO	12	000	000	000	000	000	000	000	000	000	000
131	68	08	25	0119	BT	STO	33	000	000	000	002	000	000	000	000	000	000
132	68	08	25	2230	BT	STO	29	000	000	000	000	000	000	000	000	000	000
133	68	08	27	0453	DN	STO	06	000	002	000	001	000	003	000	000	000	000
134	68	08	29	2345	BT	STO	44	000	012	000	000	002	026	000	000	000	000
135	68	08	30	2300	BH	STO	02	000	000	000	000	000	000	000	000	000	000

Attacks								US Losses				RVN Losses				VC/NVA Losses	
								Aircraft		Casualties		Aircraft		Casualties		Casualties	
NO	YR	MO	DA	HR	BASE	TYPE	RDS	DES	DAM	KIA	WIA	DES	DAM	KIA	WIA	KIA	POW
1	2	3	4	5	6	7	8	9	10	11	12	13	14	15	16	17	18
136	68	08	31	0250	DN	STO	01	000	001	000	005	000	000	000	000	000	000
137	68	09	02	0128	DN	STO	01	000	000	000	000	000	000	000	000	000	000
138	68	09	04	0529	DN	STO	02	000	000	000	000	000	000	000	000	000	000
139	68	09	08	0300	BH	STO	08	000	006	000	000	000	000	000	000	000	000
140	68	09	11	0225	BT	STO	16	000	000	000	000	000	000	000	000	000	000
141	68	09	11	2217	BT	STO	40	000	007	000	000	002	014	000	003	000	000
142	68	09	18	0515	DN	STO	03	000	000	002	007	NR	NR	NR	NR	NR	NR
143	68	09	21	0203	PK	STO	35	000	003	000	003	000	000	000	000	000	000
144	68	09	21	2330	NT	STO	23	(Losses are included with those cited for Attack No. 143)									
145	68	09	22	1408	NT	STO	04	000	004	000	009	000	000	000	000	013	002
146	68	09	29	0446	DN	STO	04	000	005	000	003	NR	NR	NR	NR	000	000
147	68	09	29	2156	BT	STO	40	000	000	000	001	000	000	000	000	000	000
148	68	10	26	2320	BH	STO	07	000	000	000	004	000	000	000	000	000	000
149	68	11	21	0132	PK	STO	24	000	000	000	008	000	000	000	000	000	000
150	68	12	23	0147	PK	STO	16	000	003	000	003	000	000	000	000	000	000
121	1968 Sub-Total						2153	028	365	070	510	013	127	041	152	323	036

	Attacks							US Losses				RVN Losses				VC/NVA Losses	
								Aircraft		Casualties		Aircraft		Casualties		Casualties	
NO	YR	MO	DA	HR	BASE	TYPE	RDS	DES	DAM	KIA	WIA	DES	DAM	KIA	WIA	KIA	POW
1	2	3	4	5	6	7	8	9	10	11	12	13	14	15	16	17	18
151	69	01	10	0200	BT	STO	62	000	000	001	004	000	000	003	005	000	000
152	69	01	10	2259	BT	STO	56	000	000	002	005	000	000	000	001	000	000
153	69	01	15	1932	PK	STO	17	000	000	000	003	000	000	000	000	000	000
154	69	01	22	0558	DN	STO	26	000	000	001	019	000	000	000	000	000	000
155	69	01	26	0015	PR	S&S	74	002	011	000	015	000	000	000	000	016	001
156	69	01	29	2138	BT	SAP		000	000	000	000	000	000	000	000	002	000
157	69	02	22	0128	PR	STO	86	000	020	000	006	000	000	000	000	000	000
158	69	02	22	2135	PC	SAP		000	000	000	001	000	000	000	000	004	001
159	69	02	23	0210	BH	STO	39	002	008	000	004	000	000	000	000	000	000
160	69	02	23	0232	BT	STO	11	000	000	000	000	000	007	000	000	000	000
161	69	02	23	0303	CRB	STO	07	000	006	000	003	000	000	000	000	000	000
162	69	02	23	0530	DN	STO	11	000	000	001	002	000	000	000	000	000	000
163	69	02	23	0622	PK	STO	02	000	001	000	002	000	000	000	000	000	000
164	69	02	24	0132	PR	STO	10	000	000	000	000	000	000	000	000	000	000
165	69	02	24	0240	NT	STO	05	000	000	000	000	000	000	000	000	000	000
166	69	02	25	0558	DN	STO	03	000	000	000	000	000	000	000	000	000	000

Attacks								US Losses				RVN Losses				VC/NVA Losses	
								Aircraft		Casualties		Aircraft		Casualties		Casualties	
NO	YR	MO	DA	HR	BASE	TYPE	RDS	DES	DAM	KIA	WIA	DES	DAM	KIA	WIA	KIA	POW
1	2	3	4	5	6	7	8	9	10	11	12	13	14	15	16	17	18
167	69	02	25	0635	PK	STO	01	000	000	000	000	000	000	000	000	000	000
168	69	03	15	0117	PR	STO	34	000	000	000	002	000	000	000	000	000	000
169	69	03	15	0554	PR	STO	07	000	000	000	000	000	000	000	000	000	000
170	69	03	16	1904	PR	STO	05	000	000	000	001	000	000	000	000	000	000
171	69	03	19	0235	PR	STO	36	000	000	000	000	000	000	000	000	000	000
172	69	03	21	0055	CRB	STO	07	000	000	000	000	000	000	000	000	000	000
173	69	03	21	0154	DN	STO	05	000	000	000	000	000	000	000	000	000	000
174	69	03	21	0624	PK	STO	03	000	000	000	006	000	000	000	001	000	000
175	69	03	21	2254	PR	STO	25	000	000	000	000	000	000	000	000	000	000
176	69	03	24	0234	PR	STO	41	000	000	000	000	000	000	000	000	000	000
177	69	03	24	0530	DN	STO	14	000	000	000	001	000	000	000	000	000	000
178	69	03	27	2229	PK	STO	01	000	000	000	000	000	000	000	000	000	000
179	69	03	29	0220	BH	DTO	02	000	000	000	001	000	000	000	000	000	000
180	69	03	31	2347	BH	STO	02	000	000	000	000	000	000	000	000	000	000
181	69	04	13	0128	PR	STO	13	000	000	000	000	000	000	000	000	000	000
182	69	04	16	0227	PC	SAP		000	000	000	001	000	000	000	000	001	000

Attacks								US Losses				RVN Losses				VC/NVA Losses	
								Aircraft		Casualties		Aircraft		Casualties		Casualties	
NO	YR	MO	DA	HR	BASE	TYPE	RDS	DES	DAM	KIA	WIA	DES	DAM	KIA	WIA	KIA	POW
1	2	3	4	5	6	7	8	9	10	11	12	13	14	15	16	17	18
183	69	04	17	0016	DN	STO	02	000	000	000	000	000	000	001	004	000	000
184	69	04	20	2308	DN	STO	03	000	001	000	000	000	000	000	000	000	000
185	69	04	21	0531	NT	STO	06	000	004	000	000	000	000	000	000	000	000
186	69	04	21	2358	PR	STO	05	000	000	000	000	000	000	000	000	000	000
187	69	04	24	0114	DN	STO	02	000	000	000	000	000	000	000	000	000	000
188	69	04	25	0545	PK	STO	01	000	001	000	000	000	000	000	000	000	000
189	69	05	11	0015	BT	STO	11	000	000	000	000	000	000	000	000	000	000
190	69	05	11	0257	PK	STO	03	000	000	000	000	000	000	000	000	000	000
191	69	05	12	0047	PR	STO	30	000	001	000	001	000	000	000	000	000	000
192	69	05	12	0122	BH	STO	05	000	003	000	000	000	000	000	000	000	000
193	69	05	12	0345	DN	STO	03	000	001	000	000	000	000	000	000	000	000
194	69	05	12	0530	PR	STO	09	000	001	000	001	000	000	000	000	000	000
195	69	05	12	2315	TSN	STO	03	000	000	000	000	000	000	000	000	000	000
196	69	05	14	0153	DN	STO	01	000	000	000	000	000	000	002	002	000	000
197	69	05	16	0021	PR	STO	22	000	000	000	000	000	000	000	000	000	000
198	69	05	17	0250	DN	STO	02	000	004	001	001	000	000	000	000	000	000

Attacks								US Losses				RVN Losses				VC/NVA Losses	
								Aircraft		Casualties		Aircraft		Casualties		Casualties	
NO	YR	MO	DA	HR	BASE	TYPE	RDS	DES	DAM	KIA	WIA	DES	DAM	KIA	WIA	KIA	POW
1	2	3	4	5	6	7	8	9	10	11	12	13	14	15	16	17	18
199	69	05	21	2001	BH	STO	02	000	000	000	000	000	000	000	000	000	000
200	69	05	22	0003	PR	STO	18	000	000	000	000	000	000	000	000	000	000
201	69	05	22	2108	PR	STO	01	000	000	000	000	000	000	000	000	000	000
202	69	05	23	0138	BH	STO	03	000	000	000	003	000	000	000	000	000	000
203	69	05	28	2234	BH	STO	04	000	000	000	000	000	000	000	002	000	000
204	69	05	31	1417	NT	STO	10	000	000	000	003	000	000	000	001	000	000
205	69	06	05	2042	BH	STO	04	000	001	000	000	000	000	000	000	000	000
206	69	06	06	0143	BT	STO	11	000	000	000	000	000	000	000	000	000	000
207	69	06	06	0303	PR	STO	15	000	001	000	003	000	000	000	008	000	000
208	69	06	06	0306	BH	STO	36	000	002	001	002	000	000	000	000	000	000
209	69	06	07	0248	DN	STO	20	002	012	004	002	000	000	000	000	000	000
210	69	06	07	0613	PK	STO	01	000	000	000	000	000	000	000	000	000	000
211	69	06	07	1620	PR	STO	03	000	000	002	008	000	000	000	000	000	000
212	69	06	09	2121	BH	STO	03	000	000	001	000	000	000	000	000	000	000
213	69	06	11	0001	PR	STO	17	000	000	000	000	000	000	000	000	000	000
214	69	06	12	0709	PK	STO	01	000	000	000	000	000	000	000	000	000	000

Attacks								US Losses				RVN Losses				VC/NVA Losses	
								Aircraft		Casualties		Aircraft		Casualties		Casualties	
NO	YR	MO	DA	HR	BASE	TYPE	RDS	DES	DAM	KIA	WIA	DES	DAM	KIA	WIA	KIA	POW
1	2	3	4	5	6	7	8	9	10	11	12	13	14	15	16	17	18
215	69	06	12	2358	BH	STO	30	000	000	000	001	000	000	000	000	000	000
216	69	06	16	1952	BH	STO	04	000	001	000	000	000	000	000	000	000	000
217	69	06	17	2333	PC	STO	18	000	000	001	001	000	000	000	000	000	000
218	69	06	18	0050	BH	STO	09	000	000	000	006	000	000	000	000	000	000
219	69	06	18	2359	PR	STO	14	000	000	000	001	000	000	000	000	000	000
220	69	06	20	1924	PR	STO	04	000	001	000	000	000	000	000	000	000	000
221	69	06	20	2147	BH	STO	08	000	000	000	000	000	000	000	000	000	000
222	69	06	29	2210	TSN	STO	03	000	000	000	000	000	000	000	000	000	000
223	69	07	08	2351	CRB	STO	12	000	000	000	000	000	000	000	000	000	000
224	69	07	10	0701	BH	STO	04	000	000	000	000	000	000	000	000	000	000
225	69	07	10	2040	BT	STO	01	000	000	000	000	000	000	000	000	000	000
226	69	07	15	1543	PR	STO	03	000	000	000	000	000	000	000	000	000	000
227	69	07	19	2325	PR	STO	11	000	000	000	000	000	000	000	000	000	000
228	69	07	20	0614	BH	STO	29	000	000	000	000	000	000	000	000	000	000
229	69	07	20	0649	PR	STO	03	000	000	000	000	000	000	000	000	000	000
230	69	08	07	0056	CRB	STO	22	000	010	000	002	000	000	000	000	000	000

Attacks								US Losses				RVN Losses				VC/NVA Losses	
								Aircraft		Casualties		Aircraft		Casualties		Casualties	
NO	YR	MO	DA	HR	BASE	TYPE	RDS	DES	DAM	KIA	WIA	DES	DAM	KIA	WIA	KIA	POW
1	2	3	4	5	6	7	8	9	10	11	12	13	14	15	16	17	18
231	69	08	12	0200	BH	STO	08	000	000	000	000	000	000	000	000	000	000
232	69	08	13	0402	DN	STO	05	000	000	000	000	000	000	000	000	000	000
233	69	08	22	0135	DN	STO	10	000	000	001	029	000	000	000	000	000	000
234	69	09	02	0631	PK	STO	01	000	003	000	000	000	000	000	000	000	000
235	69	09	04	2347	PR	STO	18	000	003	000	011	000	000	000	000	000	000
236	69	09	05	0100	BH	STO	04	000	000	000	000	000	000	000	000	000	000
237	69	09	06	0257	CRB	STO	04	000	009	000	001	000	000	000	000	000	000
238	69	09	06	0300	DN	STO	08	000	000	000	003	000	000	000	000	000	000
239	69	09	06	0619	BH	STO	18	000	000	000	000	000	001	007	012	000	000
240	69	09	13	0007	PR	STO	05	000	000	000	000	000	000	000	000	000	000
241	69	09	20	1840	PR	STO	03	000	000	000	003	000	000	000	000	000	000
242	69	10	11	0550	NT	STO	10	000	000	000	000	000	002	000	000	000	000
243	69	10	12	0557	NT	STO	03	000	000	000	000	000	000	000	000	000	000
244	69	10	25	0944	PK	STO	03	000	000	000	000	000	000	000	000	000	000
245	69	11	04	0810	PR	STO	03	000	000	000	000	000	000	000	000	000	000
246	69	11	04	1208	PR	STO	02	000	000	000	000	000	000	000	000	000	000

Attacks								US Losses				RVN Losses				VC/NVA Losses	
								Aircraft		Casualties		Aircraft		Casualties		Casualties	
NO	YR	MO	DA	HR	BASE	TYPE	RDS	DES	DAM	KIA	WIA	DES	DAM	KIA	WIA	KIA	POW
1	2	3	4	5	6	7	8	9	10	11	12	13	14	15	16	17	18
247	69	11	09	1545	PR	STO	02	000	000	000	000	000	000	000	000	000	000
248	69	11	14	0159	CRB	STO	08	000	001	001	001	000	000	000	000	000	000
249	69	11	16	0604	PK	STO	01	000	000	000	000	000	000	000	000	000	000
250	69	11	16	0815	PR	STO	01	000	000	000	000	000	000	000	000	000	000
251	69	11	21	0915	PR	STO	01	000	000	000	000	000	000	000	000	000	000
252	'69	11	25	0523	BH	STO	03	000	000	000	000	000	000	000	000	000	000
253	69	12	03	0755	PR	STO	01	000	000	000	000	000	000	000	000	000	000
254	69	12	07	0430	CRB	STO	03	000	000	000	000	000	000	000	000	000	000
255	69	12	11	0038	DN	STO	04	000	001	000	000	000	000	000	000	000	000
256	69	12	12	0625	BH	STO	11	001	000	000	003	000	000	000	000	000	000
257	69	12	14	0940	PR	STO	03	000	000	000	000	000	000	000	000	000	000
258	69	12	19	0241	TSN	STO	04	000	000	000	005	000	000	000	000	000	000
108	1969 Sub-Total						1193	007	107	017	167	000	010	011	036	023	001
259	70	01	04	0100	PC	STO	03	000	005	000	000	000	000	000	000	000	000
260	70	01	04	0645	PC	STO	02	000	000	000	000	000	000	000	000	000	000
261	70	01	05	0635	PR	STO	03	000	000	000	000	000	000	000	000	000	000

Attacks								US Losses				RVN Losses				VC/NVA Losses	
								Aircraft		Casualties		Aircraft		Casualties		Casualties	
NO	YR	MO	DA	HR	BASE	TYPE	RDS	DES	DAM	KIA	WIA	DES	DAM	KIA	WIA	KIA	POW
1	2	3	4	5	6	7	8	9	10	11	12	13	14	15	16	17	18
262	70	01	06	1833	CRB	STO	02	000	000	000	000	000	000	000	000	000	000
263	70	01	07	0658	CRB	STO	02	000	000	000	000	000	000	000	000	000	000
264	70	01	09	1808	CRB	STO	01	000	000	000	001	000	000	000	000	000	000
265	70	01	13	1906	CRB	STO	02	000	000	000	000	000	000	000	000	000	000
266	70	01	20	1905	PR	STO	01	000	000	000	000	000	000	000	000	000	000
267	70	01	21	0456	BH	STO	08	000	003	000	000	000	000	000	000	000	000
268	70	01	25	1555	PR	STO	02	000	000	000	000	000	000	000	000	000	000
269	70	02	02	NR	CRB	STO	01	000	000	000	000	000	000	000	000	000	000
270	70	02	02	0647	PC	STO	10	000	000	001	019	000	000	000	000	000	000
271	70	02	04	0029	BH	STO	04	000	000	000	000	000	000	000	000	000	000
272	70	02	11	0005	PR	SAP		000	000	000	000	000	000	000	000	002	001
273	70	02	16	2350	PR	STO	08	000	000	000	000	000	000	000	000	000	000
274	70	02	21	2235	PR	STO	05	000	000	000	000	000	000	000	000	000	000
275	70	02	27	2359	BH	STO	06	000	006	000	004	000	000	000	000	000	000
276	70	03	04	1528	PR	STO	01	000	000	001	006	000	000	001	002	000	000
277	70	03	07	0252	CRB	STO	08	000	000	000	000	000	000	000	000	000	000

Attacks								US Losses				RVN Losses				VC/NVA Losses	
								Aircraft		Casualties		Aircraft		Casualties		Casualties	
NO	YR	MO	DA	HR	BASE	TYPE	RDS	DES	DAM	KIA	WIA	DES	DAM	KIA	WIA	KIA	POW
1	2	3	4	5	6	7	8	9	10	11	12	13	14	15	16	17	18
278	70	03	07	0629	CRB	STO	03	000	000	000	000	000	000	000	000	000	000
279	70	03	12	0318	CRB	STO	04	000	000	000	000	000	000	000	000	000	000
280	70	03	14	2125	PR	STO	07	000	000	000	000	000	000	000	000	000	000
281	70	04	01	0024	PR	STO	12	000	000	000	000	000	000	000	000	000	000
282	70	04	01	0620	BH	STO	05	000	001	000	000	000	000	000	000	000	000
283	70	04	01	0935	PR	STO	02	000	000	000	000	000	000	000	000	000	000
284	70	04	04	0005	BH	STO	02	000	000	000	000	000	000	000	000	000	000
285	70	04	04	0500	PC	SAP		000	000	000	000	000	000	000	000	001	000
286	70	04	05	1513	PR	STO	01	000	000	000	000	000	000	000	000	000	000
287	70	04	06	1621	NT	STO	11	000	000	000	002	000	000	001	004	000	000
288	70	04	07	2325	PR	STO	06	000	000	000	000	000	000	000	000	000	000
289	70	04	08	0225	DN	STO	04	000	000	002	008	000	000	000	000	000	000
290	70	04	08	0227	CRB	STO	04	000	000	000	000	000	000	000	000	000	000
291	70	04	09	1021	PR	STO	01	000	000	000	000	000	000	000	000	000	000
292	70	04	19	1023	CRB	STO	03	000	000	000	000	000	000	000	000	000	000
293	70	04	20	0657	PR	STO	01	000	000	000	001	000	000	000	000	000	000

Attacks								US Losses				RVN Losses				VC/NVA Losses	
								Aircraft		Casualties		Aircraft		Casualties		Casualties	
NO	YR	MO	DA	HR	BASE	TYPE	RDS	DES	DAM	KIA	WIA	DES	DAM	KIA	WIA	KIA	POW
1	2	3	4	5	6	7	8	9	10	11	12	13	14	15	16	17	18
294	70	05	03	0045	PR	S&S	12	000	000	000	001	000	000	000	000	000	000
295	70	05	03	0140	BH	STO	06	000	000	000	000	000	000	000	000	000	000
296	70	05	03	0609	BH	STO	04	001	000	000	005	000	000	000	000	000	000
297	70	05	03	1806	BH	STO	07	000	000	000	023	000	000	000	000	000	000
298	70	05	04	0605	BH	STO	03	000	000	000	000	000	000	000	000	000	000
299	70	05	06	2105	PR	STO	06	000	000	000	000	000	000	000	000	000	000
300	70	05	07	0943	PK	STO	05	000	000	000	000	000	000	000	000	000	000
301	70	05	07	1104	PR	STO	01	000	000	000	000	000	000	000	000	000	000
302	70	05	08	0044	TH	STO	32	000	000	000	000	000	000	000	000	000	000
303	70	05	08	0258	CRB	STO	26	000	000	000	000	000	000	000	000	000	000
304	70	05	08	0535	PC	STO	04	000	000	000	000	000	000	000	000	000	000
305	70	05	12	0255	CRB	STO	03	000	000	000	000	000	000	000	000	000	000
306	70	05	15	2055	PK	STO	04	000	000	000	000	000	000	000	000	000	000
307	70	05	16	2130	PR	STO	12	000	000	000	000	000	000	000	000	000	000
308	70	05	19	0833	CRB	STO	05	000	000	000	000	000	000	000	000	000	000
309	70	05	19	1907	PK	STO	04	001	002	000	000	000	000	000	000	000	000

Attacks								US Losses				RVN Losses				VC/NVA Losses	
								Aircraft		Casualties		Aircraft		Casualties		Casualties	
NO	YR	MO	DA	HR	BASE	TYPE	RDS	DES	DAM	KIA	WIA	DES	DAM	KIA	WIA	KIA	POW
1	2	3	4	5	6	7	8	9	10	11	12	13	14	15	16	17	18
310	70	05	21	0546	PC	STO	06	000	003	000	002	000	000	000	000	000	000
311	70	05	21	2355	DN	STO	03	000	003	000	000	000	000	000	000	000	000
312	70	05	26	0230	PK	STO	04	000	002	000	001	000	000	000	000	000	000
313	70	05	30	0749	PR	STO	01	000	000	000	000	000	000	000	000	000	000
314	70	06	04	0529	PC	STO	05	000	000	000	000	000	000	000	000	000	000
315	70	06	04	0735	CRB	STO	04	000	000	000	000	000	000	000	000	000	000
316	70	06	04	1818	NT	STO	02	000	000	000	000	000	000	000	000	000	000
317	70	06	04	2348	NT	STO	03	000	000	000	000	000	000	000	000	000	000
318	70	06	06	1004	PR	STO	02	000	000	000	000	000	000	000	000	000	000
319	70	06	06	1745	CRB	STO	04	000	000	000	000	000	000	000	000	000	000
320	70	06	07	1818	NT	STO	02	000	000	000	000	000	000	000	000	000	000
321	70	06	07	2208	NT	STO	03	000	000	000	000	000	000	000	000	000	000
322	70	06	07	2348	BT	STO	06	000	000	000	000	000	000	000	000	000	000
323	70	06	10	1003	PR	STO	01	000	000	000	000	000	000	000	000	000	000
324	70	06	10	1500	CRB	STO	02	000	000	000	000	000	000	000	000	000	000
325	70	06	11	0653	BH	STO	02	000	000	000	000	000	000	000	000	000	000

Attacks								US Losses				RVN Losses				VC/NVA Losses	
								Aircraft		Casualties		Aircraft		Casualties		Casualties	
NO	YR	MO	DA	HR	BASE	TYPE	RDS	DES	DAM	KIA	WIA	DES	DAM	KIA	WIA	KIA	POW
1	2	3	4	5	6	7	8	9	10	11	12	13	14	15	16	17	18
326	70	06	12	0100	CRB	SAP		000	001	000	001	000	000	000	000	002	001
327	70	06	21	0101	DN	STO	03	000	000	000	000	000	000	000	000	000	000
328	70	06	25	1104	BH	STO	01	000	000	000	000	000	000	000	000	000	000
329	70	07	02	1020	PR	STO	02	000	000	000	000	000	000	000	000	000	000
330	70	07	04	0143	TH	STO	20	000	000	000	000	000	000	000	000	000	000
331	70	07	07	0043	BT	STO	02	000	001	000	000	000	000	000	000	000	000
332	70	07	09	0055	CRB	S&S	06	000	000	000	001	000	000	000	000	000	000
333	70	07	09	0916	PR	STO	02	000	000	000	000	000	000	000	000	000	000
334	70	07	21	0235	BT	STO	01	000	000	000	000	000	000	000	000	000	000
335	70	07	21	0747	PR	STO	01	000	000	001	000	000	000	000	000	000	000
336	70	08	01	0240	BT	STO	04	000	000	000	000	000	000	000	000	000	000
337	70	08	05	1941	PR	STO	01	000	000	000	000	000	000	000	000	000	000
338	70	08	07	1758	CRB	STO	03	000	000	000	000	000	000	000	000	000	000
339	70	08	12	0620	CRB	STO	03	000	000	000	000	000	000	000	000	000	000
340	70	08	22	0929	PR	STO	01	000	000	000	000	000	000	000	000	000	000

Attacks								US Losses				RVN Losses				VC/NVA Losses	
								Aircraft		Casualties		Aircraft		Casualties		Casualties	
NO	YR	MO	DA	HR	BASE	TYPE	RDS	DES	DAM	KIA	WIA	DES	DAM	KIA	WIA	KIA	POW
1	2	3	4	5	6	7	8	9	10	11	12	13	14	15	16	17	18
341	70	08	30	0219	CRB	S&S*	07	000	000	000	003	000	000	000	000	000	000
342	70	08	30	0448	PC	STO	06	000	000	000	000	000	000	000	000	000	000
343	70	08	30	0650	NT	STO	03	000	000	000	000	000	000	000	006	000	000
344	70	08	31	1434	PR	STO	01	000	000	000	001	000	000	000	000	000	000
345	70	09	01	0449	DN	STO	08	000	001	000	002	000	000	000	000	000	000
346	70	09	04	2347	PK	STO	02	000	000	000	000	000	000	000	000	000	000
347	70	09	16	0020	BT	STO	03	000	000	000	000	000	000	000	000	000	000
348	70	10	04	1019	PR	STO	02	000	000	000	000	000	000	000	000	000	000
349	70	10	05	0312	PC	STO	02	000	000	000	000	000	000	000	000	000	000
350	70	10	12	0030	DN	STO	02	000	000	000	000	000	000	000	000	000	000
351	70	10	21	0145	DN	STO	01	000	000	000	000	000	000	000	000	000	000
352	70	11	08	1014	PR	STO	01	000	000	000	001	000	000	000	000	000	000
353	70	11	17	0518	BH	STO	28	000	000	003	023	000	000	002	011	000	000

*Resulted in destruction of 460,000 gallons of aviation fuel and of fuel storage tanks with a combined capacity of over 2.25 million gallons.

Attacks								US Losses				RVN Losses				VC/NVA Losses	
								Aircraft		Casualties		Aircraft		Casualties		Casualties	
NO	YR	MO	DA	HR	BASE	TYPE	RDS	DES	DAM	KIA	WIA	DES	DAM	KIA	WIA	KIA	POW
1	2	3	4	5	6	7	8	9	10	11	12	13	14	15	16	17	18
354	70	11	21	2338	PK	STO	05	000	000	000	000	000	000	000	000	000	000
355	70	11	23	0703	PK	STO	03	000	000	000	000	000	000	000	000	000	000
356	70	11	24	2340	PK	STO	17	000	000	000	000	000	000	000	000	000	000
357	70	11	25	0112	PK	STO	01	000	000	000	000	000	000	000	000	000	000
358	70	11	29	1058	PR	STO	02	000	000	000	001	000	000	000	000	000	000
359	70	12	01	1928	CRB	STO	03	000	000	002	008	000	000	001	000	000	000
360	70	12	02	0515	PC	STO	03	000	000	000	005	000	000	000	000	000	000
361	70	12	06	0544	CRB	STO	04	000	000	000	000	000	000	000	000	000	000
362	70	12	16	2018	BH	STO	01	000	000	000	000	000	000	000	000	000	000
363	70	12	21	0100	DN	STO	01	000	000	000	000	000	000	000	000	000	000
364	70	12	29	0604	PK	STO	02	000	000	000	000	000	000	000	000	000	000
106	1970 Sub-Total						477	002	028	010	119	000	000	005	023	005	002
365	71	01	22	0458	BH	STO	01	000	000	000	000	000	000	000	000	000	000
366	71	02	01	0352	DN	STO	08	000	002	000	003	000	000	000	000	000	000
367	71	02	01	0508	NT	STO	NR	000	000	000	000	000	000	000	000	000	000
368	71	02	01	0610	PC	STO	06	000	000	000	001	000	000	000	000	000	000

Attacks								US Losses				RVN Losses				VC/NVA Losses	
								Aircraft		Casualties		Aircraft		Casualties		Casualties	
NO	YR	MO	DA	HR	BASE	TYPE	RDS	DES	DAM	KIA	WIA	DES	DAM	KIA	WIA	KIA	POW
1	2	3	4	5	6	7	8	9	10	11	12	13	14	15	16	17	18
369	71	02	01	0858	NT	STO	NR	000	000	000	000	000	000	000	000	000	000
370	71	02	21	0130	DN	STO	06	001	003	000	001	000	000	000	000	000	000
371	71	02	21	0449	PC	STO	04	000	003	000	000	000	000	000	000	000	000
372	71	02	22	1740	PC	STO	04	000	000	000	002	000	000	000	000	000	000
373	71	02	24	1758	PC	STO	02	000	000	000	000	000	000	000	000	000	000
374	71	02	24	2328	CRB	SAP		000	000	000	000	000	000	000	000	002	000
375	71	02	25	1335	NT	STO	02	000	000	000	000	000	000	000	000	000	000
376	71	02	25	1836	NT	STO	02	000	002	000	000	000	000	000	000	000	000
377	71	02	28	0058	PK	SAP		000	000	000	004	000	000	000	003	000	000
378	71	02	28	0150	CRB	STO	06	000	000	000	000	000	000	000	000	000	000
379	71	03	04	0433	DN	STO	10	000	000	000	002	000	000	000	000	000	000
380	71	03	16	0610	BH	STO	05	000	000	000	000	000	000	000	002	000	000
381	71	03	19	1925	CRB	STO	03	000	000	000	000	000	000	000	000	000	000
382	71	03	20	0031	CRB	STO	05	000	001	000	000	000	000	000	000	000	000
383	71	03	29	0157	DN	STO	02	000	002	000	001	000	000	000	000	000	000
384	71	03	29	0459	DN	STO	02	000	000	000	000	000	000	000	000	000	000

Attacks								US Losses				RVN Losses				VC/NVA Losses	
								Aircraft		Casualties		Aircraft		Casualties		Casualties	
NO	YR	MO	DA	HR	BASE	TYPE	RDS	DES	DAM	KIA	WIA	DES	DAM	KIA	WIA	KIA	POW
1	2	3	4	5	6	7	8	9	10	11	12	13	14	15	16	17	18
385	71	03	31	0245	PK	S&S	12	000	013	000	000	000	002	000	004	000	000
386	71	04	04	0612	PK	STO	03	000	000	000	000	000	000	000	000	000	000
387	71	04	05	0202	DN	STO	03	000	001	000	000	000	000	000	000	000	000
388	71	04	09	0054	DN	STO	01	000	000	000	000	000	000	000	000	000	000
389	71	04	16	2120	CRB	STO	03	000	000	000	000	000	000	000	000	000	000
390	71	04	25	2335	CRB	STO	03	000	000	000	000	000	000	000	000	000	000
391	71	04	26	0300	DN	STO	01	000	000	000	000	000	000	000	000	000	000
392	71	04	27	0207	DN	STO	05	000	000	000	000	000	000	000	000	000	000
393	71	04	27	0535	BT	STO	01	000	000	000	000	000	000	000	001	000	000
394	71	05	01	0009	BT	STO	03	000	000	000	000	000	000	000	000	000	000
395	71	05	05	0358	DN	STO	02	000	001	000	000	000	000	000	000	000	000
396	71	05	06	0539	PK	STO	03	000	000	000	000	000	000	000	000	000	000
397	71	05	13	0006	BT	STO	03	000	000	000	000	000	000	000	000	000	000
398	71	05	23	2115	CRB	SAP		000	000	000	001	000	000	000	000	000	000
399	71	05	30	0320	DN	STO	07	000	000	000	000	000	000	000	000	000	000
400	71	06	05	1702	DN	STO	06	000	000	000	000	000	000	006	011	000	000

Attacks								US Losses				RVN Losses				VC/NVA Losses	
								Aircraft		Casualties		Aircraft		Casualties		Casualties	
NO	YR	MO	DA	HR	BASE	TYPE	RDS	DES	DAM	KIA	WIA	DES	DAM	KIA	WIA	KIA	POW
1	2	3	4	5	6	7	8	9	10	11	12	13	14	15	16	17	18
401	71	06	07	0009	DN	STO	02	000	000	000	000	000	000	000	000	000	000
402	71	06	11	0019	CRB	STO	03	000	000	000	000	000	000	000	000	000	000
403	71	07	05	0015	DN	STO	05	000	000	005	038	000	000	000	000	000	000
404	71	07	27	2325	PR	STO	07	000	000	000	000	000	000	000	000	000	000
405	71	08	16	2319	BH	STO	02	000	000	000	000	000	000	000	000	000	000
406	71	08	25	0135	DN	STO	02	000	000	000	000	000	000	000	000	000	000
407	71	08	25	0226	CRB	S&S*	05	000	000	000	006	000	000	000	000	000	000
408	71	08	28	2347	TSN	STO	03	000	000	000	000	000	000	000	000	000	000
409	71	08	29	1920	PK	STO	06	000	000	000	001	000	000	000	000	000	000
410	71	09	13	2320	CRB	SAP		000	000	000	000	000	000	000	000	000	001
411	71	09	21	0755	PK	STO	02	000	000	000	000	000	000	000	000	000	000
412	71	09	25	0443	BH	STO	03	000	000	000	000	000	000	000	000	000	000
413	71	09	25	0854	PR	STO	03	000	000	000	000	000	000	000	000	000	000
414	71	09	29	0658	BH	STO	01	000	000	000	000	000	000	000	000	000	000
415	71	10	02	2400	DN	STO	04	000	000	000	000	000	000	000	000	000	000

*Resulted in destruction of 6,000 tons of munitions valued in excess of $10.3 million.

Attacks								US Losses				RVN Losses				VC/NVA Losses	
								Aircraft		Casualties		Aircraft		Casualties		Casualties	
NO	YR	MO	DA	HR	BASE	TYPE	RDS	DES	DAM	KIA	WIA	DES	DAM	KIA	WIA	KIA	POW
1	2	3	4	5	6	7	8	9	10	11	12	13	14	15	16	17	18
416	71	10	03	0345	BH	STO	03	000	000	000	000	000	000	002	006	000	000
417	71	11	09	1308	PR	STO	02	000	000	000	000	000	000	000	000	000	000
418	71	11	15	0001	CRB	STO	04	000	000	000	000	000	000	000	000	000	000
419	71	11	25	0248	BH	STO	03	000	000	000	000	000	000	000	000	000	000
055	1971 Sub-Total						184	001	028	005	060	000	002	008	027	002	001
420	72	01	03	0155	DN	STO	06	000	002	000	001	000	000	000	000	000	000
421	72	01	12	0157	BH	SAP*		000	000	000	000	000	000	000	000	001	000
422	72	01	16	0432	CRB	STO	04	000	000	000	000	000	000	000	000	000	000
423	72	02	05	0758	PR	STO	01	000	000	000	000	000	000	000	000	000	000
424	72	02	09	0100	DN	STO	28	000	001	000	010	000	000	001	000	000	000
425	72	02	21	0310	BH	STO	05	000	000	000	002	000	000	000	000	000	000
426	72	02	21	0825	PR	STO	02	000	000	000	000	000	000	000	000	000	000
427	72	03	06	0453	CRB	STO	03	000	001	000	003	000	000	000	000	000	000

*Resulted in destruction of munitions valued at $400,000.

Attacks								US Losses				RVN Losses				VC/NVA Losses	
								Aircraft		Casualties		Aircraft		Casualties		Casualties	
NO	YR	MO	DA	HR	BASE	TYPE	RDS	DES	DAM	KIA	WIA	DES	DAM	KIA	WIA	KIA	POW
1	2	3	4	5	6	7	8	9	10	11	12	13	14	15	16	17	18
428	72	04	07	0108	BH	STO	04	000	000	000	000	000	000	000	000	000	000
429	72	04	13	0004	CRB	STO	07	000	000	000	000	000	000	000	000	000	000
430	72	04	13	0132	DN	STO	24	001	005	001	010	000	004	000	000	000	000
431	72	04	14	2055	TSN	STO	04	000	000	000	000	000	000	000	000	000	000
432	72	04	16	0116	DN	STO	20	000	001	000	008	000	000	000	000	000	000
433	72	04	24	0149	DN	STO	13	000	000	000	009	000	000	000	000	000	000
434	72	04	25	2300	DN	STO	06	000	000	000	000	000	000	000	002	000	000
435	72	05	07	0318	DN	STO	16	001	002	000	003	000	000	000	008	000	000
436	72	05	12	0157	DN	STO	18	000	003	000	000	000	000	005	019	000	000
437	72	05	14	0149	DN	STO	18	000	002	000	000	000	000	005	019	000	000
438	72	05	23	2221	BH	STO	04	000	000	000	000	000	000	002	005	000	000
439	72	06	10	0224	DN	STO	08	000	002	000	003	000	000	000	000	000	000
440	72	06	13	2321	DN	STO	06	000	000	000	012	000	000	000	001	000	000
441	72	06	17	0045	DN	STO	04	000	000	000	001	000	000	000	000	000	000
442	72	06	22	0115	DN	STO	06	000	000	000	001	000	000	000	000	000	000
443	72	07	08	0145	DN	STO	12	000	001	001	000	000	000	000	000	000	000
444	72	07	13	0345	DN	STO	16	000	000	000	001	000	000	001	000	000	000

Attacks								US Losses				RVN Losses				VC/NVA Losses	
								Aircraft		Casualties		Aircraft		Casualties		Casualties	
NO	YR	MO	DA	HR	BASE	TYPE	RDS	DES	DAM	KIA	WIA	DES	DAM	KIA	WIA	KIA	POW
1	2	3	4	5	6	7	8	9	10	11	12	13	14	15	16	17	18
445	72	08	01	0515	BH	STO	86	000	004	001	037	000	002	006	NR	000	000
446	72	08	03	0626	DN	STO	45	000	004	001	020	000	000	000	000	000	000
447	72	08	18	0408	DN	STO		(Losses are included with those cited for Attack No. 446)									
448	72	08	18	0637	DN	STO	35	002	010	001	021	000	000	000	000	000	000
449	72	08	19	0415	DN	STO	02	000	000	000	000	000	000	000	000	000	000
450	72	08	31	0600	BH	STO	64	001	010	000	001	000	001	003	009	000	000
451	72	09	10	0952	BH	STO*	01	000	001	000	050	003	094	003	023	000	000
452	72	09	10	1745	TSN	STO	03	000	000	000	000	000	000	000	000	000	000
453	72	09	23	0500	DN	STO	27	000	003	000	000	000	000	000	000	000	000
454	72	09	27	1845	DN	STO	05	000	003	000	001	000	000	000	000	000	000
455	72	10	22	0505	BH	STO	56	000	007	000	003	000	000	002	014	000	000
456	72	10	25	0307	DN	STO	18	000	000	000	004	000	000	001	000	000	000
457	72	10	28	0302	DN	STO	27	000	008	000	003	000	000	000	000	000	000

*All, but very limited, material evidence indicated that this was a standoff attack which detonated munitions in the VNAF holding area. There was, however, a distinct possibility that these munitions were detonated by sabotage or by disregard for safety procedures.

Attacks								US Losses				RVN Losses				VC/NVA Losses	
								Aircraft		Casualties		Aircraft		Casualties		Casualties	
NO	YR	MO	DA	HR	BASE	TYPE	RDS	DES	DAM	KIA	WIA	DES	DAM	KIA	WIA	KIA	POW
1	2	3	4	5	6	7	8	9	10	11	12	13	14	15	16	17	18
458	72	11	12	0300	BH	STO		(Losses are included with those cited for Attack No. 457)									
459	72	11	12	0515	BH	STO	21	001	003	000	008	000	000	000	010	000	000
460	72	11	19	0120	DN	STO	09	000	002	000	000	000	000	000	000	000	000
461	72	11	21	0111	DN	STO	04	000	000	000	000	000	000	000	000	000	000
462	72	12	01	0500	BH	STO	28	000	000	000	000	000	014	001	009	000	000
463	72	12	04	0420	BH	STO	07	000	003	000	000	000	000	000	000	000	000
464	72	12	06	0743	TSN	STO	28	000	002	001	002	000	000	010	033	000	000
465	72	12	15	0405	BH	STO	12	000	000	000	000	000	000	000	000	000	000
466	72	12	16	0115	BH	STO	06	000	000	000	000	000	000	000	000	000	000
467	72	12	16	0915	BH	STO	03	000	000	000	000	000	000	000	000	000	000
468	72	12	26	0612	DN	STO	32	000	008	000	001	000	000	000	000	000	000
049	1972 Sub-Total						754	006	088	006	215	003	115	040	152	001	000
469	73	01	14	2307	DN	STO	07	000	004	000	001	000	000	000	000	000	000
470	73	01	17	0327	DN	STO	21	000	003	000	000	000	000	000	001	000	000
471	73	01	22	0200	BH	STO	10	000	001	000	000	000	000	000	000	000	000

Attacks								US Losses				RVN Losses				VC/NVA Losses	
								Aircraft		Casualties		Aircraft		Casualties		Casualties	
NO	YR	MO	DA	HR	BASE	TYPE	RDS	DES	DAM	KIA	WIA	DES	DAM	KIA	WIA	KIA	POW
1	2	3	4	5	6	7	8	9	10	11	12	13	14	15	16	17	18
472	73	01	26	0225	BH	STO	26	000	001	001	007	001	000	000	003	000	000
473	73	01	26	1123	DN	STO	12	000	000	000	001	000	000	000	000	000	000
474	73	01	27	0612	DN	STO	25	000	007	001	008	002	011	000	000	000	000
475	73	01	28	0628	TSN	STO	11	000	000	000	000	000	000	002	004	000	000
	(73	01	28	0800	Commencement of Cease-Fire IAW Vietnam Agreement signed at Paris 27 January 1973)												
007	1973 Sub-Total						112	000	016	002	017	003	011	002	008	000	000
475	Grand Total						6163	075	898	155	1702	025	305	154	504	385	045

Mass grave of VC/NVA soldiers who attempted to overrun Tan Son Nhut Air Base during Tet 1968. The inscription reads: ***This is the resting place of those soldiers lost on the night of the first day of Tet 1968. Their spirits beg all countrymen to wholeheartedly work so that peace will come quickly to our beloved Vietnam.***

APPENDIX 2

Summary of Attacks

YEAR	TOTAL	STO	SAP	S&S	AWP	SAB	MBN	ROUNDS
1964	001	001	000	000	000	000	000	0070
1965	003	002	000	001	000	000	000	0110
1966	008	006	001	001	000	000	000	0449
1967	017	014	001	000	001	001	000	0670
1968	121	116	003	000	000	000	002	2153
1969	108	104	003	001	000	000	000	1184
1970	106	100	003	003	000	000	000	0477
1971	055	049	004	002	000	000	000	0184
1972	049	048	001	000	000	000	000	0754
1973	007	007	000	000	000	000	000	0112
TOTAL	475	447	016	008	001	001	002	6163

APPENDIX 3

Summary of Losses

	US Losses				RVN Losses				VC/NVA Losses	
	Aircraft		Casualties		Aircraft		Casualties		Casualties	
	DES	DAM	KIA	WIA	DES	DAM	KIA	WIA	KIA	POW
	9	10	11	12	13	14	15	16	17	18
1964	005	015	004	030	002	003	000	000	000	000
1965	006	014	001	027	000	000	000	005	000	001
1966	004	098	012	173	002	036	012	051	028	004
1967	016	139	028	384	002	001	035	050	003	000
1968	028	365	070	510	013	127	041	152	323	036
1969	007	107	017	167	000	010	011	036	023	001
1970	002	028	010	119	000	000	005	023	005	002
1971	001	028	005	060	000	002	008	027	002	001
1972	006	088	006	215	003	115	040	152	001	000
1973	000	016	002	017	003	011	002	008	000	000
TOTAL	075	898	155	1702	025	305	154	504	385	045

Enemy 61-mm mortar and ammunition captured during fighting near Da Nang

APPENDIX 4

Viet Cong/North Vietnamese Army Weapons Employed in Operations Against Air Bases *

VC 7.62-mm Submachine Gun.

Description: This weapon, used extensively by the VC, was a modification of the French 9-mm MAT-49 submachine gun in which the 9-mm barrel was replaced by the 7.62-mm barrel used on the Soviet PPSh-41 or the Chicom K-50 submachine gun and the magazine altered to accept the 7.62-mm cartridge.

Characteristics: Bore, 76-mm; Ammunition, Soviet pistol cartridge Type P; Operation, blowback, automatic only; Overall length, .76 m; Weight loaded, 4.2 kg; Magazine capacity, 32 rounds; Rate of fire, 100 rpm; Muzzle velocity, 500 ms; Effective range, 150 m.

Chicom 11-mm Submachine Gun Type 36.

Description: This weapon was almost identical to the U.S. .45-cal submachine gun M3A1, and would fire the U.S. .45-cal pistol cartridge.

Characteristics: Bore, 11-mm; Ammunition, 11-mm or U.S. .45-cal cartridge; Operation, blowback, automatic only; Overall length, .75 m; Weight loaded, 4 kg; Magazine capacity, 30 rounds; Rate of fire, 100 rpm; Muzzle velocity, 280 ms; Effective range, 200 m.

Soviet 7.62-mm Carbine Model 1944, Chicom Type 53.

Description: This Mosin-Nagant carbine was a standard weapon in the Soviet ground forces. It was copied and widely used by Chicom forces. A bayonet attached to the weapon was hinged so that it might be folded to the rear. This weapon was widely used by both VC and NVA forces.

Characteristics: Bore, 7.62-mm; Ammunition, Soviet M1908 rimmed cartridge; Operation, bolt action; Overall length, 1.01 m; Weight loaded, 3.9 kg; Magazine capacity, 5 rounds; Muzzle velocity, 822 ms; Effective range, 400 m; Maximum range, 3,200 m.

Soviet 7.62-mm Assault Rifle, Model AK-47, Chicom Type 56.

Description: This was the standard infantry weapon of the USSR and most other Communist Bloc countries. The stock might be a wooden one or a folding metal variety. It was the weapon most commonly used by the VC.

Characteristics: Bore, 7.62-mm; Ammunition, Soviet M1943 rimless cartridge; Operation, gas, full or semiautomatic; Overall length, .86 m; Weight loaded, 4.3 kg; Magazine capacity, curved box, 30 rounds; Rate of fire, 100 rpm; Muzzle velocity, 710 ms; Effective range, 300 m; Maximum range, 2,500 m.

---

* USMACV Combat Experiences Lessons Learned 71, Countermeasures Against Standoff Attacks, 13 Mar 69; AFSC/FTD Report on Character of Attacks on Air Bases in SEA (FTD-CR-27-01-68, 2 Feb 68); USA/TECOM Report on Research Test of Armor, Bunker Protection Against RPG-2 and RPG-7 (Proj 1-6-8765-13, Apr 1968).

Soviet 7.62-mm Carbine, Model SKS, Chicom Type 56.

Description: This was the first Soviet carbine or rifle chambered for the 7.62-mm rimless cartridge. Widely used by Soviet forces and those of satellite countries, it had been duplicated by the Chicoms as Type 56. variously described as a rifle or a carbine, the SKS by U.S. Army standards was a rifle. It was easily identified by the attached bayonet which folded underneath the barrel when not in use, and by the triangular portion of the magazine which protruded through the underside of the stack. It was widely used by the VC/NVA.

Characteristics: Bore, 7.62-mm; Ammunition, Soviet M1943 rimless cartridge; Operation, gas, semiautomatic; Overall length, 1.02 m; Weight loaded, 4 kg; Magazine capacity, 10 rounds; Muzzle velocity, 725 ms; Effective range, 400 m; Maximum range, 2,500 m.

Soviet 7.62-mm Light Machine Gun Model DPM, Chicom Type 53.

Description: This weapon was the 7.62-mm Degtyarev Light Machine Gun Model DP, modified by the addition of a wooden pistol grip and the redesign of the recoil spring. The DPM had three sizes of gas ports which permitted adjustment of the cyclic rate of fire.

Characteristics: Bore, 7.62-mm; Ammunition, Soviet M1908 or M1930 rimmed rifle cartridge; Operation, gas, full automatic only; Overall length, 1.27 m; Weight loaded, 12.24 kg; Magazine capacity, 47 rounds; Cyclic rate of fire, 500-600 rpm; Practical rate of fire, 150 rpm; Muzzle velocity, 841 ms; Effective range, 800 m; Maximum range, 3,150 m.

VC .50-cal Antiaircraft Machine Gun.

Description: This was a standard U.S. .50-cal machine gun, modified by the addition of antiaircraft ring sights and shoulder harness. It was mounted on a Soviet 12.7-mm DSHK heavy machine gun mount which might be used for either ground or antiaircraft fire.

Characteristics: Bore, 12.7-mm (.50-cal); Ammunition, U.S. .50-cal cartridges; Operation, recoil, automatic only; Overall length, 1.44 m; Weight with mount, 38 kg; Feed drive, capacity 250 rounds (metallic belt link); Cyclic rate of fire, 800 rpm; Practical rate of fire, 250 rpm; Muzzle velocity 870 ms; Effective range, 200 m for ground targets and 1,200 m for aerial targets.

Recoilless Rifles

Chicom 57-mm Recoilless Rifle, Type 36.

Description: This weapon was a copy of the U.S. recoilless rifle, T15E16, and differed from the original only in minor aspects. Identifying features were the long, cylindrical monopod below the telescopic sight, the two protruding handles at the breech end, and the peculiarly shaped tripod.

Characteristics: Bore, 57-mm; Ammunition, HE weighing 2.5 kg and HEAT weighing 2.6 kg; Operation, recoilless; Overall length, 1.57 m; Weight with tripod, 23.8 kg; Rate of fire, 5 rpm; Muzzle velocity, 341 ms; Maximum range, 4,375 m.

Chicom 75-mm Recoilless Riflle, Type 52 and 56.

Description: This was a breech-loading, portable weapon, designed to be fired from a machine gun tripod. The barrel and breech were copied from the U.S. 75-mm Recoilless Rifle, M-20.

Characteristics: Bore, 75-mm; Ammunition, HE weighing 10 kg and HEAT weighing 9.5 kg; Operation, recoilless; Overall length, 2.08 m; Weight with mount, 85.2 kg; Rate of fire, 10 rpm; Muzzle velocity, 305 ms; Maximum range, 6,675 m.

Mortars

Chicom 60-mm Mortar, Type 31 (M1942).

Description: This was a copy of the U.S. 60-mm Mortar, M2. It was a muzzle-loaded, drop-fired, smoothbore weapon. Differences between the original and the copy were minimal—the Chicom had more brass parts, its tube was 1 inch shorter, and there was no crank on the traversing handwheel. Otherwise, the reproduction was so faithfully executed that nearly all remaining parts were interchangeable.

Characteristics: Bore, 60-mm; Ammunition HE weighing 1.5 kg; Overall length of tube, .675 m; Weight in firing position, 20.2 kg; Rate of fire, 15-20 rpm; Muzzle velocity, 157 ms; Maximum range, 1,530 m.

Chicom 82-mm Mortar, Type 53.

Description: This was a copy of the conventional, muzzle-loaded, drop-fired, smoothbore Soviet 82-mm Mortar, M1937. It could be disassembled into three 1-man loads for transport. United States, German, Japanese, French, and Italian 81-mm mortar ammunition could be fired from this weapon.

Characteristics: Bore, 82-mm; Ammunition, HE weighing 3.3 kg and Smoke weighing 3.7 kg; Overall length of tube, 1.32 m; Weight in firing position, 55.9 kg; Rate of fire, 25 rpm; Muzzle velocity, 210 ms; Maximum range, 3,040 m.

Chicom 120-mm Mortar, Type 55.

Description: This was a copy of the conventional, muzzle-loaded, drop-fired, smoothbore, Soviet 120-mm Mortar, M1943. Accurate, light, mobile, with relatively long range, this weapon was a standard item in virtually all Communist Bloc forces. A trailer was available for towing the complete assembly. However, the weapon could be disassembled into three component parts for movement over very short distances by crewmembers.

Characteristics: Bore, 120-mm; Ammunition, HE weighing 15.4 kg, Smoke weighing 16 kg, and Incendiary weighing 16.7 kg; Overall length of tube, 1.67 m; Weight in firing position, 275.5 kg; Rate of fire, 15 rpm; Muzzle velocity, 272 ms; Maximum range, 5,700 m.

Artillery

U.S. 75-mm Pack Howitzer, M-116.

Description: This was a general-purpose light artillery weapon used for either direct or indirect fire. It could be disassembled into nine separate components for transportation.

Characteristics: Bore, 75-mm; Tube length, 1.2 m; Weight, 571 kg; Rate of fire, 3-6 rpm; Muzzle velocity, 380 ms; Maximum range, 8,800 m.

Grenades/Grenade Launchers

Hand Grenades.

Viet Cong hand grenades are not described individually because of their lack of standardization. They were manufactured in relatively small munitions plants and varied considerably in their technical characteristics, reliability, and performance—features which necessitated great care in handling. Hand grenades were widely used in sapper raids and terrorist activities.

Soviet Antitank Grenade Launcher, Model RPG-2 (VC designation, B-40).

Description: The RPG-2 launcher, a smoothbore, antitank weapon was essentially a recoilless grenade launcher and a direct outgrowth of a reloadable, German *Panzerfausts* developed late in World War II. The weapon was muzzle-loaded and the warhead of the fin-stabilized HEAT projectile (PG-2), being twice the diameter of the launcher tube, projected beyond it. A 2-piece, plywood guard covered the midsection of the tube to protect the gunner from heat. A 3-foot sandbag barrier plus a standoff screen (e.g., 9-gauge chain link fence) would normally protect against the PG-2 projectile.

Characteristics: Bore, 40-mm; Ammunition, HEAT grenade (PG-2), weighing 1.5 kg; Overall length, .94 m; Weight unloaded, 2.9 kg; Rate of fire, 4-6 rpm; Muzzle velocity, 84.1 ms; Effective range, 100 m.

Soviet Antitank Grenade Launcher, Model RPG-7 (VC designation, B-41).

Description: The RPG-7 was an updated version of the RPG-2. The PG-7 projectile consisted of a shaped charge, high-explosive warhead; a point-initiating, base-detonating fuze, rocket motor; and launching-cartridge assembly. The PG-7 demanded stronger defenses than did the PG-2 projectile.

Characteristics: Bore, 40-mm; Ammunition, 85-mm HEAT warhead on a projectile weighing 2.5 kg; Overall length, .95 m; Weight unloaded, 6.6 kg; Rate of fire, 4-6 rpm; Muzzle velocity, 120 ms; Effective range, 500 m.

Rockets

Chicom 107-mm Rocket.

Description: This was a spin-stabilized, barrage rocket equipped with a high-explosive, fragmentation warhead and employed against point and area targets. The complete round, rocket and fuze, could be readily transported by one man. Due to its light weight in comparison to the 122- and 140-mm rockets, it could be introduced into otherwise inaccessible launch sites. The rocket could be fired from a standard launch tube or from earth embankments, bamboo frames, crossed stakes, etc.

Characteristics: Overall length with fuze, .83 m; Weight with fuze 19 kg; Effective range, 6,000-8,000 m, Fuze, superquick, short or long delay; Launcher weight, 22.2 kg for 2 tubes and 248.8 kg for 12 tubes.

Soviet 122-m Rocket.

Description: This was a fin-stabilized weapon and possessed a greater range and destructive power than either the 107- or 140-mm rocket. With a warhead angle-of-fall of 30°, the lethal area of this rocket for prone men in the open was 163 square meters. Like the 107-mm rocket, it could be fired from improvised positions, but launch tubes enhanced accuracy.

Characteristics: Bore, 122-mm; Overall length, 1.9 m; Weight, 46.2 kg; Range, 3,000-11,000 m; Warhead, 6.6 kg of explosives; Launcher length, 2.5 m; Launcher weight with tripod, 54.9 kg.

Soviet 140-mm Rocket.

Description: This rocket was spin-stabilized and could be launched from a single board-mounted tube or from earth mounds. Its greatest advantage was ease of deployment. The warhead fragmented into relatively few, large-sized pieces which reduced antipersonnel effectiveness. Due to its large explosive charge and optional fuze-delay settings, it had a good destructive capability against material targets. Using a 30° angle-of-fall and a superquick fuze, the lethal area for prone men in the open was 140 square meters.

Characteristics: Overall length with fuze, 1.1 m; Weight with fuze, 40.8 kg; Range, 1,000-10,000 m; Warhead, 4.1 kg of TNT explosive; Fuze, superquick, .5-second delay or 1-second delay; Launcher tube length, 1.1 m; Launcher tube weight, 10 kg.

Overcaliber Rockets.

There was frequent mention but very limited confirmed use of overcaliber 107- and 122-mm rockets, sometimes referred to as "garbage cans" because of the outward appearance of the warhead. In these adaptations, the standard rocket motors were used to boost oversize warheads containing from 12 to 90 kilograms of explosive. However, the ballistic deficiencies entailed in these modifications significantly reduced range and accuracy. Therefore, despite their great destructive power, "garbage cans" were basically short-range harassment weapons.

APPENDIX 5

Herbicides Employed in Air Base Defense Operations*

General

Antiplant agents are chemical agents which possess a high offensive potential for destroying or seriously limiting the production of food and defoliating vegetation. These compounds include herbicides that kill or inhibit the growth of plants; plant growth regulators that either regulate or inhibit plant growth, sometimes causing plant death; desiccants that dry up plant foliage; and soil sterilants that prevent or inhibit the growth of vegetation by action with the soil. Military applications for antiplant agents are based on denying the enemy food and concealment.

Antiplant agents in use

a. **ORANGE.**

(1) Description Agent ORANGE is the Standard A agent. It is composed of a 50:50 mixture of the n-butyl esters of 2,4-D and 2,4,5-T (app D and C1. TM 3-215). ORANGE appears as a dark-brown oily liquid which is insoluble in water but miscible in oils such as diesel fuel. It weighs about 10.75 pounds per gallon and becomes quite viscous as the temperature drops, solidifying at 45° F. It is noncorrosive, of low volatility, and nonexplosive, but deteriorates rubber.

(2) Rate of application. The recommended rate of application of ORANGE is 3 gallons per acre. This may vary depending on the type of vegetation. In some situations better coverage may be obtained by diluting ORANGE with diesel fuel oil, which results in a less viscous solution that is dispersed in smaller droplets. Dilution may also be required when using dispersion equipment which does not permit the flow rate to be conveniently adjusted to 3 gallons per acre.

(3) Effect on foliage. ORANGE penetrates the waxy covering of leaves and is absorbed into the plant system. It affects the growing points of the plant resulting in its death. Rains occurring within the first hour after spraying will not reduce the effectiveness of ORANGE to the extent that they reduce the effectiveness of aqueous solutions. Broadleaf plants are highly susceptible to ORANGE. Some grasses can be controlled but require a much higher dose rate than broadleaf plants. Susceptible plants exhibit varying degrees of susceptibility to ORANGE. Death of a given plant may occur within a week or less, or may require up to several months depending on the plant's age, stage of growth, susceptibility, and the dose rate.

(4) Safety precautions and decontamination. ORANGE is relatively nontoxic to man or animals. No injuries have been reported to personnel exposed to aircraft spray. Personnel subject to splashes from handling the agent need not be alarmed, but should shower and change clothes at a convenient opportunity. ORANGE is noncorrosive to metals but will remove

---

* Lib of Cong Rpt, 8 Aug 69, to the House Subcommittee on Science, Research, and Development of the Committee on Science and Astronautics, 91st Cong, 1st sess, *A Technological Assessment of the Vietnam Defoliant Matter: A Case History,* pp 67-73.

aircraft paint and walkway coatings. Contaminated aircraft should be washed with soapy water to remove the agent. Rubber hoses and other rubber parts of transfer and dissemination equipment will deteriorate and require replacement, since ORANGE softens rubber.

2. **BLUE (Phytar 560G)**

(1) Description. Agent BLUE is an aqueous solution containing about 3 pounds per gallon of the sodium salt of cacodylic acid, the proper amount of surfactant (a substance which increases the effectiveness of the solution), and a neutralizer to prevent corrosion of metal spray apparatus. BLUE is the agent normally used for crop destruction.

(2) Rate of application. BLUE may be sprayed as received from the manufacturer without dilution, if desired. The recommended application rate for crop destruction is about 1 to 2 gallons per acre. However, much higher use rates of BLUE are required to kill tall grasses, such as elephant grass or sugarcane, because of the large masses of vegetation. For hand-spray operations, two gallons of BLUE diluted with water to make 50 gallons will give a solution that can be dispersed by hand at a rate equivalent to approximately 1 to 3 gallons of pure agent per acre.

Air Force C–123s spray defoliation chemicals over the A Shau valley

A Vietnamese soldier sprays fuel oil on dense foliage to determine the effectiveness of defoliation by fire. This failed because the fire would not keep burning

(3) Effective on foliage. Enough BLUE applied to any kind of foliage will cause it to dry and shrivel, but the agent is more effective against grassy plants than broadleaf varieties. Best results are obtained when the plant is thoroughly covered, since the agent kills by absorption of moisture from the leaves. The plants will die within 2 to 4 days or less and can then be burned if permitted to dry sufficiently. BLUE in low dose rates can also prevent grain formation in rice without any apparent external effect. The plant develops normally but does not yield a crop. Spray rates higher than about one-half gallon per acre usually kill the crop. Although BLUE can produce relatively rapid defoliation, regrowth may occur again in about 30 days. Repeated spraying is necessary to provide a high degree of continuous plant kill.

(4) Safety precautions and decontamination. Normal sanitary precautions should be followed when handling BLUE. Although it contains a form of arsenic, BLUE is relatively nontoxic. It should not be taken internally, however. Any material that gets on the hands, face, or other parts of the body should be washed off at the first opportunity. Clothes that become wet with a solution of BLUE should be changed. Aircraft used for spraying this solution should be washed well afterward. When WHITE is added to BLUE, a precipitate forms that will clog the system. If the same spray apparatus is to be used for spraying agents WHITE and BLUE, the system must be flushed to assure that all residue of the previous agent is removed.

Effects of aerial defoliation

c. **WHITE (Tordon 101).**

(1) Description. The active ingredients of agent WHITE are 20 percent picloram and 80 percent isopropylamine salt of 2,4-D. Active ingredients constitute about 25 percent of the solution. A surfactant is also present. WHITE is soluble in water, noncorrosive, nonflammable, nonvolatile, immiscible in oils, and more viscous than ORANGE at the same temperature.

(2) Rate of application. WHITE usually should be applied at a rate of 3 to 5 gallons per acre on broadleaf vegetation. However, the rate may vary depending on the type of flora. Quantities required to control jungle vegetation may vary from 5 to 12 gallons per acre. This quantity exceeds the spray capability of most aircraft spray systems for a single pass. It is usually unfeasible in large-scale military operations to apply such large volumes. For ground-based spray operations, however, high volumes are necessary. Hand-spray operations cannot evenly cover a whole acre with only 3 gallons of solution. Three gallons of WHITE diluted to a 30-gallon solution can be more easily sprayed over an area of one acre. The manufacturer recommends diluting WHITE with sufficient water to make a 10-gallon solution for each gallon of agent.

(3) Effect on foliage. WHITE kills foliage in the same manner as ORANGE, since 80 percent of the active ingredient is 2,4-D. PICLORAM is more effective than 2,4-D, but acts slower. WHITE is effective on many plant species, and equal to or more effective than ORANGE on the more woody species. The material must be absorbed through the leaves. The water solution does not penetrate the waxy covering of leaves as well as oily mixtures, and is more easily washed off by rain.

(4) Safety precautions and decontamination. WHITE exhibits a low hazard from accidental ingestion. However, it may cause some irritation if splashed into the eyes. Should eye contact occur, flush with plenty of water. Splashes on the skin should be thoroughly washed with soap and water at the first opportunity. Contaminated clothing should be washed before reuse. When WHITE is used in the same equipment as BLUE, all of the WHITE should be removed before using BLUE. The two agents produce a white precipitate that will clog spray systems.

APPENDIX 6

Security Alert Conditions*

NORMAL CONDITION. This condition will not be utilized prior to the cessation of hostilities.

ALERT CONDITION WHITE. This is the day-to-day emergency security posture which will be maintained on a sustained basis in order to meet minimum security standards set forth in this manual.

ALERT CONDITION GREY. This posture should be implemented when intelligence reports indicate a need for increased vigilance. This posture can be maintained over a period of several days or weeks if necessary. It provides the commander with additional security police personnel to increase security at entry points, observation posts, and vital resources. He may also constitute additional quick reaction forces and deploy them at various locations on the base along likely avenues of approach.

ALERT CONDITION YELLOW. This posture provides the commander with an option for utilizing all security police personnel on an 8-hour per day basis. Security police support functions should be minimized and days off cancelled to provide additional security personnel. Provisions should be made for personnel from other base functions to augment the security force. The OPLAN 207-XX must specify the actions taken to provide the additional personnel required to maintain this posture and succeeding postures. This would normally be implemented when reliable intelligence data indicates that the base is going to be subjected to an attack, the timing of the attack cannot be predicted, and the advance state of preparedness may have to be maintained for a period in excess of 72 hours. This posture is a definite drain on the resources of the base and limits the capability of each organization which furnishes augmentees in performing its primary mission.

ALERT CONDITION RED (OPTION I). This posture provides the commander with the option for utilizing all security police and augmentees to provide the maximum security possible over a short period of time. Normally, personnel would be utilized in an initial maximum effort and then stabilized into a 12 on, 12 off posture. This condition would be implemented when the base is under actual attack, or when intelligence data indicates that an attack on the base is imminent.

ALERT CONDITION RED (OPTION II). This posture describes the highest security posture possible with full utilization of all available security police, augmentees, and base personnel. It is a desperation type operation to establish and to hold a secured line of defense around the perimeter of the base when the external defense forces have been overrun or are unable to cope with the threat of known enemy forces advancing toward or attacking the installation. Concurrent with the implementation of this posture all priority resources should be evacuated. Those that cannot be evacuated should be destroyed.

---

* USMACV Directive 380-18, 10 Dec 71; PACAF Manual 207-25, 20 May 68.

APPENDIX 7

Rules of Engagement and Guard Orders*

I. RULES OF ENGAGEMENT

Since the air base may be attacked by fire from outside the base or by infiltrators or agents inside the base, it shall be established policy that:

a. Guards, sentries, outposts, watchposts and patrols will fire on any force or individual committing a hostile act either within the base or from outside the base. A hostile act is defined as firing in the direction of the base, setting up weapons within range of the base (unless prior clearance has been secured by friendly forces), attempting to infiltrate or overwhelm by numbers an outpost, or failure to halt when ordered to do so when within the base.

b. All necessary force to defeat an attack shall be applied. Such force may include: small arms, automatic weapons, crew served weapons, artillery fire, armed helicopter attack, attack by aircraft, or attack by infantry or armored formation.

c. All reasonable care will be taken to reduce damage to innocent personnel and buildings, but defense of the air base will be considered as overriding.

II. GUARD ORDERS

a. I understand that it is my duty to defend the air base against any action which may threaten life or property. Effective attack may be made by mortars, small arms, low trajectory weapons, and other devices located outside the perimeter of the airfield as well as by infiltration.

b. I understand that I am authorized and directed to utilize whatever force is necessary to render an attack harmless, whether the attack comes from inside or outside the base.

c. If I observe an attack or threat from outside the base, I will report the attack or threat and take the position or force which threatens the base under fire with the most effective means at my disposal. Within the base, I will not fire unless it is either a direct assault, I see weapons being emplaced, or the personnel refuse to halt. When I observe weapons being emplaced, a direct assault, or fiashes which I can recognize as a weapon directed against the air base, I will respond with maximum firepower.

---

* Ltr, USMACV/MACCOC, to 7th AF, *et al,* subj: Tan Son Nhut Defense, 4 Jul 66.

APPENDIX 8

Tactical Situation Reports*
12-18 January 1969

PART I

Single-Use USAF Base: Phan Rang AB, Buu Son District, Ninh Thuan Province, II Corps Tactical Zone

PART II

Joint-Use USAF-VNAF Base. Tan Son Nhut AB, Capital Military District, Gia Dinh Province, III Corps Tactical Zone

PART III

Seventh Air Force Command-Wide Prospective

PART I — PHAN RANG AB, RVN

MAP REFERENCE: Sheets: CN6832 III, CN6732 II, CN6831 IV, BN6731 I 1:50,000 Topographic

I. GENERAL ENEMY SITUATION:

a. Enemy-initiated contacts rose sharply during the early part of the week and then dropped off to the previous and current low level of activity. The early actions, which coincided with, and may have been prompted by, the end of the ROKA operation, consisted of mortar and small arms attacks against nearby hamlets, local forces, and a US Army camp. During those attacks the enemy displayed a marked willingness to sustain the engagements, possibly in an effort to atone for the type of defeats customarily administered by ROKA forces. The brief increase in activity had been anticipated from information in an intelligence report received 8 Jan 1969, which suggested increased activity throughout II Corps. During the latter part of the week, however, enemy aggressiveness diminished and he resumed his harassment and propaganda operations in outlying villages.

---

* 7th AF/IGS Weekly Intelligence Summary 69-3, 21 Jan 69.

b. The following is a list of enemy units, probable strengths and probable locations:

UNIT	STRENGTH	LOCATION AND/OR LAST CONTACT (DATE)	DISTANCE/ DIRECTION FROM PRAB
X307th Local Force Bn (aka 610 NVA Ban)	120-200	BN7662	24 km S
H-13 NVA Sapper Co	30-75	Squads dispersed	18 km N
HT-111 District Force Co	20-30	BN9685	18 km E
HT-112 District Force Co	15-25	BN8268	21 km S
HT-113 District Force Co	25-30	BN6476	12 km SW
HT-115 District Force Co	10-20	BN7979	6 km SE
HT-250 District Force Co	10-30	BN5586	19 km W
HT-255 District Force Co	30-40	BP8708	21 km NW
HT-260 District Force Co	30-40	BP6616	29 km NW

II. ENEMY OPERATIONS DURING PERIOD:

a. 112147H: MAT Team 70 and a PF platoon made S/A contact with an estimated 1 squad of VC at BN865825, 7 km SE of PRAB. Artillery was fired in support. RESULTS: Friendly—two RD WIA; Enemy—one VC KIA and two hand grenades CIA.

b. 120048H: An estimated one company of VC fired an unknown number of B-40 rockets into BA THAP Hamlet (BN865915), 7 km NE of PRAB. The 160th RF Company made contact with the VC and S/A and A/W fire was exchanged. "Spooky" and artillery supported friendly elements. RESULTS: Friendly—six RF KIA, 18 RF WIA; Enemy—unknown casualties.

c. 122345H: AF OP H-12 (BN749863) observed one explosion approx 20 meters from tower. A daylight sweep was conducted; the grass approx 20 meters from the left front of H-12 was burned and suppressed by the explosion between the first and second fence. Type of explosion was a possible hand grenade. RESULTS: Negative casualties or damage.

d. 130220H: An unknown size VC force fired an estimated two rounds of B-40 rockets at the Ordnance Compound at BN774820, 2 km S of PRAB. RESULTS: Negative friendly casualties and minor damage to the compound. Enemy: unknown.

e. 130115H: C/589th Eng Bn was hit by seven mortar rds at BP481092, 27 km NW of PRAB. RESULTS: Three US WIA and minor damage to one building and three vehicles.

f. 140115H: An estimated one VC Squad infiltrated DONG ME Hamlet (BN678907), 5 km NW of PRAB. PF's and VC exchanged fire as VC withdrew. RESULTS: Friendly—negative casualties; Enemy—unknown casualties.

g. 150005H: An unknown size VC force fired six rounds of 60 mm mortars into the hamlet of TU TAM (BN786744), 10 km S of PRAB. RESULTS: Friendly—negative casualties or damage due to the rounds falling short; Enemy casualties unknown.

h. 150330H: An unknown size VC force again fired an unknown number of mortars and S/A rounds at TU TAM Hamlet (BN786744), 10 km S of PRAB. RESULTS: Negative casualties or damage reported.

i. 1510155H: Approximately five VC fired upon VN Navy Coastal personnel with S/A fire in the vicinity of BN9885, 20 km E of PRAB. RESULTS: Friendly—two VN Navy personnel WIA; Enemy—unknown casualties.

III. OTHER INTELLIGENCE FACTORS:

a. New enemy unit indentification: None reported.

b. Friendly ground activity: None reported.

c. Enemy vulnerabilities: The enemy is vulnerable to the coordinated allied harassment and interdiction program, off-base patrolling by RAAF, ROKA, and ARVN units, and USAF air-support. These corporate operations apparently reduce the enemy's mobility in the immediate vicinity of the Air Base and his inclination to initiate sapper probes or mortar attacks. The enemy's effectiveness evidently is further reduced by the nature of his own organization, locally characterized by the small independent unit. It is thought that the depth of his vulnerabilities preclude the enemy, in his present strength, from organizing the sort of mass-mobilization and general offensive which could seriously jeopardize the allied mission.

d. Enemy and personnel losses: One VC KIA.

e. Weather: Partly cloudy with rain showers for the period. The moon phase changed from a half moon to a new moon.

IV. COUNTERINTELLIGENCE: None reported.

V. NEW ENEMY TACTICS, WEAPONS AND EQUIPMENT: None reported.

VI. ENEMY CAPABILITIES: The enemy is capable of regularly sabotaging the vulnerable JP-4 pipeline, although he has not done so for 15 days, and of ambushing allied units traveling along QL 1 and QL 11, particularly in the hours of early morning and late afternoon. In spite of applied efforts to deter him, the enemy is capable of launching mortar attacks or sapper probes against the Air Base, GVN resources, and nearby communities.

VII. FRIENDLY FORCES IN 30 KILOMETER RADIUS:

a. U.S. Forces:

UNIT	STRENGTH	LOCATION	DISTANCE/ DIRECTION FROM PRAB
Hq, Rear 5/27 Artillery	214	PRAB	
589th Eng Bn	500	PRAB	
Phan Rang Logistical Support Activity (1st LOG)	195	PRAB	
116th Eng Bn	300	PRAB	
MACV Team #45	300	PRAB	
b. ARVN Forces:			
1st Bn 53rd ARVN	700	BN7470	17 km S
c. ROKA Forces:			
1st Bn 30th Regt/9th ROKA Div PRAB	950	PRAB	
d. Australian Forces:			
2nd Squadron Royal Australian Air Force (Security Force Only)	33	PRAB	

VIII. CONCLUSION: The enemy may be expected to pursue his slightly increasing endeavors in anti-US and GVN propaganda, and his more overt activities of harassing outlying allied or civilian areas with brief mortar or sniper attacks. Allied coordination in defense of the Air Base, in relation to the enemy's vulnerabilities, make sustained mortar or successful sapper attacks improbable, and virtually preclude massive ground offenses against this installation. Current local information suggests neither a repeated sudden step-up in activity nor enemy intentions to attack PRAB. The threat to the Air Base is considered to be low at this time. (ICC)

PART II-TAN SON NHUT AB, RVN

MAP REFERENCE: Sheets: XT6361 III, YT6330 I, YT6331 II, WS6360 IV, 1:50,000 Topographic

I. GENERAL ENEMY ACTIVITY:

a. Enemy initiated attacks by fire increased during the week with a slight increase in terrorist activities. Enemy units continue to be dispersed in small groups within the area as evidenced by the majority of FWMF contacts being with units of squad size or less, with the exeception of one contact with an estimated enemy platoon. Propaganda activity in and around Saigon/Tan Son

Nhut area continued at a fast pace. FWMF continued to uncover numerous VC/NVA caches in the area.

b. Enemy units in 30 Kilimeter radius:

UNIT	STRENGTH	LOCATION AND/OR LAST CONTACT (Date)	DISTANCE/ DIRECTION FROM TSN AB
1st MF Bn	150	N of Hoc Mon (1 Dec)	16 km N
2nd MF Bn	200	N of Hoc Mon (5 Dec)	15 km N
Gia Dinh Sapper Bn	250	N of Hoc Mon (10 Oct)	15 km N
8th Arty Bn	270	Unlocated SR I	N
Cu Long Regt	950		
6th LF Bn	300	Vic XS6481, dispersed in Co size elements (1 Jan)	21 km SW
308th MF Bn	300	Unlocated Southern Pineapple Plantation (26 Dec)	25 km SW
12 LF Sapper Bn	100	Elements in SR II (6 Dec)	28 km W
2nd Ind MF Bn	250	Vic XS6873 (31 Dec)	27 km SW
265th MF Bn	150	Vic XS834660 (30 Dec)	29 km S
506th MF Bn	250	Vic XS7268 (6 Dec)	29 km SW
Dong Phu MF Bn	300	Vic XS7776 (31 Dec)	21 km S
3rd Arty Bn	150	Dispersed in SR III (16 Nov)	S
D6 Hvy Wpns Bn	120	Unlocated in N SR IV	
Doan 10 Sapper Bn	180	Hq Vic YS020780 (3 Nov)	26 km SE
Thu Duc Regt	800	Dispersed Thu Duc and Nhon Trach Districts (17 Nov)	26 km SE
Dong Nai Regt	1400		
K2 Bn	250	Dispersed vic An Son (16 Dec)	
208th Arty Regt	650	Dispersed with elements in SR I II and V (21 Nov)	

II. ENEMY OPERATIONS DURING THE PERIOD:

a. Enemy initiated activity increased slightly during the past week to include mortar attacks by small units, and terrorist activities. The most significant of these enemy activities are listed below:

(1) 10010 January, XS685733 (27 km SW TSN) a 549th Regional Forces outpost received twenty rounds of B-40 rocket and small arms fire from an estimated one VC company. Fire was lifted at 0020 hours. Results: Friendly: three WIA (RF).

(2) 100445 January, XS864895 (4½ km SE TSN) a terrorist threw a grenade into the self-defense office at 295 Thuong Dung Street, 2nd Precinct, Saigon. The terrorist escaped. Results: Friendly: one civilian wounded.

(3) 101900 January, XT707195 (26½ km NNW TSN) the 2/7th (ARVN) received four rounds of 82-mm mortar which landed within the compound. Fire was lifted at 1901 hours. Results: Friendly: two WIA (ARVN).

(4) 101945 January, XS800697 (26k m S TSN) the Ki My Hamlet RD Cadre received smal arms and automatic weapons fire from an estimated VC squad. Friendlies returned small arms fire. A Popular Forces platoon en-

route to the hamlet as a reactionary force was ambushed by an unknown number of VC. Small arms and automatic weapons fire were exchanged. The VC also detonated claymore mines. Contact was lost at 2200 hours. Results: Enemy: unknown; Friendly: four KIA (PF), three WIA (PF).

(5) 101955 January XS857951 (1½ km E TSN) unknown terrorist exploded a security district guard booth. Results: Negative casualties.

(6) 102035 January, YS085881 (27½ km E TSN) an unknown number of VC fired three rounds of B-40 rocket and small arms fire at the My Hoi Hamlet Chief's house. An element of the 79th Popular Forces platoon was guarding the house. Friendlies returned small arms fire. Contact was lost at 1325 hours. Results: Enemy: unknown; Friendly: three WIA (2 PF, 1 RF), and four civilians wounded.

(7) 102100 January, XS626766 (28 km SW TSN) the Ben Luc Subsector compound received B-40 rocket, small arms, and M-79 harassment fire from an unkown number of VC. Friendlies returned small arms and automatic weapons fire. Contact was lost at 2110 hours. Results: Enemy: unknown; Friendly: two WIA (PF).

(8) 102110 January, XS554986 (26 km W TSN) the 2/49th (ARVN) received ten to fifteen rounds of 60mm mortar and small arms fire. The VC lifted fire at 2115 hours. Results: Friendly: negative

(9) 102252 January, XT836106 (13 km NNE TSN) a 3/7th (ARVN) outpost received eighteen rounds of 82mm mortar fire. Fire was lifted at 2255 hours. Results: Friendly: negative.

(10) 102315 January, XT784196 (23½ km N TSN) a 2/8th (ARVN) outpost received small arms fire and three rounds of B-40 rocket fire from an unknown number of VC. Friendlies returned small arms and automatic weapons, an unknown number of B-40 rockets and ten rouds of 60mm mortar Enemy: unknown.

(11) 110020 January, XS780820 (12 km SSW TSN) a company of the 5th Ranger (ARVN) Command Post received small arms and automatic weapons, an unknown number of B-40 rockets and ten rounds of 60mm mortar fire from an estimated VC platoon. Firing ceased at 0100 hours. At 0205 hours they again received small arms and automatic weapons fire from the same VC force. Firing ceased at 0233 hours. Launch Force Team and flareships supported both times. Results: Enemy: unknown; Friendly: seven WIA (Ranger) and three civilians KIA.

(12) 110035 January, XS741699 (27 km SSW TSN) the Rach Kien Subsector received eight rounds of 82-mm mortar fire. Fire was lifted at 0200 hours. Results: Friendly: negative.

(13) 110100 January, XS757760 (18½ km SSW TSN) a 3/50th (ARVN) outpost received ten rounds of 60mm mortar fire from an estimated VC squad. Fire was lifted at 0110 hours. Results: Friendly: three WIA (ARVN).

(14) 111100 January, XT825077 (10 km N TSN) an element of the 3rd Airborne (ARNV) received small arms and automatic weapons fire from an estimated VC squad. Friendlies returned small arms and automatic weapons fire. Firing ceased at 1115 hours. Results: Friendly: six WIA (ARVN); Enemy: unknown.

(15) 111915 January, XS980875 (16 km E TSN) the 35th Ranger (ARVN) patrol was ambushed by estimated seven to eight VC Results: Friendly: one KHA (ARVN), and three WHA (ARVN).

(16) 112045 January, XS568865 (27 km SW TSN) the 2/50th Headquarters (ARVN) received fifty rounds of 82mm mortar fire from an unknown number of VC. Thirty rounds landed inside the compound. Fire was lifted at 2300 hours. Results: Friendly: negative.

(17) 112115 January, XS819775 (16 km S TSN) a 160th Popular Forces ambush patrol was engaged by an estimated twenty enemy. Results: Enemy: one VC suspect detained, and one M-16 rifle lost, Friendly: one KHA (PF) and one captured (PF), later escaped.

(18) 112135 January, XS697816 (16 km SW TSN) B 4/12th (US) night defensive position received nine rounds of unknown type mortar. Results: Friendly: seven WHA (US).

(19) 112205 January, XT829087 (10½ km NNE TSN) the 3/7th ARVN) base camp received ten rocnds of 82mm mortar fire. All rounds landed outside of the perimeter. Fire was lifted at 2210 hours. Results: Friendly: negative.

(20) 112232 January, XS5785 (27½ km SW TSN) Fire Support Base Barger received seventeen to nineteen rounds of unknown mortar fire. Results: Friendly: thirteen WHA (US).

(21) 121905 January, XS598999 (22 km WNW TSN) the 2/49th (ARVN) received ten rounds of 82mm and 60mm mortar fire. Three rounds landed inside the compound. Fire was lifted at 1915 hours. Results: Friendly: negative.

(22) 121950 January, XS814728 (23 km S TSN) the 900th Regional Forces Company received two rounds of B-40 rocket and small arms fire from an estimated VC squad probing from the north. Firing ceased at 2005 hours. Results: Enemy: one VC (KIA); Friendly: negative.

(23) 122145 January, XS596968 (22 km W TSN) the 25th Headquarters (ARVN) at Duc Hoa received ten rounds of 82-mm mortar fire. Fire was lifted at 2305 hours. Results: Friendly: two civilians killed, and seven civilians wounded.

(24) 122300 January, XT803164 (18 km N TSN) an unknown number of VC assassinated a Chau Thanh RD Cadre trainee in his home, using a K-54 pistol.

(25) 122330 January, XT822145 (16 km N TSN) the Chau Thanh District Capital received twenty rounds of 82mm mortar fire. Results: Friendly: thirteen WIA.

(26) 122359 January, XS735974 (6 km WNW TSN) a 534th Regional Force Company received an unknown number of B-40 rocket and automatic weapons fire from an unknown number of VC. Results: Enemy: unknown; Friendly: two WIA (RF).

(27) 131250 January, XT709184 (27 km NW TSN) the 2/7th (ARVN) Compound received three rounds of 82mm mortar fire. All the rounds landed outside the compound. Fire was lifted at 1255 hours. Results: Friendly: negative.

(28) 132215 January, XS592930 (21 km W TSN) a 25th (ARVN) outpost received seven rounds of 82-mm mortar. Results: Friendly: two ARVN Policewomen KHA, and seven VN children WHA.

(29) 140205 January, XT712176 (24½ km NNW TSN) an unknown number of VC detonated an unknown amount of TNT, destroying the Ben Nay bridge. At the time of the attack the bridge was defended by thirty-one men of the 2/7th (ARVN). A diversionary attack was launched against a Popular Forces platoon 1300 meters from the bridge at the same time.

(30) 140645 January, XS846923 (4 km SE TSN) unknown terrorist placed an unknown amount of plastic explosive which detonated an exterior wall of BEQ-1, causing minor damage. Results: Friendly: negative.

(31) 142010 January, XS856925 (1½ km SE TSN) unknown terrorist caused an explosion at the Tu Duc building. Results: Friendly: negative; the National Police arrested two suspects.

(32) 152352 January, XS983770 (26 km SE TSN) two river patrol boats received an unknown number of RPG rounds: Results: Friendly: five WHA (US) and one boat took two hits.

(33) 162020 January, XS850961 (1 km SE TSN) a self-defense guard post was demolished by an unknown type explosion. Results: terrorist escaped.

III. OTHER INTELLIGENCE FACTORS:

a. New enemy unit identification: The 9th Artillery Battalion reportedly is now located in Sub-Region 1. The strength, capabilities, and exact location of the battalion are unknown. Further information on this unit will be listed as received in future reports.

b. Friendly ground activity:

(1) The majority of the FWMF initiated contacts continued to be with small enemy units. However, FWMF reported one contact with an estimated enemy platoon during the period.

(2) Although a slight decrease from last week, FWMF uncovered numerous enemy caches during the period and, reportedly, the majority of which were in good condition. Uncovered caches yielded the following items: four AK-47 rifles, one 9mm pistol, one SKS carbine, one M-79 grenade launcher, one pound of medical supplies, one pound of documents, seventy pounds of rice, five pounds of salt, two 81-mm mortar cannisters, one M-16, one M-1 carbine, fifty blank ID cards (old type), four B-40 rounds, five thousand rounds of AK ammunition, eight homemade grenades, and ten VC flags.

IV. COUNTERINTELLIGENCE:

a. Security: Documents continue to be circulated from VC Headquarters units to field units indicating that the security of their (VC) units is being endangered by the continued operations of the US/RVN Combined Intelligence Organization, commonly referred to as PHUONG HOANG. The documents cite the progress of the pacification activities of the organization and indicate that this is a threat to the overall goals of the VC in their operations to liberate the RVN. Addressees have been instructed to pay more attention to the indoctrination of cadre, soldiers, local residents, preventive actions against enemy (FWMAF/RVNAF) espionage activities, and improvement of (VC) security measures. Some of the recommended security measures to counter the programs of the (FWMAF/RVNAF) have included the establishment of a "watch-system" whereby one soldier will watch and report the activities of another soldier; a system of preventing soldiers from leaving their units in groups of less than three; a re-emphasis by military leaders that anyone (VC/NVA) attempting to desert or to Chieu Hoi will be shot; and an increase in the amount of time devoted to the political indoctrination and training of the soldiers.

b. Espionage:

(1) PW reports, as well as captured documents, mention an espionage school being conducted for VC agents in Cambodia. The students attending the courses are very young male and female teenagers, the vast majority of whom were residents of Saigon. Training emphasis for the males has been on demolitions training with a projected assignment to a sapper/sabotage unit. For the females, the emphasis has been English language training. The female is also being taught to draw pictures of military installations and equipment. The female is to be targeted against US installations. Once she has gained employment on an installation, she will select targets and then be prepared to lead the sapper/sabotage elements to it. The reason given for the emphasis on youth was that US military personnel are extremely relaxed and friendly when dealing with young VN girls and are known to allow them some freedom to move about US installations without guards.

(2) On the night of 10 Jan 69, bundle of VC documents was discovered in an abandoned bunker complex. Several sketches of US installations situated along Hwys 1 and 15 were among the documents. These sketches seemed to deal primarily with helicopter parking complexes and perimeter bunker locations. The details in the sketches would indicate that the originator had received some training in this area. The sketches appeared to have been drawn from a position along the highway; however, some of the details would indicate that the originator had a source of information located within the complex.

V. NEW ENEMY TACTICS, WEAPONS, AND EQUIPMENT: None reported.

VI. ENEMY CAPABILITIES: The enemy is capable of:

a. Increasing terrorist activities.

b. Conducting multi-battalion size attacks against Saigon/Tan Son Nhut with local forces located within the area.

c. Avoiding contact for a limited period of time.

d. Increasing harassment of installations and intensifying the interdiction of LOCs.

e. Establishing supply points and base camps in unpopulated areas.

f. Increasing rocket and mortar attacks.

g. Increasing sapper initiated activities.

VII. FRIENDLY FORCES IN 30 KILOMETER RADIUS:

a. U. S. Forces:

UNIT	STRENGTH	LOCATION	DISTANCE/ DIRECTION FROM TSN AB
199th Infantry Brigade	Unk	XS771871	18 km SW
21/3 Battalion	"	XS771871	18 km SW
3/7 Battalion	"	XS832869	9 km S
4/12 Battallion	"	XS758902	5 km S
5/12 Battalion	"	XS899874	10 km SE
2/40 Battalion	"	XS830069	9 km N
25th Infantry Division			
3/25 Brigade	"	XS8094	3 km W
4/9 Battalion	"	XS753937	6 km W
2/77 Artillery Battalion	"	XS797972	4 km W
6/15 Artillery Battalion	"	XS8491	4 km S
3/15 Artillery Battalion	"	XS8491	4 km S
3/17 Air Cavalry Battalion	"	XT9007	15 km NE
1/27 Battalion	"	XS733074	13 km NW
82nd Airborne			
505 Battalion	"	XS739998	7 km W
3/11 Cavalry	"	TSN	

b. ARVN Forces:

5th Ranger Group			
30th Ranger Battalion	"	XS894965	5 km W
33rd Ranger Battalion	"	XS720790	17 km W
35th Ranger Battalion	"	XS791889	6 km S
38th Ranger Battalion	"	X792883	12 km S
Marines			
1st Brigade	"	XS894965	5 km E
2nd Brigade	"	XS921934	10 km SE
3rd Brigade	"	XS9589	14 km SE
4th Brigade	"	XS871944	3 km E
Task Force	"	XS857949	1 km E
Airborne			
1st Brigade	"	XS858915	3 km E
3rd Brigade	"	XS814929	1 km S
5th Brigade	"	XS830834	14 km S
7th Brigade Base Camp	"	Bien Hoa	10 km E
8th Brigade	"	XS8806914	29 km NE
9th Brigade	"	XT865020	6 km NE
11th Brigade	"	XT808004	2 km N

VIII. CONCLUSION: Reports indicate the enemy has still not completed his positioning for a major attack towards the Saigon/Tan Son Nhut area. However, his reconnaissance activities and his efforts to prepare the battlefield are indicative of his intentions with continued infiltration of small enemy groups into the area. PW's, reliable agents, and documents point to 20 January as the most likely date for a significant increase in enemy activity and as Tet approaches, activity will increase and the enemy will launch his ground offensive unless spoiled by FWMF operations. During the coming week we can expect:

a. Harassing attacks in outlying areas with possible ground probes.

b. Increase in terrorist activities.

c. Possible rocket and mortar attacks.

d. Possible sapper attacks on LOC's and installations. (377th SPS)

PART III — COMMAND-WIDE PROSPECTIVE

1. General: This Prospective is prepared by the Intelligence Branch, 7AF (IGS). It is a discussion of the enemy's capabilities, vulnerabilities, past activi-

ties and the affect these factors have on the threat to the security of 7AF bases and operating locations. The conclusion portion is our estimate of what the enemy is most likely to do to 7AF bases and operating locations in the coming period. This Prospective was transmitted earlier by electrical message to all Seventh Air Force Chiefs of Security Police, PACAF Security Police Directorate, 82nd Combat Security Police Wing and the 3275 Technical Training School.

2. Discussion of enemy activity:

a. In I Corps, enemy initiated activity remained at a low level. Friendly activity was centered around Operations Taylor Common and Bold Mariner which continued with light to moderate contact. Enemy activity in II Corps remained at a low level, as friendly search and clear operations continued to destroy the Viet Cong infrastructure. In III Corps, the enemy continued his attacks by fire against outposts and LZs. There was a slight increase in small unit contacts but activity still remains at a moderate level. A sharp increase in enemy initiated activity was noted during the first part of the week in IV Corps. This was highlighted by the ground attack against Can Tho Airfield on the night of 12-13 January 1969. For the last four days activity has remained at a moderate level.

b. Bases and Operating Locations: On 15 January 1969, Pleiku Air Base received 17 rounds of 122mm rocket. This resulted in three WIA and two JP-4 bladdersets destroyed. The main gate at Tuy Hoa Air Base received approximately 30 rounds of small arms fire on the night of 13-14 January 1969. There were no casualties. This was thought to be just harassment as there was no follow up action.

3. Conclusion: The resumption of the Paris Peace Talks and the new administration in Washington make the next week to ten days a critical period in determining the enemy's most probable course of action. At this time he does not appear to be capable of launching a country-wide offensive and will need time to complete the preparation of the battlefield. Friendly operations continue to hamper his plans and he will have to make an attempt to counter our efforts. In order to do this he will have to employ attacks by fire to screen the movement of troops and supplies. We feel the enemy will increase attacks by fire against allied military installations which could include our air bases.

4. Threat estimate to 7th Air Force bases:

NOTE: Increases or decreases from previous week are noted.

a. Attack by maneuver units:

HIGH	MODERATE	LOW
	Tan Son Nhut	Cam Ranh Bay
	Bien Hoa	Nha Trang
	Da Nang	Phan Rang
	Pleiku	Phu Cat
	Tuy Hoa	
	Binh Thuy	

b. Sapper probes or attacks:

HIGH	MODERATE	LOW
Phu Cat	Nha Trang	Cam Ranh Bay
Tuy Hoa	Tan Son Nhut	
Da Nang	Phan Rang	
	Pleiku	
	Bien Hoa	
	Binh Thuy	

c. Stand-off attacks:

HIGH	MODERATE	LOW
Da Nang	Nha Trang	
Pleiku	Phu Cat	
Binh Thuy	Phan Rang	
Tuy Hoa	Cam Ranh Bay	
Bien Hoa	Tan Son Nhut	

NOTES

Chapter I

Air Base Defense Before Vietnam

1. Kenneth D. Sams, *Historical Background to the Viet Cong Mortar Attack on Bien Hoa, 1 November 1964* (HQ PACAF, Project CHECO, 9 Nov 64); ltr, 13th AF to PACAF, subj: Bien Hoa Incident, 3 Dec 64.

2. Cyril B. Falls, *The First World War* (London, 1960), pp xvii-xviii.

3. CWO Howard D. Williams, *Basic Military Training in the AAF, 1939-1944* (AAF Hist Study 49, AAF Hist Ofc, 1946), p 2.

4. *Ibid.*, p 3; ltr, Maj Gen F. L. Martin, CG Hawaiian AF, to Maj Gen Henry H. Arnold, Chief of AAF, 3 Nov 41.

5. DA Pamphlet 20-271, The German Northern Theater of Operations, 1940-45, 15 Dec 59, pp 52-60; Generalmajor A. D. Fritz Morzik, German AF, *German Air Force Airlift Operations* (USAF Hist Study 167, RSI, AU, 1961), pp 25-27, 87-105; B. H. Liddell Hart, *History of the Second World War* (New York, 1971) pp 51-63; General del Flieger Wilhelm Speidel, German AF, "Operation Yellow," Part III of "The German Air Force in France and the Low Countries, 1939-1940" (German AF Monograph 152, ASI, AU, nd), pp 60-134; B. H. Liddell Hart, ed, *The Other Side of the Hill,* rev ed (London 1951) pp 159-164; Woodford A. Heflin, ed, *The United States Air Force Dictionary* (RSI, AU, 1956), p 83.

6. Liddell Hart, *History of the Second World War,* p 135; Liddell Hart, *The Other Side of the Hill,* p 241; D. M. Davin, *Crete: Official History of New Zealand in the Second World War* (Wellington, 1953), p 114.

7. J. F. C. Fuller, *The Second World War, 1939-1945* (London, 1948), p 67.

8. Winston S. Churchill, *The Second World War,* Vol III: *The Grand Alliance* (Boston, 1950), pp 776-77.

9. Gp Capt Kinsley M. Oliver, RAF, *A Short History of the RAF Regiment* (Catterick, 1970), pp 11-14; Defense Measures for Airdromes, in IIS 35, Dir/Intel Svc, AAF, 6 Jul 42, pp 6-9; Military Attache Report 46660, London, The Royal Air Force Regiment, 10 Mar 42.

10. Memo (OCS 20602-249), DCS/G-3, U.S. Army, 12 Feb 42, quoted in Ulysses Lee, *The Employment of Negro Troops in United States Army in World War II* (OCMH, DA, 1966), pp 115-16.

11. Charles F. Romanus & Riley Sunderland, *Stilwell's Command Problems* (OCMH, DA, 1956), pp 316, 405-413; Charles Romanus and Riley Sunderland, *Time Runs Out in the CBI* (OCMH, DA, 1959), pp 164-65; Claire Lee Chennault, *Way of a Fighter* (New York, 1949), pp 324-334.

12. Pub L 80-253, 80 Stat 253 (1947).

13. Agreement, Army/Air Force, subj: Agreements as to the Initial Implementation of the National Security Act of 1947, 15 Sep 47, p 36.

14. WDTM 20-205, Dictionary of United States Army Terms, 18 Jan 44.

15. Functions of the Armed Forces and the Joint Chiefs of Staff, in JAAF Bul 13, 13 May 48.

16. AFP 5-1-1, Dictionary of United States Military Terms for Joint Usage, Jun 1950.

17. Robert F. Futrell, *Ideas, Concepts, Doctrine: A History of Basic Thinking in the United States Air Force, 1907-1964* 2 vols (USAF Hist Study 139, ASI, AU, Jun 1971), I, 341.

18. AFM 1-1, Joint Action Armed Forces, 19 Sep 51.

19. JCS Pub 2, Unified Action Armed Forces, 23 Nov 59, paras 40201-40211.

20. Futrell, *Ideas Concepts, Doctrine,* I, 342.

21. Hists, TIG, 1 Jul-31 Dec 50, II, 1-2, 1 Jan-30 Jun 51, II, 1-4, 1 Jul-31 Dec 51, II, 1.

22. Stf study, TAPM, Local Ground Defense of Air Bases, 25 June 51, para 11.

23. Air Force Council Decision 31/6, 26 May 52.

24. AFR 355-4, Local Ground Defense of Air Force Installations, 3 Mar 53.

25. Memo of agreement, DCS/Ops, DCS/Pers, TAPM, 21 Dec 54.

26. *FEAF Report on the Korean War,* 2 vols, 26 Mar 54, II 132-33.

27. *Guerrilla Warfare and Airpower in Korea, 1950-1953* (Proj AU-411-62-ASI, ASI, AU, 1964), pp 9, 35, 37.

28. Hearings before House Subcommittee on Appropriations, 83d Cong, 1st sess, *Department of Defense Appropriations for 1954,* pt 2, pp 1395-96.

29. *Estimate of the Capabilities of Subversive Elements to Deter or Obstruct, by Ground Action, the Accomplishment of the USAF Mission* (OSI, 20 Apr 56); *Estimate of Soviet Capabilities to Carry Out Guerrilla-Type Ground Tactics Against USAF Installations in the ZI, NEAC,* and *AAC* (Dir/Intel, 25 Sep 56).

30. Stf study, The Provost Marshal, Local Ground Defense of Air Bases, May 1957.

31. *Ibid.,* p 11.

32. Inaugural Address, 20 Jan 61, in *Public Papers of the Presidents of the United States: John F. Kennedy, 1961* (Ofc/*Federal Register,* NARS, 1962), p 1.

33. State of the Union Message, 11 Jan 62, in *Public Papers of the Presidents of the United States: John F. Kennedy, 1962* (Ofc/*Federal Register,* NARS, 1963, p 10.

34. Gen Maxwell D. Taylor, USA, Ret, *Swords and Plowshares* (New York, 1972), p 184.

35. Hist, 2d Air Div, 15 Nov 61-8 Oct 62, I, xvii-xviii.

Chapter II

Emergence of the Air Base Defense Mission

1. National Security Action Memo 182, Counterinsurgency Doctrine, 24 Aug 62; JCS Memo, Joint Counterinsurgency Concept and Doctrinal Guidance, 20 Nov 62.

2. Hist, CINCPAC, 1964, pp 304-306.

3. Hist, USMACV, 1964, p 102.

4. Allan E. Goodman, *An Institutional Profile of the South Vietnamese Officer Corps* (RM-6189-ARPA, The RAND Corp, Jul 1970), p 25.

5. Msg, CINCPACAF to 2d ADVON PFDAL 005, 021517Z Feb 62.

6. Msg, 2d ADVON to 13th AF, 070820Z Feb 62.

7. Memo, Dir/S&LE, 13th AF, to Comdr, 2d ADVON, subj: Staff Assistance Visit—Security and Base Defense, 21 Mar 62.

8. USMACV OPlan 61-62, 25 Oct 62.

9. Ltr, 13th AF to COMUSMACV, subj: Security Staff Visit, 5 Jan 64; ltr, IG, 13th AF, to Comdr, 13th AF, subj: Report of Staff Visit, 25 Jan 64; ltr, 13th AF to PACAF, subj: Transmittal of Staff Visit Report, 27 Jan 64.

10. Msg, 13th AF to CINCPACAF, 210855Z Aug 64; msg, 2d Air Div to PACAF and 13th AF, 121044Z Oct 64, subj: Concentration of Aircraft at Bien Hoa.

11. Ltr, COMUSMACV to 2d Air Div, subj: Airfield Defense, 15 Aug 64.

12. Msg, CINCPAC to JCS, 290-335Z Aug 64, subj: Estimate of Situation in Vietnam.

13. Msg, CSAF to CINCPACAF, 281329Z Aug 64.

14. DJSM 1491-64, Security of Air Bases in RVN, 1 Sep 64.

15. Minutes, Joint and Combined Conference on Air Base Defense, 10 Sep 64.

16. Msg, 2d Air Div to CINCPACAF, subj: Airfield Security, 21 Oct 64.

17. Taylor, *Swords and Plowshares,* p 324.

18. Hists, USMACV, 1964, pp 101-102, PACAF, 1966, p 483.

19. DJSM 1801-64, Security of US Forces and Equipment in Vietnam, 10 Nov 64; memorandums, Deputy COMUSMACV to COMUSMACV, subj: Air Base Defense, 3, 4, and 5 Nov 64; msg, COMUSMACV to CINCPAC, 070313Z Nov 64, subj: Security of Airfields.

20. Memo, Lt Gen J. L. Throckmorton, U.S. Army, Dep COMUSMACV, to Gen W. C. Westmoreland, U. S. Army, COMUSMACV, subj: Conference on Bien Hoa Air Base Defense, 15 Nov 64; MR, Lt Gen Throckmorton, subj: Bien Hoa Air Base Defense, 17 Nov 64.

21. Msg, CINCPACAF to CSAF, 112359Z Nov 64.

22. Msg, COMUSMACV to CINCPAC, 070313Z Nov 64, subj: Security of Airfields.

23. *Ibid.;* msg, COMUSMACV to CINCPAC, 021220Z Dec 64, subj: Security of Airfields.

24. Msg, JCS to CINCPAC, 232-344Z Dec 64, subj: Security of US Forces in Republic of Vietnam.

25. Hist, USMACV, 1964, pp 106-107.

26. Msg, CINCPAC to JCS, 062-219Z Jan 65, subj: Security of Forces in RVN.

27. Msg, CSAF to CINCPACAF, 221747Z Jan 65, subj: Air Base Security in RVN.

28. Ltr, CINCPACAF to CINCPAC, subj: Security of Airfields, 19 Jan 65.

29. Ltr, CINCPAC to COMUSMACV, subj: Security of Airfields, 19 Jan 65.

30. Hist, USMACV, 1965, p 424.

31. Department of Defense (The Pentagon Papers), *United States-Vietnam Relations, 1945-1967* (Washington, 1971), Bk IV, Chap IV, x, 2 [hereafter cited as *US-RVN Relations*].

32. Msg, JCS to CINCPAC, 070-001Z Mar 65, subj: Improved Security Measures in the Republic of Vietnam.

33. Hearings before House Subcommittee on Appropriations, 89th Cong, 1st sess, *Department of Defense Appropriations for 1966,* pt 3, p 388.

34. *Washington Post,* 8 Mar 65, p A1.

35. USMACV Shopping List for the Secretary of Defense, 20 Jul 65, Item 93 in JCS Files, 21 Jul 65.

36. Briefing Book for the Visit of Hon Robert S. McNamara, Sec of Defense & Party to Saigon, Jul 16-20, 1965, Item 2, Tab B, in JCS Files, 22 Jul 65.

37. The President's News Conference of July 28, 1965, in *Public Papers of the Presidents: Lyndon B. Johnson, 1965* (Ofc/*Federal Register,* NARS, 1966), II, 794-803.

38. *US-RVN Relations,* Bk IV, Chap 5, 23, 118-19.

39. *The Senator Gravel Edition, The Pentagon Papers* (Boston, 1971), IV, 308.

40. Msn Council Actn Memo 41, Minutes of Mission Council Meeting (17 Jan 66), 24 Jan 66.

41. *Gravel Pentagon Papers,* IV, 341.

42. *Ibid.,* 379.

43. National Security Action Memorandum 328, 6 Apr 65.

44. Msg. CINCPAC (For Taylor) to SECSTATE, 042058Z Apr 65.

45. Lyndon Baines Johnson, *The Vantage Point: Perspectives of the Presidency, 1963-1969* (New York, 1971), p 142.

46. White House Statement of June 9, 1945, in *Washington Post,* 10 June 65, p A1.

47. Johnson, *The Vantage Point,* p 143.

48. Jack Shulimson, *US Marine Corps Operations in the Republic of Vietnam, July-December 1965* (Hist Div, USMC, 1971), pp 6:6-6:7 and 8:2.

49. Msg, CINCPACAF to CSAF, 270339Z Aug 65.

50. *Ibid.*

51. Msg, CSAF to CINCPACAF, AFCCS 76672, 011350Z Sep 65.

52. MR, Col Charles E. Kenworthy, Dir/S&LE, subj: External Defense in Depth, 24 Sep 65.

53. *Ibid.*

54. *Ibid.*

55. JCS Memo, Security of U.S. Bases in the Republic of Vietnam, 14 Sep 65.

56. JCS Memo, Security of U.S. Bases in South Vietnam, 24 Sep 65.

57. Ltr, DCS/Plans & Ops, to DCS/R&D, subj: The Air Force Role in Base Defense, 16 Sep 69.

58. Ltr. COMUSMACV to Comdr, 2d Air Div, *et al,* subj: Tactical Employment of US Forces and Defensive Action, 10 Dec 65.

59. *Ibid.*

60. Ltr, Comdr, 2d Air Div, to All Comdrs, *et al,* subj: *Defense and Security of RVN Air Bases,* 21 Jan 66.

61. *Ibid.*

Chapter III

The Threat

1. DAP 550-106, The Communist Insurgent Infractructure in South Vietnam, Mar 1967; Study 67-023, CICV, Central Office of South Vietnam, 29 Apr 67.

2. Mao Tse-tung, *On Guerrilla Warfare,* trans Brig Gen Samuel B. Griffith, USMC, Ret (New York, 1961), p 114.

3. Newsletter 9, CICV, The Role of the Viet Cong Infrastructure in Enemy Offensive Preparations, 7 Dec 68; OOBS 69-04, CICV, The Enemy Soldier, 21 May 69; OOBS 69-02, CICV, The Viet Cong Guerrilla, 20 June 69; DID, Jul 1968, p 35.

4. Giulio Douhet, *The Command of the Air,* trans Dino Ferrari (New York, 1942), pp 53-54.

5. See notes 5, 6, and 7 to Chap I; Wesley F. Craven and James L. Cate, eds, *The Army Air Forces in World War II,* Vol III: *Europe: Argument to V-E Day, January 1944 to May 1945* (Chicago, 1951), pp. 138-227; Robert F. Futrell, *The United States Air Force in Korea, 1950-1953* (New York, 1961), pp 636-640.

6. Gen Charles Lauzin, French AF, "Operations en Indochine," *Forces Aeriennes Françaises,* Mar 1955, pp 464-65; Gen G. J. M. Chassin, French AF, "Lessons of the War in Indochina," *Interavia* VII (1952), pp 670-75.

7. EEIR 56-6-8A-1-1, OSI DO 50, 27 Jul 62.

8. *Ibid.;* OSI CID, 10 Sep 67, p. 7.

9. OSI CID, 10 Jun 69, pp 46-48; sp rprt, OSI, Viet Cong Guerrilla and Sabotage Threat to USAF Bases in South Vietnam, May 1965, pp 6-11.

10. OSI CID, 10 Jun 69, p 48; OOBS 69-02, CICV, 20 Jun 69, pp 2, 10.

11. OSI CID, 10 Sep 68, pp 6-7.

12. OSI ROI 50D27-45, 18 Oct 69.

13. DDIIR 1 665 0539 69, 15 May 69.

14. DDIIR 1 655 0219 71, 31 May 71.

15. OSI CID, 10 Jun 69, pp 52-53.

16. OSI CID, 10 Dec 66, p 3.

17. OSI CID, 10 Jun 69, p 5.

18. USMACV IB 11-68, pp 1-2.

19. Study 67-059, *VC/NVA Reconnaissance Tactics and Techniques* (CICV, 18 May 67). Unless another source is cited, this document is the principal source of data on this subject.

20. OSI CID, 10 Mar 67, pp 33-35; DDIIR 1 655 0347 66, 7 Dec 66; CAAR, 377th CSGp, 4 Dec 66.

21. OSI CID, 10 Mar 67, p 6.

22. DDIIR 1 655 0514 67, 20 May 67.

23. Study 67-061, *VC/NVA Electronic Warfare Capability* (CICV, 1 Jul 67), p 5.

24. Donzel E. Betts, *et al, Deadly Transmissions (COMSEC Monitoring and Analysis),* Cryptologic History Series: Southeast Asia (NSA/ASA/NAVSECGRU/USAFSS, Dec 1970), p 10.

25. *Ibid.*

26. OSI CID, 10 Mar 66, p 3; OSI CID, 10 Sep 66, p 4.

27. USMACV LL 67, Defense, 31 Mar 68, pp 1-2.

28. AFM 11-1, Vol I, US Air Force Glossary of Standard Terms, 2 Jan 76.

29. USMACV LL 71, Countermeasures Against Standoff Attack, 13 Mar 69, p 22.

30. *Ibid.*, pp 2-17.

31. *Ibid.*, pp 22-23.

32. *Ibid.*, p 23; OOBS 67-080, CICV, NVA Rocket Artillery Units, 1 Sep 67, pp 1, 5-7; Unit OOB Summary, CICV, The 74th NVA Artillery Regiment, 1 Feb 69.

33. USMACV LL 71, 13 Mar 69, p 23.

34. Study 67-059, CICV, 18 May 67, p 9.

35. OOBS 67-080, 1 Sep 67, pp 14-15; Study of Viet Cong Logistical System, USMACV, 12 Dec 64; hist, USMACV, 1970, III.

36. OOBS 67-080, 1 Sep 67, pp 14-15; USMACV LL 71, 13 Mar 69, p 24; DDIIR 1 655 0342 67, 29 Mar 67.

37. See note above; *Report on Character of Attacks on Air Bases in SEA* (FTD-CR-27-01-68, FTD, AFSC, 2 Feb 68), pp 24-25.

38. See note above.

39. USMACV LL 71, 13 Mar 69, p 27; USMACV LL 60, Defense Against Mortar & Recoilless Rifle Attacks, 10 Sep 66, p 3.

40. USMACV LL 60, 10 Sep 66, p 3; The Threat and Lessons Learned, Dir/SP, 7th AF, Jan 1970, p 14.

41. USMACV LL 71, 13 Mar 69, pp 27-31.

42. DID, Jan 1969, pp 24-26; DDIIR 1 655 0342 67, 29 Mar 67; USMACV LL 71, 13 Mar 69, p 31.

43. USMACV LL 71, 13 Mar 69, p 32.

44. OSI CID, 10 Dec 67, p 2.

45. DDIIR 1 655 0244 68, 29 Feb 68.

46. OSI CID, 10 Mar 66, p 37.

47. Study 69-10, *VC/NVA Sapper Tactics, Organization, Armament, Training and Effectiveness* (CICV, 23 Oct 69), pp 7-8.

48. Translation of captured VC/NVA document, in DDIIR 6 028 2631 69, 9 May 69.

49. Maj Billy J. Biberstein, U.S. Army, *A Monograph of 2Lt Nguyen Van Thong, Platoon Leader, Reconnaissance Company, 320th Regiment, 1st NVA Division* (13th Mil Hist Det, USARV, nd), p 3.

50. Study 69-10, CICV, 23 Oct 69, p 22.

51. *Ibid.*, pp 21-22. For further discussion of the importance attached to the 3-man cell, see Douglas Pike, *Viet Cong* (Cambridge, Mass., 1966), pp 229-230; Konrad Kellen, *Conversations with Enemy Soliders in Late 1968/Early 1969: A Study of Motivation and Morale* (RM-6131-1-ISA/ARPA, The RAND Corp, Sep 1970), pp 34-35; Konrad Kellen, *A Profile of the PAVN Soldier in South Vietnam* (RM-5013-ISA/ARPA, The RAND Corp, Jun 1966), pp 51-53.

52. Study 69-10, CICV, 23 Oct 69, p 22; Report on VC/NVA Sapper Units, Dir/Sp, 7th AF, 8 Mar 69, pp 1-3.

53. OSI CIM, South Vietnam: Sapper Tactics and Threat Against the USAF, 6 Apr 71, pp 1-2.

54. Study 69-10, CICV, 23 Oct 69, p 12; 7AF/IGS WEINTSUM 69-14, 7 Apr 69, pp 46-47.

55. See note above; CAAR, 377th CSGp, 25 Dec 66; DDIIR 1 655 0154 69, 6 Feb 69.

56. OSI CIM, 6 Apr 71, p 9.

57. DDIIR 1516 0239 69 (5800-05), 12 Mar 69.

58. Study 69-10, CICV, 23 Oct 69, pp 12-13; OSI CIM, 6 Apr 71, pp 8-10; USMACV LL 67, Defense, 31 Mar 68, pp 2-3; USMACV CE 4-69, pp 16-17; 7AF/IGS WEINTSUM 69-14, 7 Apr 69, pp 47-48.

59. DDIIR 1 655 0173 68, 12 Feb 68; DDIIR 1 655 0431 68, 29 Mar 68; CAARs, 377th CSGp, 9 Mar 68, 3d CSGp, 31 Jan 68.

60. Hist, USMACV, 1968, I, 130.

61. *Ibid.*, II, 895.

62. DDIIR 1 655 0173 68, 12 Feb. 68.

63. *Report on the War in Vietnam* (As of 30 June 1968) (CINCPAC, 1969), sec II, pp 157-158; OSI CID, 10 Jun 68.

64. Msg, COMUSMACV to VMAC, 300325Z Jan 68, subj: Cancellation of Tet Cease-Fire; msg, COMUSMACV to Comdr, 7th AF, 300841Z Jan 68, subj: Cancellation of Tet Cease-Fire.

65. *Report on the War in Vietnam* (As of 30 June 1968), sec II, p. 158.

66. Hist, USMACV, 1968, II, 896-97; CAARs, 377th CSGp, 9 Mar 68, 3d CSGp, 31 Jan 68.

67. DDIIR 1 655 0161 67, 20 Feb 67.

68. USMACV 1B 10-68, p 5.

Chapter IV

The Target Air Bases

1. Llewelyn Williams, *Vegetation of Southeast Asia: Studies of Forest Types, 1963-1965* (ARPA Order 424, USDA, 1965), pp 40-60.

2. *Ibid.*, p 258.

3. EOTR, Maj Carl A. Bender, SP Ops Off, Tan Son Nhut AB, 15 Apr 68.

4. R. H. Lock, "On the Growth of Giant Bamboos, with Special Reference to the Relations between Conditions of Moisture and the Rate of Growth," *Annals of the Royal Botanic Gardens,* vol II, pt II (Peradeniya, Ceylon, 1904), pp 264-65. This report was made available by Dr. Robert Soderstrom of the National Herbarium, The National Museum of Natural History, Washington, D. C.

5. Notes, Col Milton T. Pollen, Dir/SP, 7th AF (1968-69), nd [hereafter cited as Pollen Notes].

6. *Observations on Base Defense* (ARPA Order 963-67, Lockheed Missiles and Space Co, Aug 1967), pp 2-7, 2-8.

7. *Survey of Physical Security and Base Defense Actions Concerning Southeast Asia Bases* (Dir/S&LE, 1 Oct 65); EOTR, Brig Gen Albert W. Schinz, Ch/AFAG, 23 Oct 66.

8. Bender EOTR, 15 Apr 68.

9. Base Plan, Tab C-1, of Master Plan for the bases mentioned in text.

10. EOTR, Lt Col William O. Boardman, Base CE, Tan Son Nhut AB, 5 May 66.

11. Final Report, 7th AF Base Def Study Gp, 17 Aug 67, p 4 [hereafter cited as 7th AF Final Report].

12. EOTR, Col Milton T. Pollen, Dir/SP, 7th AF, 7 Jun 69, pp 10-11.

13. See note 5.

14. Base Plan, Tab C-1, of Master Plan for Tuy Hoa AB.

15. Msg. Det 9, 2d ADVON, to CINCPACAF, 211015Z Nov 61, subj: Ground Defense of Bien Hoa Airfield.

16. Ltr, COMUSMACV to CINCPAC, subj: Physical Security of US Personnel in SVN, 22 Aug 62.

17. Ltr, Dir/S&LE, 2d Air Div, to Comdr, 2d Air Div, subj: Defense and Security of Tan Son Nhut Air Base, 1 Sep 64.

18. Ltr, COMUSMACV to Comdr 7th AF, *et al,* subj: Tactical Employment of US Forces and Defensive Action, 10 Dec 65.

19. 7th AF Final Report.

20. Ltr, COMUSMACV to Comdr 7th AF, *et al,* subj: Defense of Tan Son Nhut, 20 Dec 66.

21. Staff Summary Sheet, 7th AF Dir/SP, 7th AF Status of Physical Security Aids and Ground Defense Capability, Tab A, 13 Feb 69.

22. Ltr, 7th AF to PACAF, subj: Fencing, Lighting SEAOR, 9 Apr 65.

23. *Ibid.*

24. USAF Management Summary Southeast Asia, 23 Jul 65, p 19; TO 00-25-30, 25 Jul 66.

25. Pollen EOTR, 7 Jun 69, pp 11-12; EOTR, Col Frank L. Gailer, Jr., Comdr, 35th TFWg, Phan Rang AB, Aug 1969, p D-9; Final Report, *Research Test of Armor Bunker Protection Against RPG-2 and RPG-7* (USATECOM Proj 1-6-8765-13, U.S. Army Mats and Mechs Rsch Cen, Aberdeen Proving Ground, Md., Apr 1968), p 10.

26. Pollen EOTR, 7 Jun 69, p 11.

27. PAD 69-101, 7th AF, 1969.

28. Msg, SECDEF to COMUSMACV, 051424Z Jan 69, subj: Air Force Construction Directives Lot 013.

29. Msg, 7th AF to AIG 7935, 030926Z Apr 69, subj: Ground Defense Capability.

30. *Ibid.*

31. Hist, 2d Air Div, Jul-Dec 1965, I, 75-76.

32. *Ibid.*

33. USAF Management Summary Southeast Asia, 4 Aug 67, p 51.

34. 7th AF Final Report.

35. *Ibid,;* memo, 7th AF Comdr to 7th AF C/S, 16 Oct 67.

36. Hist, PACAF, 1 Jul 69-30 Jun 70, I, pt 2, 244-266; Col Harry J. Williams, "The Hardened Aircraft Shelter in RVN," *Air Force Civil Engineer* XI (Aug 1970); hist, USMACV, 1969, II, IX-100 thru IX-102.

37. Rprt, *Considerations in Siting Hardened Aircraft Shelters in South Vietnam* (Asst for Ops Analys, PACAF, Jul 1968), note 68-7.

38. Hist (S), PACAF, 1 Jul 69-30 Jun 70, I, pt 2, 259; USAF Management Summary Southeast Asia, 25 Oct 68, p 51, and 9 Jan 70.

39. Hist, PACAF, 1 Jul 69-30 Jun 70, I, pt 2, pp 261-62; Williams, "The Hardened Aircraft Shelter in RVN."

40. 7th AF Final Report.

41. David Sylva, "Two-Story Barracks at Da Nang," in *Listen the War* (Colorado Springs, Colo., 1973), p 100.

42. Lt Col Cabell J. Fearn, "Da Nang Slab Revetments," *Air Force Civil Engineer* XI (Nov 1970).

43. *Ibid.*

44. 7th AF Final Report.

45. *Ibid.*

46. John W. Dennison and Melvin F. Porter, *Local Base Defense in RVN, January 1969-June 1971* (HQ PACAF, Project CHECO, 14 Sep 71), p 15.

47. 7th AF Final Report.

48. Msg, CINCPAC to JCS, *et al,* 291124Z, Sep 71, subj: Use of Herbisides; msg, COMUSMACV to CINCPAC, 151205Z Nov 71, subj: Perimeter Vegetation Control; *A Translation from the French: Lessons of War in Indochina,* trans V.J. Croizat (RM-5271-PR, The RAND Corp, 1967), II, 139.

49. DOD stats quoted in *Baltimore Sun,* 13 May 68, p 2.

50. Lib of Cong Rprt, 8 Aug 69, to the House Subcommittee on Science, Research, and Development of the Committee on Science and Astronautics, 91st Cong, 1st sess, *A Technological Assessment of the Vietnam Defoliant Matter: A Case History,* pp 17-19; AFM 355-2, All-Service Manual of Armed Forces Doctrine for Chemical and Biological Weapons Employment and Defense, Apr 1964, p 3.

51. *A Technological Assessment of the Vietnam Defoliant Matter,* p 20; USMACV LL 74, Accidental Herbicide Damage, nd, pp 4-5.

52. EOTR, Lt Col Donald E. Reeves, Ch/SP, Phan Rang AB, 24 Jul 69.

53. Ltr, 7th AF, to All 7th AF Wg and Gp Comdrs, subj: Lessons Learned from the Enemy Offensive During Tet, 3 Mar 68; Bender EOTR, 15 Apr 68.

54. EOTR, Maj Wayne C. Collins, SP Ops Off, Bien Hoa AB, 14 Jan 69.

55. Pollen Notes.

56. Briefing to the President's Sci Advsy Council, subj: The Use of Herbicides in Vietnam, 13 Nov 69.

57. Msg, CINCPAC to JCS, *et al,* 030115Z May 71, subj: Use of Herbicides; msg, COMUSMACV to VMAC, 300749Z Jun 71, subj: Use of Herbicides.

58. Mgs. COMUSMACV to CINCPAC, *et al,* 151205Z Nov 71, subj: Perimeter Vegetation Control.

59. Memo, Asst to the Pres for Nat Sec Affairs, to SECSTATE and SECDEF, subj: Herbicides in Vietnam, 18 Aug 71.

60. *Ibid.*

61. NSDM 141, to SECSTATE and SECDEF, Herbicides in Vietnam, 26 Nov 71; msg, SECSTATE to SAIGON, *et al,* subj: Vietnamization of Herbicide Capabilities [ca Feb 1972].

Chapter V

USAF Ground Defense Forces

1. Study, *USAF Limited War Security-Defense Force* (PACAF Lmtd War Sec Study Gp, 25 Jan 1966), pt III.

2. *Ibid.*

3. Lt Col Theodore C. Williams, Jr., U.S. Army, "The US Air Force Ground Defense System" (Thesis, U.S. Army War College, 2 Dec 68), p 16.

4. EOTR, Capt Richard L. Bofenkamp, Dir/S&LE, 2d Air Div, 11 Jul 62.

5. *Ibid.*

6. Pollen EOTR, 7 Jun 69.

7. *Ibid.*

8. SEA Trip Report, Col Leslie E. Gaskins, Dir/SP, Oct 1967.

9. *Evolutionary Base Defense* (Lockheed Missiles and Space Co, Jul 1967), p 5:3.

10. See note 6; intvw [interviewer unk], with Col Albert Feldman, Dir/SP, 7th AF, 2 Jul 69.

11. Hist, PACAF, 1967, pp 500-501.

12. See note 6; Feldman intvw, 2 Jul 69.

13. Quoted in msg, COMUSMACV to CINCPAC, 140215Z Feb 67, subj: Security of Installations in RVN.

14. Ltr, 7th AF to CINCPACAF, subj: Security of Air Bases in RVN, 18 Feb 68.

15. Msg, COMUSMACV to CINCPAC, *et al,* 181554Z Mar 68, subj: RVN Security Augmentation.

16. Hist, USMACV, 1968, I, 223-28.

17. EOTR, Maj William C. Sloan, Ch/SP, Phan Rang AB, 8 Dec 66.

18. Gailer EOTR, Aug 1969.

19. TAC rprt, *Air Base Defense in SEA, 1 Jan 1965-31 Mar 1968,* 1969, pp 3:36-3:37.

20. See note 6.

21. Collins EOTR, 14 Jan 69.

22. See note 6.

23. Rprt, *Individual Personnel Training in Support of SEA* (Dir/Pers Tng and Educ, 10 Feb 70), p 13.

24. *Ibid.,* pp 11-12.

25. *Survey of Physical Security and Base Defense Actions Concerning Southeast Asia Bases* (Dir/S&LE, 1 Oct 65).

26. *Individual Personnel Training in Support of SEA,* p 14; USAF Statistical Digest, FY 1967, p 289.

27. EOTR, Lt Col Roger W. Stinchcomb, Jr., Ch/SP, Cam Ranh Bay AB, 31 May 67.

28. Ltr, Dir/SP, PACAF, to Dir/Plans, USAF, subj: End of Tour Report —Lt Col Roger W. Stinchcomb, Jr., 8 Aug 67.

29. EOTR, Capt Richard B. Jenkins, SP Ops Off, Da Nang AB, 30 Apr 69.

30. See note 17.

31. Boardman EOTR, 5 May 66.

32. See note 6.

33. EOTR, Col Jack L. Hughes, Dir/SP, 7th AF, 5 Apr 72.

34. *Integrated Air Base Defense Program* (Lockheed Missiles and Space Co, 26 Jan 68), II, 9:1, 9:2.

35. PACAFM 207-25, Security Police Guidance for Guerrilla/Insurgency/Limited War Environments, 20 May 68, and 7th AF Sup 1 thereto, 25 Sep 68; 7th AF Reg 50-5, Security Police Training, 10 Jul 68.

36. See notes 6 and 29; AFR 50-8, Small Arms Marksmanship Training, 8 Nov 62.

37. See note 6; EOTR, Col Albert Feldman, Dir/SP, 7th AF, 4 Jun 70; EOTR, Capt James E. McCoy, Comdt, 7th AF Weapons, Small Unit Tactics, and Mortar School, 10 Feb 72.

38. McCoy EOTR, 10 Feb 72.

39. *Ibid.*

40. *Ibid.;* Feldman EOTR, 4 Jun 70.

41. See note 25.

42. See note 25.

43. LMTC TP LK-66-7, AZR77150 Air Police Combat Preparedness, 18 Mar 66; Minutes, AP Tng Conf 17-19 Oct 66, Lackland AFB, Tex.; LMTC TP LK-68-14, AZR81150 Security Police Combat Preparedness, 7 Mar 68; LMTC TP LK-70-6, AZR81150. Security Police Combat Preparedness, 19 Jan 70; LMTC TP LK-70-7, OZR8124, Security Police Officer Combat Preparedness, 19 Jan 70.

44. See note 6.

45. *FEAF Report on the Korean War,* II, 157.

46. Intvw, 1st Lt Bernard N. Hayen, 82d CSPWg, with Robert L. Garrison, Dir/SP, 28 Aug 69.

47. *Ibid.*

48. See note 46; Pollen Notes; intvw, 1st Lt Bernard N. Hayen, 82d CSPWg, with Lt Col Jim Black, Ret, Dir/SP, 30 Aug 69; *Operation Safe Side Final Report* (Dir/SP, 1 Oct 67), pp 203-04.

49. DAFM 23-31, 40-mm Grenade Launcher, M-203 and M-79, 1 May 72.

50. *Ibid.*; Pollen Notes.

51. PACAFM 207-25, 20 May 68; AFTA 538, Security Police Activities,

Organizational Small Arms Equipment, Military Dogs, Associated Equipment, Civil Disturbance and Local Ground Defense Equipment, Nov 1968; DAFM 23-11, 90-mm Recoilless Rifle, M-67, 6 Jul 65; DAFM 23-33, 66-mm HEAT Rocket, M-72A1, M-72A2, 1 Sep 65; DAFM 23-65, Browning Machine Gun, Cal .50 HB, M-2, May 1972; DAFM 23-90, 81-mm Mortar, M-29, 25 Feb 72.

52. Ltr, 3d CSGp to PACAF, subj: Special Report on Project "Fire Drum," 3 Jul 68.

53. *Ibid.*

54. Intvw, 1st Lt Bernard N. Hayen, 82d CSPWg, with Col David J. Duff, ABD Prgm Ofc, ASD, 25 Aug 69.

55. B. H. Liddell Hart, *Thoughts on War* (London, 1944), p 313.

56. See note 25.

57. Ltr, 7th AF, to All 7th AF Wg and Gp Comdrs, 3 Mar 68.

58. Ltr, 7th AF to HQ USAF, *et al,* subj: SEAOR No. 177 (FY 69), Special Purpose Security Police Vehicle, 30 Aug 68.

59. Pollen Notes; Feldman EOTR, 4 Jun 70.

60. Feldman intvw, 2 Jul 69.

61. Ltr, Maj John H. Cady, Proj Off, to Dir/S&LE, subj: Project Top Dog 45, nd.

62. *Ibid.;* figures on sentry dogs compiled by author.

63. Briefing, Lt Col Donald L. Anderson, subj: Medical Aspects of Sentry Dogs in SEA, in Minutes, 7th AF SP Comdrs Conf, 29 Oct 68.

64. DDIIR 1516 0239 69, 12 Mar 69.

65. CAAR, 377th CSGp, 25 Dec 66; CAAR, 35th TFWg, 26 Jan 69.

66. EOTR, Capt Stephen A. Canavera, SP Ops Off, Binh Thuy AB, May 1969.

67. Hist, USMACV, 1964, p 113.

68. Memo, ACS/Ops, USMACV, to Dep COMUSMACV, subj: Countermortar Radars, 29 Dec 64.

69. CAAR, 366th CSGp, 27 Feb 67.

70. Edward F. Krzysiak, *et al, RADC Handbook of Intrusion Detection Devices* (RADC, nd).

71. *Ibid.;* Pollen Notes.

72. 7th AF Plan, Phu Cat: Perimeter Detection and Surveillance Subsystem Test Plan Phases I & II, Sep 1969; Feldman EOTR, 4 Jun 70; EOTR, Col Thomas G. Monroe, 7th AF Dir/Rqmts, 11 Jun 70.

73. TC 23-22, Starlight Scopes, Small hand-held individual weapons mounted, Model No. 6060, 17 Dec 66; TC 23-13, Crew Served Weapon Night Vision Sight, 20 Jan 67; TC 23-18, Night Observation Devices Medium Range, 24 Aug 67.

74. See note above.

75. Briefing, Col Thomas A. Fleek, PACAF Dir/SP, in Minutes, 7th AF SP Comdrs Conf, 29 Oct 68.

76. *Ibid.;* briefing, Maj William Rector, in Minutes, 7th AF SP Comdrs Conf, 29 Oct 68.

77. Feldman EOTR, 4 Jun 70.

78. Ltr, 7th AF Comdr to CINCPACAF, subj: Security of Air Bases in RVN, 18 Feb 68.

79. Ltr, CSAF to TAC, subj: Combat Security Police Program, 1 Mar 68; CSAF Ltr 18 to Deputies, *et al.* subj: Enhancement of USAF Base Defense Capability in RVN, 1 Mar 68.

80. CSAF Ltr 18, 1 Mar 68.

81. *Ibid.;* ltrs, Dir/Mnpwr & Orgn to TAC, subj: Establishment of the USAF Combat Security Police Training School, 5 Mar 68, subj: Organization of the 82d Combat Security Police Wing, 5 Mar 68, subj: Organization of the 822d Combat Security Police Squadron, 22 Mar 68, subj: Activation of the 823d Combat Security Police Squadron, 2 Oct 68; msg, COMUSMACV to CINCPAC, 181554Z Mar 68, subj: RVN Security Augmentation; ltr, PACAF Dir/Prgms & Resources, to PACAF Dir/SP, subj: Safe Side Personnel, 6 Mar 69; hist, PACAF, 1 Jan-30 Jun 69, I, 17-20; hist, 82d CSPWg, Oct-Dec 1969.

82. DAFM 21-50, Ranger Training and Ranger Operations, 23 Jan 62; ltr, Dir/SP, 7th AF, to 82d CSPWg [no subj], 7 May 69; Feldman EOTR, 4 Jun 70.

83. Pollen EOTR, 7 Jun 69.

Chapter VI

Other U.S. and Allied Ground Defense Forces

1. Ltr, ACS G-3, Ops, I FFV, to DCG, I FFV, subj: Security Inspection of Phan Rang Air Base, 25 Mar 69.
2. Briefing, USMACV, subj: Saigon's Defense System, 24 Dec 68.
3. CAAR, 14th CSGp, 16 Feb 68; Reeves EOTR, 24 Jul 69.
4. Msg, JCS to CINCPAC, 070001Z Mar 65, subj: Improved Security Measures in the Republic of Vietnam.
5. Shulimson, *US Marine Corps Operations in the Republic of Vietnam, July-December 1965,* p 5:15.
6. *Ibid.*, p 5:20.
7. Jack Shulimson, *US Marines in Vietnam,* Part II: *May-December 1965* (Hist Div, USMC, 1970), p 6:18; ltr, 1st MP Bn, to CG, Marine Corps Base, Camp Pendleton, Calif., subj: Command Chronology 1st MP Battalion, 2 Feb 66.
8. OpOrd 101-67, Da Nang ABD Bn, 14 Feb 67; Ltrs, 1st MP Battalion, to Comdt, USMC, subj: Command Chronology, 2 Feb 67 and 1 Apr 69.
9. Ltr, 1st MP Bn, to CG, 3d Marine Div, subj: Personnel Weekly Summary No. 1-66, 5 Jul 66, Annex A: Civic Action; Capt William D. Parker, USMC, *US Marine Corps Civil Affairs in I Corps, Republic of South Vietnam, April 1966-April 1967* (Hist Div, USMC Dec 1970).
10. C. William Thorndale, *Defense of Da Nang* (HQ PACAF, Project CHECO, 31 Aug 69), pp 6-8; rprt, 45th Mil Hist Det, USARV, The Da Nang Infiltration Barrier, 8 Aug 68; Lt Col William J. Davis, USMC, "Da Nang Air Base Rocket Problem," *Aerospace Commentary* I (Spring 1969), 71-72.
11. Davis, "Da Nang Air Base Rocket Problem," p 65.
12. Shulimson, *US Marines in Vietnam*, Part II: May-December 1965, p 8:2.
13. EEIRs 56-715/01/14/715, OSI DO 50, 30 Jan, 17, 18, 20, and 25 Mar 65; Goodman, *An Institutional Profile of the South Vietnamese Officer Corps,* pp 13-31.
14. DDIIR 1 502 0287 75, 18 Sep 75.
15. Memo, Maj Gen Edward G. Lansdale to Amb Henry Cabot Lodge, subj: Talk with Lengoc Chan, RVN Ambassador to Tunisia, 6 Oct 66.
16. Ltr, Brig Gen William O. Quirey, U.S. Army, Ret, to Lt Col Roger P. Fox, 28 Mar 73.
17. EOTR, Brig Gen Donavon F. Smith, Ch, AFAG, Mar 1968.
18. Hist, PACAF, 1966, p 483.
19. CAAR, 377th CSGp, 25 Dec 66.
20. CAAR, 377th CSGp, 9 Mar 68.
21. CAAR, 3d CSGp, 31 Jan 68.
22. EOTR, Lt Col Bernard H. Fowle, Comdr, 3d SP Sq, Bien Hoa AB, 19 Oct 69.
23. EOTR, Maj Perry J. Rawls, Ch/SP, Pleiku AB, 30 May 69.
24. Ltr, Ch/SP Div, AFAG, to Dir/Ops, AFAG, subj: Input for End of Tour Report, 25 Sep 69.
25. Hist, Dir/SP, Jul-Dec 1971, Tab B.
26. Ltr, Dir/SP, PACAF, to Dir/SP, USAF, subj: Report of Staff Visit (RVN 5-13 Oct 71), 19 Nov 71; 1tr, Combat Sec Br, Dir/SP, to Dir/SP, subj: Trip Report, 29 Oct 71.

Chapter VII

Air Operations

1. Maj Victor B. Anthony, *Tactics and Techniques of Night Operations, 1961-1970* (Ofc/AF Hist, Mar 1973), pp iv-v, 1-23.
2. Lt Col Jack S. Ballard, *Development and Employment of Fixed-Wing Gunships, 1962-1971* (Ofc/AF Hist, Jan 1974) [hereafter cited as *Fixed-Wing Gunships*].
3. *Ibid.*, pp 45, 54-55.
4. Rprt, *Character of Attacks on Air* 2 Feb 68); ltr, 7th AF Dir/SP to 7th AF *Bases in SEA* (FTD-CR-27-01-68, FTD, Dir/Ops, subj: 26 February 1967 Attack on Da Nang Air Base, 4 Mar 67; msg, COMUSMACV to VMAC, MACCOC 1,

011020Z Feb 66, subj: Mortar Attacks on Airfields: Lessons Learned.

5. *Fixed-Wing Gunships,* p. 70.

6. Ltr, 14th ACWg to 7th AF, subj: Helicopters for Defense of Binh Thuy, 1 Jun 67; Nha Trang AB OI 60-14, 20th Helicopter Squadron (E Flight), 26 May 67.

7. *Fixed-Wing Gunships,* pp 70-71.

8. Semi-Annual Historical Report, DASC, III CTZ, 1 Jan-30 Jun 68, p 7; msg, 7th AF TACC to III DASC, 241100Z Feb 68, subj: Rules of Engagement for Air Attacks on Enemy Rocket Positions Firing on Friendly Troops and Installations; msg, 7th AF Dir/Ops to III DASC, 260500Z Apr 68, subj: Rules of Engagement for Air Attacks on Enemy Rocket Positions.

9. Ltr, COMUSMACV to 7th AF, subj: Air Attack on Enemy Rocket Positions, 2 May 1968.

10. Msg, 7th AF to III DASC, II FFV, *et al,* 200700Z May 68, subj; Rules of Engagement for Air Attacks on Enemy Rocket Positions; ltr, 7th AF to COMUSMACV, subj: Air Attacks on Enemy Rocket Positions, 20 May 68.

11. Msg, II FFV to 7th AF, *et al,* 260325Z May 68, subj: Rules of Engagement for Armed Helicopters and Air Attacks on Enemy Rocket Positions.

12. Staff Summary Sheet, 7th AF Dir/Ops to 7th AF Comdr, Rules of Engagement for Air Attacks on Enemy Rocket Positions, 29 May 68.

13. Msg, COMUSMACV to 7th AF, 280440Z May 68, subj: ROE for Armed Helicopters and Attacks on Enemy Rocket Positions.

14. Msg, 7th AF to III DASC, II FFV ALO, *et al,* 300715Z May 68, subj: Rules of Engagement for Air Attacks on Enemy Rocket Positions.

15. Ltr, 7th AF to COMUSMACV, subj: Rules of Engagement for Air Attacks on Enemy Rocket Positions, 31 May 68.

16. MR, Brig Gen William E. Bryan, Jr., Actg C/S, USMACV, subj: Evaluation of Saigon Situation, 14 May 68; msg, COMUSMACV to 7th AF, *et al,* 011125Z Jul 68, subj: Urban Warfare.

17. Msg. NMCC to COMUSMACV, 102253Z Jun 68.

18. Msg, COMUSMACV to II FFORCEV, III Corps, *et al,* 171039Z Jun 68, subj: Employment of TAC Air, Armed Helicopters and Artillery in Saigon/Cholon/Gia Dinh City.

19. Maj A. W. Thompson, *The Defense of Saigon* (HQ PACAF, Project CHECO 14 Dec 68), pp 43-46; briefing, USMACV, subj: Saigon's Defense System, 24 Dec 68.

20. Thompson, *The Defense of Saigon,* pp 46-49.

21. *Ibid.*, pp 50-52; rprt, CMAC ALO to II FFV ALO, Monthly Operations Summary, 1 Aug 68.

22. Semi-Annual Historical Report, DASC III CTZ, 1 Jan-30 Jun 68, pp 10-13; Thompson, *The Defense of Saigon,* pp 52-54; intvw, Proj CHECO hist with Maj Slayton L. Johns, Asst ALO, CMAC, 18 Jun 68.

23. Thompson, *The Defense of Saigon,* p 53.

24. Semi-Annual Historical Report, DASC, III CTZ, 1 Jan-30 Jun 68, p 7.

25. Hist, USMACV, 1966, p 204; CAAR, 377th CSGp, 25 Dec 66.

26. CHECO Digest, HQ PACAF, Feb 1968, p 8.

27. EOTR, SMSgt Raymond A. Carpenter, SP Ops NCOIC, Bien Hoa AB, 11 Jan 69; CAAR, 3d CSGp, 31 Jan 68; CAAR, 377th CSGp, 9 Mar 68.

28. EOTR, Col Frank L. Gailer, Jr., Comdr, 35th TFWg, Phan Rang AB, Aug 1969.

29. ROC 6-69, PACAF, Required Operational Capability: Gunship Program for Air Base Defense, 7 Apr 69.

30. *Ibid.*

Chapter VIII

Short Support

1. Pollen EOTR, 7 Jun 69.

2. Thompson, *The Defense of Saigon,* pp 16-19, 30-31.

3. Ltr, Brig Gen George J. Keegan, Jr., DCS/Intelligence, 7th AF, to Brig Gen Rockly Triantafellu, ACS/Intelligence, PACAF, 19 Mar 68.

4. Briefing, Lt Col Harris O. Poy, Comdr OSI DO 50, subj: Area Source Program, in Tab B, Minutes, 7th AF SP Comdrs Conf, 29 Oct 68; Ltr, OSI DO 50 to Dir/SI, USAF, subj: Briefing Package, 19 Dec 67.

5. See note above.

6. Ltr, OSI DO 50 to Dir/SI, USAF, subj: Listening Post Progress Report, 19 Oct 66; ltr, Dir/SI to TIG, subj: Japanese Information Request, 28 Sep 73.

7. Ltr, Dir/SI to TIG, 28 Sep 73.

8. *Ibid.*

9. *Study of Area Source Program in the Republic of Vietnam* (Dir/SI), 28 Aug 70), Atchs 2 and 3; MR, Dir/SI, subj: Area Source Program—Vietnam: Statistics, 5 Nov 73.

10. Ltr, OSI DO 50 to Dir/SI, subj: ASP-V Monthly Statistical Report (October 1970), 19 Nov 70.

11. PACAFM 207-25, 20 May 68, and 7th AF Sup 1 thereto, 25 Sep 68; 7th AF OPlan 533-68, Safe Side I, 1 Jul 68; OSI CID, 10 Mar 68.

12. USMACV IB 11-68, pp 6-7.

13. Ltr, DCS/Intel, 7th AF, to ACS/Intelligence, USAF, subj: The Role of Intelligence in Air Base Defense [ca Jul 1970].

14. Feldman EOTR, 4 Jun 70.

15. *Survey of Physical Security and Base Defense Actions Concerning Southeast Asia Bases.*

16. Hist, PACAF, 1966, p 493.

17. Gaskins SEA Trip Report, Oct 1967.

18. Hist, 377th CSGp, Oct-Dec 1969, App 5, Doc 24; Gailer EOTR, Aug 1969; Final Report, *XM-706 Armored Car in Military Police Operations* (Proj ACG-70F, U. S. Army Concept Team in Vietnam, 8 Jun 70), p VI-8.

19. *Integrated Air Base Defense Program,* II, 9:5.

20. Feldman EOTR, 4 Jun 70.

21. Gailer EOTR, Aug 1969.

22. *Ibid.*

23. Maj Jonas L. Blank, "The Impact of Logistics Upon Strategy," *Air University Review* XXIV (Mar-Apr 1973), 17.

24. EOTR, Maj Milton R. Kirste, Ch/SP, Phan Rang AB, 30 Mar 72.

25. Ltr. 7th AF Dir/S&LE to 7th AF C/S, subj: Resume of Viet Cong Attack Against Tan Son Nhut Airfield (13 April 1966), 20 Apr 66.

26. Pollen Notes.

27. Black intvw, 30 Aug 69.

28. Ltr, 7th AF Dir/SP to 7th AF Dir/Rqmts, subj: SEAOR-127 (FY 68), 23 May 68.

29. Pollen Notes; briefing, Col Thomas A. Fleek, PACAF Dir/SP, in Minutes, 7th AF SP Comdrs Conf, 29 Oct 68.

30. MR, Maj Robert W. Hocken, 7th AF Dir/SP, subj; TSSE and SP Equipment, 3 Dec 68; Pollen Notes.

31. *Armed Forces Journal International* III (Sep 1973), 12.

32. Kirste EOTR, 30 Mar 72.

33. EOTR, Lt Col William T. Luckett, Jr., 7th AF Dir/SP, 28 Mar 73.

34. *FEAF Report on the Korean War,* I, 133.

35. EOTR, Col Thomas G. Monroe, 7th AF Dir/Rqmts, 11 Jun 70.

Chapter IX

Getting It Together: Defense Organization in Principle and Practice

1. USMACV Dir 10-11, Organization and Functions: Command Relations and Terms of Reference for USMACV, 3 Jun 66.

2. USMACV Dir 10-4, Organization and Functions: Area Administrative Coordination, 11 Dec 65.

3. *US-RVN Relations,* Bk IV, Chap 5, 79-80.

4. Msg, COMUSMACV to CINCPAC, 15182, 8 May 65, in *US-RVN Relations,* Bk IV, Chap 5, 80.

5. USMACV Dir 10-11, 3 Jun 66.

6. Hist, USMACV, 1966, p 451.

7. Pollen EOTR, 7 June 69.

8. Hist, USMACV, 1967, I, 236-37.

9. Hist summary, May 1966, AFAG, 22 Jun 66; hist, USMACV, 1967, I, 237-38.

10. See note 7; 7th AF OPlan 533-68, Safe Side I, 1 Jul 68.

11. Msg, Gen William C. Westmoreland, U.S. Army COMUSMACV, to Lt Gen Joseph H. Moore, Comdr, 7th AF, *et al,* 031318Z Apr 66.

12. Msn Council Actn Memo 41, 24 Jan 66, p 1.

13. Reeves EOTR, 24 Jul 69.

14. Smith EOTR, Mar 1968.

15. Pollen Notes.

16. 1st Lt Thomas G. Abbey, *Attack on Cam Ranh, 25 August 1971* (HQ PACAF, Project CHECO, 15 Dec 71); CAAR, 483d CSGp, 25 Aug 71.

17. EOTR, Col Rodney H. Newbold, Comdr, 483d TAWg, Cam Ranh Bay AB, 25 Feb 72.

18. Gailer EOTR, Aug 1969.

19. EOTR, Lt Col John F. Hunter, Ch/SP, Phu Cat AB, 15 Jul 67.

20. Ltr, IG, PACAF, to Dir/Plans, USAF, subj: End of Tour Report (Captain John E. Dillon), 5 Aug 67.

21. EOTR, Col Paul F. Schwab, Ch/SP, Da Nang AB, 29 Jul 69.

22. USMACV Dir 525-13, Rules of Engagement in the RVN for the Use of Artillery, Tanks, Mortars, Naval Gunfire, Riverine Forces, and Air and Armed Helicopter Support, Aug 1969.

23. Feldman EOTR, 4 Jun 70; Hughes EOTR, 5 Apr 72.

24. Abbey, *Attack on Cam Ranh,* 25 August 1971, p. 31.

25. Hughes EOTR, 5 Apr 72.

GLOSSARY

A–1 A general-purpose attack aircraft, powered by a single reciprocating engine developed by Douglas Aircraft at the close of World War II.

A–37 This jet attack aircraft is a modified version of Cessna's 2-engine pilot trainer, used chiefly for close support of counterinsurgency operations.

AC–47 Nicknamed Spooky, this gunship was a converted C–47 transport, fitted with three 7.62-mm miniguns that could fire 3,000 or 6,000 rounds-per-minute.

AC–119G Gunship with call sign Shadow, armed with four 7.62-mm miniguns.

AC–119K Gunship with call sign Stinger, carrying four 7.62-mm miniguns and two 20-mm cannon.

AC–130 Gunship with call sign Spectre, bearing four 7.62-mm miniguns and four 20-mm cannon.

AA antiaircraft

AAC Alaskan Air Command

AAD Army Advisory Detachment

AADRS Army Advisory Detachment, United States Railway Security

AAF Army Air Forces

AAG Army Advisory Group

AB Air Base

ABD Air Base Defense

abn airborne

AC&W Aircraft Control and Warning

ACR Armored Cavalry Regiment

ACS Assistant Chief of Staff

ACSq Air Commando Squadron

Activate Put a unit into existence that has been previously constituted by name and number, so it can be organized to function in its assigned capacity.

ACWg Air Commando Wing

ADA Air Defense Artillery; Air Defense Area

ADC Aerospace Defense Command

AM Amplitude modulation, that in which the amplitude of the carrier is varied.

amb ambassador

analys analysis

ANGLICO Air and Naval Gunfire Liaison Company

Antipersonnel weapon, M–18A1 (Claymore) Weighing 3½ pounds, the Claymore can be fired by personnel or employed with tripwire. Fires a 60 degree fan of steel fragments as far as 250 meters. Is most effective up to 50 meters, and fairly so around 100 meters.

AP Air Police

ARMCO American Rolling Mill Company

ARPA Advanced Research Projects Agency, a separately organized research and development agency of the Department of Defense under the direction and supervision of the Director of Defense Research and Engineering.

arty artillery

ARVN Army of Republic of Vietnam

ASA Army Security Agency

ASD Aeronautical Systems Division

ASGp Air Support Group

ASI Aerospace Studies Institute

ASP Area Source Program

ATC Air Training Command

ATF Amphibious Task Force

AU Air University

avn aviation

A/W automatic weapon

AWS Air Weather Service

B–26 A veteran of World War II and Korea, the Douglas B–26 saw early service in South Vietnam with Farm Gate. Powered by two reciprocating engines, the plane carries eight nose-mounted .50-caliber machineguns (each packing 350 rounds). It can deliver a 4,000-pound bombload plus extra ordnance hung on external racks under its wings.

B–57 American-built, twin-jet, tactical bomber version of the British Canberra. The Martin Company built the original B–57s, some of which were

extensively modified for reconnaissance missions.
bde brigade
bk book
bn battalion
BOQ bachelor officers' quarters
BPS Balanced Pressure Sensor
br branch
Brig Gen Brigadier General
bul bulletin
C–47 A twin-engine aircraft based on the Douglas DC–3, which revolutionized air travel in the late 1930s. The C–47 flew airdrop, medical evacuation, and transport-type missions in the Vietnam War. It also served as a flareship, and was modified into the AC–47 gunship.
C–119 Twin-boom transport modified into the AC–119G Shadow and AC–119K Stinger gunships.
C–123 Built by Fairchild, this twin-engine turboprop transport was used in airlift and as a forward air control/flareship. The C–123K features two pod-mounted turbojets in addition to its piston engines.
C–130 A 4-engine, high-wing, turboprop transport, developed for the Air Force by Lockheed.
CAAR Combat Operations After Action Report
CAC Combined Action Company
Caltrop A device with four metal points, so arranged that when any three were on the ground, the fourth projected upward. The caltrop could penetrate the soles of most footwear, and puncture vehicle tires.
CAP Civic Action Program
Capt Captain
CBPAC Construction Battalion, Pacific Fleet
CBPO consolidated base personnel office
CCT Combat Crew Training
CDC career development course
CE Combat Experiences; Civil Engineer
CEIP communications-electronics implementation plan
cen center
CG Commanding General
ch chief
CHECO Contemporary Historical Examination of Current Operations
Chicom Chinese Communists
CI counterintelligence
CIA Central Intelligence Agency; captured in action
CICV Combined Intelligence Center, Vietnam
CID Counterintelligence Digest
CIM Counterintelligence Memorandum
CINCPAC Commander in Chief, Pacific Command
CINCPACAF Commander in Chief, Pacific Air Forces
CMAC Capital Military Advisory (Assistance) Command
cmte committee
co company
COC combat operations center
Col Colonel
comd command
comdr commander
comdt commandant
comm communications
Command element An element in the command echelon of an organization that exercises command. It normally consists of the commander, vice commander, deputy commanders, and sometimes the chief of staff.
COMSEC communications security
COMUSMACV Commander, United States Military Assistance Command, Vietnam
conf conference
Cong Congress of the United States
Connex A steel shipping container used in bunker construction.
const construction
CONUS Continental United States
CORDS Civil Operations and Revolutionary (Rural) Development Support. A joint U.S. civil/military staff that directed U.S. assistance to the Government of Vietnam in support of its revolutionary (rural) development program.
COSVN Central Office for South Vietnam (Viet Cong Headquarters)
Counterinsurgency Military, paramilitary, political, economic, psychological, and civic actions taken by a government to defeat subversive insurgency.
C/S Chief of Staff
CS combat support
CSAF Chief of Staff, United States Air Force
CSC central security control
CSGp Combat Support Group
CSP Combat Security Police

CSPSq Combat Security Police Squadron
CSPWg Combat Security Police Wing
CTOC corps tactical operations center
CTZ Corps Tactical Zone. Usually abbreviated "Corps," e.g., III Corps.
CWO Chief Warrant Officer
CY calendar year
DA Department of the Army
DAFM Department of the Army Field Manual
DAP Department of the Army Pamphlet
DASC direct air support center
DCS Deputy Chief of Staff
DCS/Ops Deputy Chief of Staff Operations, United States Air Force
DCS/Pers Deputy Chief of Staff Personnel, United States Air Force
DDIIR Department of Defense Intelligence Information Report
def defense
Deflection error The distance to the right or left of the target between the point aimed at and the shellburst, or the mean point of a salvo burst.
dep deputy
det detachment
DID Defense Intelligence Digest
dir director; directorate; directive
Dir/Intel Directorate of Intelligence, United States Air Force
Dir/Mnpwr & Orgn Directorate of Manpower and Organization, United States Air Force
Dir/Pers Tng & Educ Directorate of Personnel Training and Education, United States Air Force
Dir/Plans Directorate of Plans, United States Air Force
Dir/S&LE Directorate of Security and Law Enforcement, United States Air Force
Dir/SI Directorate of Special Investigations, United States Air Force
Dir/SP Directorate of Security Police, United States Air Force
div division
DJSM Director, Joint Staff, Memorandum
DMZ Demilitarized Zone
DO District Office
DOD Department of Defense
DRV Democratic Republic of Vietnam, the government of North Vietnam.
EC–121 (Navy) This modified Lockheed C–121 transport is a high-speed low-wing monoplane powered by four reciprocating engines. The EC–121K is a special search plane with bottom and top radar antennas. The EC–121M is a countermeasures aircraft with an electronic configuration.
E&E Evasion and escape. The procedures and operations whereby military personnel and other selected individuals are enabled to emerge from enemy-held or hostile areas to areas under friendly control.
EEIR Essential Elements of Information Report
elect electronics
EOTR End of Tour Report
ESP expanded security posture
F–4D Built by McDonnell-Douglas, the F–4 is a twin-engine, all-weather, supersonic, 2-place, jet fighter-bomber. The F–4D carries optical and guided bombs, other air-to-air missiles, and cannon. It features improved avionics equipment for air-to-air and air-to-ground operations.
F–8U A high-wing Navy fighter made by LTV Aerospace Corporation. Used chiefly for fleet air defense.
F–100 This single-place, turbojet, fighter-bomber has a low, thin, swept-back wing and supersonic speed. Manufactured by North American Rockwell.
F–102 Produced by General Dynamics, the F–102 is a single-place, supersonic, all-weather, delta-wing interceptor, powered by a turbojet engine.
FAC forward air control; forward air controller
Farm Gate A detachment of USAF air commandos from the Special Air Warfare Center, Eglin Air Force Base, Fla., which entered South Vietnam in November 1961. Its announced mission was to train foreign air force personnel in counterinsurgency operations.
FAT Field Advisory Training Division
FDC fire direction center
FEAF Far East Air Forces
FFORCEV Field Force Vietnam
FFV Field Force Vietnam
1st Lt First Lieutenant

Flak vest A jacket of heavy fabric containing metal plates for protection against flak.

Flash hider A device attached to the muzzle of a gun to conceal the muzzle flash.

FLC Force Logistics Command

FM Field Manual; frequency modulation

FMAW Fleet Marine Air Wing

FMFPAC Fleet Marine Force, Pacific

FOL forward operating location

Formal training Training (including special training) in an officially designated course conducted or administered in accordance with appropriate course outline and training objectives.

frag fragment; fragmentation

Frag Fragmentation operations order, the daily supplement to the standard operations order governing the conduct of the air war in Southeast Asia.

Fresnel units Mobile spotlights for illuminating the base perimeter.

FTD Foreign Technology Division, Air Force Systems Command

FWF Free World Forces. Refers to the forces of Australia, New Zealand, Korea, and Thailand, fighting with U.S. forces in Vietnam.

FWMF Free World Military Forces. (See FWF.)

FY fiscal year

GCA Ground controlled approach. The technique or procedures for talking down an aircraft during its approach so as to place it in a position for landing. Both surveillance and precision approach radar are used.

GEEIA Ground Electronics Engineering Installation Agency

Gen General

gp group

Gp Capt Group Captain (Royal Air Force, United Kingdom)

GVN Government of Vietnam

H–43 A twin-rotor, single-engine helicopter built by Kaman and designed for crash-rescue operations.

H&I harassment and interdiction

Harassment fire Fire designed to disturb the sleep of enemy troops, curtail their movement, and lower their morale by threat of losses.

Hawk Missile, MIM–23 A mobile, surface-to-air guided missile system. It is designed to defend against enemy aircraft at lower altitude and short-range rockets/missiles.

Herbicides See Appendix 5.

HQ headquarters

HQ COMD Headquarters Command

IB Intelligence Bulletin

ICC installation coordinating center

IDE intrusion detection equipment

IG Inspector General

IIS Informational Intelligence Summary

Inactivate To withdraw all personnel and return a constituted unit to the inactive list.

In-country That part of the Southeast Asia conflict within South Vietnam.

Indigenous personnel Personnel employed or drawn from indigenous populations of a foreign country for employment there.

indoc indoctrinate; indoctrination

intel intelligence

Interdiction fire Fire placed on an area or point to prevent the enemy from using the area or point.

intvw interview

IR infrared

ISA International Security Affairs, Office of the Secretary of Defense

JAAF Joint Action Armed Forces; Joint Army and Air Force

JCS Joint Chiefs of Staff

JCSM Joint Chiefs of Staff Memorandum

JDOC joint defense operations center

JGS Joint General Staff (Republic of Vietnam Armed Forces)

JP–4 Jet petroleum. A liquid jet aircraft fuel, the chief ingredient of which is kerosene.

kg kliogram (2.2046 pounds)

KHA killed by hostile action

KIA killed in action

Landline system Telephone or telegraph communication by wire over, on, or under the ground.

LAW light antitank weapon

ldr leader

LF Local Force. Directly under a provincial or district Party committee, LF units generally operated within a specific Viet Cong province or district.

Light fire teams Ground elements that attacked enemy rocket/mortar sites.

Link ammunition Cartridges fastened to one another side by side with metal links, forming a belt for ready feed to a machinegun. As the linked ammunition runs through the breech mechanism, the links and cartridge cases separate.

LL Lessons Learned

LOC line of communication

Log Logistic; also a ground flare used by FAC aircraft to create a reference point during night strikes.

LMTC Lackland Military Training Center

Lt Col Lieutenant Colonel

Lt Gen Lieutenant General

ltr letter

Machinegun, Browning, M–2, .50-caliber, heavy-barrel, flexible This weapon weighs 82 pounds and has an overall length of 65 inches. Air-cooled and recoil-operated, it is fed by a disintegrating metal link belt. Its rate of fire is 450-555 rounds-per-minute with a top range of 7,460 yards.

MAAG Military Assistance Advisory Group

MAC Military Airlift Command

MACCOC Combat Operations Center, Military Assistance Command, Vietnam

MACT Military Assistance Command, Training Directorate

MACV Military Assistance Command, Vietnam

MAF Marine Amphibious Force

Maj Major

Maj Gen Major General

Mar Marine

MAT mobile advisory team

mat material; materiel

Maverick A government vehicle stolen or misused.

MCP Military Construction Program

ME Marine Expeditionary

MEB Marine Expeditionary Brigade

mech mechanic

Meter Equals 39.37 inches.

MF Main Force. The MF units were those reporting straight to the Central Office for South Vietnam (Viet Cong Headquarters), a Viet Cong military region or subregion, and commonly serving in the corresponding territory.

MG machinegun

MI military intelligence

mil military

MIPR Military Interservice Procurement Request

MLR Main line of resistance. A line at the forward edge of a battle position, designated for the purpose of coordinating the fire of all units and supporting weapons, including air and naval gunfire. It defines the forward limits of a series of mutually supporting defensive areas, but does not include the areas occupied or used by covering or screening forces.

mm millimeter (.04 inch)

mnpwr manpower

MOB main operating base

Mortar, M–29, 81-mm Weighing 28 pounds without mount, the cannon is 51 inches long. Has elevation of 40° to about 85°, and a traverse right or left of almost 4°. Maximum range at 45° elevation is 3,885 yards. Normal rate of fire is 18 rounds-per-minute and the maximum is 30 rounds-per-minute.

Mount, gun, trailer, multiple (M–55 .50-caliber machinegun) Four M–2 .50-caliber machineguns on a M–45c armored mount, bolted to a 1-ton, 2-wheel trailer.

MOVCON Movement Control

MP Military Police

MR Military Region; memorandum for record

ms meters per second

msg message

MSL Mean sea level. It is the average height of the surface of the sea for all stages of the tide, used as a reference for elevations.

MSS Military Security Service

NA not applicable

NARS National Archives and Records Service

nat—national

NATO North Atlantic Treaty Organization

NAVADVGP Naval Advisory Group

NAVFORV U.S. Naval Forces, Vietnam

NAVSECGRU Naval Security Group

NCB Naval Construction Battalion

NCO noncommissioned officer

nd no date

NEAC Northeast Air Command

Neutralize To render an enemy force, installation, action, operation, or the like ineffective by military action.

NFLSVN National Front for the Liberation of South Vietnam (Viet Cong political arm). Also sometimes abbreviated NFL or NLF.

NF–2 Light-All unit A generator feeding up to 10 floodlights, spaced along a base's perimeter as far as 100 meters.
NMCC National Military Command Center
NOA nonoperational aircraft
NSA Naval Support Activity; National Security Agency
NSDM National Security Decision Memorandum
NVA North Vietnamese Army
NVN North Vietnam
O–1 A light, 2-seat, high-wing, single-engine monoplane. Built by Cessna, it was used for forward air control, liaison, and observation.
O–2 This Cessna 2-engine, twin-boom, monoplane replaced the O–1. Engines are mounted fore and aft of the 2-place cabin, with the booms serving to support the tail surfaces.
O&M Operation and Maintenance
OCMH Office of the Chief of Military History, United States Army
ofc office
off officer
OI Operating Instruction
OJT on-the-job training
OL operating location
OOBS Order of Battle Study
opl operational
OPlan Operation Plan
OpOrd Operation Order
opr operator
ops operations
Order of battle The identification, strength, command structure, and disposition of the personnel, units, and equipment of any military forces.
Organize To assign personnel to a unit and make it operational.
orgn organization
OSD Office of the Secretary of Defense
OSI Office of Special Investigations, United States Air Force
Out-country That part of the Southeast Asia conflict outside South Vietnam, i.e., Laos and North Vietnam.
PACAF Pacific Air Forces
PACAFM Pacific Air Forces Manual
PACFLT Pacific Fleet
PACOM Pacific Command
PAD Program Action Directive.
PAVN People's Army, Vietnam (North Vietnam)
PCS permanent change of station
PDSS Perimeter Detection and Surveillance Subsystem
Pentalateral Agreement The Agreement for Mutual Defense Assistance in Indochina. Executed at Saigon on 23 December 1950 by representatives of Vietnam, Laos, Cambodia, France, and the United States.
pers personnel
PF Popular Forces. Locally recruited South Vietnamese volunteers, organized into squads and platoons, and used chiefly as security forces in villages and hamlets.
PI photo interpreter
PLC People's Liberation Committee (Viet Cong)
plt pilot; platoon
POL petroleum, oil, and lubricants
POLWAR Political Warfare
PRAB Phan Rang Air Base
pres president; presentation
PRG Provisional Revolutionary Government (Viet Cong)
prgm program
Prime Beef (Base Engineer Emergency Forces) Worldwide base civil engineer forces. They are organized to provide trained military elements, used in direct combat support or emergency recovery from natural disaster.
proj project
prov provision; provisional; provincial
PRP People's Revolutionary Party (Communist Party in South Vietnam
pt part
pub publication
Pub L Public Law
Punji stake Made of fire-hardened and sharpened bamboo, the punji stake was smeared with excrement and hidden on trails. It could penetrate the soles of most footwear.
PW prisoner of war
QC Quan Canh, the military police of the Vietnamese Air Force and the Army of Republic of Vietnam.
QRT quick reaction team
RAAF Royal Australian Air Force
RADC Rome Air Development Center, Air Force Systems Command
RAF Royal Air Force (United Kingdom)
R&D Research and Development
R&R rest and recuperation

Rappelling Descending (as from a cliff) by means of a rope passed under one thigh, across the body, and over the opposite shoulder.

Recon Reconnaissance; to reconnoiter.

Red Horse Rapid Engineer Deployment, Heavy Operational Repair Squadrons, Engineering. Red Horse squadrons are controlled by Headquarters United States Air Force. They give the Air Force a highly mobile, self-sufficient, rapidly deployable civil engineer capability required in a potential theater of operations.

regt regiment

ret retired

rev ed revised edition

RF Regional Forces. Local South Vietnamese defense forces, recruited and used within one of the administrative regions into which the country was divided.

Rifle, recoilless, M–67, 90-mm. A lightweight (35 pounds) portable weapon 53 inches long. It is air-cooled, single-loading, and fires high-explosive antitank ammunition. Its muzzle velocity is 700 feet-per-second, and its range is 450 meters.

ROC required operational capability

Rocket, M–72, 60-mm, high-explosive, antitank (HEAT) Weighs 4½ pounds (rocket in launcher as issued). Maximum range is 230 meters for points targets and 325 meters for others. Launcher is disposable after firing rocket.

ROI Report of Investigation

ROK Republic of Korea

ROKA Republic of Korea Army

ROKFV Republic of Korea Forces, Vietnam

RPG rocket-propelled grenade

rpm rounds-per-minute; revolutions-per-minute

rprt report

rqmts requirements

RRGp Radio Research Group

rsch research

RSI Research Studies Institute

Rules of engagement Directives issued by competent military authority delineating the circumstances under which U.S. forces will begin and/or continue combat engagement with other forces met.

RVN Republic of Vietnam

RVNAF Republic of Vietnam Armed Forces

S/A small arms

SAC Strategic Air Command

SACON security alert condition

S&LE Security and Law Enforcement

SAT security alert team; special action team

sci science

Scramble To take off as quickly as possible (usually followed by course and altitude instruction).

SEA Southeast Asia

SEAOR Southeast Asia Operational Requirement

sec section; security

SECDEF Secretary of Defense

2d ADVON 2d Advanced Echelon

2d Lt Second Lieutenant

SECSTATE Secretary of State

SERVPAC Service Force, Pacific Fleet

sess session

SF Special Forces. Military personnel with cross-training in basic and specialized military skills. They were organized into small multiple-purpose detachments with the mission to train, organize, supply, direct, and control indigenous forces in guerrilla warfare and counterinsurgency operations, and to conduct unconventional warfare operations.

Short rounds Rounds of ammunition or bombs falling short of the target. Also the inadvertent or accidental delivery of ordnance, sometimes resulting in death or injury to friendly forces or noncombatants.

sig signal; signature

Slapflare A hand-held flare resembling a paper towel cylinder with a cap on the bottom. Steps for igniting are to remove the cap, hold the flare in the left hand, and slap the bottom with the right hand.

SMSgt Senior Master Sergeant

SOG Studies and Observation Group

Sortie One aircraft making one take-off and landing to conduct the mission for which it was scheduled.

sp special

SP Security Police

SPSq Security Police Squadron

spt support

sq squadron

Stage To process troops in a specified area, that are in transit from one locality to another.
Starlight scope An image intensifier using reflected light from the stars or moon to identify targets.
stat statistic
Stat Statute
stf staff
subj subject
sup supply; supplement
svc service
SVN South Vietnam
SVNLA South Vietnam Liberation Army
T–28 A 2-piece, single-engine, monoplane trainer, built by North American. The T–28D version is an attack plane, capable of carrying a variety of ordnance on counterinsurgency missions.
TAC Tactical Air Command
TACC tactical air control center
TADC tactical air direction center
TAOR Tactical area of responsibility. A defined area of land for which responsibility is specifically assigned to the commander of the area to control assigned forces and coordinate support.
TAPM The Air Provost Marshal, United States Air Force
TAWg Tactical Airlift Wing
TC Training Circular
TDY temporary duty
Tet The Lunar New Year holiday observed in Vietnam and other Asian countries. It occurs early in the Julian year.
Tet Offensive A sudden attack by the North Vietnamese and Viet Cong in the early hours of 30 January 1968 on Saigon, many other cities and towns, as well as numerous South Vietnamese and American bases and airfields. It took the U.S. and South Vietnamese forces several weeks to control this offensive.
TF task force; tactical fighter
TFWg Tactical Fighter Wing
TIG The Inspector General, United States Air Force
tng training
TO Technical Order
TOC tactical operations center
TP Training Plan
trans translator; translated by
Transceiver A radio transmitter-receiver that uses many of the same components for both transmission and reception.
Tri-Border Area The area west of Dak To, South Vietnam, at the convergence of the Cambodia, Laos, and South Vietnam borders.
trnsp transportation; transport
TRWg Tactical Reconnaissance Wing
TSN Tan Son Nhut Air Base, South Vietnam
UC–123 (Ranch Hand) aircraft A C–123 Fairchild Provider transport, converted for use in defoliation and herbicide operations.
UH–1B The Army and Marines used this Bell utility helicopter to transport personnel and supplies, and as a gunship.
UH–1F Bell helicopter used by the Air Force as a light utility cargo or personnel carrier, and as a gunship.
UE unit equipment
UNAAF United Action Armed Forces.
unk unknown
USA United States Army
USAF United States Air Force
USAFMPC United States Air Force Military Personnel Center
USAFSS United States Air Force Security Service
USAHAC United States Army Headquarters Area Command
USARPAC United States Army, Pacific

BIBLIOGRAPHIC NOTE

Governmental Sources

The Joint Chiefs of Staff papers and National Security Council documents in the USAF Directorate of Plans furnished vital data on policy and strategy, both national and military. Equally important were the records of the United States Military Assistance Command, Vietnam, located at the Washington National Records Center, Suitland, Md.

One of the most complete collections of air base defense material was assembled by the USAF Directorate of Security Police and transferred to the Office of Air Force History. Especially notable among these records were the numerous combat operations after-action reports, 7AF/IGS Weekly Intelligence Summaries, and End of Tour reports prepared by security police personnel.

The richest lode of Seventh Air Force documents was microfilmed under Project CHECO (Contemporary Historical Evaluation of Combat Operations) and deposited at the Albert F. Simpson Historical Research Center, Maxwell AFB, Ala. Also at this center is a vast assortment of base defense materials, gathered and catalogued as part of Project Corona Harvest.

For information on the enemy, the author used the principal sources maintained by the USAF Office of Special Investigations at the Washington National Records Center. Most valuable were the studies and other products of the USMACV Assistant Chief of Staff Intelligence, the Combined Military Interrogation Center, the Combined Document Exploitation Center, the Combined Materiel Exploitation Center, and the OSI. In addition, the vast number of DOD Intelligence Information Reports yielded a wealth of detail.

Helpful statistical data was obtained from the *United States Air Force Statistical Digest* and the monthly editions of the *USAF Management Summary: Southeast Asia*. Usefulness of the latter was limited by the frequent changes in format and content that prevented long-term tracking of data on specific items.

The author gleaned good overviews of air base defense and security matters from the annual histories of United States Military Assistance Command, Vietnam; Pacific Command; Pacific Air Forces; and Seventh Air Force. Histories of Air Staff directorates and those of units below numbered air force level also proved useful.

Several Project CHECO reports, written by field historians during the course of the war, gave excellent details on air base defense or selected base attacks.

Information on Marine activities came chiefly from manuscript histories, written and made available by the Historical Division, Headquarters United States Marine Corps, Washington, D.C.

A prime source of facts on sentry dogs was a manuscript account of this program by the Sentry Dog Training Branch, Department of Security Police Training, Lackland AFB, Tex.

A fund of data and insights was gained from the notes that Col. Milton

T. Pollen, Seventh Air Force Director of Security Police (1968-69) used in preparing his End of Tour report.

The so-called *Pentagon Papers* in their three versions (DOD, *New York Times,* and Gravel editions) offered high-level source documents on U.S. policy and strategy in Southeast Asia through 1967.

A reliable guide to these events from 1948 through 1973 is the seventh and final revised edition of *Background Information Relating to Southeast Asia and Vietnam,* published by the U.S. Senate Committee on Foreign Relations.

Books

Craven, Wesley F., and Cate, James L., eds. *The Army Air Forces in World War II.* 7 vols. Chicago: University of Chicago Press, 1948-1958. Vol III: *Europe: Argument to V-E Day, January 1944 to May 1945.*

Davin, D. M. *Official History of New Zealand in the Second World War: Crete.* Wellington: War History Branch, Department of Internal Affairs, 1953.

Department of Defense. *United States-Vietnam Relations, 1945-1967.* [*The Pentagon Papers*]. Washington: Government Printing Office, 1971.

Futrell, Robert F. *Ideas, Concepts, Doctrine: A History of Basic Thinking in the United States Air Force, 1907-1964.* 2 vols. USAF Historical Study 139. Maxwell Air Force Base, Ala: Aerospace Studies Institute, Air University, June, 1971.

———. *The United States Air Force in Korea, 1950-1953.* New York: Duell, Sloan & Pearce, 1961.

Heflin, Woodford A., ed. *The United States Air Force Dictionary.* Maxwell Air Force Base, Ala.: Research Studies Institute, Air University, 1956.

Lee, Ulysses. *The Employment of Negro Troops.* [*U.S. Army in World War II: Special Studies*]. Washington: Government Printing Office, 1966.

The Pentagon Papers as Published by the New York Times. New York: Bantam Books, 1971.

Public Papers of the Presidents of the United States: John F. Kennedy, 1961. Washington: Government Printing Office, 1962.

Public Papers of the Presidents of the United States: John F. Kennedy, 1962. Washington: Government Printing Office, 1963.

Romanus, Charles F., and Sunderland, Riley. *Stilwell's Command Problems.* [*U.S. Army in World War II: The China-Burma-India Theater*]. Washington: Government Printing Office, 1956.

Romanus, Charles F., and Sunderland, Riley. *Time Runs Out in CBI.* [*U.S. Army in World War II: The China-Burma-India Theater*]. Washington: Government Printing Office, 1959.

The Senator Gravel Edition, The Pentagon Papers: The Defense Department History of United States Decisionmaking on Vietnam. 4 vols. Boston: Beacon Press, 1971.

Sharp, Adm U. S. G., USN, and Westmoreland, Gen W. C., U.S. Army. *Report on the War in Vietnam (As of 30 June 1968.)* Washington: Government Printing Office, 1969.

Articles

Lauzin, Gen Charles, French Air Force. "Operations en Indochine." *Forces Aeriennes Françaises,* March 1955.

Lock, R. H. "On the Growth of Giant Bamboos, with Special Reference to the Relations between Conditions of Moisture and the Rate of Growth." *Annals of the Royal Botanic Gardens,* Peradeniya, Ceylon,

vol II, pt II. Colombo: George J. A. Skeen, Government Printer, 1904.
Williams, Col Harry J., USAF. "The Hardened Aircraft Shelter in RVN." *Air Force Civil Engineer* XI (August 1970).

Studies and Reports

Abbey, 1st Lt Thomas G., USAF. *Attack on Cam Ranh, 25 August 1971.* Hickam Air Force Base, Hawaii: Project CHECO, Headquarters Pacific Air Forces, 15 December 1971.
Anthony, Maj Victor B., USAF. *The Air Force in Southeast Asia: Tactics and Techniques of Night Operations, 1961-1970.* Washington: Office of Air Force History, March 1973.
Ballard, Lt Col Jack S., USAF. *The Air Force in Southeast Asia: Development and Employment of Fixed-Wing Gunships, 1962-1971.* Washington: Office of Air Force History, January 1974.
Biberstein, Maj Billy J., USA. *A Monograph of 2Lt Nguyen Van Thong, Platoon Leader, Reconnaissance Company, 320th Regiment, 1st NVA Division.* Saigon: 13th Military History Detachment, United States Army, Vietnam, nd.
Dennison, John W., and Porter, Melvin F. *Local Defense in RVN, January 1969-June 1971.* Hickam Air Force Base, Hawaii: Project CHECO, Headquarters Pacific Air Forces, 14 September 1971.
FEAF Report on the Korean War. 2 vols. Tokyo: Headquarters Far East Air Forces, 26 March 1954.
Parker, Capt William D., USMC. *US Marine Corps Civil Affairs in I Corps, Republic of South Vietnam, April 1966-April 1967.* Washington: Historical Division, U.S. Marine Corps, December 1970.
Sams, Kenneth D. *Historical Background to the Viet Cong Mortar Attack on Bien Hoa, 1 November 1964.* Hickam Air Force Base, Hawaii: Project CHECO, Headquarters Pacific Air Forces, 9 November 1964.
Thompson, Major A. W., USAF. *The Defense of Saigon.* Hickam Air Force Base, Hawaii: Project CHECO, Headquarters Pacific Air Forces, 14 December 1968.
Thorndale, William C. *Defense of Da Nang.* Hickam Air Force Base, Hawaii: Project CHECO, Headquarters Pacific Air Forces, 31 August 1969.
Williams, Llewelyn. *Vegetation of Southeast Asia: Studies of Forest Types, 1963-1965.* ARPA Order 424. U.S. Department of Agriculture. Washington: Government Printing Office, 1965.
Williams, Lt Col Theodore C., Jr., USA. "The US Air Force Ground Defense System." Thesis, U.S. Army War College, 2 December 1968.

Congressional Documents

U.S. Congress. Senate. Committee on Foreign Relations. *Background Information Relating to Southeast Asia and Vietnam.* 7th rev ed. 93d Cong, 2d sess, December 1974. Washington: Government Printing Office, 1975.

Non-Governmental Sources

For the most part, the author consulted published works for general background information. Of considerable worth were Bernard Fall's *Street Without Joy,* David Halberstam's *The Best and the Brightest,* and Lyndon Johnson's *The Vantage Point.*

Useful RAND Corporation monographs included Konrad Kellen's *Conversations with Enemy Soldiers in Late 1968/Early 1969,* the same author's *A Profile of the PAVN Soldier in South Vietnam,* and Alan E. Goodman's *An Institutional Profile of the South Vietnamese Officer Corps.*

Books

Chennault, Maj Gen Claire Lee, USAF, Ret. *Way of a Fighter: The Memoirs of Claire L. Chennault.* New York: G. P. Putnam's Sons, 1949.

Churchill, Winston S. *The Second World War.* Vol III: *The Grand Alliance.* Boston: Houghton Mifflin Co, 1950.

Douhet, Giulio. *The Command of the Air.* Translated by Dino Ferrari. New York: Coward McCann, 1942.

Fall, Bernard B. *Street Without Joy: Insurgency in Indochina, 1946-1963. 3d* ed. Harrisburg: Stackpole Co, 1963.

Falls, Cyril B. *The First World War.* London: Longmans, Green & Co, 1960.

Fuller, J. F. C. *The Second World War, 1939-1945: A Strategical and Tactical History.* London: Eyre & Spottiswoode, 1948.

Halberstam, David. *The Best and the Brightest.* New York: Random House, 1972.

Johnson, Lyndon B. *The Vantage Point: Perspectives of the Presidency, 1963-1969.* New York: Holton, Rinehart & Winston, 1971.

Mao Tse-tung. *On Guerrilla Warfare.* Translated by Brig Gen Samuel B. Griffith, USMC, Ret. New York: Frederick A. Praeger, 1961.

Oliver, Group Captain Kinsley M., RAF. *A Short History of the RAF Regiment.* Catterick, England: np, 1970.

Pike, Douglas. *Viet Cong: The Organization and Techniques of the National Front of South Vietnam.* Cambridge, Mass.: M.I.T. Press, 1966.

Taylor, Gen Maxwell D., USA. Ret. *Swords and Plowshares.* New York: W.W. Norton, 1972.

Articles

Chassin, Gen G.J.M., French Air Force. "Lessons of the War in Indochina." *Interavia* VII (1952).

Studies and Reports

Goodman, Allan E. *An Institutional Profile of the South Vietnamese Officer Corps.* RM-6189-ARPA. Santa Monica: The RAND Corp, July 1970.

Kellen, Konrad. *Conversations with Enemy Soldiers in Late 1968/Early 1969: A Study of Motivation and Morale.* RM-6131-1-ISA/ARPA. Santa Monica: The RAND Corp, September 1970.

____________. *A Profile of the PAVN Soldier in South Vietnam.* RM-5013-ISA/ARPA. Santa Monica: The RAND Corp, June 1966.

National Academy of Sciences. *The Effects of Herbicides in South Vietnam.* Washington: National Academy of Sciences, 1974.

INDEX

(Numbers in *italic* indicate an illustration of the subject mentioned)

A Shau Valley: 43, *215*
Advance Echelon, 2d: 13
Advanced Research Projects Agency: 88
Advisors
air base defense, role in: 115, 158–61, 165
and defoliation project: 75
group organization: 160
number assigned: 160
operating locations: 12
relations with RVNAF: 161–62
Aerospace Defense Command: 100
Aerospace Security Plan: 108
Agency for International Development: 60
Agents
enemy: 32–36
friendly: 142, 144, 171
Agreement for Mutual Defense Assistance in Indochina (1950): 158, 162
Air Base Defense School: 90
Air bases
aircraft allotments: 61–62, 71, 129
attacks on. *See* Air bases, attacks on; also by name
civil engineering at: 154
commanders, turnover of: 68
construction programs: 171
defense of. *See* Air bases, defense of; also by name
defined: 4
fire and crash vehicles: 72
flares as light sources: 66, 95–96
fuel storage: *63*
geography, effect on location: 55, 59–60
headquarters of unassigned units at: 62
insects infestation: 59, 91
joint tenancy with RVN forces: 120, 124
lighting systems, fixed and improvised: 65–66, *66,* 68, 95–96, *96, 106,* 153–54, *170*
living conditions: 88
locations and layouts: 60–64, 166, 168
mortar rounds as light source: 66, 95
motor vehicles, allotment and replacement: *98,* 145–50, 154
native population relocation: 60
overcrowding, effect of: 62
POL storage facilities: 62, 72
power plants, makeshift: 66, 72
rainfall at: 58
recreation facilities: 68
storage facilities: 63, *63,* 72
tenant status precariousness: 62–63
terrain features at: 56–58, 63
transfers to VNAF: 68
vegetation at: 58–59, *59,* 73–78, 124
water supply and purification: 63, 72–73
weather, effect on operations: 58
Air bases, attacks on by enemy (*see also* by name)
airborne units in World War II: 2

Air bases, attacks on by enemy (continued)
- ammunition supply system, 43
- artillery survey: 43
- battalion-size attacks: 50–54, 110, 152*n,* 168
- camouflage and concealment in: 43–44, 51
- chronology, number and incidence: 166*n,* 172–205
- communications, role in: 32
- deceptions and ruses in: 39–40
- Douhet theory on: 29, 31–32, 171
- early enemy avoidance: 12–13
- electronic measures in: 39–41
- espionage in: 32–33, 47
- by Germans (1941): 2–3
- grenade assaults: 44, 46, 49
- hit-and-run tactics: 45
- infiltration routes and tactics: 16, 55, 57, 128, 135–36, 168
- intelligence organization and operations: 32–43, 143
- by Japanese (1944–45): 3
- in Korea conflict: 5–6, 31
- mortar assaults: 1, 41, 44–46, 49, 104–105, 122, 128, 131–32, 170
- recoilless rifle assaults: 41, 44–46
- reconnaissance by fire: 41
- reconnaissance, ground: 16, 36–39, 43, 46–47, 55, 57, 128, 135–36, 168
- rocket artillery in: 128, 131
- rocket assaults: 36, *40,* 41, 43–46, 51, 71–72, 104–105, 128–29, 131–36, 139, *164*
- sabotage in: 54, 168
- sapper attacks: 46–50, 51, 54, 65–66, 67*n,* 68, 100*n,* 103–104, 116, 122, 137, 152*n,* 164, 168
- standoff attacks: 41–46, 58, 70, 116, 118, 128, 131–32, 139, 142, 152, 164, 168, 170
- summary of: 206
- supply system and operations: 43, 51
- terrain in aid of: 136
- threat, variance in: 83
- tunnel construction in: 51
- by Viet Minh: 31–32
- World Wars: 2–3, 31

Air bases, defense of (*see also* by name)
- advisors, role in: 115, 158–61, 165
- agents, use in: 142, 144, 171
- Air Force in ground role: 64, 79, 108, 136–37, 149, 158
- air–ground coordination: 14–15, 116, 137–38
- air operations in. *See* Air operations, tactical
- Air Police mission: 14, 27–28, 83–84
- by Army: 15, 19, 25–27, 115, 118, 158, 170
- artillery fire support in: 136, 142–43
- assessment: 168–71
- blast and fragmentation protection: 72
- bunker systems: 65, 67, *67,* 71–72
- casualties, evacuation and replacement: 86
- command and control in: 120–21, 124, 130, 136, 152, 162–63, 166, 171
- communications systems and operations: 152–53, 162, 168
- coordination and liaison in: 155–58, 161–66, 171

Air bases, defense of (continued)
counterintelligence operations: 34*n,* 35, 81, 222, 228–29
decline in defenses: 124
defoliation projects: 15, 73–74, *74,* 75–78, 171, *215–216*
detection devices in: 104–107, 117
dike construction for: *73*
doctrine and policy formulation: 1–8, 11–28, 107–14, 139, 152, 155, 158, 171
electronic measures in: 104–107
engagement rules: 166–68, 219
facilities, protection for: 72, 168
fence barriers: 65, 68, 73–74, *117*
flares and flare ships in: 125, 129–31, *131,* 137, 151, 154, *167*
ground forces in. *See* Ground defense forces; Security police squadrons
guard orders: 219
herbicides in: 74–78, 214–17
illumination devices: *106,* 125, 129–31, 137, 151
infrared devices in: 105, *105,* 142
intelligence organization and operations: 108, 117, 129, 139–45, 153, 162, 171, 220–32
joint defense operations (and centers): 34, 162–63, *163,* 164–66
Korea experience: 5–6, 107, 125, 128, 139, 145, 154
by Marine Corps: 19, 23, 116–19, 143*n,* 165, 170
mines in: 65, *65,* 73–74, 118–19
mobility as heart of: 147
mortars in: *89, 107*
by Navy: 116
night-vision devices: 105–107
observation towers in: 65, 135
on-the-job training: 86–88
organization, typical: 114
passive measures: 68–73, 166
peak period: 168*n*
personnel management: 84–88
photography, role in: 139–40
radar in: 104–106, 135
reconnaissance, aerial. *See* Air operations, reconnaissance missions
reconnaissance, ground: 16, 19, 21, 115, 117, 120, 135, *145,* 170
responsibility for: 3–5, 19, 27, 82*n,* 83, 138, 158
revetments in: 68–69, *69–70,* 70–71, *71,* 72, 130–31, *170*
by RVN Air Force: 12–13, 16, 160–61
by RVN armed forces: 12, 17–19, 26–28, 120–22, 158, 162
by RVN Army: 12, 118, 120, 159
search-and-destroy operations: 25, 143, 166, 170
security alert conditions: 165–68, 218
security measures and deficiencies: 1, 3–4, 6*n,* 8, 12–13, 15, 17–18, 21–22, 25, 27, *54,* 61–73, *138,* 140, 168, 170
security police squadrons in. *See* Security Police Squadrons

Air bases, defense of (continued)
self-help, inadequacy of: 153–54
sensor devices in: 104–105, 117–18, 125, 135
sentry dogs and handlers: 38, *38,* 73–74, 93, 96, 100–102, *102,* 103–104, 108, 117, 152
shelters in: 68, 70–71, 73, 171
spike barriers in: *92*
supervisor's guide issued: 123
tactical security support equipment: 104–107
tactical situation reports, effect on: 168, 220–32
tactics, concept of: 107–14
target designation and approval: 131–36, 166–68, 171
training programs: 79, 140, 143–44, 171
trip flares in: 73
USMACV policy and directives on: 13, 64, 149, 158
vegetation control in: 73–78, 124
warning systems: 141–42, 165–68
weapons, allotment and maintenance: 5, 13, 92–96, *150,* 150–51, 168
wire obstacles: 65, 73–74, 117–18
World Wars experience: 1, 3, 31
Air Commando Squadrons
4th: 128, 131–32
14th: 131–32
Air Commando Wing, 14th: 128, 132
Air Division, 2d: 13*n,* 14–16, 64, 82, 88, 97, 105. *See also* Moore, Joseph H.
Air Force Advisory Group: 120, 122–24, 159–60
Air Force Advisory Teams: 123
Air Force Council: 5
Air Force Logistics Command: 69, 148
Air Force Military Personnel Center: 85
Air Force Systems Command: 153–54
Air Forces
Seventh: 13, 54–55, 62, 65–71, 81 82*n,* 83–85, 87, 90–91, 97, 106–107, 110, 112–13, 115, 122–23, 128–29, 131, 134, 139, 143–44, 148, 153–55, 157, 159, 161, 165–68. *See also* Director of Security Police, Seventh Air Force; Momyer, William W.
Thirteenth: 13–15
Far East: 6
Pacific: 13, 15, 17, 82*n,* 83, 87, 102, 107–108, 129, 137, 139, 143, 148, 155
Air–ground coordination: 14–15, 116, 137–38
Air operations, strategic: 14, 23, 25, 140*n*
Air operations, tactical (*see also* by location)
aircraft allotments: 61, 131–32
armament in: 125
by Army aircraft: 125, 129–31, 135, 137–38
assessment: 131, 136, 138
commencement: 29
damage assessment: 135
dive-bombing strikes: 2
fixed-wing gunships in: 125, *126,* 126–29, *130,* 131–32
flash ranging in: 136

Air operations, tactical (continued)
forward air controllers in: 129–30, 132–36
helicopter gunships in: 137–38
by Marine Corps: 125, 129, 136
night missions: 125, 130–32
reconnaissance missions: 125, 128–30, 132–37, 139
Rocket Watch: 128, 132–36
by RVN Air Force: 125, 130–31, 136–37
short rounds incidents: 134–35
sorties, number of: 129
strafing assaults: 2
target designation and approval: 131–36
Air Police. *See also* Security Police Squadrons: *145*
alert teams: 8
air base defense mission: 14, 27–28, 83–84
establishment, expansion and reduction: 5, 7
mission: 14, 27–28, 83–84
Air Provost Marshal: 5–6
Air Staff: 87, 90, 124, 144, 146–47
Air supremacy, Allied: 3
Air Training Command: 89
Airborne Brigade, 173d: 20, 23, 25
Airborne Division, 101st: 130
Airborne units, World Wars: 2
Aircraft
allotments: 61–62, 71, 129, 131–32
damaged and destroyed: 1, 25, 46, 66–68, 70, 131–32, 139
evacuation from RVN: 14, 16
Aircraft types
A–1: 25, 68, 130–31, 136
A–2: 68
A–37: 132–34, *134*
AH–1 helicopter: *131*
B–26: 9*n*
B–57: 14, 16, 68
C–30: 67*n*
C(AC)–47: 9*n*, 67*n*, *121*, 125, 128–31, *131*, 135–37, 163
C(AC)–119: *121*, 125
C–121: 71
C–123: *38*, *74*, 75, 125, *126*, *215*
C(AC)–130: 25, 46, 67*n*, *121*, 125
F–4: 71, *169*
F–8: 68
F–100: 25, 67*n*, *69*
F–102: 25, 46
H–43 helicopter: 68
O–1: 25, 132
O–2: 133*n*, *133*, 135–36
T–28: 9*n*
U–10: 25
Alert teams: 8
American Rolling Mill Co.: 69
Ammunition
deficiencies in: 95
supply by enemy: 43
An Khe: 21
Annamite Chain: 56, 58
Area Source Program: 140–42
Armalite firearms: 92*n*
Armored personnel carriers. *See* Motor vehicles
Army Intelligence Command: 141*n*
Army Intelligence School: 144
Arnold, Henry H.: 2
Artillery fire support: 115, 136, 142–43, 162
Artillery Group, 41st: 90
Artillery survey, enemy: 43
Artillery weapons, enemy: 211
Australian forces: 115, 119

B–3 Front: 43

Barratt, Arthur S. RAF: 6*n*
Base Defense Operations Center, Seventh Air Force: 81, 113, 143
Battalion-size attacks, enemy: 50–54, 110, 152*n,* 168
Battalions
 5th, 27th Artillery: 115, 162
 56th Artillery (Air Defense): 115
Bermuda Conference (1953): 1
Bien Hoa Air Base
 accidental explosion at: 68
 air operations: 131, 133–34, 137
 Air Force arrival: 9, 12
 aircraft allotment: 61
 aircraft losses: 68
 Army troops arrival: 20, 23
 attacks on: 1, 9, 16–17, 25–27, 36, 50–52, *52,* 53–55, 85, 104, 122, 132, 136, 140*n,* 152*n*
 casualties: 68
 civil action programs: 144
 command and control: 120
 defense strength augmented: 14–17, 21, 23, 25
 defoliation projects: 77–78
 detection systems: 106
 flares employment: *131*
 intelligence operations, enemy: 33–36, 143
 joint defense operations (and center): 163
 joint tenancy with RVNAF: 120, 124
 lighting system: *170*
 location and layout: 60
 motor vehicles, allotment and replacement: 148
 phougas employment: 95
 reconnaissance operations: *145*
 reconnaissance operations, enemy: 39
 revetments: 69–70, *70*
 sabotage at: *54*
 security alert conditions: 165–68
 security measures and deficiencies: 64, 66
 sentry dogs at: 100, 102
 storage facilities: 72
 vegetation at: 64, 77
 water supply: 72
 weapons improvised: 95
Bin Thuy Air Base
 air operations: 128–29, 131
 aircraft allotments: 61
 attacks on: 34*n,* 55, 128, 131
 bunker system: 67
 communications systems and operations: 153
 defense strength augmented: 21
 defoliation projects: 78
 intelligence operations, enemy: 35
 intelligence organization and operations: 143
 joint defense operations (and center): 163
 joint tenancy with RVNAF: 120
 location and layout: 60
 sentry dogs at: 102, 104
 storage facilities: 72
 vegetation at: 59
 water supply: 63*n,* 72
Binh Khe: 21
Black troops, in air-base defense: 3
Blank, Jones L.: *149,* 150
Blitzkrieg, defined: 2
Booby traps: 91, *93*
Brigade, 3d, 82d Airborne Division: 115
Brink bachelor officers' quarters: 18

"Brinkmanship" diplomacy: 7
Brown–Rood–James: 70
Bunker systems: 65, *67*, 71–72
Burke, Edmund, quoted: 1
Buu Long Mountain: 39

Caltrops, enemy use: 91
Cam Ranh Bay Air Base
  air operations: 130
  aircraft allotments: 61
  attacks on: 55, 72, 164. *See also* Saigon
  bunker system: *67*
  engagement rules neglect: 168
  defense strength augmented: 21
  facilities, protection for: 72
  joint defense operations (and center): 164
  location and layout: 60, 63
  materiel losses: *164*
  power plant: 72
  security measures and deficiencies: 65–66
  sentry dogs at: 102–103
  storage facilities: 63, 72
  vegetation at: 74
  water supply: 73
Cambodia campaign: 34–35
Camouflage and concealment, enemy: 43–44, 51
Camp Holloway: 40*n*
Can Tho: 55, 59
Canals, enemy use of: 59
Cap St. Jacques (Vung Tau): 15, 20
Capital Military Advisory Command: 115, 135–36
Capital Military District: 115, 135, 156, 167
Carbines: 92, 150, 209–10
Casualties
  enemy: 142–43
  evacuation and replacement: 86
  friendly: 1, 18, 67–68, 78, 104
Cease-fire agreements: 51
Central Highlands area: 25, 43
Central Intelligence Agency: 35*n*
Central Office for South Vietnam, VC/NVA: 29, 32, 34–35
Central Research Directorate, VC/NVA: 32
Chief of Staff, USAF. *See* LeMay, Curtis E.: McConnell, John P.
China, 3, 42
Cholon District: 18, 135
Chu Lai: 21
Churchill, Winston: 3, *7*, 79, 113
Civic action programs: 117, 144, 171
Civil engineering: 154
Civil Engineering Squadron, 377th: 34
Civil engineers. *See* Prime Beef; Red Horse
Civil Operations and Revolutionary (Rural) Development Support: 144
Clark Air Base: 14, 16, 90, 148
Clear-and-hold operations: 118
Close air support. *See* Air operations, tactical
Colt firearms: 92–93
Combat Crew Training Squadron, 4400th. *See* Farm Gate
Combat Security Police Squadrons. *See* Security Police Squadrons
Command and control
  in air base defense: 120–21, 124, 130, 136, 152, 162–63, 166, 171
  in RVNAF: 120–21, 124
  by USARV: 156
  by USMACV: 155
  in VC/NVA: 29
Commander in Chief, Pacific Command. *See* Pacific Command

Commanders, turnover at air bases: 68
Communications Squadron, 1883d: 154
Communications systems and operations
  in air base defense: 152–53, 162, 168
  enemy: 32
  intercept, deception and jamming by enemy: 39–40
  procurement from Army: 153
Combined Campaign Plan (1967): 22
Constitution, USS: *14*
Construction programs: 171
Contractors, civilian: 69–70
Coordination and liaison in air base defense: 155–58, 161–66, 171
Coordinators, functions of: 155–58
Corps Tactical Zones (*later* Military Regions)
  I: 43, 51, 132, 156
  II: 43, 51, 119, 130, 132, 156
  III: 13, 20, 35*n*, 43, 50, 132, 156
  IV: 35*n*, 132, 156
Counterinsurgency, defined: 9*n*
Counterintelligence operations
  in air base defense: 34*n*, 35, 81, 222, 228–29
  by RVNAF: 33–34
Crash vehicles: 72
Crete, German seizure (1941): 2–3

Da Nang Air Base
  air operations: 129–30, 136
  Air Force arrival: 12
  aircraft allotments: 61
  aircraft losses: 71
  attacks on: 25, 40, *40*, 46, 51, 55, 72, 100*n*, 104–105, 116 118, 128, 142
  barrier defenses: 117–18
  coordinator, functions of: 156*n*
  deception and ruses, enemy: 40
  defense strength augmented: 14–15, 17, 21, 23
  defensive scheme and actions: 117–19
  fence barrier: *117*
  headquarters of units at: 62
  intelligence organization and operations: 142–43
  joint defense operations (and center): 163
  joint tenancy with RVNAF: 120, 124
  location and layout: 60
  Marine Corps defense of: 19, 23, 116–19, 143*n*, 165, 170
  Marine Corps deployment to: *10*, 11, 15, 20
  mines at: 118
  motor vehicles, allotment and replacement: 148
  night-vision devices at: 107
  on-the-job training at: 88
  radar employment at: 104
  rainfall average: 58
  revetments: 69, 72
  security alert conditions: 166
  security measures and deficiencies: 64–65
  sensor devices at: 118
  sentry dogs at: 100, 102
  shelters at: 71
  storage facilities: 62
  tactical importance: 20
  wire obstacles at: 118
Defense, Department of: 4, 84. *See also* Forrestal, James V.; McNamara, Robert S.; Rumsfeld, Donald H.

Defoliation projects: 15, 73–74, *74,* 75–78, 171, *215–16*
Demilitarized Zone: 118*n*
Democratic Republic of Vietnam. *See* North Vietnam; Viet Cong/North Vietnam Army
Demolitions, by enemy. *See* Sapper attacks
Deputy Chief of Staff for Operations, USAF: 5
Desertion, in RVN armed forces: 122
Detection devices: 104–107, 117
Diem, Ngo Dinh: 12
Dike construction: *73*
Direct Air Support Centers
  Alpha: 130
  II Corps Tactical Zone: 130
  III Corps Tactical Zone: 133, 136
Director of Personnel Training and Education, USAF: 87
Director (Directorate) of Security and Law Enforcement, USAF: 90, 100, 158–59, 161
Director of Security Police, Seventh Air Force: 81*n*, 88, 90, 93, 112–13, 123, 144–45
Displacement project. *See* Relocation Program
Dive-bombing assaults: 2
Doctrine and policy formulation: 1–8, 11–28, 107–14, 139, 152, 155, 158, 171
Documents, enemy, seizure and exploitation: 34–35, 41, 46, 51, 135, 162
Dodge motor vehicles: 97
Don, Tran Van: 17
Dong Ba Mountains: 39
Don Ba Thin: 21
Dong Ha Air Base: 35
Dong Tac: 60
Douhet, Giulio: 29, 31–32, 171
Duty tours. *See* Rotation system

Eisenhower, Dwight D.: *7,* 7–9
Electronic measures: 39–41, 104–107
Engagement, rules of: 166–68, 219
Engineer Battalion, 589th: 115
England Air Force Base: 110
Equipment losses. *See* Materiel losses

Face the Nation program: 20
Factionalism in RVNAF: 12–13, 16, 26, 120, 124, 166
Farm Gate: 9, 13*n,* 29, 64
Fechet, James E.: 1–2, *2*
Federal Bureau of Investigation: 141*n*
Fence barriers: 65, 68, 73–74, *117*
Field Forces, Vietnam
  I: 62
  II: 133–35
Fire and crash vehicles: 72
Fire Drum device: 95
Flak vests: 92
Flares and flare ships: 66, 95–96, 125, 129–31, *131,* 137, 151, 154, *167*
Flash ranging: 136
Flexible response policy: 7–9
Footwear: 91
Forrestal, James V.: 4*n*. *See also* Defense, Department of
Fort Campbell, Ky.: 110–11
Fort Holabird, Md.: 144
Forward air controllers: 129–30, 132–36
Forward observers, enemy: 45
Fougasse, improvised: 95
Fowle, Bernard H.: 122
Frag orders, defined: 129*n*
Fraud in VNAF: 120*n*
Free World Forces: 119, 159, 162, 170
Fuel. *See* Petroleum, oil and lubricants
Fuller, John F.: 58*n*

Gailer, Frank L., Jr.: *149,* 150
Gaines dog food: 103
Gatling gun: 125
General Electric Co.: 125*n*
Geography, effect on operations: 55, 59–60
Gia Dinh: 34, 135
Gia Dinh district: 18
Giap, Vo Nguyen: 29, 32*n*
Green Hornet. *See* Aircraft types, UH–1
Grenade assaults, enemy: 44, 46, 49
Grenade launchers: 94, 150–51, 212
Grenades: 151, 212
Ground crews training: 1–3
Ground defense forces. *See also* Security Police Squadrons
  air base defense by: 115–124
  troop authorizations and assignment: 3–5, 8, 13–19, 21–23, 25–26, 84–88, 116–17, 120, 123–24
Ground Electronics Engineering Installation Agency: 154
Guard orders: 219
  in Korea conflict: 6
  protracted warfare doctrine: 29
  World Wars experience: 1, 3
Gulf of Tonkin incident: 14, 16, 140*n*
Gunships
  fixed-wing: 125–29, 131–32
  helicopters: 137–38

Hamilton Air Force Base: 90
Harassment fire, defined: 94*n*
Harris, Hunter, Jr.: 17, 19, 26. *See also* Air Forces, Pacific
Headquarters Command, USAF: 100
Headwear: 91
Helicopter Squadron, 20th: 129
Helicopter types. *See* Aircraft types; Gunships
Herbicides: 74-78, 214–17
Hit-and-run tactics, enemy: 45
Ho Chi Minh: 29, 32*n*
Ho Chi Minh Trail: 43, 55
Hue: 21, 58
Hughes, Jack L.: 168
Humphrey, Hubert H.: 46

Infiltration tactics. *See* Reconnaissance, ground, by enemy
Illumination devices: *106,* 125, 129–31, 137, 151
Infrared devices: 105, *105,* 142
"Ink Blot" concept: 25
Insects infestation: 59, 91
Instructors, deficiencies in: 112
Intelligence organization and operations. *See also* Counterintelligence operations: 8, 51
  in air base defense: 108, 117, 129, 139–45, 153, 162, 171, 220–32
  by Army: 141*n,* 143–44
  by enemy: 32–43, 143
  by Marine Corps: 142
  by RVN Army: 142
  in security police squadrons: 108, 143, 145, 153
Insurgency operations. *See* Guerrilla forces and operations
Interdiction fire, defined: 94*n*
Internal Installation Security Program: 8
International motor vehicles: 97

Japan: 3–4
Jeeps. *See* Motor vehicles
Johnson, Lyndon B.: 20, *20*
  air operations, concern over: 135

Johnson, Lyndon B. (continued)
air strikes ordered by: 23
and combat support of RVN: 24–25
ground forces commitment: 20, 22–23
military assistance, policy on: 11–12
on rotation policy: 84
Joint Action Armed Forces (1951): 4–5
Joint Chiefs of Staff. *See also* Wheeler, Earle G.
Ad Hoc Committee for Joint Policies and Procedures: 4
and advisors program: 159
air base defense policy and directives: 4–5, 15, 18–19, 27, 120, 138, 158
aircraft allotments by: 129
and defoliation projects: 75
and ground forces security units: 20, 81, 83–84
joint operations, responsibility for: 4
Key West Agreement: 4*n*
Joint defense operations (and centers): 34, 162–63, *163,* 164–66
Joint General Staff, RVN: 14–15, 121, 124, 159, 167–68

Kadena Air Base: 102*n*
Keegan, George J.: 140, *140*
Kennedy, John F.: 8–9, *9,* 11–12
Key West Agreement (1948): 4
Khanh, Nguyen: 12, 16
Khanh Hoa Province: 39
Kirste, Milton R.: 151, 153
Korea conflict experience: 5–6, 31, 107, 125, 128, 139, 145, 154
Ky, Nguyen Cao: 12

Lackland Air Force Base: 90, 100, 102, 104*n*
Laniel, Joseph: 7
Lao Dong. *See* North Vietnam, Communist party in
Lawrence, T. E.: 1*n*
Leave policies: 85
LeMay, Curtis E.: *9,* 11, 15
Lenin, Nikolai: 29
Lettow-Vorbeck, Paul von: 1*n*
Liaison, in air base defense: 155–58, 161–66, 171
Liddell Hart, B. H., quoted: 96
Light-All unit, NF–2: 66
Lighting systems: 65–66, *66,* 68, 95–96, *96, 106,* 153–54, *170*
Limelight Project: 102
Lines of communication, enemy: 55–56
Local Forces, VC/NVA: 37*n*
Lockheed Missiles and Space Co.: 83
Lodge, Henry Cabot: 22, *22,* 162
Logistical Command, 1st: 115
Logistical systems and operations. *See* Supply systems and operations
Long Binh: *130*
Long Binh Ammunition Depot: 39*n*
Luckett, William T., Jr.: 161*n*

Machiavelli, Niccoló, quoted: 155
Machine guns: 93–95, *150,* 150–51, *169,* 210
Main Forces, VC–NVA: 37*n*, 170
Main line of resistance, defined: 65*n*
Maleme air base: 2–3
Mansfield, USS: 116
Mao Tse-tung: 29
Marine Air Wing, 1st: 116*n*
Marine Amphibious Force, III: 25, 62, 116–18, 143*n,* 155–56, 166
Marine Expeditionary Brigade, 9th: *10*, 20, 25*n*, 116

Marine Division, 3d: 116*n*
Marshall, George C.: 3
Martin, Frederick L.: 2
Materiel losses
enemy: 142
friendly: 40*n,* 54, 68, 164, *164,* 207–208
McConnell, John P.: *22,* 26–27, 110
McNamara, Robert S. *See also* Defense, Department of: *20*
air base defense policy: 16
on aircraft allotments: 131
and combined command structure: 158
on defoliation projects: 75
and ground troops commitment: 21–22
and manpower strength, USMACV: 84
withholds construction funds: 68
McNamara's Wall: 118*n*
Mechanics, shortage of: 147
Mekong Delta: 55, 58–59
Midway, battle of: 3
Military Intelligence Service, VC/NVA: 32–35
Military police, security role: 18
Military Police Battalion, 1st: 117–18
Military Regions (*formerly* Corps Tactical Zones), III and IV: 35
Military Security Service: 141*n*
Mines and mine fields: 15, 65, *65,* 73–74, 118–19
Minigun: 125
Ministry of Public Security, VC/NVA: 32
Mobility
enemy capacity: 42, 44–45, 58
need in air base defense: 147
Momyer, William W.: *22,* 70, 132, 134–35. *See also* Air Forces, Seventh
Moore, Joseph H.: 28. *See also* Air Division, 2d
Mortar assaults, enemy: 1, 41, 44–46, 49, 104–105, 122, 128, 131–32, 170
Mortars: 66, *89,* 95, *107,* 151, *208,* 211
Motor vehicles: *113, 146*
allotments and replacements: 96–99, 145–50, 154
cannibalizing practices: 148
deficiencies in: 97
losses: 68
maintenance and repair: 145–48, 154, 168
mavericks, reclaiming: 148
procurement from Army: 148
as weapons carriers: 95
Motorola Co.: 152–53

Napalm, tactical use: 95
National Liberation Front: 29
National Security Act (1947): 4
Naval Intelligence Service: 141*n*
Negro troops. *See* Black troops
Nemo (sentry dog): 104
New Jersey, USS: 116
Nha Trang Air Base
air operations: 129–30
aircraft allotment: 61
attacks on: 55, 116, 122*n*
defense strength augmented: 21
detection systems at: 106
headquarters of units at: 62
joint defense operations (and center): 163
joint tenancy with RVNAF: 163
location and layout: 60

Nha Trang Air Base (continued)
reconnaissance operations, enemy: **39**
sentry dogs at: 102
transfer to VNAF: 68
wire obstacles at: *36*
Night operations, aerial: 125, 130–32
Night vision devices: 105–107
Nixon, Richard M.: 68, 75, 78, 122, 137
Normandy campaign (1944): 3*n*
North Vietnam. *See also* Viet Cong/North Vietnam Army
air assaults against: 14, 23, 25, 140
attack on U.S. Navy: 14
Communist party in: 29
Nuclear warfare policy: 7–9

Observation, ground. *See* Reconnaissance, ground
Observation towers: 65, 135
Office of Investigations, VNAF: 141
Office of Special Investigations, USAF: 140–42, 153
Officers, allotments to air base defense: 85–86
Oklahoma City Air Materiel Area: 153*n*
On-the-job training: 86–88
O'Neal unarmed defense course: 90
Oxford rifle sight: 105

Pacific Command: 15, 19, 84, 155
Parks Air Force Base: 90
Passenger cars. *See* Motor vehicles
Passive defense measures: 68–73, 166
Patrols. *See* Reconnaissance
Pentalateral Agreement (1950): 158, 162
People's Revolutionary Party: 29, 32
Perimeter Detection and Surveillance Subsystem: 105–106, 154
Personnel carriers. *See* Motor vehicles
Personnel management: 84–88
Petit, Robert L.: 81
Petroleum, oil and lubricants storage: 62, *63,* 72, *73, 164*
Phan Rang Air Base
air operations: 130, 137, 142
aircraft allotment: 61
Army complement at: 115
attacks on: 55, 116, 152*n,* 163
counterintelligence operations: 222
defense force strength: 21
defoliation project: 77
fuel supply: 63
ground forces allotments: 74, 110–11
intelligence organization and operations: 222
joint defense operations (and center): 164
joint tenancy with RVNAF: 162
location and layout: 60, 63, 115
native population relocation: 60
night vision devices at: 107
on-the-job training at: 88
Safe Side squadron at: 110
security measures and deficiencies: 66
sentry dogs at: 102–104
storage facilities: 63, 72
tactical situation reports: 220–23
training program: 90
water supply: 63, 72

Phan Rang Air Base (continued)
weapons allotment and maintenance: 151
weapons improvised: 95
Philco—Ford agency: 148
Photography, role in air base defense: 139–40
Phougas employment: 95
Phu Bai: 21
Phu Cat Air Base
air operations: 130
aircraft allotment: 61
attacks on: *42*, 50, 55, 103
bunker system: 67
detection systems at: 106, 154
fence barrier: 68
ground forces allotment: 84, 112*n*
intelligence organization and operations: 142
joint defense operations (and center): 164–65
lighting system: *66*
location and layout: 60, 63
mines at: *65*
mortars in defense: *89*
night vision devices at: 107
native population relocation: 60
security measures and deficiencies: 65
sentry dogs at: 102–104
training program: 90
weapons improvised: 95
Pistols: 93, 150
Pleiku Air Base: 58, *152*
air operations: 128, 130, 142
aircraft allotment: 61
attacks on: 19, *45*, 51, 55, 122*n*, 128, 142
deception and ruses, enemy: 40
ground forces allotment: 21, 84
headquarters of units at: 62
joint defense operations (and center): 162–63
joint tenancy with RVNAF: 120, 124
location and layout: 60
revetments at: *71*
sentry dogs at: 102, 104
storage facilities: 62, 72
water supply: 63*n*, 72
Political crises: 12–13, 16, 120*n*
Popular Forces: 36*n*, 115, 117, 120, 159
Population relocation. *See* Relocation program
Power plants: 66, 72
Press reports: 41
Prime Beef (Base Engineer Emergency Forces): 69
Prisoners of war, enemy: 34, 36, 38–39, 41, 45, 50–51, 103, *157*, 162
Propaganda, enemy: 135
Provisional Revolutionary Government: 35*n*
Punji stakes, enemy use: 91, *93*

Quan Canh: 162
Qui Nhon: 19, 21
Quirey, William O., USA: 121, *121*, 167

Radar systems: 104–106, 135
Radio communications. *See* Communications systems and operations
Radio Research Group, 59th: 115
Radio sets captured by enemy: 40*n*
Rainfall, effect on operations: *58*
Ranger units, ARVN: 36, 39
Rappelling, defined: 112*n*

Rawls, Perry J.: 122
Raymond-Morrison-Knudson: 70
Recoilless rifle assaults, enemy: 41, 44–46
Recoilless rifles: 95, *150*, 151, 210–11
Reconnaissance operations
  aerial: 125, 128–30, 132–37, 139
  by fire: 41
  ground: 16, 19, 21, 115, 117, 120, 135, *145*, 170
  ground, by enemy: 6, 36–39, 43, 46–47, 55, 57, 128, 135–36, 168
Recreation facilities: 68
Red Horse (Rapid Engineer Deployment, Heavy Operational Repair Squadrons, Engineering): 70, 154
Regional Forces: 16*n*, 17, 115, 120, 122, 159
Relocation program: 60–61
Rennie (sentry dog): *102*
Repair parts. *See* Maintenance and repair
Replacements. *See* Rotation program
Republic of Korea forces: 119, 142, 163–65
Republic of Vietnam
  Communist party organization: 29–30
  ground forces commitment to: 11
  political crises: 12–13, 16, 120*n*
  USMACV deference to: 171
  withdrawal of U.S. forces: 68, 73
Republic of Vietnam Air Force
  advisors, relations with: 161–62
  air base defense by: 12–13, 16, 160–61
  air bases, transfer to: 68
  air operations by: 125, 130–31, 136–37
  fraudulent practices in: 120*n*
  headquarters site: 62
  initiative, lack of: 124
  joint base tenancy: 120
  operational relationship with USAF: 158–61
  training program: 122–24
  staff inefficiency: 124
  23d Defense Group: 122
  33d Wing: 35, 121
  41st: 116
  74th Wing: 34
  2d Security Company: 35
  4th Security Company: 35
Republic of Vietnam Armed Forces
  air base defense by: 12, 17–19, 26–28, 120–22, 158, 162
  combat effectiveness and morale: 12, 16, 23, 120, 122, 124
  command and control deficiencies: 120–21, 124
  counterintelligence operations: 33–34
  deficiencies in: 12
  factionalism in: 12–13, 16, 26, 120, 124, 166
  joint base tenancy with USAF: 120, 124
  leave policies: 166
  operational relationship with USMACV: 158–59
  security mission: 18
Republic of Vietnam Army
  air base defense by: 12, 118, 120, 159
  and defoliation projects: 75

Republic of Vietnam Army (continued)
- intelligence organization and operations: 142
- desertion from combat posts: 122
- joint base tenancy with USAF: 120
- Ranger units: 36, 39
- I Corps: 62
- II Corps: 62
- 2d Service Battalion: 122, 124
- 57th Battalion: 36

Rest and recreation program. *See* Leave policies
Revetments, in air base defense: 68–69, *69–70*, 70–71, *71*, 72, 130–131, *170*
Revolutionary Development Program: 171
Revolvers: 93, 150
Rifle sight, Oxford: 105
Rifles: 92–93, 150, 209
Rocket artillery, enemy: 128, 131
Rocket assaults, enemy: 36, *40*, 41, 43–46, 51, 71–72, 104–105, 128–29, 131–36, 139, *164*
Rocket launchers: *42*, *44–45*, *129*, 212
Rocket Watch: 128, 132–36
Rockets: 95, 151, 212–13
Roles and missions: 4, 6, 138
ROLLING THUNDER Operation: 23
Rotation program: 84–88, 144
Rome Air Development Center: 105
ROX automotive store: 148
Royal Air Force: 3–4
Rumsfeld, Donald H.: 88. *See also* Defense, Department of
Ruses, enemy: 39–40
Rusk, Dean: 20. *See also* State, Department of
Russia. *See* Soviet Union

Sabotage, enemy: 8, 13, 54, 168
Safe Side programs: 81, 82*n*, 110–14, 143
Saigon: 43, 55
- air bases at: 55
- air operations: 135
- attacks on: 18, *19*, 45–46, 51–54
- intelligence organization and operations: 143
- rainfall average: 58

Saigon International Airport: 34, 62
Sapper attacks, enemy: 46–51, 54, 65–66, 67*n*, 68, 100*n*, 103–104, 116, 122, 137, 152*n*, 164, 168
Savage firearms: 95
Schofield Barracks: 110–11
Scramble, defined: 130*n*
Search-and-destroy operations: 25, 143, 166, 170
Sears, Roebuck & Co.: 105
Secretary of Defense. *See* Forrestal, James V.; McNamara, Robert S.; Rumsfeld, Donald H.
Secretary of State. *See* Rusk, Dean
Security alert conditions: 165–68, 218
Security Division, VNAF: 141
Security measures: 1, 3–4, 6*n*, 8, 12–13, 15, 17–18, 21–22, 25, 27, *54*, 61–68, 73, 108, *138*, 140, 168, 170
Security measures, enemy: 43, 47, 49, 51
Security Police Squadrons. *See also* Air Police; Ground defense forces
- command and control of: 112

Security Police Squadrons (continued)
communications systems and operations: 152–53
equipment, personal: 91–93
instructors, deficiencies in: 112
intelligence organization and operations: 108, 143, 145, 153
manpower allotments: 82–83, 171
motor vehicles, allotments and replacement: 96–99, 147–48
officers, allotments: 85–86
on-the-job training: 86–88
organization and tactical mission: 78–81, 84, 110–12, 114, 139
performance assessed: 113
Safe Side program: 81, 82*n*, 110–14, 143
training programs: 85–91, 107–13, 154
troop strength, periodic: 81–88, 90, 107, 111, 113, 124
uniform, headwear and footwear: 91
weapons, allotment and maintenance: 92–96, 150–51
weapons training: 90–91, 110
35th: 84, 90
37th: 90, 154
377th: 153*n*
821st: 82*n*, 84, 90, 110–11, 143
822d: 82*n*, 110–11, 143
823d: 82*n*, 110–11
1041st: 82*n*, 112*n*
Combat Security Police Training School: 110–11
Combat Security Police Wing, 82d: 110
Combat Support Groups
3d: 122
377th: 115, 122, 156*n*
633d: 130*n*
Security Service, VC/NVA: 32
Self-help, inadequacy of: 153–54
Sensor devices: 104–105, 117–18, 125, 135
Sentry Dog Training Center: 102*n*, 104*n*
Sentry dogs and handlers: 38, *38*, 73–74, 93, 96, 100–102, *102*, 103–104, 108, 117, 152
Shadow aircraft. *See* Aircraft types, C(AC)–119
Shelters, in air base defenses: 68, 70–71, 73, 171
Short, Walter C.: 2
Short rounds incidents: 134–35
Shotguns: 94–95
Showa, Japan: 102*n*
Siesta custom: 58
Sighting devices: 104
Signal Battalion, 69th: 115
Slap flares: 66
Smith, Donavon F.: 163
Song Dong Nai River: 136
South Vietnam. *See* Republic of Vietnam
Southeast Asia Deployment Programs: 84
Southeast Asia Intrusion Detection Equipment Program: 105
Southeast Asia Operational Requirement 22: 105
Soviet Union: 42
Spectre aircraft. *See* Aircraft types, C(AC)–130
Spike barriers: *92*
Spooky aircraft. *See* Aircraft types, C(AC)–47
Standoff attacks, enemy: 41–46, 58, 70, 116, 118, 128, 131–32, 139, 142, 152, 164, 168, 170

Starlight scope: 92*n*, 106, *106*
State, Department of: 24, 75. *See also* Rusk, Dean.
Status of forces agreement: 158, 162
Stevens firearms: 94–95
Stinger aircraft. *See* Aircraft types, C(AC)–119
Storage facilities: 62–63, *63*, 72, *73*, *164*
Strafing assaults: 2
Strategic Air Command: 6, 100
Submachine guns: 93, 209
Supply operations and systems, enemy: 43, 51, 55, 59
Surprise, enemy application: 51

Tactical Air Command: 82*n*, 100, 110
Tactical air support. *See* Air operations, tactical
Tactical Air Wing, 366th: 116, 166
Tactical situation reports: 168, 220–32
Tactics, air base concept: 107–14
Tan Son Nhut Air Base: *60*, *62*, *64*, *86*
- air operations: 128, 131, 133–34, 137
- Air Force arrival: 12, 128
- aircraft allotment: 61
- Army units at: 115
- attacks on: 38, 46, 50–55, 65, 93, 95, 104, 122*n*, 131–32, 136–37, 139, 152, *225*
- civic action program: 144
- command and control, RVN: 120–21, 124
- communications systems and operations: 152, 153*n*
- coordinator, functions of: 156*n*
- counterintelligence operations: 228–29
- detection systems at: 106
- engagement rules neglect at: 167–68
- flares, use at: *167*
- ground forces allotments: 14–15, 21, 27, 84, 89*n*
- headquarters of units at: 62
- intelligence operations, enemy: 34–35, 38–39
- joint defense operations (and center): 162–63, *163*
- joint tenancy with RVNAF: 120, 124
- living conditions: 88
- location and layout: 60
- mines, use at: *119*
- motor vehicles, allotment and replacement: 146, 148
- night vision devices at: 107
- organization for defense: 114
- POL storage facilities: 72
- reconnaissance operations, enemy: 38
- revetments at: 69, *69*
- security measures and deficiencies: 64–65, *138*
- sentry dogs at: *38*, 100, 102
- storage facilities: 62, 72
- tactical situation reports: 223–32
- vegetation at: 59, 64, 77
- weapons improvised: 95
- target designation and approval: 131–36, 166–68, 171

Task Force 35: 115
Taylor, Maxwell D.: *15*, 15–17, 20, 23, 158
Technical School, 3275th: 90–91
Technicians. *See* Ground crews
Telephone—telegraph communications. *See* Communications systems and operations

Terrain, effect on operations: 56–58, 63, 136
Terrorist attacks: 18
Tet offensive: 31, 46, 50–54, 58, 67, 73, 77, 81, 84–85, 95, 97, 107–108, 110, 116, 122, 132, 137, 139, 144, 150, 157, 161, 163, 168, 170, *205*
Throckmorton, John L., USA: 17, *17*, 19–20, 26–27
Top Dog Project 45: 100, 102
Totem Pole lighting system: 95–96, *170*
Training programs: 1–3, 79, 85–91, 107–13, 122–24, 140, 143–44, 146–47, 154, 171
Training programs, enemy: 29–31, 36*n*, 38–39, 42, 46–50, 54, 73–74, 103
Transceivers, tactical use: 152
Transportation facilities, enemy: 42, 44–45, 58
Transportation Group, 110th: 115
Transportation squadrons: 145–50
Triantafellu, Rockey: 140, *140*
Tri-border area: 43
Tri-Service Ammunition Storage Area: 164
Trip flares: 73
Troop carriers. *See* Motor vehicles
Trucks. *See* Motor vehicles
Tunnel systems, enemy: 51
Tuy Hoa Air Base
  air operations: 130
  aircraft allotment: 61
  aircraft losses: 66, 67*n*
  attacks on: 55, 66, 67*n*, 68
  casualties: 67*n*
  dike construction: *73*
  fence barrier at: 68
  illumination at: *106*
  intelligence organization and operations: 142–43
  location and layout: 60, 63
  native population relocation: 60
  recreation facilities: 68
  security measures and deficiencies: 65–66
  sentry dogs at: 102–103
  shelters at: 70
  terrain features: 63–64
  vegetation at: 59
Typhoons, incidence: 58

Unconventional forces. *See* Guerrilla forces and operations
Unified Action Armed Forces (1959): 5
Uniforms: 91
United Press International: 35*n*
United States Air Force
  autonomy established: 4
  bases, defined: 4
  deployment to RVN: 9
  in ground role: 64, 79, 108, 136–37, 149, 158
  joint base tenancy with RVNAF: 120, 124
  operational relationship with VNAF: 158–61
  roles and missions: 4, 6, 138
  security forces strength: 14*n*
  strength in RVN, periodic: 87
United States Army
  air base defense by: 15, 19, 25–27, 115, 118, 158, 170
  air operations by: 125, 129–31, 135, 137–38
  bases, defined: 4
  communications equipment, procurement from: 153
  ground troops commitment: 20
  intelligence organization and operations: 141*n*, 143–44

United States Army (continued)
motor vehicles, procurement from: 148
roles and missions: 4, 6
security mission: 18, 108
weapons, procurement from: 151
United States Army Air Forces, activated: 2*n*
United States Army, Vietnam
command and control by: 156
headquarters moves: 62*n*
Special Troops: 115
United States Marine Corps
air base defense by: 19, 23, 116–19, 143*n*, 165, 170
air operations by: 125, 129, 136
bases, defined: 4
intelligence organization and operations: 142
roles and missions: 4
United States Military Assistance Command, Vietnam. *See also* Westmoreland, William C.
activated: 155
air base defense, policy and directives: 13, 64, 149, 158
aircraft allotments by: 129
attack on headquarters: 46
command and control by: 155
defoliation project: 75, 78
engagement rules: 166, 168
expansion of forces: 9
Government of Vietnam, deference to: 171
and ground forces security units: 83–84, 121
headquarters moves: 62*n*
operational relationship with RVNAF: 158–59
organization and mission: 155–56
rotation program: 84–88
security alert conditions plan: 165–68
security measures: 64
troop strength, periodic: 84–85, 135
United States Naval Forces, Vietnam: 155
United States Navy
air base defense by: 116
aircraft losses: 71
attack on by VC/NVA: 14
bases, defined: 4
roles and missions: 4
United States Overseas Mission: 18

Vegetation, effect on operations: 58–59, *59*, 73–78, 124
Viet Cong/North Vietnam Army
agents, recruitment and operations: 32–36
cadre, mission and functions: 33–34, 36
combat efficiency and ingenuity: 54, 171
combat unit organization: 42, 46–49
command and control structure: 29
genesis and political organization: 29, 47
infrastructure in South: 33
lines of communication: 55–56
Local Forces: 37*n*
Main Forces: 37*n*, 170
mobility and transportation: 42–45, 58
propaganda campaigns: 135
security measures: 43, 47, 49, 51
supply system and operations: 55, 59
surprise, application by: 51

Viet Cong/North Vietnamese Army (continued)
training, armament and equipment: 29–31, 36*n*, 38–39, 42, 46–50, 54, 73–74, 103
weapons, description and characteristics: 209–13
Viet Minh: 32
Vietnamization program: 82, 120, 122, 137, 161*n*
Vinh Cuu District: 36
Volunteer Informant Program: 144
Vung Tau (Cap St. Jacques): 15, 20

Walt, Lewis W., USMC: 25, 116, *116*
War Zone D: 25, 43
Warner Robins Air Materiel Area: 146
Warning systems: 141–42, 165–68
Water supply and purification: 63, 72–73
Weapons (see also by type)
allotments and maintenance: 5, 13, 92–96, *150*, 150–51, 168
enemy: 209–13
improvised: 42, 95
procurement from Army: 151
Weapons and Small Unit Tactics School: 113
Weather, effect on operations: 58
Westmoreland, William C., USA. *See also* United States Military Assistance Command, Vietnam: *25*
air base defense, policy and directives on: 11, 14–18, 22, 27–28, 133–35, 167, 170
and combat support of RVN: 24–25, 27
and combined command structure: 158
on ground troops commitment: 20–22
operational relationship with RVN: 159
on relations with RVNAF officers: 161–62
and security measures: 27
Wheeler, Earle G., USA: 20, *20*. *See also* Joint Chiefs of Staff
Wire obstacles: 65, 73–74, 117–18
World Wars, experience from: 1, 3, 31

☆U.S. GOVERNMENT PRINTING OFFICE: 1979 631-351 1-3

INTERVAL TRAINING FOR LIFETIME FITNESS